MOON

D0342928

PACIFIC
NORTHWEST

Road Trip

ALLISON WILLIAMS

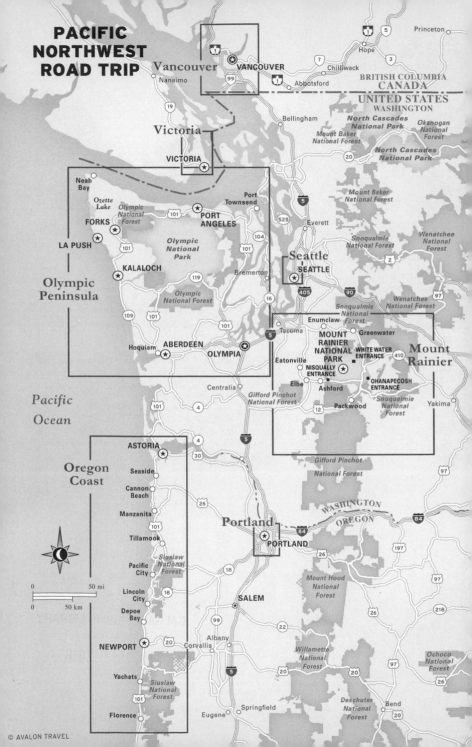

PACIFIC NORTHWEST ROAD TRIP

BRITISH COLUMBIA CANADA

Princeton

Hope

Chilliwack

Vancouver

VANCOUVER

Nanaimo

Abbotsford

UNITED STATES
WASHINGTON

Bellingham

North Cascades National Park

Okanogan National Forest

Mount Baker National Forest

North Cascades National Park

Victoria

VICTORIA

Neah Bay

Port Townsend

Port Angeles

PORT ANGELES

Mount Baker National Forest

Ozette Lake

Olympic National Forest

FORKS

Everett

LA PUSH

Olympic National Park

Snoqualmie National Forest

Wenatchee National Forest

KALALOCH

Bremerton

Seattle

SEATTLE

Olympic Peninsula

Olympic National Forest

Snoqualmie National Forest

Enumclaw

Wenatchee National Forest

Hoquiam

ABERDEEN

OLYMPIA

Tacoma

Greenwater

MOUNT RAINIER NATIONAL PARK

WHITE WATER ENTRANCE

Mount Rainier

Centralia

Eatonville

NISQUALLY ENTRANCE

Elbe

Ashford

OHANAPECOSH ENTRANCE

Snoqualmie National Forest

Yakima

Pacific Ocean

Gifford Pinchot National Forest

Packwood

ASTORIA

Gifford Pinchot National Forest

Oregon Coast

Seaside

Cannon Beach

Manzanita

Tillamook

WASHINGTON
OREGON

Portland

PORTLAND

Siuslaw National Forest

Pacific City

Mount Hood National Forest

Lincoln City

0   50 mi

0   50 km

SALEM

Depoe Bay

NEWPORT

Albany

Corvallis

Willamette National Forest

Yachats

Siuslaw National Forest

Ochoco National Forest

Florence

Eugene

Springfield

Deschutes National Forest

Bend

PLANNING YOUR TRIP

Where to Go

Seattle

The future is waiting around every corner of this waterfront city—from the towering **Space Needle** to the collection of spacecraft at the **Museum of Flight.** Wake early for the **Seattle Art Museum** and bustling **Pike Place Market,** but prepare to stay up late for farm-to-table **dining** and a diverse selection of **live music.**

Vancouver

Mountains tower over Vancouver, Canada—so close that **Grouse Mountain** skiers practically slide down next to the city's skyscrapers. Bike or walk around downtown's **Stanley Park,** browse the wares on offer at the **Granville Island Public Market,** and take in some **Olympic**

history with a day trip to **Whistler.** At night, sample the myriad options on offer from Vancouver's **international culinary scene.**

Victoria

Victoria may be only a short ferry ride away, at the tip of Vancouver Island, but a visit here feels like crossing the pond to Britain. This is the **capital of British Columbia,** and a tour of the **British Columbia Parliament Buildings** provides a primer on the parliamentary system of government. Enjoy the delicate elegance of afternoon tea in the **Fairmont Empress Hotel** as it holds court over Victoria's Inner Harbour, and then visit **The Butchart Gardens,** a world-class garden housed in an old quarry.

Olympic Peninsula

Washington's "green thumb" is a promontory of land rich in natural features. **Olympic National Park** is home to **Hurricane Ridge,** with its sweeping ridgetop vistas, and the verdant mists of the **Hoh Rain Forest.** The peninsula's **beaches and bays** stretch from the town of **Port Angeles** to **Neah Bay** and continue down the coast.

Oregon Coast

Driving down U.S. 101, it seems like the **beaches** of the Oregon Coast never end. From **Astoria,** the sand stretches for miles past **Cannon Beach** and **Tillamook Bay.** Along the way, follow the footsteps of Lewis and Clark at **Fort Clatsop,** explore the tide pools at **Haystack Rock,** and nibble bites of cheese at the **Tillamook Cheese Factory.**

Portland

Few cities have more personality than Portland. Each small block is packed with **unique shops, creative eateries, tasty brewpubs,** and residents **biking** across the bridges between them. Stop and smell the roses that line the **International Rose Test Garden** (one of the world's largest)

VANCOUVER

25 mi/
40 km

NEAH
BAY

70 mi/
113 km

141 mi/
227 km

71 mi/
114 km

VICTORIA

PORT
ANGELES

83 mi/
134 km

157 mi/
253 km

SEATTLE

60 mi/
98 km

65 mi/
104 km

OLYMPIA
50 mi/
80 km

ABERDEEN

GREENWATER

45 mi/
72 km

Pacific
Ocean

77 mi/
123 km

115 mi/
185 km

PARADISE

ASTORIA

140 mi/
225 km

97 mi/
156 km

134 mi/
215 km

PORTLAND

NEWPORT

135 mi/
217 km

© AVALON TRAVEL

clockwise from top left: First Nations totem poles in Vancouver's Stanley Park; Seattle Space Needle; Oregon Coast view.

in **Washington Park,** gaze in awe at the **Pittock Mansion**'s three-story staircase, and wander amid the giant playground that is the **Oregon Museum of Science and Industry.**

Mount Rainier

When "The Mountain" is out, it's one of the most spectacular sights in the Northwest—a giant dotted with **glaciers** and flanked by **wildflower meadows.** Stop at the **Jackson Visitor Center** in the aptly named **Paradise,** or spend the night at the historical **Paradise Inn.** Add a side trip to **Mount St. Helens** and drive up to the **Johnston Ridge Observatory** for a firsthand look at where the mountain blew in 1980.

When to Go

If there's one thing you can depend on in the Pacific Northwest, it's that you *can't* depend on the weather. The region is known for **rain,** but it doesn't fall in regular intervals. **Summer** is the driest and sunniest season. Occasionally temperatures can soar above 90 degrees, and the lack of widespread air-conditioning can make it uncomfortable. **Fall** can vary between brisk, beautiful days and soggy, gray ones. **Winter** rarely brings much snow outside of the mountains and passes (but when it does snow in the city, stay off the streets). Mountain roads, such as those around Mount Rainier, are prone to **seasonal closures** and may require chains in winter months. **Spring** is often the rainiest time of year, but it doesn't tend to pour in the region—instead, expect drizzles with the occasional shower. (Sometimes it's even sunny!) In general, when the rain falls in the region it's of this gentler variety—which is why you'll notice the locals make do with hats and hoodies rather than umbrellas, and don't tend to let it stop them from getting out and about.

Before You Go

It's nice to leave room for the unexpected in a trip to the Pacific Northwest, but some things should be arranged in advance. International visitors will most likely need a visa, though Canadian neighbors can make due with only their **passport.** Residents of a country other than the United States or Canada should know in advance if they plan to **cross the border** on their trip. Most visitors will enter through the international airports in Seattle, Portland, or Vancouver; all have some form of public transportation running to the center of town, but not all run 24 hours.

Hotels in big cities like Seattle and Portland can fill quickly during popular times: the middle of summer, winter holidays, and around big conventions and sporting events. Given the **limited accommodations in smaller towns** on the Olympic Peninsula and Oregon Coast, sellouts are possible. **Campgrounds** that take reservations are likely to fill up in advance during the summer, as are big national park or mountain lodges. Rental cars are less in danger of being completely out of stock, but **train and bus tickets** are also best reserved in advance. **Ferry reservations** in Washington and British Columbia should be arranged as soon as travel plans are set; the former releases availability in batches (only for San Juan Island and Victoria trips; the rest of the Puget Sound ferries don't take advance bookings).

As for attractions and dining, book ahead only if you need to ensure availability at a certain time, or have your heart set on a particular fine dining restaurant. **Tickets for sporting events** like professional football and even soccer should also be scheduled in advance. Otherwise, once you've secured the bones of a Pacific Northwest trip, there's lots of room to explore, improvise, and discover things along the way.

Best Rainy-Day Distractions

It doesn't rain *every* day in the Pacific Northwest, but it could. Fortunately there are plenty of ways to have fun indoors.

- **Pike Place Market:** Seattle put its farmers market under a roof, so even the famous flying fish are covered (page 26).

- **Seattle Art Museum:** Several floors of galleries and free public tours offer shelter at this downtown museum (page 28).

- **Museum of History and Industry:** Follow Seattle's historic rise to tech giant, and then check the weather through the working periscope (page 35).

- **Vancouver Police Museum:** A gray day sets the mood for murder exhibits in the city's old morgue (page 85).

- **University of British Columbia Museum of Anthropology:** Tall windows provide sanctuary in the museum's airy totem pole gallery (page 89).

- **Fairmont Empress Hotel:** Warm up with the hotel's famous Afternoon Tea

and linger over your mini meal (page 130).

- **Northwest Maritime Center:** Watch craftspeople build wooden boats inside a warm boat shop (page 153).

- **Hoh Rain Forest:** Don't hide from the rain—embrace it in the thick forest of Olympic National Park (page 174).

- **Tillamook Cheese Factory:** How many cheese samples can you eat at once (page 212)?

- **Oregon Coast Aquarium:** There are plenty of creatures in the touch tanks to take up a whole afternoon (page 222).

- **Pittock Mansion:** The historical home of a Portland luminary is crammed with beautiful antique furnishings (page 249).

- **Oregon Museum of Science and Industry:** Seek shelter inside a submarine that sits in the Willamette River (page 251).

- **Paradise Inn:** The giant fireplaces inside this historical hotel provide plenty of warmth (page 302).

Driving Tips

It's best to use **headlights even during the day** to appear visible to approaching vehicles. Also take care to watch for animals on the road, because hitting a deer at high speeds can be lethal to the driver as well as the deer. Passing is discouraged except in very open areas, and on roads that travel uphill there are often passing lanes built in to keep drivers safer.

Mountain roads, such as those around Mount Rainier, are especially prone to seasonal closures and may legally require

snow chains in winter months. However, this is only an issue on roads that climb to high elevations and isn't a problem on I-5 or coastal roads.

Take note of your gas-tank level on all roads other than interstates, though **large regions without services** are often signed. In the Pacific Northwest, it's very important to have working **windshield wipers**—you'll encounter rain in every season here, and driving is impossible without them. Also locate your **bright lights** in advance of needing them, as they may be necessary in cases of fog or on rural highways without streetlights.

HIT THE ROAD

Circle the Pacific Northwest in this **two-week drive.** Start in Seattle, Washington, and head north to Vancouver, British Columbia. After a brief stop in Victoria, ferry over to the Olympic Peninsula and drive down the Oregon Coast. Loop inland to Portland, and then head north with stops at Mount St. Helens and Mount Rainier before returning to Seattle. Alternatively, start in Portland or Vancouver and follow the loop from there.

For directions on each leg of the trip, see the *Getting to* sections in each chapter and notes on where to stop in between.

The 14-Day Best of the Pacific Northwest

Days 1-2
SEATTLE
Spend two days visiting the many sides of Seattle (see details and suggestions on page 27). Wander the city's bustling **downtown,** watch the fish fly at **Pike Place Market,** spot volcanoes from atop the **Space Needle,** and indulge in one of **Capitol Hill's restaurants.** Add a day trip to the winemaking hub of **Woodinville,** or **hop a ferry** to see more of sparkling Puget Sound.

Days 3-5: Vancouver
SEATTLE TO VANCOUVER
141 miles, 3 hours
Head north on **I-5** to Vancouver, British Columbia. Leave plenty of time for delays at the **Peace Arch border crossing** between the United States and Canada because lanes back up on weekends and holidays.

Spend two days exploring downtown Vancouver (see details and suggestions on page 79). Bike around sprawling **Stanley Park,** tour the city's **Olympic sights,** and drive north of the city to ride the tram up **Grouse Mountain.** Add a day trip to **Whistler** and make reservations for tomorrow's ferry to Victoria.

Day 6: Victoria
VANCOUVER TO VICTORIA
113 kilometers (70 miles), 3 hours
From Vancouver, drive 35 kilometers (22 miles) south on **Highway 99** to the **Tsawwassen ferry terminal** and board the **B.C. Ferry** to Victoria. The 90-minute boat trip arrives in **Swartz Bay.** Follow **Highway 17** for 32 kilometers (20 miles) south to Victoria. It's a quick trip into the city, though traffic can build in the early morning.

Explore Victoria's Inner Harbour (see details and suggestions on page 130). Reserve an Afternoon Tea at the **Fairmont Empress Hotel,** take the Harbour Ferry to **Fisherman's Wharf,** and cap the night in bustling **Chinatown** and its historical Fan Tan Alley.

Days 7-8: Olympic Peninsula
VICTORIA TO FORKS
80 miles, 3 hours
Take the **Black Ball Ferry Line** across the Strait of Juan de Fuca, arriving in **Port Angeles,** Washington. Follow **U.S. 101** west as it passes through Olympic National Park. Take care on the two-lane highway, as trucks and cars alike can speed on the tight turns.

Spend at least one day enjoying the verdant wonders of **Olympic National Park** (see details and suggestions on page 150). Stop at **Hurricane Ridge Visitor Center** for sweeping views, and then spend the night at **Lake Crescent** or continue south to **Forks.** Day two brings quick access to the crashing waves at **La Push,** or explore the park's **Hoh Rain Forest** and **Lake Quinault.**

Best Roadside Attractions

A drive across the Pacific Northwest is beautiful, but the best part of any trip is the strange or unusual stop that breaks up a day on the road.

- **Taylor Shellfish Farms:** Oysters and clams are some of the region's best delicacies, and this outpost of one of the region's biggest purveyors is close to where they're harvested (page 22).

- **Chateau Ste. Michelle:** Woodinville's biggest winery is inside a French-style chateau surrounded by green lawns ripe for picnicking (page 39).

- **Deception Pass State Park:** Cross from Puget Sound's Whidbey Island to the mainland over a dramatic chasm, and then visit a tiny museum that celebrates the workers that built the classic park structures (page 74).

- **Capilano Suspension Bridge:** Dare to look down from the swinging wooden structure or tree houses just outside Vancouver (page 92).

- **The Butchart Gardens:** An old quarry has become a lush series of gardens, complete with a winter skating rink and boat tours (page 133).

- **Port Gamble:** The site of an old lumber town has become a quaint village with manicured lawns, a church, and a reputation for ghosts (page 149).

- **Makah Museum:** This cultural center celebrates the Native American tribe that lives in a remote corner of the Olympic Peninsula (page 178).

St. Paul's Church in Port Gamble

- **Olympia Farmers Market:** The capital city's food and craft market is right on the waterfront, near lumberyards and marinas (page 186).

- **Pelican Pub & Brewery:** Leave U.S. 101 for a tiny town on Cape Kiwanda, where you can enjoy a locally brewed beer right on the beach (page 215).

- **Sea Lion Caves:** Ride an elevator down into a cavern crowded with barking sea lions (page 230).

- **Edgefield:** This hotel property includes a brewery, movie theater, golf course, and music venues (page 255).

- **Northwest Trek Wildlife Park:** At this wildlife preserve, bison, elk, and bobcats are nursed back to health (page 313).

Day 9: Olympic Peninsula to the Oregon Coast
FORKS TO ASTORIA
185 miles, 4 hours
It's a long trip on **U.S. 101** from **Forks** down to **Astoria** on the Oregon Coast, so start early. Traffic is less likely to be an issue, but any small backup or accident on the road can cause problems. Plan to arrive in Astoria in time for a casual dinner in the industrial waterfront town.

Best Hikes

Vancouver

- **Grouse Grind:** The haul up Vancouver's city ski mountain is a challenge to the lungs and legs, but it comes with plenty of summit rewards (page 105).

Olympic Peninsula

- **Mount Storm King:** Brave some elevation gain through Olympic forest to reach lookout buildings with Lake Crescent views (page 170).

- **Sol Duc Falls:** One of the classic waterfalls of the famously lush Olympic Peninsula is just a short loop from the trailhead (page 170).

- **Hoh River Trail to Glacier Meadows:** Charge into the rain forest on a flat route along one of the Northwest's most picturesque rivers (page 174).

Oregon Coast

- **Devil's Churn:** The wild Pacific waves turn a section of Cape Perpetua into a frothing, active cauldron of seawater (page 230).

- **Hobbit Trail:** Reach the sands of the Oregon coastline through a magical, short hike that recalls a fantasy landscape (page 230).

Mount Rainier

- **Skyline Trail:** Take the first steps up giant Mount Rainier through alpine meadows, with views of the peak's giant glaciers (page 302).

- **Grove of the Patriarchs:** A suspension bridge links sections of a flat and easy ramble through the Rainier area's biggest trees (page 304).

- **Eruption Trail:** The gaping crater of Mount St. Helens provides a backdrop to an educational walk through volcanic rock and wildflowers that thrive in the ashy dirt (page 319).

Day 10: Oregon Coast
ASTORIA TO FLORENCE
183 miles, 4.5 hours
This simple drive down the Oregon Coast follows **U.S. 101** south, with worthwhile stops along the way (see details and suggestions on page 198). Stop for lunch on the sand in **Cannon Beach,** visit the aquarium in **Newport,** or take a sand dune tour in **Oregon Dunes National Recreation Area.** Exploring the **Three Capes Loop** will add extra time (and 50 miles) to this leg of the trip.

Days 11-12: Portland
FLORENCE TO PORTLAND
173 miles, 3 hours
Leave Florence early, following **U.S. 126** east for 56 miles to I-5. Take **I-5** north for 115 miles to Portland. You'll roll into the city just after the morning traffic jams.

You can see a lot of Portland in two days (see details and suggestions on page 242). Spend one day exploring downtown sights such as **Powell's City of Books** and the **South Park Blocks.** On day two, cross the Willamette River to visit the southeast neighborhoods and the **Oregon Museum of Science and Industry.**

Day 13: Mount Rainier
PORTLAND TO MOUNT RAINIER
137 miles, 2.5 hours
Leave Portland early (before rush-hour traffic). Head north on **I-5,** then take **U.S. 12** east for 30 miles. At Morton, follow **Highway 7** north for 15 miles to **Highway 706.** Turn east and take Highway 706 to Mount Rainier's **Nisqually Entrance.**

Spend the day hiking through wildflower meadows at **Paradise,** or enjoy a

clockwise from top left: Yaquina Bay Lighthouse on the Oregon Coast; Portland's Arlene Schnitzer Concert Hall; hiking in Mount Rainier National Park.

Best Scenic Drives

Astoria-Megler Bridge

- **Vancouver to Whistler:** Leave Vancouver behind and follow Highway 99, the Sea to Sky Highway, as it traces Horseshoe Bay in tight turns before climbing into steep mountains (page 104).

- **Hurricane Ridge:** From Port Angeles, ascend Hurricane Ridge Road through thick Olympic National Park forest before rising to the alpine meadows of Hurricane Ridge (page 166).

- **Astoria to Manzanita:** Cross the dramatic Astoria-Megler Bridge, then drive south down U.S. 101 along the dramatic Oregon Coast (page 197).

- **Paradise Road:** The road from the Nisqually Entrance of Mount Rainier National Park to the visitor hub at Paradise is a slow trek through thick trees past the historical buildings of Longmire and with frequent stops for wildlife, waterfalls, and mountain vistas (page 301).

---

scenic drive through the national park to **Sunrise** (see details and suggestions on page 296).

Day 14: Return to Seattle
MOUNT RAINIER TO SEATTLE
86 miles, 2 hours
In summer, head north out of the national park on **Highway 410,** driving through Enumclaw back to Seattle. When the roads are closed, exit back through the Nisqually Entrance on **Highway 706** toward Ashford and circle back to **I-5** and Seattle.

Options for Shorter Trips
SEATTLE TO VANCOUVER
Hit the region's two biggest cities in a short road trip. Start in **Seattle** and spend two days exploring the downtown sights. Drive north on **I-5,** stopping in **Anacortes**

or the tiny towns of **Bow** and **Edison.** Arrive in **Vancouver** and enjoy some outdoorsy side trips to the mountains north of the city or to **Whistler.**

PORTLAND LOOP
An easy loop from Portland includes the best of both city and nature. Spend two days discovering **Portland**'s neighborhood gems, and then take **I-5** north into Washington and drive 44 miles to Longview. At Longview, jog west on **Highway 432** to **U.S. 30** and continue 45 miles to **Astoria** on the coast. Spend a day or two following **U.S. 101** south along the coast with stops to walk on the beach or watch whales. At Newport, take **U.S. 20** east for about 63 miles to the towns of Corvallis and Albany, where it meets up with I-5. From Albany, follow **I-5** north for 70 miles to return to Portland.

Best Brewpubs and Taprooms

Rhein Haus beer garden

Seattle

* **Rhein Haus:** The bocce courts are always active and the beer steins always overflowing at this Bavarian-themed beer garden in Seattle (page 42).

Vancouver

* **Granville Island Brewing:** Tucked into Vancouver's waterfront arts and culture hub, this brewery crafts one of British Columbia's most popular brands of beer (page 95).

Victoria

* **CANOE Brewpub:** The Victoria brewer offers waterfront views and welcomes children much of the day, all in a historical brick building downtown. The brewery also hosts live music three nights a week (page 134).

Olympic Peninsula

* **Fish Tale Brewpub:** In Olympia, a town once synonymous with a cheap, fairly light beer, a new generation of thoughtful brewers is creating organic ales and creative ciders, all served next to their striking mural-covered building (page 189).

Oregon Coast

* **Fort George Brewery and Public House:** This brewer set up shop in an old service station, often hosts big public events, and likes to bring a sense of humor to brewpub decor and beer names (page 201).

* **Pelican Pub & Brewery:** Catch some salt air at this beachfront brewery in Pacific City, with a thorough menu of both pours and food options (page 215).

* **Rogue Ales Brewery:** One of Oregon's most popular beers is made here in Newport (page 224).

Portland

* **BridgePort Brewpub:** Hops are king at a classic Portland brewery known for IPAs, the region's hallmark beer (page 257).

* **Hopworks Urban Brewery:** Green practices and organic brewing give this bike-friendly beer spot an upbeat do-gooder vibe (page 257).

CONTENTS

DISCOVER
The Pacific Northwest

I t's not unusual to think of the Pacific Northwest as green and lush. But you must tour the entire region to truly appreciate how many shades of the color blanket this corner of the world.

There's the deep evergreen of Douglas fir trees and the dusty pale green of rainforest moss. The electric green of Seattle's hometown sports jerseys. A green ethos keeps Portland running on bicycle power and compost. And then there is all that green cash that companies like Starbucks, Nike, Microsoft, and others bring to the region. And envy? It seems like everyone's jealous of the great Pacific Northwest; population growth is off the charts.

Between nature and culture, every possible shade of green appears in the Pacific Northwest. The best way to see the treasures of Washington, Oregon, and British Columbia is to follow the roads connecting vibrant cities like Seattle, Vancouver, and Portland with the wild green places in between—an untamed coast, a deep forest, and a legendary mountain (or two).

Seattle

More than half a century has passed since a World's Fair transformed this Northwestern port into a global city. Just look at the Space Needle for evidence of Seattle's endless optimism and vision.

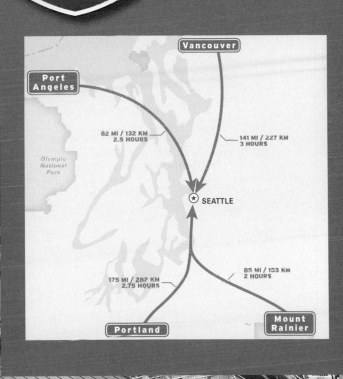

Vancouver

Port Angeles

82 MI / 132 KM
2.5 HOURS

141 MI / 227 KM
3 HOURS

Olympic National Park

⊛ SEATTLE

85 MI / 153 KM
2 HOURS

175 MI / 282 KM
2.75 HOURS

Portland

Mount Rainier

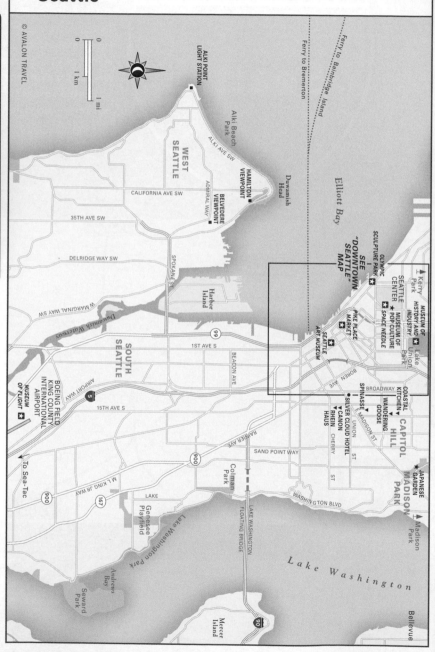

Seattle

© AVALON TRAVEL

Highlights

★ **Pike Place Market:** Fish are tossed through the air with the greatest of ease, but that's not this bustling farmers market's only famous seller—a little coffee shop called Starbucks started here in 1971 (page 26).

★ **Seattle Art Museum:** A 48-foot-tall *Hammering Man* sculpture stands at the entryway to this collection of world-class art. (page 28).

★ **Olympic Sculpture Park:** Giant art pieces by Alexander Calder and Richard Serra fit into the many terraces and levels of this waterfront space that used to be an oil transfer facility (page 31).

★ **Space Needle:** Seattle's retro emblem may date back to the city's 1962 World's Fair, but the views are timeless (page 32).

★ **Museum of History and Industry:** Ensconced in an old art deco armory building on Lake Union are city artifacts (like the city's favorite beer sign), a working periscope, and a flag made out of petticoats (page 35).

★ **Museum of Flight:** The giant building abuts an airfield and has planes of every type, including an old Air Force One and a space shuttle replica you can walk through—plus astronaut ice cream in the gift shop (page 38).

★ **Volunteer Park:** Designed by the same visionaries that laid out New York City's Central Park, the city's prettiest green space crams lawns, fountains, a conservatory, an art museum, and a castle-like tower into only 48.3 acres (page 48).

Built on a bumpy series of hills between a lake and a bay, Seattle has grown into a mature metropolis.

The vibe is more about achievement than status; it's not cool to work so hard that you can't, say, kayak a little before dinner or jam with your folk rock quartet on the weekend. A healthy arts and music scene has grown beyond Seattle's rush of '90s grunge. But never fear—the city hasn't completely moved beyond its youthful exuberance. It's still the home of the bustling coffee shop and the ambitious start-up. Creative energy explodes from tech minds, performers, and chefs who, like the Space Needle, reach for the stars.

Evidence of past success is around every corner in Seattle. Starbucks, once a tiny coffee shop near Pike Place Market, occupies downtown with the same ubiquity it's achieved around the world. The online bookstore turned tech monolith, Amazon, has colonized the South Lake Union neighborhood and helped turn its forgotten blocks into a bustling cultural center. There are signs everywhere not only of Microsoft—it began here and is headquartered just outside town—but also of the entities it helped build, like the campus of the philanthropic Bill & Melinda Gates Foundation and Paul Allen's football stadium and music museum.

Most of the country lies to the east of Seattle, but the city faces west toward Puget Sound and the Pacific Ocean. With just enough history to build considerable civic pride, there's enough optimism to look to the horizon—or perhaps just to the sunsets that illuminate the Olympic Mountains on clear nights. Sure, it rains sometimes, but it makes the beautiful days all the sweeter.

Getting to Seattle

Driving from Vancouver
141 miles, 3 hours

The drive from Vancouver to Seattle takes about 2.5 hours, though border delays can vary. Leave downtown Vancouver by taking Granville Street south over Granville Bridge. Continue south on **Highway 99** through the residential neighborhoods of greater Vancouver. Despite the frequent stoplights, traffic moves quickly outside of rush hours.

Follow Highway 99 south as it turns left on Park Drive and then south on Oak Street. Highway 99 crosses the Oak Street Bridge to become the Vancouver-Blaine Highway through the Richmond suburbs. Speeds slow at the Canada-U.S. border, and cars are directed into waiting lanes to be questioned by border control agents. Once clear of customs, pass the massive white Peace Arch monument, which claims to be the first monument built and dedicated to world peace.

The route is now called **I-5**, a freeway that runs from the Canadian border to Tijuana, Mexico. Follow I-5 south through the town of **Bellingham,** Washington, and the expansive Skagit Valley, home of a spring tulip festival. Freeway traffic may start to slow around **Everett,** an industrial hub 30 miles north of Seattle and home to some of Boeing's largest airplane factories and runways.

Express lanes, which change direction depending on time of day, may be open about 8 miles north of downtown Seattle. They are often faster than the freeway, but offer fewer off-ramps. The multilane I-5 narrows as it enters downtown Seattle, where the freeway darts through tunnels and under buildings, with exits springing both left and right.

Stopping in Bow and Edison

Leave I-5 at Bow Hill Road for a detour to the towns of Bow and Edison; both are located off scenic Chuckanut Drive/

Best Accommodations

★ **Hotel Max:** Artsy decor gives this downtown hotel the energy of a hip gallery hosting an after-party (page 61).

★ **Edgewater:** The only Seattle hotel that's actually on the water—a pier, in this case—has views that can't be beat (page 61).

★ **Ace Hotel:** This was the first in a now global chain that emphasizes style and a youth-first vibe (page 62).

★ **Sorrento Hotel:** From atop one of the city's hills, this historical, Italian-style building exudes old-world charm (page 62).

★ **Hotel Ballard:** Head here for a forward-thinking boutique property in a distant but incredibly popular neighborhood (page 63).

Highway 11, which connects to I-5 in Burlington. Each tiny town boasts bakeries, cheesemongers, and cafés. Ask for a local pint at the **The Old Edison** (5829 Cains Ct., Bow, 360/766-6266, www.theoldedison.com, 11:30am-11pm Sun.-Thurs., 11:30am-midnight Fri.-Sat.). Then follow Chuckanut Drive north to find fried oysters and a Samish Bay view at **Taylor Shellfish Farms** (2182 Chuckanut Dr., Bow, 360/766-6002, www.taylorshellfishfarms.com, 9am-5pm daily) before returning to I-5 at Burlington.

Driving from the Olympic Peninsula
82-140 miles, 2-3.5 hours
From **Forks, Port Angeles,** or **Port Townsend** on the northern Olympic Peninsula, follow U.S. 101 east to Highway 104, which runs 14 miles east to the Hood Canal Bridge. Cross the floating bridge and continue east for 9 miles on small, sometimes-winding Highway 104 through Port Gamble and to Kingston. Board the Washington State Ferry to Edmonds, a community just north of Seattle's city boundaries. From the ferry dock in Edmonds, take Highway 104 east for 5 miles to I-5, and then follow I-5 south for 13 miles to Seattle.

From **Aberdeen** on the southern Olympic Peninsula, follow Highway 8 east for 50 miles to Olympia. In Olympia, merge onto I-5 North and drive 60 miles to Seattle.

Stopping in Olympia
Right on I-5 and sitting at the bottom tip of Puget Sound is the capital city of Olympia, with a thriving downtown district, including the **Olympia Farmers Market** (700 Capitol Way N, 360/352-9096, www.olympiafarmersmarket.com, 10am-3pm Thurs.-Sun. Apr.-Oct., 10am-3pm Sat.-Sun. Nov.-Dec.), hawking fresh berries and local meats.

Driving from Portland
175 miles, 2.75 hours
Seattle is 175 miles north of Portland along I-5, about 2.75 hours without traffic; with traffic the drive can take closer to 3-3.5 hours. Exit central Portland on **I-405** North, which crosses the Willamette River over the arch of the Fremont Bridge. Join **I-5** North, which runs through residential Portland before crossing the wide Columbia River and entering Washington.

After traversing the city of Vancouver, Washington (not to be confused with Vancouver, British Columbia), I-5 runs north through rural farmland and along the Columbia River, past the small cities of Kelso, Longview, Chehalis, and Centralia.

The state capitol dome is visible from the freeway as I-5 turns northeast in

Best Restaurants

★ **Matt's at the Market:** Though the peekaboo views of Pike Place's crowds are neat, the food is also among the best downtown (page 50).

★ **Le Pichet:** A touch of Paris in downtown Seattle, this spot is perfect for a quick glass of wine with cheese plate on a rainy day (page 54).

★ **Local 360:** With all ingredients sourced from within a few hundred miles of Seattle, this playful eatery gathers the best of what's around (page 54).

★ **Canlis:** A classic, this beloved fine-dining establishment in a midcentury building has *Mad Men* style to spare (page 55).

★ **Toulouse Petit:** When it's time for a social cocktail or beignets at midnight, Queen Anne's hot spot is never boring (page 56).

★ **Portage Bay Café:** Eat breakfast the way it's meant to be done—with unlimited toppings for pancakes and waffles (page 56).

★ **Sitka and Spruce:** Like the trees it's named for, everything is Northwest in this Capitol Hill favorite, from the fresh cuisine to the funky space (page 57).

★ **Wandering Goose:** As adorable as a storybook, this biscuit bakery offers buttery treats ideal for a special-occasional breakfast (page 58).

★ **The Walrus and the Carpenter:** Oysters and shareable plates are worth the wait at this gleaming-white seafood hangout (page 59).

★ **Bastille Café:** A classy stop on busy Ballard Avenue, this is where casual French fare meets the social crowds (page 59).

Olympia; the scenic view of the Nisqually National Wildlife Refuge marks your last stretch of uninterrupted greenery. Traffic can get thick through the Joint Base Lewis McChord and the industrial city of **Tacoma,** about 35 miles south of Seattle. As you follow I-5 North into downtown Seattle, the freeway narrows and passes through several short tunnels.

Driving from Mount Rainier
85 miles, 2 hours
From the **Nisqually Entrance** on the southwest side, follow Highway 706 west for 35 miles until the road becomes Highway 7. Continue north on Highway 7 for 10 miles, and then turn right onto Highway 161/Eatonville-LaGrande Road. Follow Highway 161 north for 15 miles into Puyallup, and then take Highway 512 East to Highway 167 North. Follow Highway 167 north for 22 miles to I-405 South, which quickly heads west to I-5 in

about 2.5 miles. Once on I-5, continue 10 miles north to Seattle.

From the **White River Entrance** on the east side, follow Highway 410 north for 33 miles through Greenwater to the town of Enumclaw. Past Enumclaw, turn right onto Highway 164, which continues north for 7 miles through a hybrid of farmland and suburban residential blocks to Highway 18 in Auburn. Take Highway 18 west for 3 miles to I-5, and then follow I-5 north for 24 miles to Seattle.

By Air or Train
Air
Sea-Tac International Airport (SEA, 17801 International Blvd., 206/787-5388 or 800/544-1965, www.portseattle.org/sea-tac) is located 15 miles south of downtown Seattle. From I-5, follow Highway 518 about 1 mile west. The airport is a busy terminus that receives both domestic and international flights. At its center

Downtown Seattle

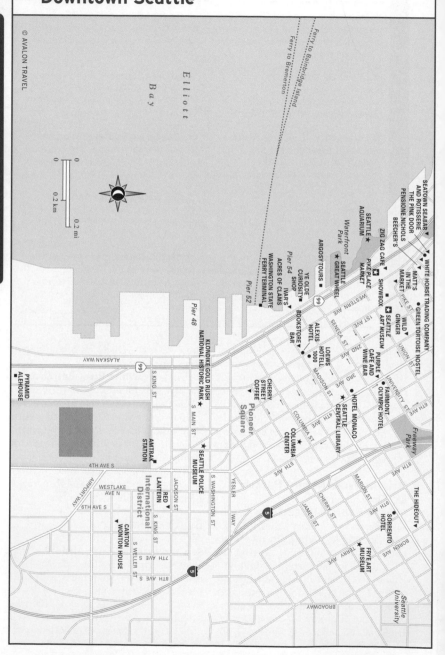

© AVALON TRAVEL

Elliott Bay

Ferry to Bainbridge Island

Ferry to Bremerton

0
0.2 km
0
0.2 mi

SEATOWN SEABAR AND ROTISSERIE
THE PINK DOOR
PENSIONE NICHOLS
BEECHER'S
WHITE HORSE TRADING COMPANY
GREEN TORTOISE HOSTEL
MATT'S IN THE MARKET
WILD GINGER
ZIG ZAG CAFE
SHOWBOX
PURPLE CAFE AND WINE BAR
SEATTLE ART MUSEUM
Waterfront Park
SEATTLE AQUARIUM
PIKE PLACE MARKET
ARGOSY TOURS
SEATTLE GREAT WHEEL
Pier 54
YE OLDE CURIOSITY SHOP
IVAR'S ACRES OF CLAMS
WASHINGTON STATE FERRY TERMINAL
Pier 52
Pier 48
ALEXIS HOTEL
LOEWS HOTEL 1000
BOOKSTORE BAR
FAIRMONT OLYMPIC HOTEL
HOTEL MONACO
KLONDIKE GOLD RUSH NATIONAL HISTORIC PARK
ALASKAN WAY
CHERRY STREET COFFEE
SEATTLE CENTRAL LIBRARY
COLUMBIA CENTER
Pioneer Square
PYRAMID ALEHOUSE
AMTRAK STATION
SEATTLE POLICE MUSEUM
THE HIDEOUT
SORRENTO HOTEL
FRYE ART MUSEUM
WESTLAKE AVE N
RED LANTERN
International District
CANTON WONTON HOUSE
Freeway Park
Seattle University

ALASKAN WAY
WESTERN AVE
1ST AVE
2ND AVE
3RD AVE
4TH AVE
5TH AVE
6TH AVE
7TH AVE
8TH AVE
9TH AVE
BOREN AVE
TERRY AVE
MINOR AVE
BROADWAY
AIRPORT WAY
6TH AVE S
7TH AVE S
8TH AVE S
AIRPORT WAY S
4TH AVE S
UNION ST
UNIVERSITY ST
SENECA ST
SPRING ST
MADISON ST
MARION ST
COLUMBIA ST
CHERRY ST
JAMES ST
YESLER WAY
S KING ST
S MAIN ST
S JACKSON ST
S WASHINGTON ST
S KING ST
S WELLER ST
99
5

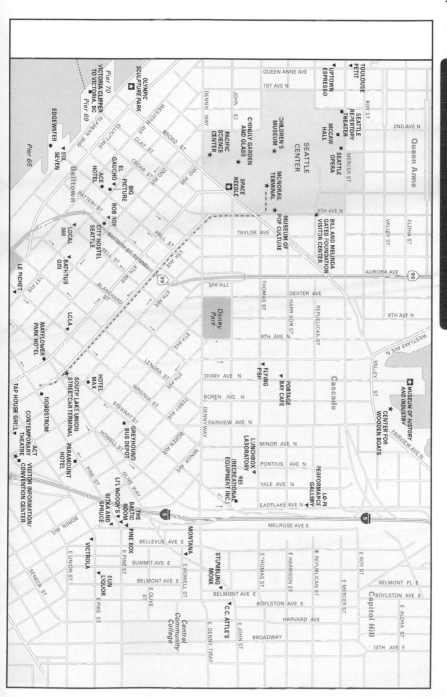

is a large glass atrium lined with rocking chairs and outposts of local restaurants. Parking ($3-4 per hour), car rentals (3150 S. 160th St.), and public transportation are available.

A taxi from the airport to the downtown core costs a flat rate of $40. The **Central Link light rail** (www.soundtransit. org, 5am-1am Mon.-Sat., 6am-midnight Sun., $3) traces a 40-minute ride through Seattle's southern neighborhoods before stopping in the downtown underground transit tunnel. The **Downtown Airporter** (425/981-7000, https://downtownairporter.hudsonltd.net) provides shuttle service from the airport to select hotels downtown.

Train

Amtrak (800/872-7245, www.amtrak. com) trains arrive and depart daily from Seattle's King Street Station (303 S Jackson St.), located near Pioneer Square just south of downtown. The *Cascades* route travels from Vancouver, BC, to Eugene, Oregon, with stops in Tacoma, Portland, and Salem; the *Empire Builder* route runs east all the way to Chicago; and the *Coast Starlight* travels south from Seattle with stops in Portland, Oregon, and throughout California.

Sights

It doesn't matter what the weather is—the open-air farmers market is open even in the rain, and the top of the Space Needle is a thrill even on a cloudy day. Much of the city's sights revolve around the futuristic, innovative energy of the city, from the *Hammering Man* in front of the art museum to the Tomorrowland-like Seattle Center.

Downtown

The hilly core of Seattle is a tight space, perched on hills that spill down to the dark waters of Elliott Bay, a part of the deep V of saltwater Puget Sound. The urban core first grew up around Pioneer Square, just south of today's busiest and biggest buildings, where the white Smith Tower is just one architectural gem preserved from an earlier era. More recent buildings, like the skyscraping Columbia Tower, are reflective glass giants, while at their feet is a walkable, if sometimes vertical, city.

★ Pike Place Market

Looking for some flying fish? Just follow the crowds to **Pike Place Fish Market** (86 Pike St., Pike Place Market, 206/682-7181, www.pikeplacefish.com, 6:30am-6pm Mon.-Sat., 7am-5pm Sun.). One of downtown's most popular attractions is the market's tossed halibut, salmon, and crabs—from one fishmonger to another, so don't worry about catching them yourself. Why throw fish? If you ask the loud, jovial workers, they'll probably just answer "Why not?" The practice started early in the fish market's life, simply to hurry the purchased wares back behind the counter, where they were weighed and wrapped. Soon they began having fun with all the fish tossing, and crowds began to gather for the show, not the seafood itself. The centrally located fish stand, topped with a "World Famous" sign, sells oyster shooters in souvenir shot glasses ($3.50) and cookbooks, as well as fresh seafood. Kids may notice the mouth of a dead fish moving—it's a trick the staff performs using fishing line and fish with particularly gruesome mouths.

But that's only the beginning of the sights and sounds to take in at Pike Place Market. Around every corner are accomplished buskers, and stalls sell local vegetables, flowers, and crafts. A row of more permanent stores face the public market, with local cheesemonger **Beecher's** (1600 Pike Pl., 206/956-1964, www.beechershandmadecheese.com, 9am-7pm daily) offering a glimpse of its curds, whey, and giant metal mixers in the signature Flagship cheddar assembly line.

Also facing the market is a little coffee

Two Days in Seattle

Seattle is an international city with arts, food, science, and the outdoors to explore. To get the most in a short trip, focus first on the city's core, and then venture out onto the water or to one of the city's parks.

Day 1

Start the day like any other day—at **Starbucks** (page 28). The location in Pike Place Market isn't quite as "original" as the T-shirts and mugs would have you believe, but it's an interesting reminder that the chain used to be just another local coffee stand. Java in hand, explore **Pike Place Market** (page 26) and its long rows of craft and food stands. Watch fish fly at **Pike Place Fish Market** (page 26), and venture past the **Gum Wall** (page 28).

Walk two blocks south along 1st Avenue to the *Hammering Man* at the **Seattle Art Museum** (page 28), and venture inside for one of the West Coast's best art collections. From there it's only three blocks down University Street (head down the steps at the *Hammering Man*) to the waterfront—just head for the big, round **Seattle Great Wheel** (page 29). Take a boat ride on **Argosy Cruises** (page 39) or hop a big white **Washington State Ferry** (page 66).

Once you're back on dry land, take a cab to the **Seattle Center** (page 32). You're probably starving, and the Armory hosts small outlets of some of the city's best cheap eats. The Seattle Center alone contains enough entertainment for a week, so pick your (fun, cool) poison: science at the **Pacific Science Center** (page 33) or rock and roll and pop culture at the **Museum of Pop Culture** (page 34). Topping either one will take something big—like, say, the **Space Needle** (page 32). Travel to the observation deck at the top and catch views in every direction.

For dinner, head to Belltown and hit up one of the city's memorable restaurants: **El Gaucho** (page 54) is known for steak, while **Six Seven** (page 51) earns acclaim for both seafood and its waterfront location. If you still have energy, return downtown for a symphony show at **Benaroya Hall** (page 44) or rock at the **Showbox** (page 42).

Day 2

Start the day with French toast and the breakfast toppings bar at **Portage Bay Café** (page 56) in South Lake Union. Walk 0.5 mile east on Harrison Street and then turn right on Yale Avenue for some quick shopping at **REI** (page 46). Or simply follow Terry Avenue north to Lake Union Park and the **Museum of History and Industry** (page 35) to learn the story of Seattle and its high-flying, computer-inventing ways. Before you leave South Lake Union, head back down Terry Avenue and grab a massive meal at **Lunchbox Laboratory** (page 56).

Drive northwest to **Discovery Park** (page 36) and ramble out to the beach. Enjoy your lunch and explore the tide pools and historical lighthouse. The former fort is big enough that you'll forget you're in the middle of the Northwest's biggest city.

Reenter civilization by driving north on 15th Avenue West and across one of the city's many drawbridges to reach Ballard, a former fishing center. Turn west on NW Market Street to reach the **Hiram M. Chittenden Locks** (page 49). The locks are more than an engineering marvel, though it's fun to watch the gates open and the locks fill as boats move in and out. But there's also a fish ladder with underground viewing windows and a botanical garden.

Before leaving Ballard, try some of the neighborhood's fine dining. Back on NW Market Street, turn south on 22nd Avenue to reach Ballard Avenue and the French fare at **Bastille Café** (page 59). Or wait for the city's best oyster bar at the superb **The Walrus and the Carpenter** (page 59), a mere three blocks away. Bars in Ballard are among the city's best, so stay on Ballard Avenue and take a tipple at **Noble Fir** (page 41) or **King's Hardware** (page 41), and drink as the anglers once did on these very streets. Finish the night in Capitol Hill—dancing at **Q** (page 42) and drinks at the bustling **Quinn's Pub** (page 57) go late.

Tillicum Village

Seattle may have gained global prominence in the 20th century, but **Tillicum Village** (Pier 55, 1101 Alaskan Way, 206/622-8687, www.tillicumvillage.com, $84 adults, $75 seniors, $32 children 4-12, children under 4 free; cruise only: $40 adults, $20 children 4-12, children under 4 free) is a reminder that people have lived along Puget Sound for centuries. The village is located on Blake Island, a state park about 8 miles from Seattle and birthplace of Chief Seattle. The buildings are re-creations of those built by the Coast Salish people. Tillicum Village is only accessed by a boat tour and meal experience, though boaters can land on the rest of forested Blake Island for free. The potlatch—a Native American festival—includes traditional dances done in elaborate costume and storytelling by a native of a local tribe, plus steamed clams and salmon cooked on cedar planks over alderwood fires in the longhouse. Trips take about four hours total.

shop that goes by the name of **Starbucks** (1912 Pike Pl., 206/448-8762, www.starbucks.com, 6:30am-9pm daily). The chain's first location was a few doors down, but this early outpost retains a few old-timey touches, like a logo whose mermaid mascot is more bare-breasted than the version that's been exported worldwide. Lines for a latte or vintage-style Starbucks swag often snake out the door.

Seattle's stickiest attraction is the **Gum Wall** (1428 Post Alley between Pike St. and Pike Pl.), located down an alley near the entrance to Pike Place Market. It started when theatergoers of a nearby improv theater began leaving their gum on the building's exterior. Now it's a giant mess of multicolored blobs—some people even spell out names with their bubblegum. The attraction was rated the second-germiest in the world (second only to the kissable Blarney Stone).

On the north end of the market, **Victor Steinbrueck Park** (2001 Western Ave., 206/684-4075, 6am-10pm daily) offers waterfront views, two traditional cedar totem poles, and a rather gritty assortment of park visitors.

★ Seattle Art Museum
Just look for the hammering man—the moving sculpture that stands guard in front of the **Seattle Art Museum** (1300 1st Ave., 206/654-3100, www.seattleartmuseum.org, 10am-5pm Wed. and Fri.-Sun., 10am-9pm Thurs., $20 adults, $18 seniors, $13 students, children free) takes a break only on Labor Day. The art on display ranges from the cutting edge—a life-size tree made of small wooden pieces hangs in the foyer—to the traditional, with artists like John Singer Sargent and Jackson Pollock represented. There are also galleries of Northwest art: Outside, a line of video screens displays nature and city images, and occasionally even live shots from below the museum. Admission is free the first Thursday of the month, and periodic SAM Remix events open the galleries extra late on Friday nights and feature a raucous dance party.

Seattle Aquarium
From its spot on two piers, **Seattle Aquarium** (1483 Alaskan Way, 206/386-4300, www.seattleaquarium.org, 9:30am-5pm daily, $29.95 adults, $19.95 children 4-12, children under 4 free) dangles over the waters it celebrates. In the lobby a giant Window on Washington Waters tank is filled with local fish, and throughout the day divers pop inside to show off its inhabitants. Look for the mottled orange of the rockfish, which can live up to 100 years but develops eye problems in captivity. The Seattle Aquarium's vet has done extensive work on eye surgery and even hopes to provide prosthetic eyes for the creatures. The aquarium has

touch tide pools and bird exhibits, plus weird-looking sea creatures like the octopus and hundreds of jellyfish. Larger habitats house sea and river otters, and a new amphitheater-style area holds three harbor seals. Check at the front desk for the schedule of daily animal feedings. The café has pizzas, sandwiches, some seafood entrées (sustainable ones only, of course), and microbrews, and the outdoor balcony is open on days with decent weather.

Seattle Great Wheel
When the **Seattle Great Wheel** (1301 Alaskan Way, 206/623-8600, www.seattlegreatwheel.com, 10am-11pm Sun.-Thurs., 10am-midnight Fri.-Sat., shorter hours in winter, $14 adults, $12 seniors, $9 children 4-11, children under 4 free) popped up on Seattle's waterfront in 2012, it took the city by surprise—but it carried a million riders in its first year. The 175-foot ride is the tallest of its kind on the West Coast, and the enclosed cars can hold eight people each. From inside each gondola, the views shift from downtown Seattle to Elliott Bay and the Olympic Mountains across Puget Sound, and the Ferris wheel's end-of-the-pier location means that you'll dangle over the dark blue water. One of the cars is not like the others: The VIP gondola has leather seats and a glass floor, and a ride inside ($50) comes with a champagne toast, free T-shirt, and the ability to skip the line.

Ye Olde Curiosity Shop
Ye Olde Curiosity Shop (1001 Alaskan Way, 206/682-5844, www.yeoldecuriosityshop.com, 9am-9pm daily summer; 10am-6pm Sun.-Thurs., 9am-9pm Fri.-Sat. winter) is indeed a shop, but it's also a historical Seattle attraction. In 1899 it opened as the Free Museum and Curio, mainly showing off artifacts from Alaska that gold rushers had brought back. The preserved mummy named Sylvester is the shop's biggest attraction; the body was supposedly dug from the Arizona

desert in 1895 and may have been mummified by natural dehydration, though a CT scan revealed the bullet that killed him. There's also a large collection of shrunken human heads, Siamese cow bodies, walrus tusks, and the Lord's Prayer engraved on a single grain of rice. The wares for sale are a little less exotic—souvenirs, porcelain collectibles, and saltwater taffy, plus Northwest Native American totem poles and masks. You can also buy a shrunken head replica made of goat hide.

Seattle Central Library
There are a million books inside **Seattle Central Library** (1000 4th Ave., 206/386-4636, www.spl.org, 10am-8pm Mon.-Thurs., 10am-6pm Fri.-Sat., noon-6pm Sun., free) and nearly as many glass panels on the unusual exterior. Being inside is something like visiting a greenhouse, but one that grows books. The windowed building was designed by Dutch architect Rem Koolhaas and has enough glass to cover more than five football fields. Groups of five or larger can book free tours of the space, but everyone can wander for free and access the cell phone tour (206/686-8564). Readings and events occur daily in the library's auditorium and other meeting spaces, and the expansive 3rd floor has a café, reading areas, and computers with Internet access. For the best views in the building, head to level 10, the Betty Jane Narver Reading Room.

Columbia Center Sky View Observatory
How high do you want to go? Visit **Columbia Center Sky View Observatory** (701 5th Ave., 206/386-5564, www.skyviewobservatory.com, 8am-11pm daily, $14.95 adults, $9.75 seniors, students, and children 6-12, children under 6 free) for the absolute tallest observation point in the city (yes, taller than the Space Needle). The view at 902 feet off the ground makes it the highest publicly

accessible spot west of the Mississippi. On the way up, visit the 40th-floor Starbucks, the chain's highest outpost in the world.

Frye Art Museum

The charming **Frye Art Museum** (704 Terry Ave., 206/622-9250, www.fryemuseum.org, 11am-5pm Tues.-Wed. and Fri.-Sun., 11am-7pm Thurs., free) isn't too far from downtown, tucked away among the hospitals of First Hill, but it has a quieter vibe (and free parking). The Fryes, a Seattle couple who lived in the early 20th century, left a collection of European paintings, and the museum has since taken on a collection of contemporary art and hosting of temporary exhibits as well. The Fryes stipulated that their art be shown for free and in particular arrangements; the building was designed by modernist architect Paul Thiry and is made up of large concrete forms and sharp right angles. Free public tours are given daily at 1pm, and the museum also houses a café.

Pioneer Square

Pioneer Square (Yesler Way and 1st Ave., www.pioneersquare.org), located on the south end of downtown, is the city's oldest neighborhood. Much of the architecture is classic Victorian and Edwardian styles, built on fill that buried the first story of many of the town's buildings after a fire ravaged the area. During the Klondike gold rush, the Pioneer Square neighborhood was full of outfitters and saloons where prospectors would prepare for the trip to Alaska. During the Great Depression, a shantytown emerged and the area fell into disrepair. Since the 1960s, the Pioneer Square buildings have been preserved and protected. Although the whole neighborhood carries the name, Pioneer Square itself is at the corner of Yesler Way and 1st Avenue, a relatively small patch of grass and an ornate pergola that dates back to the 1909 Alaska-Yukon-Pacific Exposition.

Klondike Gold Rush National Historical Park

When you think "gold rush," you probably either picture California or Alaska, not Seattle. But the **Klondike Gold Rush National Historical Park** (319 2nd Ave. S, 206/220-4240, www.nps.gov/klse, 9am-5pm daily summer, 10am-5pm daily winter, free), run by the National Park Service, is located in the middle of the Pioneer Square neighborhood. The museum tells the story of how Seattle served as the gateway to the Klondike. Old newspaper reports reveal the great excitement that arose in 1897 when gold from the Klondike River in Alaska and Canada arrived via steamship at the American ports. Prospectors came to Seattle to be outfitted for the trip north—even Seattle's own mayor quit to join the stampede. The Canadian Mounties, worried that all those people were going to starve in the wilderness, began requiring that each person bring a year's worth of food. Fun hands-on exhibits and gold-panning demonstrations show how the Seattle economy grew from that gold rush—and how poorly most prospectors fared.

Underground Tour

If someone tells you a separate city exists underneath the streets of Seattle, they're not pulling your leg (probably). The **Underground Tour** (608 1st Ave., 206/682-4646, www.undergroundtour. com, 9am-7pm daily summer, 10am-6pm daily winter, $22 adults, $20 seniors and students, $10 children 7-12, children under 7 free) began in the 1960s when renovation of the Pioneer Square area reminded locals that the original first story of many buildings had been buried with dirt to stabilize the marshy tidal area. A *Seattle Times* reporter began leading people down dark stairways to the buried sidewalks and edifices. Now the tour is incredibly popular and even has an occasional adult-oriented version that points out old opium dens and red-light districts. The walking tour is fascinating, even if the underground spaces are a bit more cramped than one would imagine when they hear the phrase "buried city."

Smith Tower

The Space Needle is weirder and the Columbia Tower is taller, but the **Smith Tower** (506 2nd Ave., 206/622-4004, www.smithtower.com, 10am-9pm daily, $19 adults, $15 seniors, students, and children 6-12, children under 6 free) is a beautiful historical building that used to be the tallest in the West. Built in 1914, the pointy white tower was long a symbol for the city. On the 35th floor—reached on an original Otis elevator with operator—an observation deck offers a 360-degree view of the city, waterfront, and distant mountains. The outdoor viewing deck is surrounding by ornate white gates, and the room is a lovely destination with breathtaking views. Though it once held Chinese artifacts, it's now part of a larger historical tour and experience, with a bar that serves retro speakeasy-style cocktails.

Belltown
★ Olympic Sculpture Park

An oil company's waterfront land was reborn as **Olympic Sculpture Park** (2901 Western Ave., 206/654-3100, www.seattleartmuseum.org, sunrise-sunset daily; pavilion: 10am-5pm Tues.-Sun. summer, 10am-4pm Tues.-Sun. winter, free), a series of zigzagging green spaces that hold massive works of art. The centerpiece is Alexander Calder's *The Eagle*, a twisted figure in red visible to the ferries that cross Elliott Bay. A glass bridge is decorated with images of the skyline, and the piece *Love & Loss* has a prominent ampersand on a tall spike. A Z-shaped path crosses the green space as it leads down to the water. The vivarium, a narrow building with a 60-foot nurse log

from top to bottom: Seattle Aquarium; Seattle Central Library; Pike Place Market.

Seattle's World's Fair

Even Elvis discovered Seattle in 1962 when the Century 21 Exposition put the city on the map. The World's Fair was meant to show off Washington State as the center of jet-age progress, proving it was more than an out-of-the-way region often confused with Washington, D.C.

Over breakfast meetings in the city's finest hotel, the Olympic, a group of businessmen dreamed up the infrastructure that would become Seattle's icons—the Seattle Center, the monorail, the Space Needle. In the middle of the space race against the Soviet Union, the home of Boeing had to show off its science and technology above all. A giant replica of a dam had water falling down six spillways, and a giant glass elevator called the Bubbleator took riders through a World of Tomorrow exhibit. There was even a visit from a famous cosmonaut, Gherman Titov, but his notoriety was religious, not technological—at his World's Fair press conference, he proclaimed, "I don't believe in God. I believe in man." Four days later, U.S. astronaut John Glenn agreed that he didn't see God in space, but only because God was too big for such an appearance.

For all the showing off, the fair was mostly about fun. The country tasted its first Belgian waffles in a popular stand on the outdoor area called the Gayway. Rides and games for the kiddies were out front, but an observant visitor could find Show Street, where the bawdy Gracie Hanson hosted a topless girlie show.

The Shah of Iran, a British prince, Bob Hope, and Lassie all popped by the six-month fair, but of the almost 10 million visitors, none was more adored than Elvis Presley. He shot the film *It Happened at the World's Fair* and, in his off hours, avoided crowds by going on double dates with a production assistant—one was even to see an Elvis movie.

When the Century 21 Exposition finally closed in October 1962, its most anticipated guest, President John F. Kennedy, bowed out, claiming a cold. The festivities went on without him, and a few days later it was revealed that the Cuban Missile Crisis, not congestion, had kept JFK away.

inside, showcases an intersection of art and nature—illustrating how a dying tree serves as an incubator for new plants. Outside, the sculpture park includes ginkgo and dawn redwood trees, plus meadow grasses and a shoreline often visited by seals. A pavilion holds restrooms and offices, plus a large space for events.

Queen Anne
Seattle Center

Born as the fairgrounds of the 1962 World's Fair, the **Seattle Center** (305 Harrison St., 206/684-7200, www.seattlecenter.com) is a giant play space, workshop, stage, and meeting spot. Beyond its signature tall white arches—part of the Pacific Science Center, designed by the same architect that designed New York City's World Trade Center—is the domed International fountain and 74 acres of performance spaces, museums, and parks. The Seattle Center serves as the city's collective backyard, or perhaps its welcoming parlor, as a number of festivals take place on the grounds celebrating music, art, and culture. One lawn has a giant, multicolored outdoor glass mosaic by Paul Horiuchi, and a pagoda made of Japanese cypress wood houses a bell that was given to the city by its sister city, Kobe, Japan.

★ Space Needle

The city's retro icon was born as a sketch on a cocktail napkin by one of the 1962 World's Fair planners, but the 605-foot **Space Needle** (400 Broad St., 206/905-2100, www.spaceneedle.com) was built in less than a year. During the World's Fair, the space-age elevators were operated by pretty young women; today the operators (of both genders) tell a quick story of the tower during the trip to the top. At 520 feet, the **Observation Deck** (10am-11pm Mon.-Thurs., 9:30am-11:30am Fri.-Sat., 9:30am-11pm Sun., $19-29 adults, $16-22 seniors, $13-18 youth 4-12, children 3 and under free) features indoor and outdoor binoculars and information on what you can see (or what you'd see if the clouds would clear); a snack bar and gift shop are located inside. Timed tickets can be purchased in advance; lines often wrap the Space Needle base, so plan ahead. The revolving **SkyCity Restaurant** is undergoing renovations but slated to reopen in spring 2018, and will eventually feature a glass floor.

Pacific Science Center

Life-size dinosaurs and bigger-than-life IMAX films live at the kid-friendly **Pacific Science Center** (200 2nd Ave. N, 206/443-2001, www.pacificsciencecenter.org, 10am-5pm Mon. and Wed.-Fri., 10am-6pm Sat. Sun., $19.75 adults, $17.75 seniors, $14.75 children 6-15, $11.75 children 3-5, children under 3 free). During the 1962 World's Fair, this was the U.S. Science Pavilion, and there's a retro mid-century feel to the outdoor pools and boxy buildings. The exhibits inside are much more up to date, featuring a live-weather globe and interactive health displays. Warm and humid, the Tropical Butterfly House is filled with 500 tropical butterflies every week; animal exhibits, such as the East African naked mole rat, include residents known to be a little less glamorous. Outside, the *Sonic Bloom*'s sculptured flowers show off the power of solar radiation by glowing with solar-powered energy. Laser shows take place regularly, arranged to pop or psychedelic tunes, and large visiting history and art exhibitions come to the newly renovated gallery space. Two IMAX theaters show nature films and popular cinema (shows and special exhibitions require additional tickets).

Seattle Children's Museum

Located downstairs in the Armory, the **Seattle Children's Museum** (305 Harrison St., 206/441-1768, www.thechildrensmuseum.org, 10am-5pm Mon.-Fri., 10am-6pm Sat.-Sun., $11.50 adults and children, $10.50 seniors, children under 1 free) appeals to tots 10 and younger—in fact, you have to have a kid of that age to enter. Exhibits are hands on and image based, like the Global Village where the dresser drawers and table are filled with clothing and food from around the world. There is a construction zone, play bus, and a big art studio.

Although the building has had many uses both during and after the World's Fair, today the Armory serves as a pavilion boasting a truly gourmet food court. Some of Seattle's most popular restaurants have outposts here, including Skillet Street Food, Mod Pizza, Bigfood BBQ, and Eltana Wood-Fired Bagels. Order from the counter and then head outside if the weather's good; public bathrooms are also available in the building.

Chihuly Garden and Glass

You can't go far in the Northwest without seeing some spectacular glass art. **Chihuly Garden and Glass** (305 Harrison St., 206/753-4940, www.chihulygardenandglass.com, 11am-8pm Sun.-Thurs., 11am-9pm Fri.-Sat., $29 adults, $22 seniors, $18 children 5-12, children under 5 free) celebrates the country's most famous glassblower, Dale Chihuly, with a gallery of his works and a fanciful garden of glass flowers and sculpture. Prepare to feel like Alice wandering around Wonderland. Chihuly's signature bulbs are lit creatively inside. One room consists of a glass ceiling overflowing with anemone-like works, while another turns the pieces into a light installation. The attached Collections Café reflects Chihuly's penchant for collections—each table center has handfuls of his tin toys, or accordions, or carnival masks, or other items housed under glass.

Museum of Pop Culture

What would you do with a billion dollars? Microsoft cofounder Paul Allen started, among other things, the Experience Music Project in honor of Jimi Hendrix and his hometown's musical heritage, and the Frank Gehry-designed building morphed into the EMP Museum and now the **Museum of Pop Culture** (325 5th Ave. N, 206/770-2700, www.mopop.org, 10am-7pm daily summer, 10am-5pm daily winter, $33 adults, $30 seniors and students, $24 children 5-17, children under 5 free), dedicated to pop culture. Outside the museum's guitar tower are interactive booths for trying out keyboards or turntables. Downstairs an animatronic dragon overlooks a fantasy exhibit (pull his tail—he'll move), which also has a giant magical tree and interactive exhibits about fantasy archetypes. Also downstairs, a science fiction exhibit includes a *Star Trek* captain's chair and *Doctor Who* props.

Seattle Center Monorail

The lumbering old metal **Seattle Center Monorail** (Harrison and Broad Sts., 206/905-2600, www.seattlemonorail.com, 7:30am-11pm Mon.-Fri., 8:30am-11pm Sat.-Sun. summer; 7:30am-9pm Mon.-Thurs., 7:30am-11pm Fri., 8:30am-11pm Sat., 8:30am-9pm Sun. winter, $2.25 adults, $1 seniors and children 5-12, children under 5 free) skates down a mile-long track to the center of downtown, a reminder of the city's once-extensive plans for public transportation. The trip is great fun for transportation junkies or tourists looking to see the city from a few stories up, but it's not much of a commuter time-saver, running from the Seattle Center to the Westlake Mall. Still, the train rumbling above 5th Avenue or through the Experience Museum Project, which was built around it, remains one of the enduring sights of Seattle.

Seattle Center Monorail passing through the Museum of Pop Culture

Bill & Melinda Gates Foundation Visitor Center

Although Bill Gates first made his mark as the founder of Microsoft, he's now trying to solve the world's biggest problems of health and extreme poverty through his foundation. The **Bill & Melinda Gates Foundation Visitor Center** (440 5th Ave. N, 206/709-3100, www.gatesfoundation. org, 10am-5pm daily, free) is a chance to highlight for visitors what the foundation does. The ash and apple wood displays explain how the Gates' money helps smaller organizations deliver health care and crop assistance. A giant interactive wall offers a timeline of the Gates family and the group itself. But perhaps the biggest emphasis is on toilets: In an effort to bring sustainable sanitation to people living in unhygienic conditions, the foundation's Reinvent the Toilet Challenge produced a waterless solar-powered toilet prototype that now stands in the lobby.

South Lake Union
★ Museum of History and Industry

When the **Museum of History and Industry** (860 Terry Ave. N, 206/324-1126, www.mohai.org, 10am-5pm Fri.-Wed., 10am-8pm Thurs. summer; 10am-5pm daily winter, $19.95 adults, $15.95 seniors, $13.95 students, children free) moved to this waterfront ex-armory building in 2012, it spurred a renewed interest in the museum's mix of artifacts, hands-on exhibits, and curiosities. The working World War II-era periscope offers a chance to peek out onto Lake Union, and displays explain the impact of events like the Great Seattle Fire of 1889 and the 1962 World's Fair. An old notepad bears the scribbling of a young Bill Gates, and the city's preeminent beer sign, from the old Rainier brewery, gets center stage. Outside are several historical ships and tugboats and a small pond with model sailboat rentals.

South Lake Union Streetcar

The city of Seattle has almost as many forms of transportation as it has hills. The **South Lake Union Streetcar** (206/553-3060, www.seattlestreetcar.org, 6am-9pm Mon.-Thurs., 6am-11pm Fri.-Sat., 10am-7pm Sun., $2.25 adults, $1 seniors, $1.50 children 6-17, children under 6 free) begins at Stewart Street and Fifth Avenue and travels through the South Lake Union neighborhood and up the east side of Lake Union. The neighborhood has quickly become home to new restaurants and stores in recent years, thanks to the relocation of the Amazon campus to the once-sleepy neighborhood.

Capitol Hill
Seattle Asian Art Museum

The **Seattle Asian Art Museum** (1400 E Prospect St., 206/654-3100, www.seattleartmuseum.org) is operated by the Seattle Art Museum, but is located in the middle of Volunteer Park in a beautiful 1933 building that once housed the entire SAM collection, with pieces of Chinese,

Indian, Korean, Japanese, and Southeast Asian origin. Replicas of Ming dynasty camel statues sit outside among well-kept flower beds, perfect as props in a photo. The museum is currently closed for renovations but anticipates reopening in 2019.

University District

Locals say "UW" or the shorter "U-Dub" when they're talking about the sprawling **University of Washington** (1401 NE Campus Pkwy., 206/543-9686, www.washington.edu). The campus was first a fairground, host to the 1909 Alaska-Yukon-Pacific Exposition. Students crowd the central Red Square between classes or relax on grassy quads, but the busiest gathering space on game days is the rebuilt Husky Stadium on Lake Washington.

Burke Museum of Natural History and Culture

What's cooler than dinosaur skeletons? How about the bones of a giant sloth, remains that were found at Seattle-Tacoma airport and delivered to the **Burke Museum of Natural History and Culture** (17th Ave. NE and NE 45th St., 206/543-5590, www.burkemuseum.org, 10am-5pm daily, $10 adults, $8 seniors, $7.50 students and children 5 and older, children under 4 free) at the University of Washington. The fossils of a mastodon and stegosaurus are even more massive, and the museum holds treasures that didn't come out of the dirt as well. A survey of the Pacific cultures that influenced the Northwest includes exhibits from Japan, Korea, China, and Hawaii. A new building opens in 2019, and throughout the move the old building will show the behind-the-scenes work of moving specimens to the new space.

Henry Art Gallery

The University of Washington's **Henry Art Gallery** (15th Ave. NE at NE 41st St., 206/543-2280, www.henryart.org, 11am-4pm Wed. and Fri.-Sun., 11am-9am Thurs., $10 adults, $6 seniors, students and children under 14 free) is not only a repository for art, it's one of the university's hubs for arts and cultural events. Originally founded by a local philanthropist as the first public art museum in the state, it started with 19th- and 20th-century paintings but later grew to have a substantial photography collection and new-media installations. There are also textiles from around the world, including rugs from Central Asia and costumes from Eastern Europe. The gallery's café (8am-4pm Tues.-Fri., 10:30am-2pm Sat.-Sun.) has salads, sandwiches, and coffee, plus pastries and wraps.

Ballard

Nordic Heritage Museum

Although much of the Northwest can trace some roots to Scandinavia, Ballard in particular was founded by people of Northern Europe. So it's no wonder the **Nordic Heritage Museum** (3014 NW 67th St., 206/789-5707, www.nordicmuseum.org, 10am-4pm Tues.-Sat., noon-4pm Sun., $8 adults, $7 seniors and students, $6 children 5-18, children under 5 free) is located in Ballard. The building was an elementary school built in 1907, so the museum houses classrooms, an auditorium, and a library as well as exhibit spaces. Those exhibits show off photos and artifacts that tell the story of Nordic immigrants to the United States in the 19th century, especially their work in the fishing and lumber industries. The Folk Art Galleries have costumes, textiles, and furniture with roots in the Nordic countries: Denmark, Finland, Iceland, Norway, and Sweden. Visiting exhibitions explore specific artists or themes.

Greater Seattle

Discovery Park

The large waterfront **Discovery Park** (3801 Discovery Park Blvd., 206/386-4236, www.seattle.gov, park: 4am-11pm daily, cultural center: 8:30am-5pm Tues.-Sun., free), near the Seattle neighborhood of Magnolia, used to be a military installation called Fort Lawton, though the army presence there was never very large. In World War II it served as a POW camp for Germans and Italians, and some of the latter were allowed to socialize with Seattle residents. More than 500 acres became Discovery Park in the 1970s, named for George Vancouver's ship, including areas around the 1881 West Point Lighthouse on Puget Sound. The park has more than 2 miles of beaches, plus wooded bluffs and meadows with great views. Trails cross the park; it's a 1.5-mile walk to the beach from the parking lots, passing some old military buildings and a radar that serves as backup for the Seattle-Tacoma airport. There are tennis courts and a playground, and tide pools are visible during low tides on the north beach. The visitors center at the main entrance has park staff and limited exhibits.

Woodland Park Zoo

The 92 acres of **Woodland Park Zoo** (550 Phiney Ave. N, Green Lake, 206/548-2500, www.zoo.org, 9:30am-6pm daily spring-summer, $20.95 adults, $18.95 seniors, $12.95 children 3-12, children under 3 free; 9:30am-4pm daily fall-winter, $14.95 adults, $12.95 seniors, $9.95 children 3-12, children under 3 free) hold more than 1,000 animals of more than 300 species, many of which are endangered. Nearly a million people visit the zoo every year, so it's one of the city's busiest attractions. An African Savanna area has giraffes, hippos, gazelles, and zebras, and the Tropical Asia exhibit has orangutans. Keepers give demonstrations with different raptor species, and grizzly bears are fed salmon every day even though their exhibit has a stream stocked with fish. Ask about when the gorillas get their afternoon snack packs filled with food and toys. The zoo gives discounts

from top to bottom: Olympic Sculpture Park; Museum of History and Industry; Space Needle.

for taking public transportation; check the website before going.

University of Washington Arboretum

The **University of Washington Arboretum** (2300 Arboretum Dr. E, Madison Park, 206/543-8800, http://depts.washington.edu, visitors center 9am-5pm daily, free) is more than a simple garden, it's a tree sanctuary that holds more than 20,000 of them over 230 acres, including well-regarded collections of maple, pine, oak, and mountain ash. Trails circle the park, and yes, there are plenty of flowers, too. Wetlands on Lake Washington are especially populated with waterfowl.

The nearby **Japanese Garden** (1075 Lake Washington Blvd. E, 206/684-4725, www.seattle.gov/parks, noon-5pm Mon., 10am-5pm Tues.-Sun. Mar. and Oct.; noon-7pm Mon., 10am-7pm Tues.-Sun Apr. and Aug.; noon-8pm Mon., 10am-8pm Tues.-Sun. May-July; noon-6pm Mon., 10am-6pm Tues.-Sun. Sept.; 10am-4pm Tues.-Sun. Nov., $6 adults, $4 seniors, students, and children 6-17, children under 6 free) is operated by the city, not the university, so there's a fee to enter. The garden is especially popular when the cherry blossom trees bloom. Tea ceremonies are held occasionally, and a community center inside the formal Japanese garden has periodic art displays.

Bellevue Arts Museum

Who says Seattle has all the culture? Across Lake Washington in the posh city of Bellevue is the **Bellevue Arts Museum** (510 Bellevue Way NE, Bellevue, 425/519-0770, www.bellevuearts.org, 11am-5pm Wed.-Sun., $12 adults, $10 seniors and students, children under 6 free). It focuses on Northwest creations, with an emphasis that puts crafts and design works next to paintings and sculptures.

★ Museum of Flight

You might think you like airplanes, but until you've been to the **Museum of Flight** (9404 E Marginal Way, South Seattle, 206/764-5720, www.museumofflight.org, 10am-5pm daily, $23 adults, $19 seniors, $14 children 5-17, children under 5 free), you don't really understand what it means to be obsessed with flight. The building is located next to Boeing Field, an airstrip used by Boeing and private aircraft, whose tarmac is often lined with new and experimental aircraft. The museum has 150 planes and flying machines, many hanging in a giant glass pavilion—there's the Mach 3 Blackbird, the fastest plane ever built, and early airmail biplanes, a sailplane, WWI fighters, and a Huey helicopter. A big red barn—the original Boeing airplane factory—traces the history of flight and the Boeing industry in Seattle. Outdoors is a kind of parking lot for cool old airplanes, including a supersonic Concorde jet and the first jet to serve as Air Force One—you can walk through the 707 and see where President Kennedy sat on his flights. The 3-D theater and flight simulators let you feel like you got off the ground.

One of the most exciting parts of the Museum of Flight is the space exhibits, including a full-size replica of an International Space Station lab and a Soyuz module used by Charles Simonyi, a billionaire who used his Microsoft money to visit space (and built the gallery that houses many of the museum's space artifacts). In the center of the room is the giant Space Shuttle Trainer, a full-scale replica of the now retired spacecraft. It never went to space, but every shuttle astronaut trained on it. **Tours** ($20-25, reservations recommended) are available for a peek inside the crew compartment, though any museum visitor can look inside the cargo bay—Queen Elizabeth once dined inside it when she visited NASA in Houston, Texas.

Sightseeing Tours

When is a bus like a boat? When you're riding one of the amphibious craft at **Ride**

Day Trip to Woodinville Wine Country

Most of Washington's famed wine-making takes place east of Seattle, across the mountains. But go just a little east of the city for a town that's become a kind of emissary for the far-off vineyards. **Woodinville** is just 30 miles from the Space Needle but can feel like a different world, one with a slower pace and finer appreciation for sitting around and sipping spirits.

In the center is **Chateau Ste. Michelle** (14111 NE 145th St., 425/488-1133, www. ste-michelle.com, tastings and tours 10am–5pm daily, free), a French-style behemoth that should look utterly out of place in rural Washington. Instead the quaint shutters and giant wooden doors on the estate are welcoming, if a bit weird, and the winery gives tastings and hosts summer concerts on its well-trimmed lawns.

Besides the big French castle, dozens of other establishments have tasting rooms around Woodinville, and two thirds of the 99 wineries in town actually produce wine here. Nearly half produce fewer than 2,000 cases, compared to Chateau Ste. Michelle's more than two million. It's possible to wander on foot between tasting rooms in the industrial part of town, or simply stop at one of the larger establishments for a snack and a lengthy tasting.

Drinks may be taken care of, but there's always dinner to consider, and the town has a clear favorite dining spot in **The Herbfarm** (14590 NE 145th St., 425/485-5300, http://theherbfarm.com, seatings at 4:30pm or 7pm, $205-265). Originally home to an educational meal on the site of a small local farm, now it's relocated to a flowery spot across the street from Ste. Michelle. Meals are a single-seating, nine-course affair preceded by a garden tour and introduction to swine named Basil and Borage—they're pets, not future pork dishes. As befits the wine-loving town, the restaurant chooses pairings from a 26,000-bottle cellar.

the Ducks (516 Broad St., 206/441-3825, www.ridetheducksofseattle.com, 10am-4pm Mon.-Fri., 9:30am-4pm Sat.-Sun., $35 adults, $32 seniors, $20 children 4-12, $5 children under 2). These vehicles were originally used in World War II, but now they're rollicking tour vessels that show off Seattle by land and sea. Tours begin with goofy introductions by the driver, who'll likely wear a silly hat the entire trip. Expect a little bit of history and a lot of loud music and games, like screaming "ka-ching" every time you pass a Starbucks, and the humming of duck-shaped kazoos that some riders purchase. After a loop through the downtown streets, the Duck open-air vehicles travel to the north end of Lake Union, where they head into the water and become boats. The water tour passes Gasworks Park and the floating homes that were popularized in the movie *Sleepless in Seattle*.

Not only does **Argosy Cruises** (Pier 55, 1101 Alaskan Way, 888/623-1445, www.argosycruises.com, $27-84 adults, $22-75 seniors, $13-32 children 4-12, children under 4 free) run the Tillicum Village experience, it also has a whole slate of boat tours around Puget Sound and Lake Washington. The harbor cruise, a narrated one-hour experience, visits the city's industrial waterfront and shipping terminal, providing water views of the Space Needle. The Locks Cruise (2.5 hours) includes a trip through the Ballard Locks and peeks at the houseboats on Lake Union. Other tours that visit Lake Washington—with its floating bridges, waterfront mansions, and stadium views—leave from marinas in South Lake Union or Kirkland. Dining and murder-mystery-game cruises are scheduled regularly, and in the winter the Christmas Ship, decked in white lights, travels to 45 different waterfront communities and broadcasts the caroling performance of the onboard choir.

The tradition reaches back more than 60 years, and once the schedule is posted, the residents of each Seattle waterfront community make a point of greeting the ship as it passes. Tickets can be booked on both the Christmas Ship with its choir or the Parade Boat that follows it.

Entertainment and Events

It's been a long time since the city was just known for grunge music. Culture in Seattle ranges from a strong jazz tradition to thriving independent movie theaters. Cocktail culture is nationally recognized, but the city's quirky sensibilities are still found in watering holes, clubs, and music venues.

Nightlife
Bars and Clubs
Downtown

Down the stairs from Pike Place Market is the quintessential Seattle cocktail bar, **Zig Zag Café** (1501 Western Ave., No. 202, 206/625-1146, www.zigzagseattle. com, 5pm-2am daily). Bartenders in neat black vests take pride in crafting memorable cocktails and remembering customer's faces, making it a local's favorite even as tourists wander up the steps outside. Stroll down the alley that runs just uphill from the market and look for a half-open Dutch door; that's **White Horse Trading Company** (1908 Post Alley, 206/441-7767, 4pm-midnight Mon.-Thurs., 4pm-2am Fri.-Sat.), a snug British drinkery crowded with old-timey golf clubs, bookshelves, and paintings of red-coated fox hunters. Besides British ales, the bar serves Pimm's Cup highballs, a drink that's to Brits at Wimbledon what a mint julep is to Southerners at the Kentucky Derby.

For an even more literate quaff, **Bookstore Bar & Café** (Alexis Hotel, 1007 1st Ave., 206/624-3646, www.bookstorebar.com, 7am-10pm Mon.-Fri., 8am-10pm Sat.-Sun.) sits under rows of books for sale. Any tome is $5, and dishes at happy hour (3pm-6pm daily) aren't much more. The best reading in the house, however, is the menu of 70 single-malt Scotch whiskeys and almost as many American whiskeys.

To call **The Hideout** (1005 Boren Ave., 206/903-8480, www.hideoutseattle.com, 4pm-2am Mon.-Fri., 6pm-2am Sat.-Sun.) an art bar is a vast understatement—nearly every inch of the 16-foot-high walls are plastered with canvases, a thoughtful still life next to a frantic modern collage. The signage outside is modest, perhaps to best fit in with the surrounding hospitals in First Hill, or "Pill Hill." Be sure to swing by the art vending machine in the bar's dark corner before ordering from the bar. You can get a beer, a decent cocktail, or an artwork price list and flashlight to shop the gallery around you.

Belltown

Peek down an alleyway and look for a metal placard noting the entrance to neo-speakeasy **Bathtub Gin and Co.** (2205 2nd Ave., 206/728-6069, www.bathtubginseattle.com, 5pm-2am daily), a thin, multi-level establishment that does more than trade on its twee theme. Great dates take place in the bar's intimate nooks, but sit at the small bar to have the talented bartenders create original cocktails. When it comes time to pay, request a receipt—they'll usually handwrite one, complete with doodles of beer bottles or cocktail glasses.

For cocktails just as fancy but easier to find, **Rob Roy** (2332 2nd Ave., 206/956-8423, www.robroyseattle.com, 4pm-2am daily) isn't far away. Even classic cocktails here are on the obscure side (ever heard of a Jungle Bird?), and if you're lucky, ice will be chopped by hand to fit the glass. Original creations are even more eyebrow raising—the Gunpowder Punch includes rum, gin, spices, and actual gunpowder. Just a little, though.

South Lake Union

Despite its location as a lonely club on a somewhat quiet street, **Lo-Fi Performance Gallery** (429 Eastlake Ave., 206/254-2824, www.thelofi.net, hours vary) is definitely best known as a dance club, especially on its most popular theme nights. A '60s soul night steers away from overplayed hits, while the massively popular monthly '90s dance party is full of chart toppers.

Capitol Hill

Sun Liquor (607 Summit Ave. E, 206/860-1130, www.sunliquor.com, 5pm-2am daily) was one of the first bars to capture cocktail cool in Seattle, soon opening a distillery outpost a few blocks away. The original bar is tucked into a mostly residential neighborhood and serves drinks made from house-made syrups and their own gin and vodka. The area's real cocktail cathedral, however, is the prim and proper **Canon** (928 12th Ave., 206/552-9755, www.canonseattle.com, 5pm-2am daily), where bartenders, whiskeys, and bitters are the stars. No one is let inside unless a seat is available, so there's no throwing elbows to reach the bar. Not that there isn't a sense of humor here—page 63 of the massive menu is labeled "hardcore porn" for bottles like a $1,225 Canoe Club whiskey from 1898 or a Maker's Mark named for the Triple Crown-winning horse Seattle Slew.

As the home of the city's party scene, Capitol Hill isn't all good behavior. There's an obvious Western theme at **Montana** (1506 E Olive Way, 206/422-4647, www.montanainseattle.com, 4pm-2am daily), where specials are scrawled on a blackboard. Bearded young men in flannel shirts fill the wooden booths, and even the women here are likely to be wearing plaid.

Every other pattern under the sun is represented at **The Unicorn** (1118 E Pike St., 206/325-6492, www.unicornseattle.com, noon-2am Mon.-Fri., 11am-2am Sat.-Sun.), a veritable assault on the senses. Decorated like a circus seen through an acid trip, it even has horned beasts mounted on the walls—real taxidermy ones, not unicorns. Downstairs is even wilder: a basement bar called the Narwhal, named for the unicorns of the sea. Pinball machines, a photo booth, and sticky floors are a good match for the cheap cocktails and bowls of popcorn.

Though located in Capitol Hill, **The Baltic Room** (1207 Pine St., 206/625-4444, www.balticroom.com, 10pm-2am Mon.-Sat.) is just a bridge away from downtown, so it pulls scenesters from both neighborhoods. It hosts a wide range of DJs and the usual mix of pop, R&B, and house-music nights, but you can also find odder things taking place on the dance floor, like a live art painting event while speakers thump dance music around the artists.

Ballard

The spacious **King's Hardware** (5225 Ballard Ave. NW, 206/782-0027, www.kingsballard.com, 3pm-2am Mon.-Fri., noon-2am Sat.-Sun.) isn't the only bar in Seattle with Skee-Ball, but it's probably the best. Linda Dershang, Seattle's expert on great casual hangouts, helped create the bar in an old hardware space, taking care to include must-haves like an outdoor patio, a vintage Donkey Kong game, burgers, and a jukebox.

Slightly more upscale is the nearby **Noble Fir** (5316 Ballard Ave. NW, 206/420-7425, www.thenoblefir.com, 4pm-midnight Tues.-Thurs., 4pm-1am Fri.-Sat., 1pm-9pm Sun.), a sleek establishment that gets more natural light than most firs in the forest. The beer menu shows evidence of fastidious selection, and one corner has a hiking and travel book library nook.

Brewpubs and Taprooms
Downtown

There are bars with impressive beer selections, and then there's the **Tap House Grill** (1506 6th Ave, 206/816-3314, http://taphousegrill.com, 11am-1am Sun.-Thurs.,

11am-2am Fri.-Sat.) A curved wall behind the bar has 160 taps, claimed to be the largest selection in the region. The Tap House Grill carries international styles like Belgians and bitters, but, this being the hoppy Pacific Northwest, more than two dozen IPAs are featured. Almost all local breweries are represented, and bartenders offer tastes to help customers find the perfect choice. The basement space is a large, corporate-style restaurant, but happy hour flatbreads topped with chicken sausage or bacon and pineapple are a great deal. The rest of the menu is broad, encompassing nearly as many food styles as beer varieties: jambalaya, prime rib, pad Thai, and more.

Capitol Hill

The barn-like **Rhein Haus** (912 12th Ave., 206/325-5409, www.rheinhausseattle.com, 3pm-2am Mon.-Fri., 10am-2am Sat.-Sun.) is a German theme park unto itself, with multiple bars, indoor bocce courts, a fireplace, and long beer-hall tables popular with students from Seattle University across the street. Beer comes in glasses that range from a two-ounce taste to a full-liter mug, and most pours hail from Germany and Austria. A special machine spirals potatoes thin, so they can be fried on a stick like a never-ending potato chip.

The idea of a beer bar in a mortuary sounds grim, but in practice at **Pine Box** (1600 Melrose Ave., 206/588-0375, www.pineboxbar.com, 3pm-2am Mon.-Fri., 11am-2am Sat.-Sun.) it's a perfect fit. With its giant curved windows and high molded ceilings, the space feels like a warm church dedicated to the worship of beer and hanging out. The bar has a few dozen beers on tap, and the food menu is split between "less," "more," and pizza dishes, all the kind of spicy, saucy eats that pair well with a high-alcohol specialty beer. For all the grandeur of the former place of mourning, including a loft overlooking the whole space, it's a loud and crowded beer hall.

Local beer is crucial to the Northwest drinking scene; since most of the nation's hops are grown here, the bitter IPA practically flows from the water taps, and every week there's a new brewery putting out IBUs from a suburban garage or Ballard bike shed. **Stumbling Monk** (1635 E Olive Way, 206/860-0916, 6pm-2am daily), a fixture that sits between two busy hubs of Capitol Hill, takes a different approach to beer appreciation by specializing in Belgians and other imports. It's as dark as a European pub, with high-backed booths and wooden tables that look like they have as much history as the Habsburgs. Though the bottle menu attracts aficionados, the selection of board games is a clear sign that the joint isn't about beer snobbery.

Gay and Lesbian

With its white walls and floor, sleek surfaces, and high-concept lighting, **Q** (1426 Broadway, www.qnightclub.com, 9pm-2am Wed.-Thurs., 10am-3am Fri.-Sat.) can feel more like an Apple Store than a dance club. But then the music kicks up and drinks start flowing, featuring house-made infused vodkas in Hickory Bacon or Chocomint flavors.

While it's common to find a mixed crowd on Q's dance floor, **The Cuff** (1533 13th Ave., 206/323-1525, www.cuffcomplex.com, 2pm-2am daily) is unapologetically a gay bar. It's popular among the leather, bear, and fetish crowds, but the dance floor draws a diverse mix of men, and the spot's disco ball has hung in local gay bars since the 1970s. It's a more chill scene at **C.C. Attle's** (1701 E Olive Way, 206/726-0565, www.ccattles.net, 3pm-2am Mon.-Fri., 2pm-2am Sat.-Sun.), a bear bar with pool and more sunlight than many drinking holes on the Hill.

Live Music

The art deco styling of the downtown **Showbox** (1426 1st Ave., 206/628-3151, www.showboxpresents.com) doesn't lie. The theater has been around since the

1930s and once hosted burlesque superstar Gypsy Rose Lee in her hometown. Today the space creates intimacy with the audience spread over several levels, making it a popular stop for rock, indie, and R&B acts.

Born as a Beaux-Arts vaudeville and movie theater in the 1920s, the **Paramount Theatre** (911 Pine St., 206/902-5500, www.stgpresents.org/paramount) now welcomes traveling Broadway shows, big headlining musicians, and massive political rallies. The old dame of a theater was renovated in the 1990s by a Microsoft executive with a flair for the dramatic; she donated the theater to a nonprofit group to manage it.

More intimate performances take place at downtown's **The Triple Door** (216 Union St., 206/838-4333, www.thetripledoor.net), with plush booth seating and an Asian fusion menu. The stage at **Dimitriou's Jazz Alley** (2033 6th Ave., 206/441-9729, www.jazzalley.com) is surrounded by two levels of tables and upscale diners.

Neumos (925 E Pike St., 206/709-9442, www.neumos.com) got its name because it's the "New Moe's," the resurrection of a '90s club that welcomed Radiohead, Pearl Jam, and Neil Young; even President Bill Clinton popped in for a show when he was in town. Today the performance space is the center of a complex that includes a fish fry eatery, a casual bar, and a more-intimate stage.

The Arts
Theater

It may be more than 3,000 miles from **5th Avenue Theatre** (1308 5th Ave., 206/625-1900, www.5thavenue.org) to Broadway, but the trip feels quicker for the musicals produced here that have gone on to successful Broadway runs—including two Tony Award winners for Best Musical. Besides future blockbusters like *Memphis*

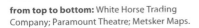

from top to bottom: White Horse Trading Company; Paramount Theatre; Metsker Maps.

and *Hairspray*, the theater hosts touring productions.

Seattle Repertory Theatre (155 Mercer St., 206/443-2222, www.seattlerep.org) dates back to the arts enthusiasm that arose after the 1962 World's Fair left the city with a number of performance spaces. The group has premiered plays by big-name playwrights like August Wilson and Neil Simon, and its theater in the Seattle Center is recognized as the city's foremost nonmusical theater stage. The downtown **ACT Theatre** (700 Union St., 206/292-7660, www.acttheatre.org) specializes in contemporary productions and commissions new works from up-and-coming playwrights.

Classical Music, Opera, and Dance

As the home of the Seattle Symphony, **Benaroya Hall** (200 University St., 206/215-4800, www.seattlesymphony. org/benaroya) performances are most often under the direction of electric conductor Ludovic Morlot, though the stage also hosts talks and even film events. A giant Dale Chihuly sculpture decorates the main hall, and giant glass windows open to a downtown view. **McCaw Hall** (321 Mercer St., 206/733-9725, www.mccawhall.com) in Seattle Center shares its stage with **Seattle Opera** (www.seattleopera.org) and **Pacific Northwest Ballet** (www.pnb.org), the latter a nationally recognized dance troupe.

Modern dance works are a highlight of the Queen Anne-based **On the Boards** (100 W Roy St., 206/217-9886, www.ontheboards.org), whose summer NW New Works Festival encourages artists to take big risks in theater performances.

Cinema

The giant 70-foot curved screen of **Cinerama** (2100 4th Ave., 206/448-6680, www.cinerama.com) harks back to an earlier era when movies had intermissions and IMAX didn't exist. The retro theater hosts first-run movies, classic movie nights, and special events, and even the popcorn is special—coated in chocolate.

The menu's much broader at **Big Picture** (2505 1st Ave., 206/256-0566, www.thebigpicture.net), a small basement theater with a full bar outside. Order a drink before the lights dim to get in-seat delivery in the middle of the flick.

Festivals and Events

Wintergrass (Bellevue, www.acoustic-sound.org, Feb.) is an annual bluegrass music event that draws banjo players and fiddle masters just east of Seattle every winter. Hotel ballrooms fill with music performances, but the hallways and sidewalks are just as likely to be packed with folk tunes as musicians gather and jam.

Seattle is known as a nerd town, so it's no wonder that the **Emerald City ComicCon** (www.emeraldcitycomicon.com, Mar.) has grown into a giant festival of comic books, superheroes, and fantasy. Actor appearances, book signings, and film screenings draw attendees, and thousands of people don costumes for the event.

Seattle's annual **Pride Parade** (www.seattlepride.org, June) now celebrates the legalization of same-sex marriage in Washington. The parade usually starts at 11am and runs north down 4th Avenue to Denny Way. Billed as the largest free Pride festival in the country, Seattle **PrideFest** (www.seattlepridefest.org, June) fills Seattle Center (305 Harrison St., 206/684-7200, www.seattlecenter.com) with vendors and performers.

Things go fast at **Seafair** (www.seafair.com, June-Aug.), the city's annual summer festival that stretches from June to August. Hydroplanes race around Lake Washington at more than 150 miles per hour, and fighter jets turn loops above a boat flotilla that forms on the lake. But not everything is in a rush—the annual Torchlight Parade and Parade of Ships are no faster than a mosey.

Once an upstart neighborhood event, the **Capitol Hill Block Party** (www.

capitolhillblockparty.com, July) has grown into a raucous July weekend party. Independent musicians appear on stages throughout the hipster enclave of South Capitol Hill, though the festival's growth has meant more and more recognizable names on the bill.

Even before Washington legalized recreational marijuana use in 2012, **Hempfest** (www.hempfest.org, Aug.) has been the largest pot-themed gathering in the world. Bands, bong sales, and activist work fill the now three-day festival held the third weekend in August, always free and always 100 percent volunteer run.

The city's biggest music festival is named for something locals are proud to do without—umbrellas, or in British slang, **Bumbershoot** (www.bumbershoot. org, Sept.). Every Labor Day weekend, the Seattle Center grounds fill with arts of every stripe, from headlining bands playing Key Arena to art shows and poetry readings.

Shopping

Who says Seattle doesn't have style? It's a common joke, what with all the polar fleece and hiking boots worn on the street. But there is also a quirky sophistication on display, with local designers often incorporating outdoorsiness into attractive and, dare we say it, refined clothes and home decor.

Downtown
Books

The downtown **Barnes and Noble** (600 Pine St., 206/264-0156, www.barnesandnoble.com, 9am-10pm Mon.-Thurs., 9am-11pm Fri.-Sun.) doesn't look too big on the street level—just magazines, a few shelves of books, and some checkout stands. Go down the escalators for the full store with a children's section, travel section, Starbucks, and DVD shelves. The basement store opens to the lower lobby

of the Pacific Place shopping center and parking garage.

The cozy **Seattle Mystery Bookshop** (117 Cherry St., 206/587-5737, www.seattlemystery.com, 10am-5pm Mon.-Sat., noon-5pm Sun.) has none of the menace of all the mystery books it holds. The store specializes in Northwest mystery authors—many of whom stop in to sign copies of their books—but it also carries an impressive selection from around the world.

The charming **Arundel Bookstore** (214 1st Ave. S, 206/624-4442, www.arundelbookstores.com, 11am-6pm daily) is a sweet store in Pioneer Square that is dedicated to the printed word. It specializes in art and rare books and also runs a publishing operation so small that it uses a hand-cranked press.

Clothing and Shoes

Downtown boutique **Baby & Company** (1936 1st Ave., 206/448-4077, www.babyandco.us, 10am-6pm Mon.-Sat., noon-5pm Sun.) has carried the torch for Seattle fashion since the 1970s, carrying quirky brands that defy the city's fleece-and-hiking boots reputation. The feel is one part Bohemian, one part urban chic, in a glistening white space decorated with palm fronds.

There may not be many Seattle occasions for a fancy chapeau from **Goorin Brothers Hat Shop** (1610 1st Ave., 206/443-8082, www.goorin.com, 10am-7pm Mon.-Thurs., 10am-8pm Fri.-Sat., 11am-7pm Sun.), but the staff specializes in personal service and fittings. Learn the difference between a cloche and a fedora, or pick up feathered pins to decorate your own grubby ball cap. **Diva Dollz** (624 1st Ave., 206/652-2299, www.divadollz.com, noon-6pm daily), in Pioneer Square, is a different kind of throwback, where pinup and rockabilly-style dresses create '60s silhouettes. It's not hard to imagine Bettie Page rocking these frocks—when she wore clothes at all, that is.

Department Stores

The downtown **Nordstrom** (500 Pine St., 206/628-2111, http://shop.nordstrom. com, 9:30am-9pm Mon.-Sat., 10am-7pm Sun.) serves as both the shopping chain's flagship and the city's retail anchor. The store's roots are in shoe sales, but the giant has since grown to include high-end clothing, jewelry, and makeup. Some days a piano player serenades shoppers as they glide up and down the store's escalators. But anyone priced out of the main store can head underground next door to **Nordstrom Rack** (400 Pine St., 206/448-8522, http://shop.nordstrom. com, 9:30am-9pm Mon.-Sat., 10am-7pm Sun.). The outlet for the department chain has heavily discounted high fashion and rows of shoes on sale.

The nearby **Macy's** (300 Pine St., 206/506-6000, www.macys.com, 10am-8pm Mon.-Wed., 10am-9pm Thurs., 10am-10pm Fri.-Sat., 11am-7pm Sun.) takes a slightly broader approach, carrying more housewares, furniture, and linens. Seattle was one of three cities to first receive **City Target** (1401 2nd Ave., 206/494-3250, www.target.com, 7am-11pm daily), a slightly smaller version of the cheap big-box retailer meant for the urban dweller. There are fewer large items for sale in the three-floor store, and food selections include ready-made lunches.

Gift and Home

Go ahead, let locals claim they don't carry an umbrella. That pride has probably meant a miserable walk or two, and they're missing the plethora of bumbershoots at **Bella Umbrella** (1535 1st Ave., 206/297-1540, www.bellaumbrella.com, 10am-6pm Mon.-Sat., 11am-5pm Sun.). Besides selling and renting a variety of styles (the latter for large events, not an unexpected downpour), the proprietor shows off selections from her own vintage collection.

It's worth getting lost in **Metsker Maps** (1511 1st Ave., 206/623-8747, www. metskers.com, 9am-8pm Mon.-Fri., 10am-8pm Sat., 10am-6pm Sun.), a travel store with enough inspiration for several trips around the world. Besides a selection of travel books and folded maps of every corner of the globe, the store specializes in map art, including gorgeous woodcut charts of the Salish Sea. There are gifts galore in **Watson Kennedy Fine Home** (1022 1st Ave., 206/652-8350, www. watsonkennedy.com, 10am-6pm Mon.-Sat., noon-5pm Sun.), but you'll likely be tempted to shop for yourself among the vintage-style glassware, framed art, and fine treats. Local touches can be seen in the Fran's chocolates (a Seattle brand favored by President Obama) and weathered signs listing ferry destinations around Puget Sound.

Gourmet Goodies

As one corner of the mighty Pike Place Market, **DeLaurenti** (1435 1st Ave., 206/622-0141, www.delaurenti.com, 9am-6pm Mon.-Sat., 10am-5pm Sun.) has a prime location for its fine-food wares. A long cheese and meat counter sits toward the back, while prepared deli foods up front cause out-the-door lines to form at lunchtime. Head up the steps to a wine room that hosts tastings.

Not everything from **Paris-Madrid Grocery** (1418 Western Ave., 206/682-2827, www.spanishtable.com, 10am-6pm Mon.-Sat., 11am-5pm Sun.) hails from France and Spain, but most of it does—there's also quite a bit from Portugal. A cheese counter doles out Manchego and pâté, and a selection of cookbooks provides instruction on how to achieve Iberian flavors.

South Lake Union
Outdoor Equipment

Outdoor store **REI** (222 Yale Ave. N, 206/223-1944, www.rei.com, 9am-9pm Mon.-Sat., 10am-7pm Sun.) is still the same co-op it was when it was founded by a group of Seattle hikers, only supersized. The flagship's rock climbing wall, stone fireplace, indoor hiking trail, and

Gallery Hopping

Pioneer Square is home to many of the city's art galleries. The area is centered on the intersection of Washington Street and 3rd Avenue South and is a good destination on the first Thursday of every month, when the **First Thursday Seattle Art Walk** (www.firstthursdayseattle.com, noon-8pm) keeps galleries open. **Foster/White Gallery** (220 3rd Ave. S, 206/622-2833, www.fosterwhite.com, 10am-6pm Tues.-Sat.) is Northwest-artist focused, and next door is the **Greg Kucera Gallery** (212 3rd Ave. S, 206/624-0770, www.gregkucera.com, 10:30am-5:30pm Tues.-Sat.), known for contemporary paintings, prints, and sculptures, often highlighting works with a political focus.

Located downtown, close to the Seattle Art Museum, **Patricia Rovzar Gallery** (1111 1st Ave., 206/223-0273, www.rovzargallery.com, 11am-5pm daily) has bright contemporary works. **Sisko Gallery** (3126 Elliott Ave., 206/283-2998, www.siskogallery.com, 11am-5pm Fri.-Sun.), near the Olympic Sculpture Park, displays contemporary work and hosts a reservation-only life-drawing club on Sunday.

Capitol Hill's art scene tends to be looser, younger, and less expensive. **Vermillion** (1508 11th Ave., 206/709-9797, 4pm-midnight Tues.-Thurs., 4pm-1am Fri.-Sat., 4pm-11pm Sun.) is an art gallery with a fantastic secret—a bar behind the display space. The funky space has a good-sized serving area, a blackboard displaying food items, a good wine list, exposed brick walls, and friendly bartenders.

outdoor bike route allow customers to really try out the merchandise, and the rental counter downstairs loans out snowshoes, sleeping bags, and tents. The focus is cozier at the nearby **Feathered Friends** (119 Yale Ave. N, 206/292-2210, www.featheredfriends.com, 10am-8pm Mon.-Fri., 10am-6pm Sat., 11am-5pm Sun.), a fluffy foundry of down everything—coats, booties, sleeping bags, and featherbeds. The store also carries a smaller selection of the same outdoor gear found at REI, but the staff is more reliably knowledgeable.

Capitol Hill
Books

In literate Seattle, **Elliott Bay Book Company** (1521 10th Ave., 206/624-6600, www.elliottbaybook.com, 10am-10pm Mon.-Thurs., 10am-11pm Fri.-Sat., 11am-7pm Sun.) is practically a church. Readers gather among bookshelves, in the café, or in a basement reading room that fills almost daily for names big and small. This is the kind of indie bookstore where the staff recommendations are spot-on and the café seats are a hot commodity.

Clothing and Shoes

In a city this fanatical about recycling, it's unsurprising that we'd have a shop like **NuBE Green** (1527 10th Ave., 206/402-4515, www.nubegreen.com, 11am-6pm Mon.-Thurs, 10am-6pm Fri.-Sat., 10am-5pm Sun.), where home decor and fashion meet sustainability. The in-house line remakes pieces using vintage and thrift goods, and everything sold is in some way U.S. made or recycled.

In a stylish, vast space, the wares of **Totokaelo** (1523 10th Ave., 206/623-3582, www.totokaelo.com, 11am-7pm Mon.-Sat., 11am-6pm Sun.) get a chance to breathe. The menswear, women's wear, and home furnishings are so fashionable that the local store has more customers in New York City than in Seattle.

Gourmet Goodies

There are two options at **Melrose Market** (1501-1535 Melrose Ave., 206/568-2666, www.melrosemarketseattle.com): Buy meats and cheeses for a meal at home, or indulge in the handful of restaurants that sit around the two stands. The indoor gourmet market is abutted by **Taylor**

Shellfish Farms (1521 Melrose Ave., 206/501-4321, www.taylorshellfishfarms. com, 11am-9pm Sun.-Thurs., 11am-11pm Fri.-Sat.), where local oysters and mussels are ready to be slurped and steamed.

University District
Books

Not only does the **University Book Store** (4326 University Way NE, 206/634-3400, www.bookstore.washington.edu, 9am-8pm Mon.-Fri., 10am-7pm Sat., noon-5pm Sun.) carry many of the Northwest authors that are taught at the University of Washington next door, but there's also every kind of Husky shirt, bag, sticker, and flag imaginable. The large store often holds events with visiting writers.

Greater Seattle
Books

The first place is home and the second place is work. **Third Place Books** (6504 20th Ave. NE, 206/525-2347, www.third-placebooks.com, 8am-9pm Sun.-Thurs., 8am-10pm Fri.-Sat.) is meant to be a third important part of a Seattle resident's life, and sells new and used books in two locations in the city. (This is the Ravenna spot, closest to downtown.) The downstairs **Pub at Third Place** (206/523-0217, 3pm-11pm Mon.-Thurs., 3pm-midnight Fri.-Sat., 3pm-10pm Sun.) features 18 beer taps, most with local brews, and an international selection of wine. On-site **Vios Café** (206/525-5701, 8am-9pm daily) offers Greek-inspired menus.

Sports and Recreation

Parks
★ Volunteer Park

Green space impresarios the Olmstead Brothers (who designed Central Park, among other spaces) designed Capitol Hill's **Volunteer Park** (1247 15th Ave. E, 206/684-4075, www.seattle.gov/parks, 6am-10pm daily)—less than 50 acres, but with a little bit of everything. A stately brick water tower offers panoramic views from the top, and a glass conservatory blooms even when the weather's at its worst outside. Lawns dot the space around the Seattle Asian Art Museum, guarded by twin camel statues, and the Isamu Noguchi sculpture *Black Sun* has a keyhole view of the Space Needle.

Kerry Park

For the absolute best view of the Space Needle, head to **Kerry Park** (211 W Highland Dr., 206/684-4075, www.seattle.gov/parks) on Queen Anne Hill. This tiny space is known primarily for how it looms over the landmark. It fills quickly on New Year's Eve, when fireworks shoot from the top of the tower.

Green Lake

The very urban **Green Lake** (7201 E Green Lake Dr. N, 206/684-4075, www.seattle.gov) is one busy oasis. A walking and biking trail surrounds the lake that's about 3 miles around, and a swimming beach is available (though the lake sometimes closes for algae blooms). The calm waters are perfect for beginning kayakers and stand-up paddleboarders, and an impressive old bleacher stand faces the water near a boathouse. The 3-mile loop is popular for families, dog walkers, and inline skaters, and the fields around the lake fill with sports team. Boat rentals are available at **Green Lake Boat Rental** (7351 E Green Lake Dr. N, 206/527-0171, www.greenlakeboatrentals.net, 9am-7pm daily spring-fall, $22-30 per hour), including sailboats and paddleboats. Next to the lake, the **Green Lake Pitch & Putt** (5701 E Green Lake Way N, 206/632-2280, www.seattle.gov/parks, 9am-dusk Mar.-Oct., $7) is a nine-hole, par-three golf course.

Gasworks Park

There's something beautiful about the industrial ruins in **Gasworks Park** (2101 N Northlake Way, 206/684-4075, www.seattle.gov/parks, 6am-10pm daily), even if state ecologists are still testing the metal refineries and tanks for pollution. No swimming is allowed in the waterfront park because of contaminants, but the city views—and the kite-flying—are perfect from atop the park's biggest hill.

Hiram M. Chittenden Locks

For the mechanically minded, there's nothing like an afternoon watching the **Hiram M. Chittenden Locks** (3015 54th St. NW, 206/783-7059, www.nws.usace. army.mil), operated by the U.S. Army Corps of Engineers and opened almost a century ago. On a scenic stretch of the ship canal in Ballard, next to a manicured botanical garden, the water elevator lets boats come and go. An underground passage shows off the fish ladder that allows the fish to do the same.

Beaches

Don't laugh. There really is sand on **Alki Beach Park** (1702 Alki Ave. SW, 206/684-4075, www.seattle.gov/parks, 4am-11:30pm daily), in West Seattle on a peninsula that protrudes farther into Puget Sound than downtown. Even when it isn't all that sunny, locals toss Frisbees, bike along the sandy stretch, or warm themselves around fire pits.

Located north of the city, **Golden Gardens Park** (8498 Seaview Pl. NW, 206/684-4075, www.seattle.gov/parks, 6am-11:30pm daily) is barbecue central, with room for a volleyball net and an off-leash area for pets. The view of Salmon Bay feels hopelessly far from downtown Seattle.

In a beach that's more about being seen than swimming, **Madison Park** (E Madison St. and E Howe St., 206/684-4075, www.seattle.gov/parks, 4am-11:30pm daily) buzzes with chatter, stereos playing, and even some splashing on summer afternoons. Lifeguards overlook the swimmers in the Lake

from top to bottom: Volunteer Park; view from Kerry Park; Center for Wooden Boats.

Washington waters, more bearable than the chilly Puget Sound.

Biking

Cars have the freeway, bikes have the lengthy **Burke-Gilman Trail** (206/684-7583, www.seattle.gov/parks), which stretches almost 19 miles from Ballard to Bothell. Enter the trailhead at NW 45th Street and 11th Avenue NW; the trail turns into the Sammamish River Trail around NE Bothell Way and 73rd Avenue NE, in Bothell. Hardy cyclists can pedal all the way to the wineries of Woodinville. Commuting bikers are known to buzz the more leisurely walkers on the path if they don't pay attention to lane markings.

It's impossible to get lost on the **Green Lake Trail** (7201 E Green Lake Dr. N, 206/684-4075, www.seattle.gov/parks), a biking and running route around one of the city's more residential lakes. Pass swimming spots, roller skaters, dog parks, an amphitheater, and sports fields in the 3-mile loop.

Bike Rentals

Downtown's **Bicycle Repair Shop** (68 Madison St., 206/682-7057, www.thebicyclerepairshop.com, 8am-6pm Mon.-Fri, 10am-6pm Sat., noon-6pm Sun.) is right on the waterfront, offering hybrid and road bikes ($9-15 per hour) from a spot near the Great Wheel and ferry dock. Self-guided tour maps are free. Seattle has a mandatory helmet law, so all bike rentals come with free headwear.

Boating

You have two choices: Rent a kayak or stand-up paddleboard at **Agua Verde Café and Paddle Club** (1303 NE Boat St., University District, 206/545-8570, www.aguaverde.com, $18-24 per hour) *before* you try the fresh Mexican quesadillas and margaritas, or *after*. The latter allows you to work off the calories you gained, but you might lose the willpower to paddle up the ship canal to Lake Washington or

even peek at the nearby houseboats on Lake Union.

As an organization, **Center for Wooden Boats** (1010 Valley St., 206/382-2628, www.cwb.org, 12:30pm-5pm or dusk Sat.-Sun., $30-60 per hour), on the south end of Lake Union, promotes shipbuilding and sailing. On a clear day, they do so by renting rowboats, pedal boats, or sailboats. For those nervous about their seafaring skills, there's no shame in picking up a model version for use on a nearby pond.

Hiking

Although it begins south of downtown near the stadiums, the best place to hop on the **Elliott Bay Trail** (www.mtsgreenway.org) is in the Olympic Sculpture Park. Look for the trail running along Puget Sound; as the trail heads north, it passes a rose garden, rocky beaches, and picturesque (really!) waterfront grain elevators. The route travels from Myrtle Edwards Park at Alaskan Way and Broad Street to Smith Cove Park at 23rd Avenue West and West Marina Place in Magnolia.

Food

Of course there's seafood here. We can practically fish mussels and salmon right from Seattle's downtown piers. But the city is also becoming world-renowned—think James Beard Award-winning chefs—for its local sourcing. And then there's the Asian influence in the thriving International District and in popular fusion restaurants across town. There's even a place for classics like the Canlis salad, a high-end dish that hasn't changed in 50 years.

Downtown
Pacific Northwest

The beloved ★ **Matt's at the Market** (94 Pike St., No. 32, 206/467-7909, www.mattsinthemarket.com, 11:30am-2:30pm and 5:30pm-10pm Mon.-Sat., lunch $10-16, dinner $28-34) started as a tiny 23-seat eatery and is not that much bigger now. The 2nd-story location keeps it feeling like something of a secret, even though the big curved windows look directly at the iconic Pike Place Market sign. Chefs shop the market daily to create their menus, usually a short list of seafood or other meat dishes and simple, fresh salads.

Seafood

It's no wonder that **Six Seven** (2411 Alaskan Way, 206/269-4575, www.edgewaterhotel.com, 6:30am-9pm Sun.-Thurs., 6:30am-9:30pm Fri.-Sat., lunch $10-16, dinner $29-48), located in the pier-built Edgewater Hotel, specializes in seafood—it's practically in Puget Sound. The jazzy atmosphere and killer western views (try to make it here for sunset) almost overshadow the delicate preparations, which are careful not to overpower the halibut, scallops, or salmon. There are also a number of meat dishes, but they're clearly not the stars of the show. The dessert menu includes a thick, delicious honey lavender crème brûlée. The outdoor deck opens when weather permits, seating diners mere feet from the dark waters of Elliott Bay.

The **Seatown Seabar and Rotisserie** (2010 Western Ave., 206/436-0390, www.tomdouglas.com, 11am-9pm Mon.-Thurs., 11am-10pm Fri., 9am-10pm Sat., 9am-9pm Sun., breakfast $8.50 15.50, lunch $10.50-25, dinner $10.50-28.50), located right next to Pike Place Market, is restaurateur Tom Douglas's most direct take on seafood. Oysters are popular with the after-work crowd, when the long bar fills quickly. There are also several kinds of Alaskan crab on the menu, plus rotisserie chicken. The Rub with Love Shack next door sells the spices and rubs used at the Tom Douglas restaurants in town.

The popular **Ivar's Acres of Clams** (1001 Alaskan Way, 206/624-6852, www.ivars.com, 11am-10pm Mon.-Thurs.,

11am-11pm Fri.-Sat., $10-32) is Seattle's iconic, signature fast food. Locations are throughout the region, but the downtown waterfront spot is the most popular. Ivar Haglund, a colorful Seattle character, opened the chowder and fish-and-chips spot in 1938, bringing in crowds not only with food but also with octopus wrestling and eating contests. The Pier 54 spot has a regular dining room and dockside fast food. It offers both white and red clam chowder, so chowder purists can argue over which is best. Fish-and-chips are made with Alaskan cod and Ivar's tartar sauce. Ivar's own motto was "keep clam," and a statue commemorating him stands near the restaurant.

American

Located across from Matt's at the Market and also featuring curved windows, **Radiator Whiskey** (94 Pike St., No. 30, 206/467-4268, www.radiatorwhiskey.com, 4pm-midnight Mon.-Sat., $14-22) has a completely different feel. This is a hangout joint, one where not only the kitchen is open but the shelves are stacked with dishes and napkins. The menu is scrawled across a blackboard, and there are barrels behind the bar. Those barrels hold special whiskeys and barrel-aged cocktails, none of which come cheap; the lengthy whiskey menu is also easy to get lost in. Despite being in the middle of a tourist favorite, on the 2nd floor of a market location, the bar draws locals and restaurant industry folk with a happy hour menu of tot-chos—nachos made with tater tots—and a "dirty" sandwich that comes with a side of a Rainier tall boy and a shot of whiskey. Regular dinner still feels like a happy hour thanks to the crowds and buzz of the joint, though meat dishes like a lamb neck sloppy Joe and beef brisket are certainly substantial enough. A smoked half-pig head ($60) will feed the whole table but must be ordered in advance.

The grill is the thing at meat-centric **Miller's Guild** (612 Stewart St,

206/443-3663, http://millersguild.com, 7am-10pm daily, $25-54), attached to Hotel Max. The wood-fired grill in the restaurant cooks beef that was dry-aged for 75 days, plus a daily selection that can include Wagyu ribeye and lamp chops; look to the handwritten "From the Inferno" menu. The nose-to-tail butchery is taken seriously, and even the morning breakfast is hearty, drawing on foraged mushrooms for the frittata. The modern interior keeps it from feeling like an old-fashioned steak house; seats at the bar are the best way to get a look at the monster grill.

You almost have to lean back to see the top of the wine tower in the two-story **Purple Café and Wine Bar** (1225 4th Ave., 206/829-2280, www.thepurplecafe.com, 11am-11pm Mon.-Thurs., 11am-midnight Fri., noon-midnight Sat., noon-11pm Sun., $13-35). The cavernous space fills with diners during happy hour and on weeknights, feeding as many business diners as theater patrons. The menu is filled with the kind of rich bites that pair well with wines—wild boar rillettes and cheese flights, plus a killer braised bacon poutine. It's almost overkill, what with the sandwiches, pizzas, pastas, and other entrées fighting for attention, but the wine list has international scope and wit—the madeira varietal, for example, is described as "the Chuck Norris of wine."

Coffee

In a town that seems to have a Starbucks on every corner, **Cherry Street Coffee** (103 Cherry St., 206/621-9372, www.cherrystreetcoffee.com, 6:30am-5pm Mon.-Fri., 8am-3pm Sat.-Sun., $4.50-9.50) is a nice combination of independent coffee spot and consistent chain, with eight locations downtown. Each location features local artists, and the Cherry Street flagship has an underground seating area with an antique bank vault. Besides a wide array of coffee drinks with their own blends, the café serves sandwiches, salads, and quiches. Because most

Ivar's Acres of Clams

locations have large seating areas, any Cherry Street Coffee is a good place to sit a spell and soak in the so-called "coffee culture" of Seattle.

Pioneer Square's artsiest coffee stop, **Zeitgeist Coffee** (171 S Jackson St., 206/583-0497, http://zeitgeistcoffee. com, 6am-7pm Mon.-Fri., 7am-7pm Sat., 8am-6pm Sun., $5-9), dates to the 1990s, when coffee culture became a defining characteristic of the city. The decor, however, feels very of-the-moment, as the name implies: There's exposed brick, exposed ducts hanging from tall ceilings, and warm blond wood panels on the wall. Art is the shop's secondary calling, with original pieces on the wall and large gatherings on First Thursday Seattle Art Walk nights. The written word gets its share of the space, with newspaper racks and a dictionary on display. There's breathing room and a number of tables to enjoy the lattes topped with delicate foam art, plus a sandwich if you want to linger over the dictionary.

Asian

Considering Seattle's spot on the Pacific Rim, it's no surprise that an Asian fusion restaurant like **Wild Ginger** (1401 3rd Ave., 206/623-4450, www.wildginger. net, 11:30am-3pm and 5pm-11pm Mon.-Fri., 11:30am-3pm and 4:30pm-11pm Sat., 4pm-9pm Sun., lunch $7-22, dinner $13-33) would do so well for so long. Inspirations come from throughout Asia, particularly Malaysia, Indonesia, China, and Vietnam. Pad Thai shares the menu with satay and grilled boar. There's a special vegan menu and a live tank supplying clams and mussels. The restaurant's signature dish is the fragrant duck, served with puffy white steamed buns and plum sauce. The quarter-duck size probably isn't big enough for your table, unless you're dining alone—it's that good. The large restaurant is across from Benaroya Hall, so the staff is adept at getting diners out in time for shows and concerts.

You don't go to **Canton Wonton House** (608 S Weller St., 206/682-5080, 11am-11pm Tues.-Thurs. and Sun., 11am-midnight Fri.-Sat., $4-7, cash only), in the International District, for the fancy digs. The storefront is plain, and the tables are the plain Formica found in cafeterias and company lunchrooms. You come for the steaming dishes: Find all sorts of varieties of noodle soup, noodles with meat and vegetables, and congee. The restaurant is family run, and customers are firm devotees of their favorite variety of wonton soup. The spot has the hole-in-the-wall feel that makes fancier furniture—or a floor that's not linoleum—unnecessary.

Many of the International District eateries sacrifice ambience in favor of flavor and flavor only, but **Red Lantern** (520 S Jackson St., 206/682-7211, www. redlanternseattle.com, 11am-2:30pm and 5pm-9:30pm Mon.-Sat., lunch $8-12, dinner $9-16) manages to deliver both in a space that stays simple but nevertheless decorates with wood tables and sleek red light fixtures. The food hails from northern China and Korea, which means both familiar bites like pot stickers and sweet-and-sour beef, plus brown-braised pig feet and duck cooked in shaoxing wine. Certain house specialties, like Sichuan peppercorn crab and steamed ginger fish, require calling ahead. The dessert menu has red tea tiramisu and black tea crème brûlée.

French

The small ★ **Le Pichet** (1933 1st Ave., 206/256-1499, www.lepichetseattle.com, 8am-midnight daily, lunch $10-12, dinner $10-20) is a taste of France in the middle of downtown Seattle, complete with sidewalk café, mirrors on the walls, and white-tile floors. The menu is so French it's actually written in the language (with translations), but the most important thing to know is that the roasted whole chicken for two people takes an hour to cook. Good thing there are plenty of drinks and charcuterie selections to keep you occupied—it's worth the wait. For all the French quality, there's nothing fussy about the restaurant. In fact, it's been voted both "Best Hangover Meal" and "Best Ambiance" in the city.

Italian

The Pink Door (1919 Post Alley, 206/443-3241, www.thepinkdoor.net, 11:30am-11:30pm Mon.-Thurs., 11:30am-1am Fri.-Sat., 4pm-10pm Sun., lunch $11-22, dinner $16-26) is a strange combination of restaurants. The outdoor patio, overlooking the waterfront and Pike Place Market, is a casual dining spot, but inside is a candlelit dining room where the Italian menu is served under hoops and swings used by occasional cabaret and trapeze performers. Still, the reliable and large saucy dishes are local favorites, and shows (with cover) can include burlesque performers and a balloon artist. The restaurant is indeed behind a pink door located on Post Alley, but it's much less hidden than it sounds. Look for a hanging pointed finger directing the way.

Belltown
Pacific Northwest

Imagine Seattle in the middle of a circle with a radius of 360 miles. At ★ **Local 360** (2234 1st Ave., 206/441-9360, www.local360.org, 9am-10pm Sun.-Thurs., 9am-11pm Fri,-Sat., brunch $5-15, lunch $8-18, dinner $9-26), almost every ingredient comes from within that circle, including the lengthy spirits list. The restaurant goes for a funky feel, what with the rough-hewn wood walls, candlesticks, and peanut-butter-and-jelly bonbons on the menu (they come with a shot of milk, naturally). The young crowd comes here for snacks to go with their cocktails, or perhaps even a whole meal with fried chicken or a pork shank. A slight touch of a Southern influence is evident from the grits, collard greens, and tasting flight of locally brewed moonshines.

American

A gaucho is a South American cowboy, but there's nothing rough-and-tumble about **El Gaucho** (2505 1st Ave., 206/728-1337, www.elgaucho.com, 4pm-10pm Sun.-Thurs., 4pm-midnight Fri.-Sat., $37-78). The steak house has restaurants in Seattle, Portland, Tacoma, and across the lake in Bellevue. If you close your eyes, you can almost imagine you're back in the swinging '50s—indeed, it was inspired by a supper club of that era. It's almost dinner theater: An open charcoal grill isn't far from patrons dressed to the nines, and a Bananas Foster is set aflame as it's served at a leather banquette. Lobster tail and diver sea scallops are on the menu, but it's a shame to order anything but a dry-aged steak or perhaps the Chateaubriand tenderloin, carved tableside.

Mediterranean

Although Tom Douglas has fun with his restaurant themes, **Lola** (2000 4th Ave., 206/441-1430, www.tomdouglas.com, 6am-midnight Mon.-Thurs.,

6am-2am Fri., 7am-2am Sat., 7am-1am Sun., $17-39) is refreshingly grown up. The Mediterranean- and North African-inspired menu makes use of local seafood and lots of Greek favorites, pita, tagines, and lamb in a number of forms—the lamb burger comes with chickpea fries. Daily brunch is popular, especially the made-to-order doughnuts. The ceiling is hung with orange wire light fixtures, and the restaurant is decorated in warm oranges and yellows. The round bar is a good, social spot for a drink, but in the dining room the booths block the bustle well.

Queen Anne
Pacific Northwest

To be precise, ★ **Canlis** (2576 Aurora Ave. N, 206/283-3313, www.canlis.com, 5:30pm-9:30pm Mon.-Thurs., 5:30pm-10pm Fri., 5pm-10pm Sat., $85-125) isn't exactly a restaurant—it's more of an experience, a destination, a landmark. It was opened in 1950 by Peter Canlis and is run today by his grandsons in a beautiful midcentury building with a stone fireplace and angled windows overlooking Lake Union. Its signature service is all about personal touches, like the valet that doesn't take a name or offer a ticket, just remembers each driver's face and delivers the car as if by magic (the coat check works the same way). Meals come in a variety of tasting menus, but the Canlis salad is a must-try: greens and a dressing made of lemon, olive oil, and coddled egg prepared tableside. Main dishes are simple, well-prepared classics: grilled sea bass, slow-roasted chicken that takes an hour to prepare, and Muscovy duck breast for two. Dining at Canlis is an all-evening affair, and men are required to wear a suit or sport coat.

Sorry, but there's no wolf on the menu at **How to Cook a Wolf** (2208 Queen Anne Ave. N, 206/838-8090, www.ethanstowellrestaurants.com, 5pm-11pm daily, $14-24). The name comes from a book by midcentury food writer M. F. K. Fisher.

The eatery does have endless fresh and finely crafted dishes, so it's just as well. Situated in the local's neighborhood on the top of Queen Anne, it's more regularly visited by discerning Seattle diners, not tourists. Dishes are simple and rustic, drawing from Italian inspiration. The short menu usually has a handful of pastas and several small, sharable appetizers like chicken liver mousse or black bass. Order several of each to fill up, but expect a few extra tastes here and there from the kitchen.

American

What kind of restaurant is **The 5 Spot** (1502 Queen Anne Ave. N, 206/285-7768, www.chowfoods.com, 8:30am-midnight Mon.-Fri., 8:30am-3pm and 5pm-midnight Sat.-Sun., breakfast $8-11, lunch $9-13, dinner $12-20)? It's a diner, plus a Florida seafood joint. Or a New Mexico cantina. Or a Texas barbecue restaurant. The menu has a stable half and a changing half, and goofy decor rotates with the theme. (The artwork is often connected to the door; look to see what changes when the front door swings.) Not every American cuisine tackled here is perfectly realized, but no one can say the cooks are unadventurous. The comfy diner has a signpost noting all the places the menu has been, plus a cheap late-night menu and a hearty breakfast. It's where to go when you're fine with ending up just about anywhere.

Coffee

Part of a local chain, **Uptown Espresso** (525 Queen Anne Ave. N, 206/285-3757, www.velvetfoam.com, 5am-10pm Mon.-Thurs., 5am-11pm Fri., 6am-11pm Sat., 6am-10pm Sun.) earns character points with its collection of dining room tables and walls laden with a hodgepodge of mirrors, framed oil paintings, and historical photographs. It's a quiet respite on a busy block of Queen Anne, where students hunker down with laptops or chat in small groups. The house coffee is known as Velvet Foam, a roast almost as creamy as the hot chocolate topped with whipped cream.

Southern

Very little is small about the New Orleans-themed ★ **Toulouse Petit** (601 Queen Anne Ave. N, 206/432-9069, www.toulousepetit.com, 8am-2am daily, breakfast $8-25, lunch $9-22, dinner $14-42). Located a 10-minute walk from Belltown or the Seattle Center, the restaurant is crowded on weekend nights with flirty young professionals enjoying the late-night happy hour and tossing back sweet cocktails. Some ornate furnishings, as might befit the French Quarter, hang over booths and tables. The endless menu has appetizers, entrées, salads, seafood, charcuterie, "curiosities," oysters, pastas, steaks, and a prix fixe option—if you can't find something to eat at Toulouse Petit, you must really not like food. Some but not all dishes have a Louisiana twist, and there is plenty of shrimp and spicy sausage. At brunch the party continues, this time with mimosas flowing freely and house-made fried beignets served with a chicory crème anglaise. The generous hash will sop up any mistakes you made the night before.

South Lake Union
Seafood

While the raw halibut soar through the air at Pike Place Market, the dishes at **Flying Fish** (300 Westlake Ave. N, 206/728-8595, www.flyingfishrestaurant. com, 11:30am-2pm and 4pm-10pm Mon.-Thurs., 11:30am-2pm and 4pm-11pm Fri., 4pm-11pm Sat., 4pm-10pm Sun., $23-32) arrive in a much calmer fashion. Seafood-first restaurants should be a dime a dozen in Seattle, but they're really not. This is one of the few in the neighborhood that is unapologetically fishy. But that's not its only claim to fame. After 18 years, a neighborhood move, and numerous accolades, the chef sold to a Chinese restaurant group and started incorporating

Asian flavors into the menu—Thai crab cakes, cod served with Sichuan broth, and mussels with chili-lime dipping sauce. But the menu still emphasizes organic, wild ingredients, and the space has the same happy din. The colors are bright, with none of the all-shades-of-blue cliché found in so many sea-themed eateries.

American

When it's time for brunch, the lines form at ★ **Portage Bay Café** (391 Terry Ave. N, 206/462-6400, www.portagebaycafe.com, 7:30am-2:30pm daily, breakfast $8.50-16, lunch $11.50-15). The South Lake Union location is one of three around the city, but this location has two big rooms of seating. In the center is the breakfast bar filled with seasonal fruits, nuts, and organic maple syrup. Choose from the five French toast or five pancake options, then top it from the breakfast bar. The menu has many vegan and vegetarian options, and most of the French toasts can be made gluten-free. Rowing sculls hang from the ceiling inside, and during weekend brunches the waiting crowd outside is its own social scene.

The mad scientist who came up with **Lunchbox Laboratory** (1253 Thomas St., 206/621-1090, www.lunchboxlaboratory.com, 11am-11pm daily, $11-14) had some strange experiments—how else do you explain burgers made of churken (chicken and turkey), a lamb patty topped with feta, or a dork (duck and pork) concoction? For all the strange combos, the upbeat burger joint is a cheery and tasty joint, and each offering is almost big enough to split. They do homage to the Dick's burger, a cheap drive-in Seattle classic, and plenty of normal combinations as well. Sweet potato fries are the best side dish (then come skinny fries, homemade chips, and tater tots), and the milkshakes come either with alcohol or not. Weekly specials are billed as experiments and are even crazier than the regular menu. The brightly colored spot is close to REI and, like the outdoor store, is a whimsical destination for grown-ups.

Capitol Hill
Pacific Northwest

The crown jewel of Melrose Market, a collection of food-based shops and eateries in Capitol Hill, is ★ **Sitka and Spruce** (1531 Melrose Ave., 206/324-0662, www.sitkaandspruce.com, 11:30am-2pm Mon., 11:30am-2pm and 5:30pm-10pm Tues.-Thurs., 11:30am-2pm and 5:30pm-11pm Fri., 10am-2pm and 5:30pm-11pm Sat., 10am-2pm and 4:30pm-9pm Sun., $10-29). The restaurant excels at local cuisine, headed up by rising-star chef Matthew Dillon. The kitchen isn't just open—it's an equal part of the small space, with cooks bustling around the chopping blocks and stoves with bundles of greenery. Diners sit at the windows, at small tables, or at a large, blocky communal table. Seasonal veggies are served without unnecessary fanfare, and diners share flavorful chicken, salmon, chanterelles, mussels, or whatever's freshest that day. The menu is short but aggressively local. On Mondays the restaurant serves a special menu inspired by Mexican cuisine, for a very different feel from the rest of the week but prepared with the same exacting standards.

Seafood

You're always at the coast at **Coastal Kitchen** (429 15th Ave. E, 206/322-1145, www.coastalkitchenseattle.com, 8am-midnight daily, $13-28), even though the location of the coast changes. The seafood restaurant has a rotating focus that shifts every three months. The destinations are specific, like Veracruz, Mexico, or New Orleans, Louisiana. The regular menu includes seafood standbys, like fish-and-chips, oysters, and calamari, plus a few entrées other than seafood. The space is open late and has $5 drinks at the three "Don't Judge Me" happy hours (one's from 8am-10am). Art pieces on the wall rotate with the changing menu, and humorous language lessons play in the bathroom. The large restaurant has several counters and bars, plus tables and a garage door that's open on nice days. On Mondays the restaurant hosts jazz performances.

American

Only one thing at **Li'l Woody's** (1211 Pine St., 206/457-4148, www.lilwoodys.com, 11am-11pm Mon.-Thurs., 11am-3am Fri.-Sat., 11am-10pm Sun., $4.50-8) is "li'l"—the quarter-pound burger that comes with Tillamook cheese and basic toppings. The rest of the burgers are a third of a pound and loaded with bacon and horseradish, or green chiles, or pickled figs with gorgonzola cheese. You can even load a burger with peanut butter. Skinny skin-on fries come plain, with house-made cheese, or with "crack," a small bowl of milkshake for dipping. With a few local beers on tap, a loft seating area, and a window-front counter, the small restaurant manages to be an eat-in joint, not just a burger counter. The location is in Capitol Hill, but on the edge, just across the freeway from the convention center, making it the best burger close to downtown.

Everybody goes to **Quinn's Pub** (1001 E Pike St., 206/325-7711, www.quinnspubseattle.com, 3pm-1am daily, $8-24), a two-story restaurant that occupies a prime location on one of Capitol Hill's busiest streets. It's nice enough for a business meal (well, a casual, impress-with-the-food kind of business meal), dim enough for a date, rowdy enough for dinner with friends, and flavorful enough for a special occasion. The burger is one of the most popular menu items, but it's no burger joint; the bistro fare includes a Scotch egg and grilled Vermont quail. Desserts are small and, at $3 each, meant to be ordered in multiples. The bar, with access to the knowledgeable bartenders pouring Trappist ales, is prime seating but hard to score. Upstairs tables have less ambience, which can mean more elbow room. Besides the 14 beer taps, the alcohol offerings lean toward bourbons and whiskeys.

Coffee

Capitol Hill was once known for its coffee shops, but many have been forced out in recent years, unable to keep up with sky-rocketing rents in the hip neighborhood. One survivor is **Victrola** (411 15th Ave. E, 206/325-6520, www.victrolacoffee.com, 6am-10pm Mon.-Sat., 6am-9pm Sun.), where the usual bustle of baristas and students hums under a kind of art gallery for local artists. The space has hosted radio events, movie nights, and even an insect safari. It also serves up more pedestrian fare like sandwiches and salads. The company's second café is located farther down Capitol Hill (310 E Pike St.), with free educational coffee tastings on Wednesdays at 11am; Victrola does its roasting at this building in Capitol Hill's old auto row.

Starbucks began as a modest coffee shop near Pike Place Market, and it has grown to include outposts on nearly every Seattle corner, plus a global headquarters south of the stadiums. But its pinnacle might be Capitol Hill's **Starbucks Reserve Roastery and Tasting Room** (1124 Pike St., 206/624-0173, http://roastery.starbucks.com, 6:30am-11pm daily), an airy space meant to show off the company's claim to high-end coffee mastery. It doesn't serve the normal Starbucks menu, but rather its limited Reserve line roasted here and brewed in a variety of methods—pour-over, Clover, French press, and more. The coffee show happens in a room filled with copper pipes and beans running through pneumatic tubes, so it's meant to be appreciated by the coffee lover.

Asian

The cheery **Poppy** (622 Broadway E, 206/324-1108, www.poppyseattle.com, 5:30pm-11pm Sun.-Thurs., 5:30pm-midnight Fri.-Sat., $11-27) is a less common take on Indian dining. The menu is based around *thali* platters of many small dishes, using local ingredients and traditional Indian spices. The *thalis*, which might include soup, salad, nigella-poppy naan, some kind of pickle, and a braised meat or fresh fish, change daily. The cocktails use fresh juices and flavors that match the complex *thalis*. The small garden out back has both outdoor seating and the restaurant's herb garden. Inside it's all exposed brick and bright orange design accents.

Italian

In a city where new American pub cuisine and creative seafood concepts get all the attention, **Spinasse** (1531 14th Ave., 206/251-7673, www.spinasse.com, 5pm-10pm Sun.-Thurs., 5pm-11pm Fri.-Sat., $12-32) excels at Italian fare and a sophisticated atmosphere. The food is from Northern Italy and relies on local ingredients and handmade pastas. Salads, antipasti, and meaty rabbit or pork belly are all delicious, but the *tajarin*—egg pasta served with ragu or butter—is the simple, delectable standout. It may be one of the best single dishes in Seattle, so splurge for the bigger portion. If the table doesn't devour the shareable plates, it makes for killer leftovers. Some seats face the open kitchen. The sister bar next door, Artusi, also has small Italian bites, plus expert bartenders and a sunny, modern space.

Southern

The ★ **Wandering Goose** (403 15th Ave. E, 206/323-9938, www.thewanderinggoose.com, 7am-4pm daily, $5-13) sounds like a fairy tale character, and indeed the owner has written a children's book. The restaurant itself is sweet and comfortable, with counter service and wooden chairs at little wooden tables. The food is Southern and breakfast-inspired: biscuits, grits, ham, gravy, plus some salads for lunch and baked goods. The honey is house-made and sourced from beehives on the roof. On Fridays, a special fried-chicken meal is served at 5pm: three pieces of buttermilk chicken, a biscuit, and three sides, like collard greens or coleslaw. If a farmhouse café was neatly blended with a Southern diner, it would look and feel—and luckily taste—something like this.

University District
Mexican

You have two choices at **Agua Verde Cafe** (1303 NE Boat St., 206/545-8570, www.aguaverde.com, 11am-9pm Mon.-Sat., $7-15), located on Portage Bay between Lake Washington and Lake Union: Eat Mexican food and then rent a kayak, or kayak first and then bliss out on tacos, Mexican beer, and margaritas. Well of course you can skip the boat rentals altogether, but the view and proximity are very tempting. The restaurant has dishes with a Baja California vibe—empanadas, enchiladas, and open-face tacos, ordered from a counter and then served in a funky, beachy space. The attached **Agua Verde Paddle Club** (206/545-8570, $18-24) rents single and double kayaks and stand-up paddleboards. Routes go to Lake Washington or to Lake Union for views of downtown and Gasworks Park. Occasional tours lead kayakers to the University of Washington Arboretum or on moonlit paddles.

Ballard
Seafood

Both stories of **Ray's Boathouse** (6049 Seaview Ave. NW, 206/789-3770, www.rays.com, 5pm-9:30pm daily, $13-39) have views of Shilshole Bay and the distant peaks of the Olympics. The pier-side restaurant serves seafood specialties, some local as well as Maine lobster and Gulf prawns. The café upstairs is more casual, but the downstairs bar faces the water and is topped with blown-glass light fixtures.

An oyster bar named for the poem in *Alice in Wonderland,* ★ **The Walrus and the Carpenter** (4743 Ballard Ave. NW,

206/395-9227, www.thewalrusbar.com, 4pm-10pm Sun.-Thurs., 4pm-11pm Sat.-Sun., $8-12) has wait times that are hard to believe—up to or even surpassing two hours, even on a weeknight. The small space has a handful of tables and a bar, and all the seafood is locally sourced. A handful of veggie dishes complement the oysters and shellfish, especially the fried Brussels sprouts. Steak tartare and cheese plates complete the menu, but the spot isn't a good bet for anyone hoping to avoid seafood. And yes, the wait is worth it for a table in the sparkling white space and handfuls of shareable plates. To ease the pain of the line, leave a phone number at the door and head to another bar on Ballard Avenue for a drink—they'll call when you're next up for oysters.

French

The French ★ **Bastille Café** (5307 Ballard Ave. NW, 206/453-5014, www.bastille-seattle.com, 5:30pm-midnight Mon.-Thurs., 5:30pm-1am Fri.-Sat., 10am-3pm and 5:30pm-midnight Sun., brunch $9-15, dinner $11-26) is a lovely, adult addition to a bar-heavy neighborhood that's matured in recent years. The walls are rustic exposed brick and gleaming white tiles, and menus are scrawled on mirrors; chandeliers hang from exposed beams. The outdoor patio and indoor fire hearth fill for weekend brunches and casual dinners. Sconces and other touches try to evoke a hip French bistro (or maybe a very fancy metro station). Honey is sourced from 50,000 honeybees living on hives up on the roof.

Mexican

It's a long way from Seattle to the Mexican border, but **La Carta de Oaxaca** (5431 Ballard Ave. NW, 206/782-8722, www.lacartadeoaxaca.com, 5pm-11pm Mon., 11:30am-3pm and 5pm-11pm Tues.-Thurs., 11:30am-3pm and 5pm-midnight Fri.-Sat., $6-17) serves authentic Mexican fare in a small, crowded space. The guacamole is made by hand, and the open kitchen proves that the mole is made here. A wall of framed photographs lightens the restaurant, but everyone is concentrating on shoveling in tortillas, tostadas, and *entomatadas*. Reservations are not accepted, and the spot's quality is well known, so expect a wait.

Greater Seattle
American
Although Bellevue doesn't have the range of dining options that Seattle does, it does have **Bis on Main** (10213 Main St., Bellevue, 425/455-2033, www.bison-main.com, 11:30am-11pm Mon.-Thurs., 11:30am-midnight Fri., 5:30pm-midnight Sat., 5pm-9pm Sun., $23-49). There's free valet parking on most nights. The restaurant is a stellar example of how the area's second city is no slouch. The menu has straightforward American classics like filet mignon and maple leaf duck breast but also includes a touch of luxury in truffle French fries and a $60 special rack of lamb. The unassuming class of the space makes it popular for business dinners—the 300-bottle wine list probably doesn't hurt—and service is friendly.

Asian
You'll travel to the 2nd floor of a mall building to find **Din Tai Fung Dumpling House** (700 Bellevue Way NE #280, Bellevue, 425/698-1095, www.dintai-fungusa.com, 11am-10pm Mon.-Fri., 10am-10pm Sat.-Sun., $3.50-8), but lines often form for the giant space—in fact they were over three hours long when the spot opened. The chain originated in Taiwan and has locations around the world, including in Seattle's downtown and University District—but the Bellevue location was the first in the area. Specialties include soft buns filled with pork, vegetables, or pastes, and steamed soup dumplings (a.k.a. *xiao long bao*) that are delicate and flavorful. (And hot! Take care with your chopsticks or spoon.) Folks with ties to Asia often flock to Din Tai Fung for a taste of home; besides the food, there are Asian beers. Windows in front show the staff folding the buns.

Italian
Café Juanita (9702 NE 120th Pl., Bellevue, 425/823-1505, www.cafejua-nita.com, 5pm-9pm Tues.-Thurs., 5pm-10pm Fri.-Sat., $16-55) isn't really near anything of note in a quiet neighborhood north of Lake Washington, and it's hard to find. But the Italian restaurant has a great reputation (they've racked up awards) and ardent fans. The Northern Italian fare includes homemade pastas and rich dishes like braised rabbit. Even though it's tucked away, the refined food and classy setting give it a sense of occasion.

Accommodations

Being a well-appointed hotel in Seattle is not enough—you have to have a personality. Often that's expressed in art collections and modern decor, but it's also manifested in views, in-house dining, and programming for locals and visitors alike.

Downtown
Under $150
Few properties in the city can boast a location more convenient than that of the **Green Tortoise Hostel** (105 Pike St., 206/340-1222, www.greentortoise.net, $38-65 dorms), across the street from Pike Place Market and within walking distance of downtown, Pioneer Square, Belltown, and, with a little trek, the Seattle Center. The hostel has bunk beds with private lights, fans, and power outlets, plus curtains for a small amount of privacy. Some bunk beds are doubles. There's free wireless Internet and continental breakfast, and three times a week the hostel serves free dinner.

$150-250
The homey **Pensione Nichols** (1923 1st

Ave., 206/441-7125, www.pensionenichols.com, $180-300 shared bath) is a bed-and-breakfast with killer views of Elliott Bay and an unbeatable location next to Pike Place Market. The antique furnishings lean slightly toward the grandmother's-living-room aesthetic, but the house dogs are plenty welcoming.

Over $250

Every door in ★ **Hotel Max** (620 Stewart St., 206/728-6299, www.hotelmaxseattle.com, $340-450) is covered in local artwork, and each floor has a theme. Bold colors and mature art give the property an adult vibe, and meaty dishes from the wood-fired grill in the restaurant next door can be sent up as room service 24 hours a day.

The more traditional **Mayflower Park Hotel** (405 Olive Way, 206/623-8700, www.mayflowerpark.com, $278-323) is decked out in Queen Anne style, complete with chandeliers and brass knobs, a mark of its 85-year history. The central location is between downtown and Belltown, with the Mediterranean eatery **Andaluca** (6:30am-11am Mon., 6:30am-11am and 5pm-9pm Tues.-Fri., 7am-noon and 5pm-10pm Sat.,7am-noon and 5pm-9pm Sun.) just downstairs.

The electric colors of **Hotel Monaco** (1101 4th Ave., 206/621-1770, www.monaco-seattle.com, $310-385) start in the lobby—where walls are blue and patterns are bright—and continue in guest rooms, where even the bathrobes are vivid in animal prints. The downtown location is close to the Seattle Central Library and walkable to major attractions. Despite all the design pizzazz, the staff wants you to feel at home—so much so that you can get a complimentary loaner goldfish to act as your pet while you're there. The nearly 200 rooms are modern and equipped with high-end electronics, furniture, and linens.

While there's a bookish theme to the **Alexis Hotel** (1007 1st Ave., 206/624-4844, www.alexishotel.com, $405-485),

the very modern decor in the lobby is less reminiscent of a library, though rooms have intricate headboards and classic furnishings. The hotel has bikes available for guest use, and there's a free wine reception in the lobby every evening. Valet parking is $42 per night, but hybrid vehicles get it at half price. The cozy **Bookstore Bar & Café** (7am-10pm Mon.-Fri., 8am-10pm Sat.-Sun.) sells tomes ($5) along with whiskeys and salads.

The Beatles stayed at the waterfront ★ **Edgewater** (2411 Alaskan Way, 206/728-7000, www.edgewaterhotel.com, $409-629) when they came to town, famously posing with fishing poles out their window. The chic Northwest decor includes gas fireplaces and stuffed footstools shaped like brown bears.

When presidents like John F. Kennedy visited Seattle, they stayed in the historical rooms of the **Fairmont Olympic Hotel** (411 University St., 206/621-1700, www.fairmont.com, $373-529). Not only was it the site of the original University of Washington, this longtime landmark was also the site of much planning for the city's World's Fair. Its rooms are decked in pale luxury, with classic Victorian-inspired furniture and gray marble in the bathrooms. The large lobby is home to 2nd-floor interior balconies, red-carpeted stairs, and potted palms, while a tucked-away swimming pool sits inside a glass solarium, perfect for Seattle's not-so-warm days.

The luxe **Loews Hotel 1000** (1000 1st Ave., 206/957-1000, www.hotel1000seattle.com, $401-520) is a boutique property with easy access to downtown, the waterfront, and Pioneer Square. Bathrooms are large and include bathtubs whose faucets are on the ceiling. The rooms have creative but tasteful decor and fine linens. The basement Spaahh (206/357-9490) offers a variety of treatments, while the virtual Golf Club (8am-10pm daily) brings the links of the world to a small room. The hotel also has a restaurant.

Belltown
Under $150

Don't be fooled by the beautiful building that looks more like an embassy than a cheap place to crash. **City Hostel Seattle** (2327 2nd Ave., 206/706-3255, www.hostelseattle.com, $38-40 dorms, $99-120 private rooms) is indeed a hostel. The property has breakfast and free luggage storage, plus kitchens and an outdoor grill for guest use. Most rooms use shared hall bathrooms. Each room is decorated with a different kind of mural or painting, many with glaringly bright colors, and the hostel also has a 20-seat movie theater.

In an old boardinghouse, a collective of creative entrepreneurs opened the ★ **Ace Hotel** (2423 1st Ave., 206/448-4721, www. acehotel.com/seattle, $129-219), putting turntables and reclaimed wood furniture in every room. Some rooms share hall bathrooms, and some rooms have original wood floors. Original art in the rooms comes from the likes of Shepard Fairey. A large black table sits in the lobby, and a breakfast room serves waffles and coffee in the morning.

Queen Anne
$150-250

Billed as a historical property, the **Inn at Queen Anne** (505 1st Ave. N, 206/282-7357, www.innatqueenanne.com, $179-199) definitely has the dark corners of an older property. Rooms are simple, but all have private bathrooms and some have stoves, and the Seattle Center is right across the street.

The age of the nearby **MarQueen Hotel** (600 Queen Anne Ave. N, 206/282-7407, www.marqueen.com, $239-339) manages to convey a bit more luxury, with beveled glass doors and Alaskan marble in the floors. Some rooms have awkwardly placed but charming sitting parlors.

Capitol Hill
Over $250

As one of the only hotels in Capitol Hill, **Silver Cloud Hotel** (1100 Broadway, 206/325-1400, www.silvercloud.com, $289-359) earns cool points just for being so close to the city's best restaurant and bar scene. Otherwise the chain is standard but well appointed, with an indoor pool and in-room refrigerators and microwaves. The artsy vibe is meant to echo the apartments on trendy Capitol Hill.

The ★ **Sorrento Hotel** (900 Madison St., 206/622-6400, www.hotelsorrento.com, $259-379) is like an Italian transplant next to the city's collection of world-class hospitals. It features the crooked, charming rooms of a historical building. The cozy Fireside Room hosts a monthly silent reading party.

University District
$150-250

The **Watertown Hotel** (4242 Roosevelt Way NE, 206/826-4242, www.watertownseattle.com, $209-309) is owned by the Pineapple Hospitality Group, a fact only notable because the lobby is stocked with pineapple cupcakes; otherwise there's nothing tropical about the hotel. The location is a few blocks from the university, and the hotel offers free bike rentals. Free daily shuttles go to downtown Seattle, and there is a free laundry machine for guest use. A related property down the street has an outdoor pool that guests can use. Some rooms have downtown views.

Over $250

The name of the **Hotel Deca** (4507 Brooklyn Ave. NE, 206/634-2000, www.hoteldeca.com, $309-329) refers to the art deco aesthetic that inspired the hotel, and in fact the property dates back to art deco's heyday in the 1930s. Rooms are more modern and some have great views. There's also an in-house restaurant, the **District Lounge** (6:30am-2pm and 5pm-10pm Mon.-Fri., 7:30am-noon and 5pm-10pm Sat.-Sun.), and a coffee shop. The street is a busy one, especially on weekend nights, but the building is tall enough that most disturbances are minimized. It's one of the few properties walkable to the main part of the University of Washington campus.

Ballard
$150-250
Ballard Inn (5300 Ballard Ave. NW, 206/789-5011, www.ballardinnseattle. com, $189-239) has the same owners as the Hotel Ballard, which is right next door, but a cozier feel. Many rooms share hall baths, and all are smaller than those in its sister property.

Over $250
The ★ **Hotel Ballard** (5214 Ballard Ave. NW, 206/789-5011, www.hotelballard-seattle.com, $399-499) is unusual in that it's an upscale boutique Seattle hotel, but isn't in downtown. It sits on Ballard's busiest street, right across from the buzziest bars, restaurants, and performance spaces, and above the high-end Olympic Athletic Club—sharing access to the club's giant saltwater pool. The top-floor open-air patio has a view of Ballard's industrial waterfront. Rooms are luxe and decorated in a modern European style, and the bathtubs are sizable. The downstairs restaurant specializes in wood-fired pizzas.

Greater Seattle
Over $250
In the Bellevue suburb of Kirkland, the luxury **Heathman Hotel** (220 Kirkland Ave., Kirkland, 425/284-5800, www. heathmankirkland.com, $309-409) makes the most of quiet streets next to the shores of Lake Washington. Northwest farm-to-table cuisine is top rate at the in-house Trellis restaurant, and rooms are spacious and filled with the kind of linens that makes you want to steal. Even farther from the center of Kirkland, **Woodmark Hotel** (1200 Carillon Point, Kirkland, 425/822-3700, www.thewoodmark.com, $299-459) is a calming spot next to a marina and flanked by two good dining spots, ideal for a city getaway that almost feels remote.

Information and Services

This is a tech-heavy city, and it's not afraid to show off how much information it has. Look around Pike Place Market or the Convention Center area for tourist info, and head to the Central Library for the glass cathedral full of books and free Internet access.

Visitor Information
To obtain maps, book tours, and get information, head to one of downtown's two visitors centers operated by the city. **Seattle Visitor Center and Concierge Services** (Washington State Convention Center, 7th Ave. and Pike St., 866/732-2695, www.visitseattle.org, 9am-5pm daily summer, 9am-5pm Mon.-Fri. rest of the year) is on the uphill end of downtown, while the **Market Information Center** (Pike Place Market's southwest corner, First Ave. and Pike St., 866/732-2695, www.visitseattle.org, 10am-6pm daily) is closer to the waterfront.

Though nowhere near as comprehensive, **Travel Gay Seattle** (614 Broadway Ave. E, 206/363-9188, www.travelgay-seattle.com, 9am-5pm Mon.-Thurs., 9am-6pm Fri., 10am-2pm Sat.) is a visitor information booth located in a 1st Security Bank branch in Capitol Hill, traditionally the city's most LGBT-friendly area. They have maps showing businesses that specifically support the city's growing gay and lesbian travel industry.

Media and Communications
For a long time Seattle was a two-daily town, but when the *Seattle Post-Intelligencer* newspaper folded its print operation, the older *The Seattle Times* (www.seattletimes.com) became the only major paper in town. The *Times* is printed seven days a week and is available at newsstands, in newspaper boxes, and at many cafés and delis. It has local and

international news, business, sports, and lifestyle coverage.

The *Seattle Weekly* (www.seattle-weekly.com) has long provided independent weekly coverage, including music performance information and news and political reporting. The slightly, well, stranger weekly in town is *The Stranger* (www.thestranger.com), published bi-weekly in Capitol Hill and featuring sex-advice columnist Dan Savage. It also has news and culture reporting as well as performance listings. Both are distributed for free in newspaper boxes, and both have websites with much of the same information.

Services

The central **Seattle Post Office** (301 Union St., 206/748-5417, www.usps.com, 8:30am-5:30pm Mon.-Fri.) branch is in the middle of downtown. A small stand in the lobby sells packing materials while the official desk has national and international shipping options. Look for the automated postage machine in the lobby for faster service.

Seattle's train station and Amtrak depot, the 1906 **King Street Station** (303 S Jackson St., 206/296-0100, www.amtrak.com, 6am-11pm daily) is a real beauty. Its signature 12-story brick tower, modeled after the famous San Marco bell tower in Venice, is visible from around the south side of downtown. A renovation finished in 2013 fixed the historical plasterwork and cleaned up the shiny white interior. However, the station still doesn't have many eateries, but there is **luggage storage** for a fee.

For urgent but not emergency cases of medical need, try one of the city's many urgent care clinics, like **ZoomCare** (531 Broadway, 206/971-3728, www.zoomcare.com/clinic/capitol-hill, 8am-midnight Mon.-Fri., 9am-6pm Sat.-Sun.). Appointments can be booked online or over the phone, and doctors can treat minor injuries and illnesses. The city's major emergency room is at **Harborview**

King Street Station

Medical Center (325 9th Ave., 206/744-3300, www.uwmedicine.org/harborview), where helicopters often land carrying trauma patients from around the Northwest.

Getting Around

San Francisco may be known as the hilliest West Coast city, but Seattle makes its case for steep slopes. While a grid governs most of central and north Seattle, the many hills and waterways make for some confusing routes—and traffic is no joke around rush hour.

Car

Seattle is not an easy city to navigate by car because the downtown neighborhood is hilly and filled with one-way streets, and the traffic is notorious. **Rush hour** is far longer than an hour (7am-9am and 4pm-6pm), and the I-5 freeway through the city is often clogged with cars. The

I-90 freeway, Highway 99, and surface streets are also known for rush-hour jams. A car isn't needed if staying in a downtown hotel. Most attractions are within walking distance, and cabs frequent the area.

The only **toll road** in Seattle is the bridge that crosses Lake Washington on Highway 520. It has no toll booths, but cameras will capture license plates and mail bills to drivers without a prepaid sticker. Rates range from $3.25 to $5.40, with free periods in the middle of the night.

Parking in downtown Seattle is in street parking or private lots. Meters for street parking accept credit cards, and rates range $1-4 per hour; hours are generally 8am-8pm.

To rent a car in downtown Seattle, look to **Hertz** (1501 8th Ave., 206/903-6260, www.hertz.com, 7:30am-6pm Mon.-Fri., 8am-2pm Sat., 9am-2pm Sun.), **Budget** (801 4th Ave., 206/682-8989, http://locations.budget.com, 7am-6pm Mon.-Fri., 8am-4pm Sat.-Sun.), or **Avis** (1919 5th Ave., 206/448-1700, http://locations.avis.com, 7am-7pm Mon.-Fri., 8am-5pm Sat.-Sun.). All the major car rental chains have desks in Sea-Tac Airport's car rental facility.

Taxi

To hail a taxi in Seattle, try **Yellow Cab** (253/872-5600, www.yellowtaxi.net) or hail one on the street in the downtown core. Taxi rates in Seattle are $2.70 per mile with an initial charge of $2.50. The city also has private car companies like **Uber** (www.uber.com), which uses a phone app to assign cars to customers.

Seattle is also covered in **car2go** (877/488-4224, http://seattle.car2go.com) SmartCar rentals, where very small cars are rented by the minute, gas included, and can be picked up on the street around the city or at the airport. Advance registration is required because users get a card that opens and activates their rental car.

Ferry

The iconic green and white **Washington State Ferry** (Pier 52, 801 Alaskan Way, 888/808-7977, www.wsdot.wa.gov/ferries, $8 adults, $4 seniors and children) boats are constantly crossing Puget Sound in front of downtown. They allow commuters to travel to islands around Puget Sound and from the Olympic Peninsula on a daily basis, but can also be a fun, cheap ride for tourists. Walk on to a Bainbridge-bound ferry to get the great views in both directions. Check the schedule ahead of time, or head to the terminal to catch the next boat (but prepare to wait). Tickets can be purchased from machines in the terminal lobby. On the Bainbridge side, walk to the nearby **Bainbridge Island Museum of Art** (550 Winslow Way E, 206/842-4451, www.bi-artmuseum.org, 10am-6pm daily, free), grab a bite of poutine at the English-inspired **Harbour Public House** (231 Parfitt Way SW, 206/842-0969, www.harbourpub.com, 11am-midnight daily, $10-16), a 10-minute walk away, or just ride the boat back.

The **King County Water Taxi** (Pier 50, 801 Alaskan Way, www.kingcounty.gov, $5.25 adults and children 6-18, $2.25 seniors, children under 6 free) is a shorter ride on a smaller boat but offers many of the same breathtaking downtown views. It travels to West Seattle, and despite it being a long walk from that dock to Alki Beach, there is a waterfront trail and the Hawaiian-inspired food at **Marination Ma Kai** (1660 Harbor Ave. SW, 206/328-8226, www.marinationmobile.com/ma-kai, 9am-8pm Tues.-Thurs. and Sun., 9am-9pm Fri.-Sat., $3-10.50). Inspired by a local food truck, this great spot on the water has outdoor tables and a small bar.

RV

Renting an RV in Seattle is not easy because companies are based in Everett, about 28 miles north of the city, or in southern suburbs. Those flying into Sea-Tac Airport can look to **Five Corners RV** (16068 Ambaum Blvd. S, 206/241-6111, www.fivecornersrv.com, 8:30am-4pm Mon.-Fri.), located very close to the airport.

To park an RV in Seattle, look east to **Issaquah Valley RV Park** (650 1st Ave. NE, Issaquah, 425/392-9233, www.ivrvpark.com, $44-50). Although it's located very close to I-90, about 16 miles from downtown Seattle, it's also very close to the area's great outdoor recreation and is a neat, well-run facility. The **Vasa Park Resort** (3560 E. Lake Sammamish Pkwy., Bellevue, 425/746-3260, www.vasa-parkresort.com, $32-40), also in the suburbs east of Seattle, is on the shores of Lake Sammamish and has a boat launch and swimming beach.

Public Transit

The Seattle city bus system, **King County Metro Transit** (206/553-3000, http://metro.kingcounty.gov, $2.50-3.25 adults, $1 seniors, $1.50 children 6-17, children under 6 free) has an extensive web of routes all over the city, including bus tunnels that run under downtown and subway-like stations. Drivers only accept exact change, but the downtown underground bus stations have vending machines for ORCA cards, which can hold a balance for bus fare. Bikes can be loaded onto bike racks on the front of most buses.

ORCA cards are also accepted on the **water taxis** (206/553-3000, http://metro.kingcounty.gov/tops/watertaxi, $5.25 adults, $2-2.50 seniors, $3-5.50 children 6-17, children under 6 free) that travel from downtown Seattle at 801 Alaskan Way, south of the ferry docks, to Vashon Island and West Seattle. The former is mostly a commuter route, but the latter ends at a dock with a beautiful view of the city and an eatery.

Though only useful for travelers on a very specific route, **South Lake Union Streetcar** (206/553-3060, www.seattlestreetcar.org, 6am-9pm Mon.-Thurs., 6am-11pm Fri.-Sat., 10am-7pm Sun.,

$2.25 adults, $1 seniors, $1.50 children 6-17, children under 6 free) could be the future of Seattle transit. It goes from a stop behind Westlake Center, at 5th Avenue and Olive Way, to the Eastlake neighborhood. Station platforms have ticket machines, and cash is accepted on board. It's most useful for tourists looking to go from downtown to Lake Union, where the Museum of History and Industry and the Center for Wooden Boats are located.

Vancouver

Has there ever been a city that can legitimately claim both the mountains and the water like Vancouver can? Glass towers gleam with modern ambition, while deep forest gorges and mountains topped with ski resorts sit within city neighborhoods.

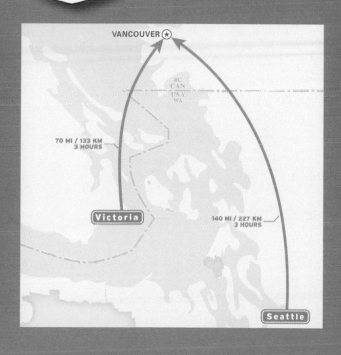

VANCOUVER ★

BC
CAN
USA
WA

70 MI / 133 KM
3 HOURS

Victoria

140 MI / 227 KM
3 HOURS

Seattle

Vancouver

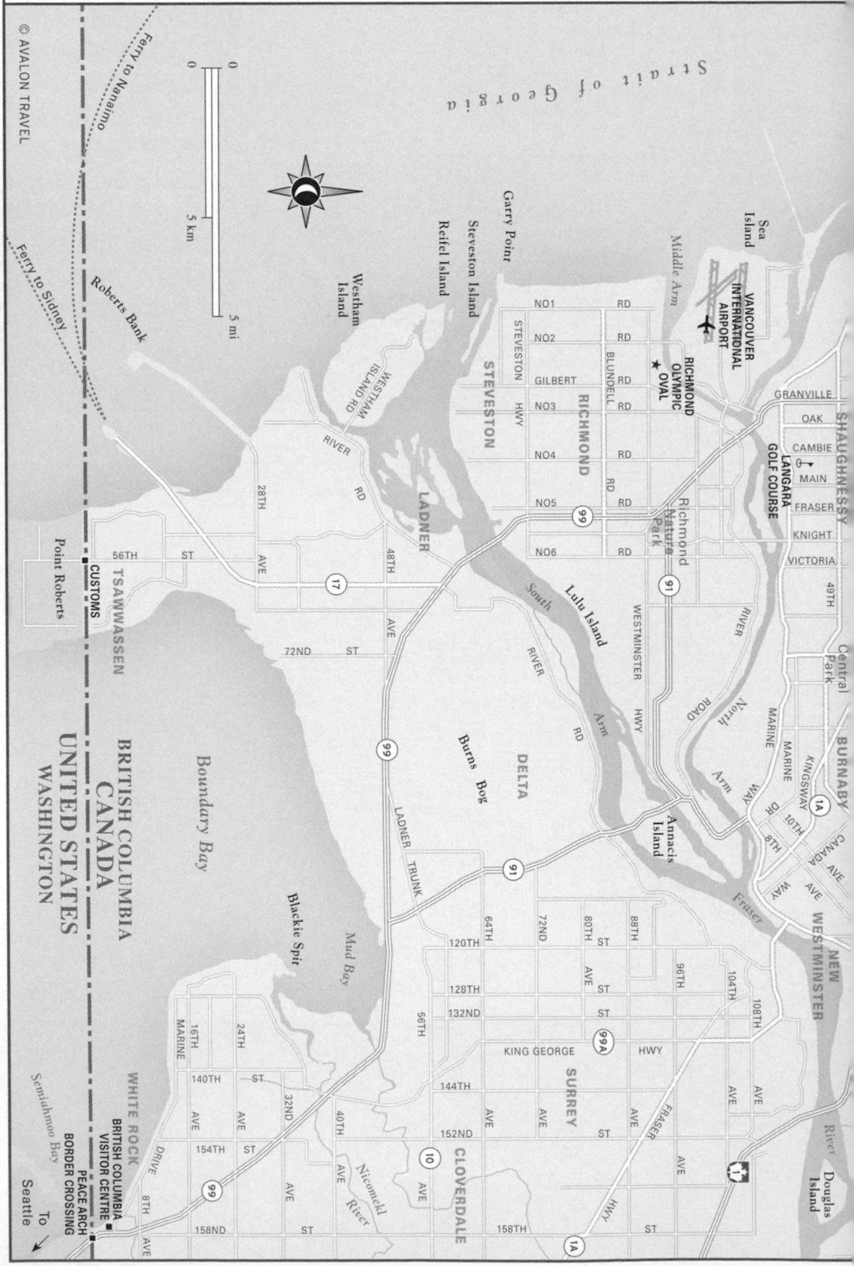

© AVALON TRAVEL

Ferry to Nanaimo

Ferry to Sidney

Roberts Bank

0

5 km

0

5 mi

Strait of Georgia

Sea Island

Middle Arm

VANCOUVER INTERNATIONAL AIRPORT

Garry Point

Steveston Island

Reifel Island

Westham Island

RICHMOND OLYMPIC OVAL

GRANVILLE

OAK

CAMBIE

MAIN

FRASER

KNIGHT

VICTORIA

SHAUGHNESSY

LANGARA GOLF COURSE

NO1 RD

NO2 RD

STEVESTON HWY

GILBERT

BLUNDELL

NO3 RD

NO4 RD

NO5 RD

NO6 RD

STEVESTON

RICHMOND

LADNER

Richmond Nature Park

49TH

Central Park

BURNABY

WESTHAM ISLAND RD

RIVER RD

28TH

48TH AVE

Point Roberts

CUSTOMS

TSAWWASSEN

56TH ST

72ND ST

17

99

91

Lulu Island

South Arm

River Arm

WESTMINSTER HWY

RIVER ROAD

North Arm

MARINE WAY

MARINE DR

KINGSWAY

10TH AVE

8TH AVE

CANADA WAY

1A

NEW WESTMINSTER

BRITISH COLUMBIA
CANADA
UNITED STATES
WASHINGTON

Boundary Bay

Blackie Spit

Mud Bay

Burns Bog

DELTA

Annacis Island

LADNER TRUNK

64TH ST

72ND ST

80TH ST

88TH ST

96TH ST

104TH

108TH

Fraser River

Douglas Island

99

91

WHITE ROCK

BRITISH COLUMBIA VISITOR CENTRE

PEACE ARCH BORDER CROSSING

Semiahmoo Bay

To Seattle

120TH

128TH

132ND

56TH ST

16TH AVE

24TH AVE

MARINE DRIVE

32ND ST

40TH AVE

140TH ST

144TH AVE

152ND ST

154TH ST

158ND AVE

158TH ST

8TH AVE

Nicomekl River

KING GEORGE HWY

SURREY

CLOVERDALE

FRASER HWY

10

1A

99A

99

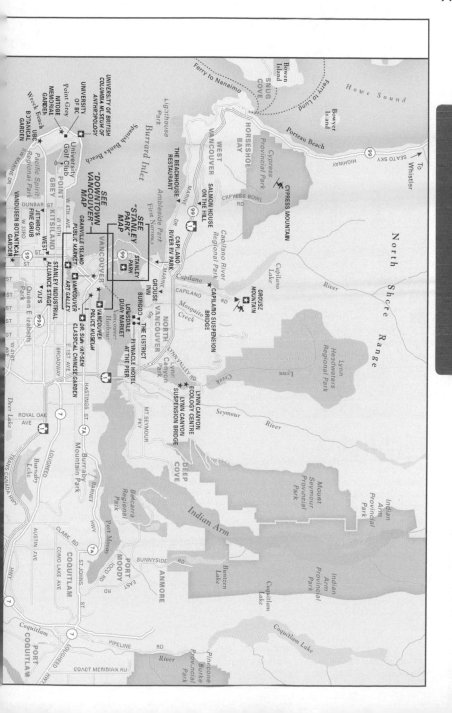

Highlights

★ **Stanley Park:** The forested acres of this massive downtown park are best seen from the seat of a bicycle (page 78).

★ **Vancouver Art Gallery:** Canadian treasures, including those by local standout Emily Carr, are displayed in a building from the province's most famous architect (page 83).

★ **Vancouver Police Museum:** Everything you wanted to know about Canadian crime prevention is here, plus some things you can't believe they let you see (page 85).

★ **Dr. Sun Yat-Sen Classical Chinese Garden:** More a historical manor house than a simple garden, this site is the jewel of Vancouver's Chinatown (page 86).

★ **Granville Island Public Market:** Shop for food, flowers, soaps, jewelry, or just about anything else you can imagine among the endless stalls (page 89).

★ **University of British Columbia Museum of Anthropology:** Totem poles receive a regal, light-filled display at this museum celebrating culture both at home and around the world (page 89).

★ **Grouse Mountain:** Ski in the winter, hike in the summer, and take in the mountaintop views year-round (page 91).

Culturally rich with native history and international industry, Vancouver is one of the most cosmopolitan spots on the west coast of North America.

Already on its way at the turn of the century, the city swelled with the attention that came with the 2010 Olympic Games. Today it has a growing culinary scene and is poised to become the business, recreation, and tourism jewel of Canada.

Vancouver's downtown is almost an island, bordered on three sides by False Creek, English Bay, and Vancouver Harbour. Shops crowd the Robson and Granville Streets, while the renovated neighborhoods of Yaletown and Gastown have become known for their culinary choices. Another reinvention, Granville Island, has turned a once-industrial site into a giant market, theater center, and shopping district. And throughout the city, international flavors abound—crowds flock to the night market and exquisite gardens in Chinatown, and the most popular restaurant is an Indian joint hidden on an unassuming street outside the downtown core. Nowhere is the area's native history better recognized than at the Museum of Anthropology's glass-walled gallery of totem poles.

But the outdoors is never far away, with waterfront areas, a spectacular city park, and mountains right next to downtown. The Stanley Park bike path takes pedal pushers past woods, beaches, and rocky shores, while just across the harbor is Grouse Mountain, with skiing or snowshoeing accessible by city bus.

Although Vancouver's population is slightly smaller than Seattle's, it feels bigger thanks to its great variety and modern, glassy architecture. Canadians show off their famously friendly disposition on the city streets, and even the mountains that tower over Vancouver feel welcoming.

Getting to Vancouver

Driving from Seattle
140 miles, 3 hours

The main route through Seattle is **I-5.** This multilane road is infamous for its traffic snarls, which are worst during early morning and late afternoon rush hours. The 8-mile-long express lanes, which change direction depending on where the bulk of cars are heading, can be a useful bypass.

Traveling north, I-5 reaches the city of **Everett** 30 miles north of Seattle. From Everett, there's usually little to slow drivers until they reach the border crossing 80 miles north in **Blaine,** Washington.

Stopping in Anacortes

Though it's a 20-minute drive from the freeway, the town of **Anacortes** is worth the detour. From I-5, take exit 230 and follow Highway 20 west for 11.5 miles across farmland and the tidal waters of several sloughs, then take the Highway 20 spur north to Anacortes, about 4.5 miles. Anacortes is best known as the departure point for San Juan Island ferries, including one that continues west to Victoria on Vancouver Island. Stop for a bite at **Adrift** (510 Commercial Ave., 360/588-0653, www.adriftrestaurant. com, 8am-9pm Mon.-Thurs., 8am-10pm Fri.-Sat., 8am-2pm Sun., breakfast $5-13, $15-34), a seafood joint better known for its wide variety of burgers and ice cream floats made with stout or champagne. Or try the barbecue and biscuits at **Dad's Diner** (906 Commercial Ave., 360/899-5269, 7am-4pm Tues.-Thurs. and Sat.-Sun., 7am-9pm Fri., $8-20). After lunch, walk along the waterfront where boats

Best Accommodations

★ **Burrard Hotel:** Here's a retro, renovated hot spot where the rooms open to a central courtyard and the bike rentals are free (page 114).

★ **Listel Hotel:** It may be a hotel, but it feels like an art gallery with all the contemporary paintings and sculptures decorating the hallways (page 114).

★ **Fairmont Pacific Rim:** A paragon of modern luxury lives up to the high standards of its chain, but with unique touches (page 115).

★ **Shangri-La Hotel:** An international chain hosts a deluxe spa among downtown's busy streets, plus an outdoor pool for all guests (page 116).

★ **Opus Hotel:** Find a touch of attitude and playfulness in a chummy neighborhood, and the best place in town for pampered pets (page 116).

sit neatly parked in the bustling marina. Drive south to **Deception Pass State Park** (Hwy. 20 and Rosario Rd., www.parks. wa.gov), which expands onto Whidbey Island. The bridge that connects to the island is either picturesque or terrifying, depending on your fear of heights! Park and cross by foot for the best views.

Crossing the Border

Two options are available for crossing the border: the Peace Arch crossing at the end of **I-5** and the Pacific Highway crossing on **Highway 543.**

To reach the Peace Arch crossing, stay on I-5 north as it slowly funnels cars directly into the border-crossing lanes. The actual arch sits in a large green park between crossing stations. Take care when letting passengers out to explore the field while the driver waits in line because everyone will need to be back in the car well before the crossing station. Upon entering Canada, the route immediately becomes the **Canadian Highway 99.**

For the Pacific Highway Crossing (also called Truck Customs, for its use among commercial vehicles), take exit 275 off I-5. Follow Highway 543 for less than a mile before meeting the border. Once through the border crossing, follow **Canadian Highway 15** for several blocks, turn left on 8th Avenue, and then take a right at the roundabout at Highway 99. Though less scenic than the waterfront

Peace Arch crossing, the Pacific Highway crossing often has a shorter wait.

From the Border to Vancouver
48 kilometers (30 miles), 45 minutes
Highway 99, also called the Vancouver-Blaine Highway, swings north through the open plains that sit just south of Vancouver's suburbs. In about 30 kilometers (19 miles), Highway 99 passes through a tunnel under the Fraser River, emerging in the suburb of Richmond.

From Richmond, Highway 99 continues across the Oak Street Bridge. Turn left on West 70th Avenue and continue north on Highway 99/Granville Street for about 16 kilometers (10 miles) toward the Granville Bridge and downtown Vancouver. Although the route narrows from a highway to surface streets, traffic flows well into the downtown core.

After crossing the Granville Bridge, you'll arrive in the heart of Vancouver. Follow Seymour Street northeast to continue to the waterfront area and Gastown. Note that several downtown byways are one-way, so check all traffic signs before making any turns.

From Victoria
113-195 kilometers (70-121 miles), 3 hours
Two ferry routes travel between Victoria and Vancouver. The **Swartz Bay** (Hwy. 17, www.bcferries.com, $17.20 adults, $8.60

Best Restaurants

★ **Smoke's Poutinerie:** Embrace Canada's signature dish with make-your-own combos of fries, gravy, and cheese curds (page 105).

★ **Hapa Izakaya:** Share plates of Japanese fare at a busy downtown eatery with excellent people-watching, inside and out (page 107).

★ **Café Medina:** Brave the line for one of the city's best brunches, or take a cooking class next door while you wait (page 107).

★ **Bao Bei:** The heart of Vancouver's Chinatown is marked by its neon sign, while artisanal Asian plates are dished in the narrow dining room (page 107).

★ **Finch's Tea and Coffee House:** Canada does tea well, especially in this organic treasure box of a café (page 109).

★ **Homer Street Café and Bar:** A brilliant white dining room is actually quite cozy when it's serving warm roast chicken and delicious desserts (page 110).

★ **Vij's:** The city's longtime blockbuster Indian restaurant is worth the wait, even after a move from its original location (page 112).

children 5-12, children under 5 free, vehicles $57.50, surcharges for fuel and large vehicles) route departs from the Saanich Peninsula, 32 kilometers (20 miles) north of Victoria at the end of Highway 17, just north of the town of Sidney. The boat travels to **Tsawwassen,** located south of the Vancouver-Blaine Highway, a 90-minute trip. From the Tsawwassen ferry terminal (1 Ferry Causeway, Delta), drive north on Highway 17A for 13 kilometers (8 miles), and then take Highway 99 north to Vancouver. The ferry travels 8-17 times per day in each direction. Reservations are recommended.

The second ferry departs from **Nanaimo** (www.bcferries.com, $17.20 adults, $8.60 children 5-12, children under 5 free, vehicles $57.50, surcharges for fuel and large vehicles), about 110 kilometers (68 miles) north of Victoria along Highway 1. Arrival is at **Horseshoe Bay** (6750 Keith Rd., West Vancouver), approximately 20 kilometers (12 miles) northwest of Vancouver. The trip lasts about one hour and 40 minutes; ferries run 7-12 times per day in each direction; reservations are recommended. From Horseshoe Bay, drive southeast on Highways 1 and 99 for 20 kilometers (12 miles) to North Vancouver. Highway 99 continues south across the Lions Gate Bridge into downtown Vancouver.

By Air, Train, or Bus
Air
Vancouver International Airport (YVR, 3211 Grant McConachie Way, Richmond, 604/207-7077, www.yvr.ca) is located on Sea Island, just 20 kilometers (12 miles) southwest of the city (technically in the suburb of Richmond). Canada's second-busiest airport sees daily arrivals from around the Pacific Rim. For **car rentals,** head to the ground floor of the airport terminal for a selection of rental companies. The drive into the center of Vancouver takes 20 minutes without traffic, longer during morning and evening rush hours.

A **taxi** from the airport to downtown Vancouver costs about $36. Alternatively, look for signs for the **Canada Line** (604/953-3333, http://thecanadaline.com, $9 adults, $7.75 seniors, students, and children 5-13, children under 5 free), a rapid rail link. The rail line takes 26 minutes to get to downtown Vancouver

VANCOUVER

Downtown Vancouver

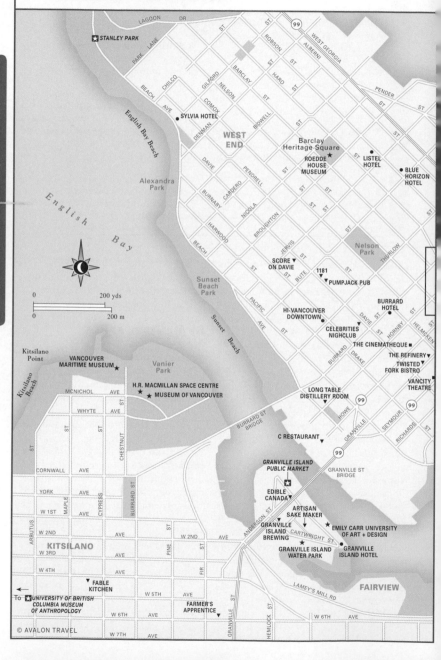

LAGOON DR

🏕 STANLEY PARK

PARK LANE

BEACH

CHILCO

GILFORD

NELSON

BARCLAY

COMOX

ROBSON ST

HARO ST

ALBERNI ST

WEST GEORGIA

99

PENDER ST

● SYLVIA HOTEL

English Bay Beach

DENMAN

BIDWELL

WEST END

Barclay
Heritage Square

ROEDDE ★
HOUSE
MUSEUM

● LISTEL
HOTEL

● BLUE
HORIZON
HOTEL

Alexandra
Park

DAVIE

PENDRELL

CARDERO

NICOLA

BROUGHTON

E n g l i s h

B a y

BURNABY

HARWOOD

BEACH

Nelson
Park

THURLOW

0   200 yds
0   200 m

Sunset
Beach
Park

PACIFIC

BEACH

JERVIS ST

BUTE ST

SCORE ▾
ON DAVIE

1181
▾ PUMPJACK PUB

HI-VANCOUVER
DOWNTOWN ●

BURRARD
HOTEL

DAVIE ST

HORNBY ST

HELMCKEN

Kitsilano
Point

**VANCOUVER
MARITIME MUSEUM** ★

Vanier
Park

Sunset Beach

AVE

BURRARD

DRAKE

CELEBRITIES
NIGHCLUB

THE CINEMATHEQUE ■

THE REFINERY ▾
TWISTED
FORK BISTRO

Kitsilano
Beach

MCNICHOL AVE

★ H.R. MACMILLAN SPACE CENTRE
★ MUSEUM OF VANCOUVER

LONG TABLE
DISTILLERY ROOM ▾

HOWE

99

VANCITY
THEATRE

WHYTE AVE

SEYMOUR

RICHARDS

99

BURRARD ST
BRIDGE

CHESTNUT

C RESTAURANT ▾

GRANVILLE

CORNWALL AVE

99

**GRANVILLE ISLAND
PUBLIC MARKET**

GRANVILLE ST
BRIDGE

YORK AVE

MAPLE

CYPRESS

BURRARD ST

W 2ND

PINE ST

W 2ND AVE

AVE

🚼 EDIBLE
CANADA

ANDERSON ST

ARTISAN
SAKE MAKER ▾

ARBUTUS

KITSILANO

W 1ST AVE

W 3RD

W 4TH AVE

AVE

FIR ST

GRANVILLE
ISLAND
BREWING ▾

CARTWRIGHT ST

★ EMILY CARR UNIVERSITY
OF ART + DESIGN

GRANVILLE ISLAND
WATER PARK

★ GRANVILLE
ISLAND HOTEL

← ▾ FABLE
KITCHEN

To 🏕 UNIVERSITY OF BRITISH
COLUMBIA MUSEUM
OF ANTHROPOLOGY

W 5TH AVE

W 6TH AVE

FARMER'S
APPRENTICE ▾

LAMEY'S MILL RD

GRANVILLE ST

HEMLOCK ST

FAIRVIEW

W 6TH AVE

© AVALON TRAVEL

W 7TH AVE

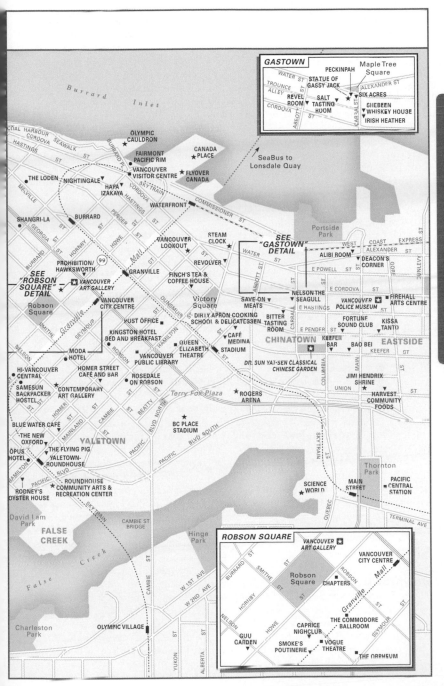

and ends at the Waterfront station (W Hastings St. between Howe St. and Seymour St.).

Train

Amtrak (800/872-7245, www.amtrak. com, $32-75) has two trains daily to Vancouver. The *Cascades* route departs King Street Station (303 S Jackson St.) in Seattle's Pioneer Square neighborhood with stops in Edmonds, Everett, Stanwood, Mount Vernon, and Bellingham, Washington. Arrival is at Vancouver's **Pacific Central Station** (1150 Station St., 604/683-8133, 5am-1am daily). Amtrak also has several bus departures between Seattle and Vancouver ($45).

Bus

The Greyhound-owned **BoltBus** (877/265-8287, www.boltbus.com) offers four daily Seattle-Vancouver trips, leaving Seattle at 5th Avenue South (at S King St.) and arriving in Vancouver at **Pacific Central Station** (1150 Station St., 604/683-8133, 4:45am-12:30am daily). Limited $1 fares are available online, but most trips cost about $24-28. The bus has wireless service, and most trips take a little over four hours.

The Seattle **Greyhound** station (800/231-2222, www.greyhound.ca, $15-32) is at 811 Stewart Street (206/628-5526, 7am-12:30am) and has three departures daily to Vancouver ($23, discounts for early and web bookings); the trip takes just over four hours.

Sights

Downtown

The core of Vancouver almost feels like an island. It's surrounded by water on most sides—False Creek, English Bay, Burrard Inlet, and Vancouver Harbour. Only the area near Chinatown has a land connection to the rest of the city. Otherwise the main entrance points to

downtown are over the Granville Bridge and over the Lions Gate Bridge near Stanley Park. In such limited space, the city packs row after row of shiny, tall apartment and commercial buildings, the windows almost blinding when the sunlight hits just right. The downtown area has one-way streets, bike lanes, water taxi and ferry terminals, and a SkyTrain (actually located underground), so leave some time for traffic and getting a little lost. The good news is that the city is very walkable, particularly between the downtown, Gastown, and Yaletown neighborhoods.

★ Stanley Park

Vancouver is proud of **Stanley Park** (604/257-8531, http://vancouver.ca) and rightfully so—its 1,000 acres are full of bike paths, beaches, viewpoints, tennis courts, and swimming pools. With half a million trees, it's even bigger than Central Park. It opened to the public in 1888, named for the Governor General of Canada, Lord Stanley.

The 8.8-kilometer (5.5-mile) **Seawall Promenade** that circles the park is perhaps its most popular attraction; the seawall itself extends around the city, but the park section is the most scenic. Two lanes are marked off, one for walkers and one for bikers and inline skaters, the latter traveling counterclockwise only. The promenade passes a number of statues including figures of *Harry Jerome,* a runner, and the *Girl in a Wetsuit* perched on a rock just offshore.

On a circular trip around the park, one of the first major stops is **Brockton Point,** where a collection of nine totem poles stands against the backdrop of Stanley Park greenery. Most are replicas of the originals, now in museums, but they are intricately carved and painted in bright colors.

Other park attractions include the **Variety Kids Water Park** (next to the seawall at Lumbermen's Arc, 10am-6pm daily June-Sept., free), full of creative,

Two Days in Vancouver

It's impossible to see all of Vancouver in two days, but that's enough time to poke around downtown, glimpse some of the funky neighborhoods of Gastown and Yaletown, and head either to the wild North Shore mountains or the culture-filled West End.

Day 1

Start downtown at **Canada Place** (page 84). Just look for the big white sails on the north end of downtown. View the Olympic Cauldron from the 2010 Winter Games, or ride a virtual flight at FlyOver Canada.

From Canada Place, head southwest on Howe Street, then turn left on West Cordova Street. In three blocks, bend east (toward the water) on Water Street to explore the Gastown neighborhood. Enjoy photo ops at the **Steam Clock** (page 85) and the **Gassy Jack Statue** (page 85) before turning south on Carrall Street. Grab some breakfast or a cup of Stumptown coffee at **Revolver** (page 109), and then continue down Carrall Street to wander through the (re-created) 15th century at **Dr. Sun Yat-Sen Classical Chinese Garden** (page 86).

It's a 2-kilometer (1.2-mile) walk west along Pacific Boulevard to **David Lam Park** (page 88), or opt for a shorter stroll to the Plaza of Nations Ferry Dock (south of Pacific Boulevard, across from BC Place Stadium). From either place, catch the tiny False Creek Ferry to **Granville Island** (page 89). Sample a beer tasting at **Granville Island Brewing** (page 95), or stop for lunch at the **Granville Island Public Market** (page 89). And don't forget to pick up a new sweeper from the **Granville Island Broom Company** (page 101).

It might seem early for dinner, but you'll want to get to **Vij's** (page 112) early—the Indian eatery always has a line. Catch a cab, put your name on the list at the door, and then enjoy some free snacks while you wait. After dinner, cab it downtown to **Caprice Nightclub** (page 93) for dancing, or catch a show at the **Commodore Ballroom** (page 96).

Day 2

For breakfast, grab a quick doughnut and coffee at a **Tim Hortons** (page 105), and spend the morning in **Stanley Park** (page 78). Rent a bike from **Spokes Bicycle Rental** (page 103) and cycle the 10-mile Seawall Promenade, soaking in the great views along the periphery. Or explore the undersea galleries and wildlife shows at **Vancouver Aquarium** (page 82).

For a day trip, leave the park and drive north on Highway 99 across the Lions Gate Bridge. At Marine Drive, turn right, then turn left and head north on Capilano Road for 2 kilometers (1.2 miles) to **Capilano Suspension Bridge** (page 92) to test your fear of heights. Then ride the tram up to the top of **Grouse Mountain** (page 91). If your vertigo hasn't kicked in yet, continue to the top of Grouse's Eye of the Wind windmill for a quick lesson in renewable energy and outstanding views.

Not an outdoors fan? Then make the neighborhood of Kitsilano your destination. From Stanley Park, follow Beach Avenue south to cross the Burrard Bridge. Head west on 4th Avenue to the **University of British Columbia Museum of Anthropology** (page 89). Be sure to take in the totem pole gallery and outdoor exhibits. On the way back downtown, turn left on Arbutus Street and follow it to Chestnut Street to stop at Vanier Park, home to both the **Museum of Vancouver** (page 90) and the **Vancouver Maritime Museum** (page 90).

You'll want to make it back downtown for dinner. Scoot over to Chinatown for Asian small plates at **Bao Bei** (page 107). If you still have energy on the way home, head to the top of the **Vancouver Lookout** (page 84) for a view of the sparkling city from right in the middle of it.

Stanley Park

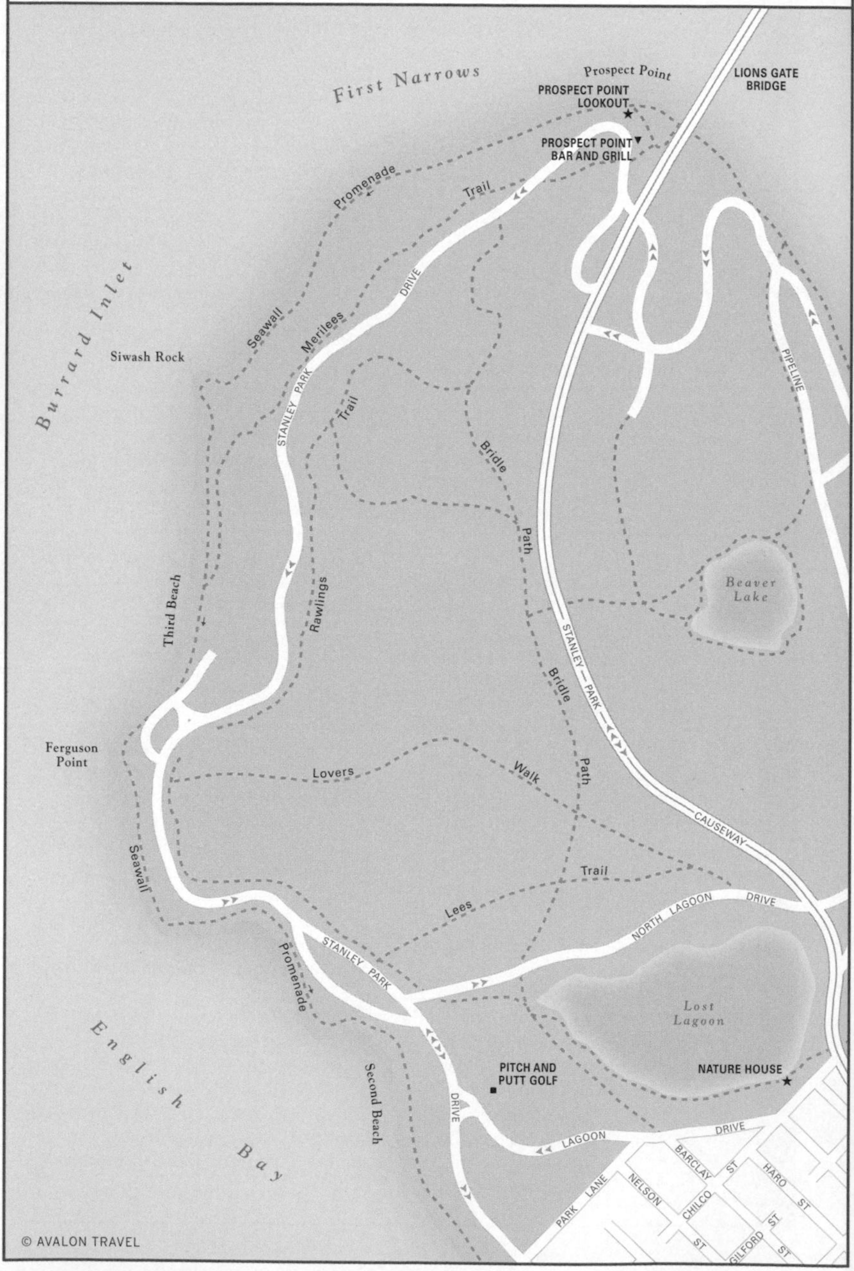

First Narrows

Prospect Point

PROSPECT POINT
LOOKOUT ★

LIONS GATE
BRIDGE

PROSPECT POINT
BAR AND GRILL ▼

Promenade

Trail

Burrard Inlet

Seawall

Merilees

DRIVE

Siwash Rock

STANLEY PARK

Trail

Bridle

PIPELINE

Beaver
Lake

Path

Third Beach

Rawlings

STANLEY PARK

Ferguson
Point

Lovers

Walk

Bridle
Path

CAUSEWAY

Seawall

Trail

Lees

NORTH LAGOON
DRIVE

Lost
Lagoon

Promenade

STANLEY PARK
DRIVE

PITCH AND
PUTT GOLF ■

NATURE HOUSE ★

English

Bay

Second Beach

DRIVE

LAGOON

DRIVE

BARCLAY
ST

HARO
ST

PARK LANE

NELSON
ST

CHILCO
ST

GILFORD
ST

© AVALON TRAVEL

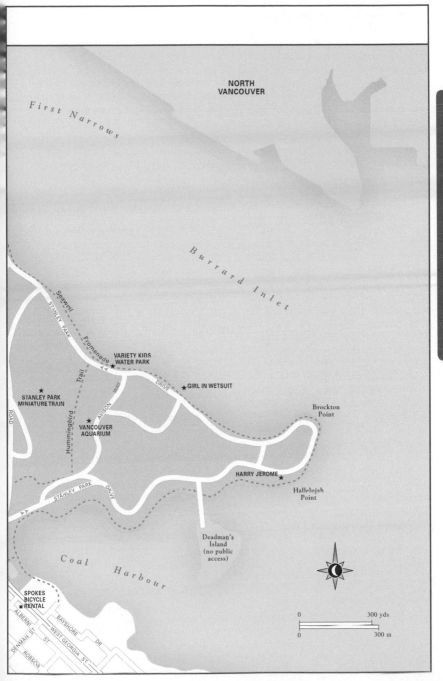

large sprinklers, and the **Pitch & Putt** 18-hole golf course (604/681-8847, http://vancouver.ca, 8am-8pm daily mid-Mar. to mid-Oct., limited services and weather dependent mid-Oct. to mid-Mar., $14.25 adults, $10.50 seniors and children under 18). No trip to Vancouver is complete without a short trip to Stanley Park, even if it's just a quick drive through the Stanley Park Causeway and across the **Lions Gate Bridge** that travels to North Vancouver.

Vancouver Aquarium

Located near the center of Stanley Park, the **Vancouver Aquarium** (845 Avison Way, 604/659-3474, www.vanaqua.org, 10am-5pm daily, $39 adults, $30 seniors, students, and youth 13-18, $22 children 4-12, children under 4 free, discount with transit pass) is the wettest spot within its borders. More than 50,000 sea creatures are inside, including false killer whales, jellyfish, penguins, and harbor porpoises; the aquarium plan to bring beluga whales, a onetime central attraction, back in 2019. Outdoor seating and underground galleries allow for views above and below the water, and regular shows introduce the aquarium residents and educate visitors. A 4-D theater plays films about local wildlife, adding wind, mist, and scents to the experience. The aquarium also has a gift store and café.

Stanley Park Miniature Train

Kids—and rail buffs—make a beeline to the **Stanley Park Miniature Train** (10am-4pm Sat.-Sun. May-June, 11am-4pm daily late June-early Sept., seasonal holiday hours Oct. and Dec., $6.80 adults, $4.86 youth 13-18 and seniors, $3.40 children under 13). The railway was built in a clearing that emerged after the 1964 Hurricane Frieda felled a number of trees in the park. The train itself is a replica of Canada's first transcontinental train, and the two-kilometer (1.2-mile) ride is supplemented on holidays with ghosts, Easter characters, native culture, or bright lights.

Stanley Park Nature House

Located on the shores of Lost Lagoon, the **Stanley Park Nature House** (north end of Alberni St., 604/257-8544, http://stanleyparkecology.ca, 10am-4pm Sat.-Sun. Sept.-June, 10am-5pm Tues.-Sun. July-Aug., free) provides a peek at the natural side of the park. **Lost Lagoon** is a mudflat turned lake, formed when the Stanley Park causeway was created. It's now a sanctuary for birds, filled with rushes and grasses. The Nature House serves as a kind of ranger station where you can ask questions about the wildlife and check out interactive displays about the flora and fauna. The children's area has more exhibits and coloring. Birders will want to check for updates on the migrations of warblers, shorebirds, the area's four pairs of bald eagles, and the great blue heron colony.

Prospect Point

Though a trip around the edge of Stanley Park hits a number of landmarks and attractions, you have to sweat—or drive—up an incline to get the best view. **Prospect Point** (5601 Stanley Park Dr., http://vancouver.ca, 11:30am-6pm daily), west of the Lions Gate Bridge, is the highest point in the park at 210 feet. Soak in the Lions Gate Bridge, Burrard Inlet, and the mountains that rise above North Vancouver. Stop for a bite at the **Prospect Point Bar and Grill** (604/669-2737, www.prospectpoint.ca, 9am-sunset daily), which reopened after renovations in summer 2017; there's also a café and ice cream counter.

Second and Third Beaches

Within Stanley Park, there are two major destinations that appeal to different kinds of beach lovers. **Second Beach** (8501 Stanley Park Dr., 604/681-8029, http://vancouver.ca) is located at Stanley Park Drive and North Lagoon Drive on the western shore near the golf course. This family-friendly area includes a giant, heated outdoor pool, a playground, washrooms, and pay parking nearby. **Third Beach** (Ferguson Point, http://vancouver.ca) is a bit harder to reach by car. Located farther north, it's more popular with cyclists and single adults. The beach faces directly into Burrard Inlet and even stretches up toward North Vancouver. Washrooms and pay parking are available.

Roedde House Museum

The Victorian **Roedde House Museum** (1415 Barclay St., 604/684-7040, www.roeddehouse.org, 11am-4pm Tues.-Sat., 1pm-4pm Sun., $5 adults and children over 5, children under 5 free, Sunday tea $8), built in 1893 in the Queen Anne style, was the home of a bookbinder and is now a historical museum. Visitors can roam the rooms freely (no velvet-rope path) and touch some of the artifacts. On Sundays, the Tea and Tour includes a guided look at the house and a tea tasting. And unlike some preserved houses, this spot doesn't show off the lifestyles of the once rich and prosperous. Instead, it has been restored to show how the middle class lived in the late 19th century.

★ Vancouver Art Gallery

The 1906 building that holds downtown's **Vancouver Art Gallery** (750 Hornby St., 604/662-4700, www.vanartgallery.bc.ca, 10am-5pm Wed.-Mon., 10am-9pm Tues., $24 adults, $20 seniors, $18 students, $6 children 5-18, children under 5 free) was designed by British Columbia's most famous architect, Sir Francis Mawson Rattenbury, a British man who made his name designing major buildings in Vancouver and Victoria, like the landmark Empress Hotel. The gallery moved

---

from top to bottom: Dr. Sun Yat-Sen Classical Chinese Garden; sea otters at the Vancouver Aquarium; bike path in Stanley Park and the Lions Gate Bridge.

to the courthouse building in 1983, but the collection is much older, begun in 1931 and greatly expanded in the 1950s to include works by notable local artist Emily Carr. (A long-term plan to move the gallery to its own, new building elsewhere in Vancouver has been underway for years, but so far only preliminary designs exist.) Exhibits from the collection show off Canadian and specifically British Columbian artists, as well as 17th-century Dutch works and photos by the likes of Ansel Adams and Margaret Bourke-White. Vancouver Art Gallery also hosts touring exhibitions.

Vancouver Lookout

The round observatory of the **Vancouver Lookout** (555 W Hastings St., 604/689-0421, www.vancouverlookout.com, 8:30am-10:30pm daily summer, 9am-9:30pm daily winter, $17.50 adults, $14.50 seniors, $12.50 students and youth 13-18, $9.50 children 6-12, children under 6 free) pops above the Harbour Centre building like a jaunty hat. The glass elevators have as good a view as you'll get at the top (though you'll need a ticket to ride them), but the lookout isn't quite tall enough to tower over the city. Still, placards are well positioned to explain notable Vancouver buildings and the cities in the distance. No, the skyline you see a few miles away isn't Seattle, the signs announce. Daytime visitors can keep their tickets and return the same night.

Canada Place

The roof of the waterfront pavilion at **Canada Place** (999 Canada Pl., 604/665-9000, www.canadaplace.ca, free) resembles sails, or perhaps snow-topped mountains—you can see both from the outdoor walkways. Inside is a space built for Expo '86, the World's Fair held in Vancouver in 1986. It's the site of festivals, like the Aboriginal Spirit Celebration or Canada Day events, and cruise ships dock here before leaving for Alaska. Temporary exhibits highlight

aspects of Vancouver's history, as well as the Canadian Trail path that leads to permanent installations about history, and at noon the Heritage Horns—giant aluminum horns that play at 115 decibels—sound the first four notes of Canadian national anthem "O Canada" at noon. Try the **FlyOver Canada** (604/620-8455, www.flyovercanada.com, 9:30am-10pm daily, $27 adults, $21 seniors, students, and youth 13-17, $17 children 4-12) simulation ride for an eight-minute "flight" over Canadian landscapes.

BC Place Stadium

The giant retractable roof over **BC Place Stadium** (777 Pacific Blvd., 604/669-2300, www.bcplacestadium.com) is the biggest of its kind on the world, something that was useful during the 2010 Winter Olympic Games, when the arena held the Opening and Closing Ceremonies. Now it's home to the **Vancouver Whitecaps FC** soccer team (604/669-9283, www.whitecapsfc.com) and the **BC Lions Football Club** (604/589-7627, www.bclions.com), which plays a sport similar to American football but not identical. It's also where the major music acts play in Vancouver; a U2 concert crowded the venue even more than the Olympics. A smaller interior roof can make the venue smaller for more intimate concerts (like ones with only 25,000 spectators), and a new LED light system decorates the interior.

Science World British Columbia

It's easy to spot **Science World British Columbia** (1455 Quebec St., 604/443-7440, www.scienceworld.ca, 10am-5pm Mon.-Fri., 10am-6pm Sat.-Sun. summer; 10am-5pm Tues.-Fri., 10am-6pm Sat.-Sun. winter, $22.50 adults, $18.50 seniors, students, and children 13-18, $15.25 children 3-12, children under 3 free), thanks to its giant geodesic dome—the one that looks like a big golf ball, made up of 766 triangles—which was made for Expo '86 and based on the famous design by R. Buckminster Fuller. Today it holds the

OMNIMAX giant movie theater. Most of the center is a kid's paradise, with live hourly science shows, puzzles and interactive exhibits, and live animals. A *Bodyworks* gallery explains the inner workings of the human body, and a nature area includes a real beaver lodge, bear pelts, and the cast of a T. Rex. A sizable science store sells puzzles, lab kits, and models. A burger joint is also on-site.

Gastown and Chinatown

Today it's home to hip bars, high-end shopping, and one weird clock. But Gastown was almost demolished to become a freeway, the pet project of mayor Tom Campbell in the 1960s. The buildings were mostly slums at the time, and the idea was that the route would be like Seattle's downtown waterfront freeway (now scheduled for removal). A community campaign halted the project, and businesses began buying up buildings. The neighborhood funded the construction of the Gastown Steam Clock, which is nowhere near as old as it looks—it was installed in 1977.

In a way, the story is similar to New York City's SoHo neighborhood, which had an influx of artists while a freeway project was slowly debated for the area. The road was never built and SoHo became the artist center of the city. Gastown, too, was spared a major demolition and is now one of the city's most popular neighborhoods.

Steam Clock

What do you get when you combine a locomotive and a timepiece? You get something like the **Steam Clock** (Cambie St. and Water St.) of Gastown, a street corner oddity that draws large groups of admirers. A miniature steam engine inside it is powered by steam from the downtown heating network. Even stranger is that it isn't as old as it looks—it was built in 1977 in an attempt to give Gastown a historical look (it even has electric fans inside). Clockmaker Ray Saunders basically

guessed at how to make it, though he's made several other clocks since. The charming tower makes for a pretty picture, and the whistle and chimes mark the time at the quarter hour.

Gassy Jack Statue

Let the kids giggle. One Gastown attraction really is called **Gassy Jack Statue** (Alexander St. and Water St.), though not for any embarrassing personal habits. Captain John Deighton got the nickname for his tendency to speak at length—and he got the statue because he started one of the first establishments in Gastown, which was eventually named for him (and since that district later grew to become Vancouver, the entire metropolis could have ended up named for the endless talker). The original saloon served whiskey he brought in a barrel down the Fraser River—which is why Gassy Jack now poses on a barrel.

★ Vancouver Police Museum

You didn't misread it; the building that now holds the **Vancouver Police Museum** (240 E Cordova St., 604/665-3346, sinsofthecity.ca, 9am-5pm Tues.-Sat., $12 adults, $10 seniors, $8 students, children under 6 free) does indeed read "Coroner's Court." This used to be the city morgue, but you wouldn't know it from the front half of the second-story museum. Exhibits are charming, if dated and a bit cluttered. One traces the evolution of police uniforms for women; another pays tribute to canine cops. One con man's series of fake IDs takes up a whole wall, and a display of dangerous weapons confiscated by the police has everything from throwing stars to brass knuckles in the shape of a pair of lips. Not that the museum is living in the past; interactive exhibits invite visitors to examine a crime scene, and a computer offers the chance to re-create a perp's face using an automated sketch artist.

But where the museum gets really memorable is in the back (where it's obvious that the museum is not associated with the Vancouver Police Department). The sign that reads, "Exhibits beyond this point are graphic in nature" ain't kidding. The one-time morgue and autopsy suite are not for little children. Behind the rows of stainless steel morgue doors, the first room holds cases illustrating some of Vancouver's biggest murders—including replica skulls (the real skulls used to be in the case) and facial casts of two children killed in Stanley Park circa 1947 in an unsolved mystery.

The next room is tiled with two autopsy tables set up—the very room where the body of Errol Flynn was once examined (the erstwhile Robin Hood died of a heart attack while in town to buy a boat). Tissue samples, of flesh hit with bullets or brains wrecked by aneurysm, line the walls. The entire effect is grisly, but fascinating. Museum staff clearly approach the serious exhibits with a slight sense of humor—the doctor names on the old autopsy blackboard belong to *Harry Potter* and Shakespeare characters.

The museum is also the kicking-off point for **Sins of the City Walking Tours** ($18 adults, $14 students and seniors), which visit sites associated with the city's gangsters and biggest crimes. Tours last 90 minutes and focus on red-light districts (4pm-5:30pm Sat.) and opium dens (6pm-7:30pm Fri., 11am-12:30pm Sat.)— so the tours may not be appropriate for children. Book on the Vancouver Police Museum's website, or call.

★ Dr. Sun Yat-Sen Classical Chinese Garden

One of the first things tour guides at **Dr. Sun Yat-Sen Classical Chinese Garden** (578 Carrall St., 604/662-3207, http://vancouverchinesegarden.com, 10am-6pm daily May 1-June 14 and Sept., 9:30am-7pm daily June 15-Aug. 31, 10am-4:30pm daily Oct., 10am-4:30pm Tues.-Sun. Nov.-Apr., $14 adults, $11 seniors, $10 students, children under

Science World British Columbia

5 free) explain is that the popular attraction isn't just a garden. It's more of a re-creation of a Ming Dynasty scholar's home, complete with courtyards, study, and yes, gardens. The 15th century is re-created in beautiful white and red architecture, and all materials came from China, even the rocks. Although the style is centuries old, it was built in the 1980s and named for a Chinese leader from the early 20th century who traveled the world to raise money for China's nationalist movement and was later named the Republic of China's first president. Hour-long tours of the grounds, free with admission, run 4-6 times a day and include hands-on activities like Chinese character drawing, and traditional tea is served.

Next door is the free **Dr. Sun Yat-Sen Park,** which has a similar feel to the Chinese Garden's grounds, but was built using more modern techniques (and American materials). Ironically, it has more of a garden feel than its next-door neighbor, with a few short paths to wander.

Jimi Hendrix Shrine

Though guitar god Jimi Hendrix hailed from Seattle, a **shrine** (206 Union St., 604/669-0377, noon-6pm Mon.-Sat., by donation) is set up in Chinatown where his grandmother lived and worked at a chicken shack that played host to famous black musicians like Louis Armstrong and Nat King Cole. The young Jimi was often left here with relatives. The small red shack and garden are open irregular hours, and the area smells strongly of marijuana. Still, music fans will enjoy the kitsch and Hendrix paraphernalia, and it's a refreshingly undermanaged sight in a city that's otherwise quite polished.

Yaletown

Located south of downtown, the Yaletown neighborhood sits between the busy commercial thoroughfare of Granville Street and the calm waters of False Creek. The streets used to be lined with warehouses, most of which are now home to upscale restaurants and shops—some even use the raised loading docks for outdoor patios. High-end condos rise above the once-utilitarian streets now filled with shoppers and tourists.

Roundhouse Community Arts & Recreation Center

Yaletown's **Roundhouse Community Arts & Recreation Center** (181 Roundhouse Mews, 604/713-1800, www.roundhouse.ca) sits in a building that used to service steam locomotives and once served as an exhibition hall for Expo '86. Now it has a performance center, exhibition hall, art studios, a gym, a café, and other rooms. The outdoor plaza has seating and a working crane that can be moved during performances. A schedule of what's playing at all the center's stages is online. The complex also houses the Engine 374 Pavilion, home to the engine that pulled the first transcontinental train

Olympic Sites

For 17 days in February 2010, Vancouver hosted more than 2,500 athletes for the Winter Olympic Games. The region is still dotted with the venues and monuments of the games.

The most notable addition to Vancouver's landscape is the **Olympic Cauldron** (www.vancouverconvention-centre.com), located outside the Vancouver Convention Centre (1055 Canada Pl.), which served as the International Broadcast Centre during the games. The 10-meter (33-foot) sculpture is still lit occasionally for Canada Day. Inside the convention center is an Olympic Legacy display case full of medals and torches.

If you're really an Olympic nerd, you know the **Richmond Olympic Oval** (6111 River Rd., Richmond, 778/296-1400, www.richmondoval.ca, $19.50 adults, $13.70 seniors and youth 19-25, $11 children 13-18, $5 children 6-12, children under 6 free; rentals extra) was built especially for the games to host speed skating. Located about 20 minutes from downtown, the ice skating rink now has limited drop-in hours (children under 13 are required to wear a helmet). There's also a museum with sports simulators to re-create the feeling of doing a ski jump or riding a Paralympic sit-ski.

Cypress Mountain (6000 Cypress Bowl Rd., West Vancouver, 604/926-5612, www.cypressmountain.com, 9am-4pm daily Nov. to mid-Dec., 9am-10pm daily mid-Dec. to Mar., limited hours Apr.), located about 30 minutes from downtown Vancouver, was the site of the freestyle ski and snowboarding events. This is where Canada won its first Olympic medals on home snow when they scored the gold in men's moguls, women's snowboard cross, women's ski cross, and men's parallel giant slalom. In winter, you can ski the same slopes ($62 adults, $40 seniors, $46 children 13-18, $26 children 6-12, $8 children under 6) on six chairlifts, or the hit the snow-tube park ($18). During the summer, the area has disc golf and hiking trails through the yellow cypress fir trees, some of which are more than 1,000 years old, plus interactive displays in the Cypress Creek Lodge.

More skiing events took place in Whistler at the **Whistler Blackcomb** (4545 Blackcomb Way, 604/967-8950, www.whistlerblackcomb.com, two-day tickets: $176-206 adults, $147-181 seniors and children 13-18, $81-104 children 7-12, children under 7 free, $68 summer), a much larger ski mountain, and the **Whistler Sliding Centre** (4910 Glacier Ln., 604/964-0040, www.whistlerslidingcentre.com, 9am-5pm daily, rides $179, walking tours $10), where today visitors can climb into a bobsled or onto a skeleton luge and ride the same track the Olympic athletes did.

An epic final-medal hockey game, the Canadians versus the United States, was held at **Rogers Arena** (800 Griffiths Way, 604/899-7400, www.rogersarena.com). When Canada clinched the gold, a raucous celebration erupted in Vancouver's streets.

The logo for the Vancouver Olympics was the *inukshuk,* based on an Inuit rock symbol (though some Inuits were angered, saying that this version, a person-shaped *inukshuk,* was the sign that someone had died). A large *inukshuk* sculpture stands near **English Bay Beach** (Beach Ave., http://vancouver.ca), while nearby smaller handmade rock cairns, inspired by the form, line the beach.

into Vancouver. After getting rusted and weathered by the elements in Kitsilano Park, it was restored and now has an indoor home.

David Lam Park
Downtown the **David Lam Park** (1300 Pacific Blvd., http://vancouver.ca, 10am-dusk daily) is located along the seawall that borders False Creek—an ideal place for urban strolling—and its large lawns and playfields are often filled with Frisbee-throwers and soccer players. Stages are often set up in the park for

major festivals, such as the Vancouver International Jazz Festival. The False Creek Ferries water taxi dock leads pedestrians to Granville Island or farther up False Creek.

Contemporary Art Gallery

The downtown **Contemporary Art Gallery** (555 Nelson St., 604/681-2700, www.contemporaryartgallery.ca, noon-6pm Tues.-Sun., free) is dedicated to visual art. Visiting exhibitions highlight photography, sculpture, video, and paintings by artists from around the world with a focus on Canadians. It also hosts gallery talks and family art-making days.

Granville Island

Granville Island isn't an actual island. The original area was sandbars and tidal flats that were eventually reclaimed with fill to become an industrial area that's connected to the Fairview neighborhood. It was used for shipping, mining, and construction until it was no longer practical for modern industry, at which point it was converted to recreational and commercial use by the Canadian government. Some old tenants remain, like a concrete factory and a drill bit manufacturer.

In addition to the Granville Island Public Market, the area now includes the **Emily Carr University of Art and Design** and the Arts Club Theatre Company. The **Granville Island Water Park** (1318 Cartwright St., www.falsecreekcc.ca/waterpark.htm, 10am-6pm daily summer only, free) is the largest free water park in North America, and features a big yellow waterslide (though constant repairs to the waterslide mean it's not always open). There's also a great deal of shopping and many art studios, plus the Granville Island Brewing microbrewery.

To reach the area from downtown, you must cross the Granville Street Bridge and backtrack (the auto route soars above Granville Island before connecting with the Fairview neighborhood), or go by sea. Two boat services cross False Creek: **False Creek Ferries** (604/684-7781, www.granvilleislandferries.bc.ca, $3.50-6 adults, $2.25-4 seniors and children) has stops at Granville Island, Aquatic Center at the foot of Thurlow Street, the Maritime Museum, David Lam Park, Stamps Landing, Spyglass Place, Yaletown at Quayside Marina, Plaza of Nations, and Science World. The rainbow-colored **Aquabus** (604/689-5858, www.theaquabus.com, $3.50-5.50 adults, $1.75-3.75 seniors and children) goes to Granville Island, Hornby Street, David Lam Park, Stamps Landing, Spyglass Place, Yaletown at Quayside Marina, Plaza of Nations, and The Village, not far from Science World.

★ Granville Island Public Market

There's so much more than food at the **Granville Island Public Market** (1661 Duranleau St., 604/666-6477, www.granvilleisland.com, 9am-7pm daily). Booths in the covered structure –the building used to be a machine shop, evidence of Granville Island's previous life as an industrial center—sell jewelry, art, stained glass, and soap. And, yes, a good amount of local produce is available too, especially in the seasonal farmers market held just outside, in addition to goodies like jam, cured meats, and prepared foods. The candy and chocolate stalls are ideal for gift-buying. Grab bites or a carton of fresh berries to eat as you wander the aisles, or sit at one of the tables scattered throughout the indoor market space.

West Side
★ University of British Columbia Museum of Anthropology

It's worth the drive out to Vancouver's university area to visit the **University of British Columbia Museum of Anthropology** (6393 NW Marine Dr., 604/822-5087, www.moa.ubc.ca, 10am-5pm Wed.-Mon., 10am-9pm Tues., $18 adults, $16 students and seniors, children under 7 free), a world-class collection of local artifacts and cultural traces gathered worldwide. The indoor spotlight is a totem pole collection in the **Great Hall,** made by First Nation tribes like the Haida, Gitxsan, and Oweekeno. Though the structures, many more than 100 years old, are safely inside, they're lit by sunlight that pours through the ceiling-high windows. The building was designed in 1976 based on traditional structures. In the Bill Reid Rotunda, his wood sculpture called *The Raven and the First Men* gets center stage. If it looks familiar, that might be because the iconic shape also appears on the Canadian $20 bill.

Even though the carvings are reason enough to visit the museum, the Multiversity Galleries of more than 10,000 worldwide anthropological artifacts are equally intriguing. Chinese teacups, Mexican masks, Indonesian carvings—all get space behind glass, and you can pull open the drawers full of more treasures that sit under display cases. Touch-screen computers allow for virtual browsing. Outside is a **Haida House** exhibit, built in the 1950s and 1960s, resembling the villages that once populated Haida Gwaii (the Queen Charlotte Islands of British Columbia).

UBC Botanical Garden

The green grounds of the **UBC Botanical Garden** (6804 Marine Dr. SW, 604/822-4208, www.botanicalgarden.ubc.ca, 9:30am-4:30pm daily, $9-24 adults, $7-18 seniors, students, and children 13-17, $5-12 children 5-12, children under 5 free) contain a number of separate gardens, including a physics garden around a central sundial, containing plants used for drugs throughout early European history—plaques explain how and why doctors and apothecaries used them. There are also alpine, rainforest, and food gardens. Fruits and vegetables harvested from the latter are donated to a soup kitchen downtown. Ticket prices vary depending on whether you want to incorporate specific attractions: The **Nitobe Memorial Garden** (9:30am-5pm

daily Apr.-Oct., 10am-2pm Mon.-Fri. Nov.-Mar.) is a traditional Japanese garden, complete with a teahouse that is especially popular in spring when the cherry blossoms are in bloom, and the **Greenheart Canopy Walkway** (10am-4pm daily) tour climbs above the forest, crossing bridges 50 feet in the air. Guided tours last 45 minutes.

Museum of Vancouver

One goal of the **Museum of Vancouver** (1100 Chestnut St., 604/736-4431, www.museumofvancouver.ca, 10am-5pm Mon.-Wed. and Sun., 10am-8pm Thurs., 10am-9pm Fri.-Sat., $19 adults, $16 students and seniors, $9 youth 5-17, children under 5 free) in Vanier Park is to tell the story of the city from the 1900s to 1970s. The building is an impressive sight—the dome is meant to resemble the woven baskets made by First Nation people in the area. Outside is a stainless steel crab sculpture that stands more than six meters (20 feet) tall. Inside are permanent exhibits, many dedicated to individual decades in Vancouver's 20th-century history. (*Neon Vancouver, Ugly Vancouver* rescued the city's neon signs from junkyards and relit them to tell the story of Vancouver's urban transition.) The **H. R. MacMillan Space Centre** (www.spacecentre.ca, 10am-3pm Mon.-Fri., 10am-5pm Sat., noon-5pm Sun., $18 adults, $15 seniors and children 12-18, $13 children 5-11, children under 5 free) that shares the space is a planetarium with space-minded exhibits. Evening astronomy shows and open observatory times take place on Friday and Saturday nights, for a reduced admission charge.

Vancouver Maritime Museum

With so much of the city backing up onto waterfront, it's no wonder the city has the **Vancouver Maritime Museum** (1905 Ogden Ave., 604/257-8300, www.vancouvermaritimemuseum.com, 10am-5pm Fri.-Wed., 10am-8pm Thurs., $12.50 adults, $10 seniors, students, and children 6-18, children under 6 free) to tell the story of the city's ships and shipping. It's located right near the Museum of Vancouver in Vanier Park, and water taxis dock outside. The building is a tall A-frame structure that holds exhibits and model ships (including one made of bone by French prisoners of war), plus a children's center and a re-creation of the forecastle of George Vancouver's ship. The museum also has hand-drawn charts from Captain Cook's expedition and the Arctic exploration vessel *St. Roch*—the first ship to sail the Northwest Passage and the first to circumnavigate North America—but it's often undergoing renovations. Outside is the *Ben Franklin,* a NASA underwater vessel, plus the boiler of the first steamship in the region.

North Vancouver
★ Grouse Mountain

The peaks behind North Vancouver are more than just a postcard backdrop. **Grouse Mountain** (6400 Nancy Greene Way, 604/980-9311, www.grousemountain.com, 8:45am-10pm daily, $45-59 adults, $40-55 seniors, $26-40 youth 13-18, $16 children 5-12, children under 5 free) is the easiest ski area to access from downtown Vancouver, though it's more than a one-season destination; the mountaintop complex also includes attractions and activities that are open year-round. It's accessed via the **Skyride** tram (every 15 min., 8:45am-10pm daily), which leaves from a spot within North Vancouver's residential streets and climbs a mile up to an area with a lodge, skating pond, trails, and ski area. Ticket prices vary depending on what you plan to do on Grouse Mountain, but all include the Skyride passage.

A turbine called **Eye of the Wind** generates some of the power that runs the compound, and visitors can go up the

from top to bottom: Museum of Vancouver; Capilano Suspension Bridge; University of British Columbia Museum of Anthropology.

20-story tower for an even better view of the mountains and city. The **Grouse Mountain Refuge for Endangered Wildlife** is home to two grizzly bears, both orphans found in British Columbia, and wolves retired from appearing in movies. Summer activity options include zip-lining, hiking, a lumberjack show, and paragliding. Truly brave souls can tackle the **Grouse Grind,** a hike from the tram's base to the top. Record holders do it in around 30 minutes, but you'll want to leave considerably longer unless you have thighs of steel.

In winter you can rent snowshoes ($20) to explore the woods surrounding the ski slopes, or sit back on a sleigh ride. Skiing is open during the day, but the night skiing is where Grouse Mountain truly shows off. The lights of Vancouver seem right at the base of each run on clear nights.

Year-round dining ranges from a casual coffee bar to an outdoor bistro and indoor fine dining at **The Observatory** (604/980-9311, 5pm-10pm daily, entrées $25-36, five-course prix fixe $130), which includes the cost of the tram ride up.

In summer, there's a free shuttle ride from downtown Vancouver, provided you've purchased a tram ticket, or you can take the SeaBus to Lonsdale Quay from downtown, then catch bus 236 to Grouse Mountain. To drive from downtown Vancouver, take Highway 99 through Stanley Park and across Lions Gate Bridge, then turn right on Marine Drive. Take the first left a hundred yards later onto Capilano Road, and follow it for six kilometers (3.7 miles); the road becomes Nancy Green Way along the way. The Grouse Mountain Skyride has a number of parking lots around the base; pay for parking at central kiosks.

Capilano Suspension Bridge Park

At one time it took a wilderness trek to reach the **Capilano Suspension Bridge** (3735 Capilano Rd., 604/985-7474, www.capbridge.com, daily: 9am-5pm Jan.-Feb and Oct.-Nov., 9am-6pm Mar. to mid-Apr. and Sept., 9am-7pm mid-Apr. to mid-May, 8:30am-8pm mid-May to Aug., 11am-9pm Dec.-Jan.; $43 adults, $39 seniors, $34 students, $27 children 13-16, $15 children 6-12, children under 6 free), but now it's a short drive from downtown, reachable by city bus. But the park is no less spectacular, still known for its signature bridge built in 1889. (Yes, it's safe. It was rebuilt in the 1950s, but you'll have trouble remembering that when you're 230 feet in the air above the Capilano River.)

On the other side of the forested canyon is a series of tree-to-tree bridges (not nearly so scary); come back across to where you started for the **Cliffwalk,** a narrow, cantilevered walkway overlooking the river. Very little here is appropriate for anyone afraid of heights, but it's all quite solid and an easy way to peek at British Columbia's signature nature. Drop into the Story Centre near the park entrance, next to its signature totem pole, for more history of the area.

Lynn Canyon Suspension Bridge

Though less popular than its Capilano cousin, the **Lynn Canyon Suspension Bridge** (3993 Peters Rd., www.lynncanyon.ca, 7am-9pm daily summer, 7am-7pm daily spring and fall, 7am-6pm daily winter) is no less dramatic—what's more, it's free. Built in 1912, it crosses more than 160 feet above Lynn Canyon and connects to walking trails in the heavily forested area. The **Lynn Canyon Ecology Centre** (3663 Park Rd., 604/990-3755, http://dnv.org/ecology, 10am-5pm Mon.-Fri., noon-4pm Sat.-Sun., $2 donation) has nature exhibits and puppet shows. Swimming holes are popular—well, in the summer, anyway.

Entertainment and Events

Nightlife
Bars and Clubs
Downtown

There's nothing particularly new about the speakeasy bar, but **Prohibition** (801 W Georgia St, 604/673-7089, 7pm-1am Thurs., 7pm-2am Fri.-Sat., cover charge after 8pm) in the Rosewood Hotel Georgia manages to feel special and a bit elusive—just like good gin during the Prohibition era. Head toward the big wooden doors from the hotel lobby for the bar, where the dim room is brightened with teal stools and a lot of mirrors, as much '80s excess as '20s style. A beautiful ringed chandelier sets the fancy mood, and well-blended cocktails, small bites, and live music complete the decadent scene.

The **Caprice Nightclub** (967 Granville St., 607/685-3288, www.capricenightclub.com, 10pm-3am Tues.-Sat.) on busy Granville Street attracts dancers to a main dance floor and second-level mezzanine and lounge. Weekdays the soundtrack includes Latin, Brazilian funk, Reggacton, and more, while weekends are more about Top 40 tunes. The sleek decor and lighting recalls a Miami nightclub, and the young crowds that come to dance tend to favor tight clothing and slicked-back hair, but the scene is a little calmer upstairs.

Gastown and Chinatown

The cocktail menu at Gastown's **Revel Room** (238 Abbott St., 604/687-4088, www.revelroom.ca, 4pm-1am Tues.-Thurs., 4pm-2am Fri.-Sat., 4pm-midnight Sun.) is as much fun as a night out on the town—even during its "Sour Hour" (4pm-6pm Tues.-Sun.), a happy hour with sour drink specials. Seasonal offerings might include a Stay Puft S'more (it's a *Ghostbusters* reference, but yes,

there are toasted marshmallows) or the Mother in Law (a bourbon-based tipple from New Orleans that's "perfect for settling arguments"). Food at the establishment is from the American South, hailing from the Southwest or New Orleans, and a house band plays jazz and blues every Sunday.

Menus at the **Six Acres** (203 Carrall St., 604/488-0110, www.sixacres.ca, 11:30am-11:30pm Sun.-Thurs., 11:30am-12:30am Fri.-Sat.) are bound in old children's books, but what's inside is decidedly grown-up. There is a rotating selection of bottled beers for the pickiest of beer nerds, and any nerd can enjoy the soundtracks playing in the bathroom—they rotate from radio plays to language tapes. The two-story bar is in the oldest brick building in the city and has an outdoor patio that faces one of the busiest intersections in Gastown. Still, the place has an intimate feel and is proud of the fact that it sits behind Gassy Jack's statue (and so patrons get to stare at his bronzed behind). Snacks include sliders and a very sharable plate of poutine with gravy made from St.-Ambroise stout. Happy hour is all day, every day, until 6pm.

The **Shebeen Whiskey House** (210 Carrall St., 604/688-9779, www.shebeen.ca, 5pm-midnight Tues.-Thurs., 5pm-2am Fri.-Sat.) isn't hidden, exactly, but you do have to walk through the Irish Heather Gastropub to find the bar. It's owned by the same guy, Sean Heather, who can't stop creating eateries in the area. Shebeen is one of his most modest, though the whiskey list doesn't hold back. The scotch menu separates the Scottish Isle of Islay selections from the Isla of Jura ones (wouldn't want to throw them all together), and even has whiskey selections from India and Japan. Bartenders aren't fussy, though, and the space is a bit less fussy than other Heather establishments.

Although **Salt Tasting Room** (45 Blood Alley Sq., 604/633-1912, www.salttastingroom.com, 4pm-11pm daily) is one of the more heavily designed spots run by

Heather, it's earned its popularity. It sits on Blood Alley in Gastown, so named either for the refuse tossed by butchers onto the cobblestones, or for the crime that was committed in the area. The bar is decked out in brick and wood beams, with square metal stools and a wall-sized chalkboard that advertises the food offerings; it's mostly meat and cheese. Assemble a wine flight or nibble some snacks while the bartender selects a few two-ounce pours; personalized service is a stated goal, so don't be intimidated by the chic vibe.

Forget a wine list—the beer list at **Alibi Room** (157 Alexander St., 604/623-3383, www.alibi.ca, 5pm-11pm Mon.-Thurs., 5pm-12:30am Fri., 10am-12:30am Sat., 10am-11:30pm Sun.) changes so frequently that it celebrated its 400th tap rotation after only about six years of operations. They're most proud of their selection of cask beers and rare microbrews, but the menu of upscale pub food is also popular.

The menu at **Darby's Gastown** (16 W Hastings St., 604/558-4658, www.darbys-gastown.pub, 3pm-12:30am Sun.-Thurs., 3pm-1:30am Fri.-Sat.) is all about craft beers and local wines, specializing in Canadian flavors. There's an all-day breakfast wrap made with local veggies and Cajun chips, but the small bites—tacos, meatball sliders—pair well with the beers, or go for an elaborate wine and meat plate.

If a mad scientist decided to open a bar, it would look something like Chinatown's **The Keefer Bar** (135 Keefer St., 604/688-1961, http://thekeeferbar.com, 5pm-1am Sun.-Thurs., 5pm-2am Fri.-Sat.). There are vials and flasks in every corner, anatomical designs behind the bar, and bottles lit to look more like potions than simple spirits. But drinks are certainly potions of a sort, made carefully with bitters and fresh juices for a well-heeled, hip young crowd. The food selections are the strongest reminder of the neighborhood, including Peking duck sliders and

Vancouver skyline

shrimp miso shitake tacos, though drinks do use some Asian-inspired ingredients like dragon-fruit gin, sake, and syrup made from mushroom-infused tea.

In a space that used to be a Chinese restaurant, Chinatown's **Fortune Sound Club** (147 E Pender St., 604/569-1758, www.fortunesoundclub.com, hours vary) now blasts dance music. For a late-night club, it's very proud of its ecofriendly decor, including sustainable materials on the bar surface and a reclaimed-wood dance floor. A wall installation from street artist Shepard Fairey is in the front walkway. Inside, DJs and performers take turns in the DJ booth and stage.

Yaletown

No need to be stuffy, old chap; **The New Oxford** (1144 Homer St, 604/609-0901, http://donnellygroup.ca/new-oxford, 11:30am-1am Mon.-Thurs., 11:30am-2am Fri., 11am-2am Sat., 11am-1am Sun.) is a British sports pub, sure, but it's hardly filled with cigar smoke and fuddy-duddies. The interior has a mix of comfy leather chairs and bright pop art, and the televisions showing sports manage to be somewhat unobtrusive among the wood-paneled and exposed-brick walls. Find a mix of local and British drafts (including Guinness, of course), plus a mix of house-made tonics and original cocktails.

The bright white and worn wood of **Rodney's Oyster House** (1228 Hamilton St., 604/609-0080, www.rodneysoysterhouse.com, 11:30am-11pm daily) recalls the boats where the food is caught; even the hooks on the walls look like they belong on a boat. Come for the clams, oysters, and "Oysters Rockerfellah," but stay for a drink called a Caesar—imagine a Bloody Mary, but one made with Clamato juice and topped with a big prawn. Canadians swear by them.

Just outside Yaletown, **Long Table Distillery Room** (1451 Hornby St., 604/266-0177, www.longtabledistillery.com, 1pm-6pm Wed.-Thurs., 1pm-9pm Fri.-Sat.) sits on a quiet street, claiming the title of the city's first microdistillery. Tastings of their gin and vodka are held in the space also occupied by shiny copper equipment and, yes, a big long table.

Granville Island

If the Public Market is the crown jewel of Granville Island, then **Granville Island Brewing** (1441 Cartwright St., 604/687-2739, www.gib.ca, 11am-9pm daily) is its best ambassador. It began in the 1980s as the country's first microbrewery, though it is now owned by a subsidiary of Molson Coors and most of its beer is actually made in Kelowna, a city 320 kilometers (200 miles) inland. But the original taproom on Granville Island serves the beers that still bear the name of Vancouver neighborhoods and landmarks, plus small-batch brews not largely available. Tours ($9.75) include three 5-ounce tasters of beer, and the taproom serves 12.5-ounce servings.

Echoing the brewery's landmark establishment 30 years ago, **Artisan Sake Maker** (1339 Railspur Alley, 604/685-7253, www.artisansakemaker.com, 11:30am-6pm daily) has staked a claim as Canada's first fresh sake maker. The small space opens its garage door to welcome tasters and tour takers, showing off one variety that is made from organically grown rice harvested in the Fraser Valley. Larger servings of sake are also available, as well as a small menu of snacks.

West Side

Although it was known primarily as an LGBT spot when it opened a few decades ago, **Celebrities Nightclub** (1022 Davie St., 604/681-6180, www.celebritiesnightclub.com, 10pm-3am Tues. and Fri.-Sat.) is now a dance mecca for straight and gay crowds alike. It has a programmable light system, so some 20,000 LED lights flash in patterns in the large dance area, accompanied by a powerful sound system. Weekly parties are held, including karaoke Tuesdays and the long-running Stereotype Fridays, first launched to be proudly genre-free—not constrained to one type of music—and devoid of club culture clichés.

Gay and Lesbian

The vibe at **PumpJack Pub** (1167 Davie St., 604/685-3417, www.pumpjackpub.com, 1pm-2am daily) is a little less lavish than the party clubs of Vancouver; there are two pinball machines and cheap drinks. That doesn't mean there isn't a line, even on days other than Friday and Saturday. The joint is popular with the leather and bear communities, and there are often few women inside.

The small **1181** (1181 Davie St., 604/787-7130, www.1181.ca, 6pm-3am daily) is the watering hole for much of Vancouver's stylish, well-chiseled gay scene. It can get crowded but achieves more of an upscale lounge feel than its fellow gay bars. The good-looking bartenders are pretty friendly, and DJs spin even though there isn't much of a dance floor.

Score on Davie (1262 Davie St., 604/632-1646, www.scoreondavie.com, 11am-1am Mon.-Thurs., 11am-2am Fri., 10am-2am Sat., 10am-midnight Sun.) is a sports bar with a gay clientele, there to watch hockey or football. The bar serves all meals and has a 30-bottle beer list. Food is a step above normal fare—the burger comes on a brioche bun and has horseradish and Dijon aioli, and "handhelds" are fry cones with toppings. On Sunday mornings, the Bloody Caesars, topped with burgers, brownies, sandwiches, and more, are a meal unto themselves.

Live Music

Open since 1929, the **Commodore Ballroom** (868 Granville St., 604/739-4550, www.commodoreballroom.com) has a mix of the old and the new—pillars alongside the dance-floor-or-standing-room area, art deco wrought-iron handrails on the stairs, and complicated light shows from above. It has hosted everyone from Tom Waits to Tina Turner, David Bowie to Patti Smith. A neon sign outside calls it "The Fabulous Commodore Ballroom," and the big-name acts it gets help it live up to the moniker. Events are often for ages 19 and older and include Canadian and American rock, pop, and indie acts.

Even though it's best known as the home of the Vancouver Canucks hockey team, **Rogers Arena** (800 Griffiths Way, 604/899-7400, www.rogersarena.com) also hosts the city's major music shows. This is where Kanye and Beyonce perform when they're in town. It opened in 1995 with, what else, a Bryan Adams concert and was renamed Canada Hockey Place during the 2010 Olympics as it hosted the hockey matches, including the gold-medal game between Canada and the United States, considered to be one of the best hockey games in history (at least to the Canadians, who won).

The art deco-style **Vogue Theatre** (918 Granville St., 604/569-1144, www.vogue-theatre.com) was originally an Odeon movie theater built by a bootlegger and opened in 1941. It's currently rumored to be inhabited by a ghost wearing a tuxedo (not the bootlegger, at least from what anyone can tell). The giant landmark sign out front has a neon figure of the Roman goddess Diana, and inside a recent restoration turned a once-crumbling relic back into a historical gem. A high-definition screen is available for film screenings. Otherwise the theater hosts bands, comics, and parts of the Vancouver International Jazz Festival and Vancouver International Film Festival.

The Arts

Classical Music, Opera, and Dance

Major folk and rock acts play the historical **Orpheum Theatre** (601 Smithe St., 604/665-3050, http://vancouver.ca), but it's also home to the **Vancouver Symphony Orchestra** (604/876-3434, www.vancouversymphony.ca), which plays more than 140 concerts per year as the country's largest performing-arts organization west of Ontario. The Orpheum also hosts the Vancouver Bach Choir, which has performed Bach and contemporary pieces since 1930, and the Vancouver Chamber Choir. The theater has an elegant scalloped backdrop, ornate ceiling, and red carpets in the elegant lobby. It dates back to 1927, when the Spanish baroque revival building was constructed to be a vaudeville house.

The lobby of the **Queen Elizabeth Theatre** (649 Cambie St., 604/665-3050, http://vancouver.ca) is hung with chandeliers that resemble snowflakes, a delicate juxtaposition to the mid-20th-century style of the building. The theater has been renovated several times since it was built in the 1950s and dedicated by Queen Elizabeth II. The theater hosts touring Broadway Across Canada shows, the Vancouver Christmas Market, and other touring productions. It's home to **Ballet British Columbia** (604/732-5003, www.balletbc.com) and the **Vancouver Opera** (604/683-0222, www.vancouveropera.ca), the country's second-largest opera company.

Theater

The buildings that house the **Firehall Arts Centre** (280 E Cordova St., 604/689-0926, www.firehallartscentre.ca) clearly used to be a fire station—actually the first motorized fire hall on the continent, built in 1906. From its place in a neighborhood underserved by the arts, the Firehall puts on plays, dance performances, art shows, and more. Art in the gallery sometimes links to the shows on stage, but not always. The campus also has an enclosed courtyard where audiences can hang between acts and get concessions.

The **Arts Club Theatre Company** (1585 Johnston St., 604/687-1644, www.artsclub.com) has put on 50 seasons of theater and is now performing at three theaters. One is on Granville Island, and the others are in the southeast end of the city. The **Granville Island Stage** (1585 Johnston St.) hosts popular plays and musicals, while the **BMO Theatre Centre** (162 W 1st Ave.) is not far, closer to the end of False Creek. The **Stanley Industrial Alliance Stage** (2750 Granville St.) is a longer trek from downtown but is the group's flagship theater, home to its biggest productions, often shows that premiered on Broadway.

Cinema

Although membership is required to see films at **The Cinematheque** (1131 Howe St., 604/688-8202, www.thecinematheque.ca, $11-16 adults, $9-14 seniors and students), it's only an annual $3 fee. Plus, if you decide to stay for a double feature, you can upgrade to the double-bill price without buying a full second ticket. Not only that, but the concession stand sells popcorn and candy that won't actually cost more than a theater ticket.

The movies are foreign and independent flicks, often part of film festivals and series.

Vancity Theatre (1181 Seymour St., 604/683-3456, www.viff.org/theatre) not only hosts the Vancouver International Film Festival in September and October but also plays movies all year. Series include shorts programs and a BC spotlight, but all films are international, independent Canadian, documentary, or art movies. Beer and wine are sold at most films, but not flicks meant for kids—though few of the films even allow those under 18. Tickets include an annual $2 fee.

Festivals and Events

The **PuSh International Performing Arts Festival** (www.pushfestival.ca, Jan.-Feb.) brings performances and parties to some otherwise quiet months in the city. Recent years have brought hundreds of artists from around the globe for 150 dance, theater, musical, and literary events. The overarching theme emphasizes contemporary expression and cutting-edge creativity. One event screened a movie that was filmed only an hour before the screening began. Parties and galas are also part of the series.

Spring's prettiest celebration is the **Vancouver Cherry Blossom Festival** (www.vcbf.ca) in March or April, inspired by the Japanese Sakura festivals and starring the 40,000 ornamental cherry trees in the city, many of which came from Japan in the 1930s. Events include the Cherry Jam Downtown Concert, which starts with culinary demos, held at the Burrard Skytrain Station (Burrard and Dunsmir Sts., 604/953-3333, www.translink.ca), the Umbrella Dance near the Vancouver Art Gallery (750 Hornby St.), and the Sakura Days Japan Fair in the VanDusen Botanical Garden (5251 Oak St., 604/257-8335, http://vancouver.ca), located in a residential neighborhood. To experience the blooms without the crowds, find maps on the festival website with hundreds of locations of cherry trees, or find a walk held around the city.

On a day in early May, the **BC Spot Prawn Festival** (www.chefstablesociety.com/spotprawnfestival, May, $19.75) celebrates a local delicacy, a kind of shrimp—no, they're not actually prawns. The bash takes place at False Creek Fisherman's Wharf just west of Granville Island, near where West 1st Avenue meets Pennyfarthing Drive. Tickets get you entrance to a Spot Prawn Boil featuring the sweet, firm little creatures, plus the chance to see chef demonstrations and grab a few pounds to make them at home. A food tent also serves coffee, wine, and other bites. The season goes from May into early summer, and fresh catch is often sold at the False Creek Fisherman's Wharf.

About half a million people attend the **Vancouver International Jazz Festival** (www.coastaljazz.ca, June), made up off 300 concerts around the city in late June. Half of the concerts are free, and big names show up—the likes of Herbie Hancock and Esperanza Spalding. The Downtown Jazz Weekend, part of the festival, was relocated to the grounds of the Vancouver Art Gallery, where a free village of music and arts stages is set up alongside a family zone and artisan market, plus a dance party. It's been known to attract more than 150,000 over just two days.

The idea of Shakespeare performed al fresco is nothing new, but **Bard on the Beach** (604/737-0625, www.bardonthebeach.org, June-Sept.) takes it up a notch and moves the iambic pentameter to Vanier Park (1000 Chestnut St., http://vancouver.ca) in Kitsilano. Almost 90,000 people attend the festival, which produces four plays on two tented stages June-September. The bigger of the two has an open end, so the audience can see the water and mountains behind, while the smaller stage does lesser-known plays and unusual Shakespeare stagings. The

Bard Village has concessions, bars, and a gift shop and also holds educational events.

What's better than fireworks? A fireworks competition. The **Celebration of Light** (http://hondacelebrationoflight.com, July) is a renowned international battle between three countries in the art of pyrotechnic. Spectators—almost half a million of them—head to the beaches of English Bay to watch over three nights in late July and early August. Entrants are judged on concept, color, and music correlation, but the event is more about 25-minute segments of nonstop dazzle.

November brings the **Eastside Culture Crawl** (www.eastsideculturecrawl.com, Nov.), a four-day arts festival attended by more than 30,000 people. Hundreds of artists show off their art in dozens of buildings within the bounds of Main Street, 1st Avenue, Victoria Drive, and the waterfront (so just east of Gastown and including some of Chinatown). Galleries hold special events and exhibits, but it's more fun to visit the studios open to the public for the day.

Shopping

There's an equal balance between large chain stores and artsy boutiques in Vancouver. The American and Canadian dollars are usually close in value, but consumer goods—clothing, electronics, and food—are mostly more expensive in Canada.

Downtown
Department Stores
Hudson's Bay (674 Granville St., 604/681-6211, www.thebay.com, 9:30am-9pm Mon.-Sat., 11am-7pm Sun.) department stores purport to be the oldest business in North America, and because they were trading for furs back in the 17th century, no one's challenging them for the title. The store in downtown Vancouver, a.k.a. The Bay, has come a long way since the

days of bartering with First Nations people over blankets and beads. Now there's Lancôme and BCBG wares for sale in the downtown department store. But you can still purchase the Hudson's Bay Company signature multicolored striped wool blanket or Canada-labeled workout gear that's been sold since the 2010 Winter Olympics were held in Vancouver.

Fur used to matter in Canada because so many department stores were born of the fur trade. **Holt Renfrew** (737 Dunsmuir St., 604/681-3121, www.holtrenfrew.com, 10am-7pm Mon.-Tues., 10am-9pm Wed.-Fri., 10am-8pm Sat., 11am-7pm Sun.) emerged from a store that didn't collect them from trappers, but rather sold them to rich Europeans from Quebec City. Today the Vancouver store is a destination for shoppers of luxury brands like Armani, Gucci, and Valentino. The Holts Salon and Spa offers pampering if the gleaming white walls and skylights aren't calming enough.

Clothing and Shoes
If Canada had its own Gap, it would probably be **Le Château** (813 Burrard St., 604/682-3909, www.lechateau.com, 10am-7pm Sat.-Wed., 10am-9pm Thurs.-Fri.). The chain store has more than 200 outposts around Canada selling its mid-priced casual wear and special-occasion outfits for both men and women. Styles are trendy but generally affordable.

Style is at a premium at **Aritzia** (1110 Robson St., 604/684-3251, www.aritzia.com, 10am-10pm Mon.-Sat., 10am-9pm Sun.), which was originally a single women's wear boutique in Vancouver. In 30 years it's grown into a chain with more than 50 stores, many in the United States. The store caters to the young set bent on looking effortlessly casual, even if it takes a little work and a little cash. The online website even includes a magazine full of style profiles and artist interviews.

Who cares what you wear to yoga? Everyone, ever since **Lululemon Athletica** (970 Robson St., 604/681-3118, www.

lululemon.com, 9am-10pm Mon.-Sat., 9am-9pm Sun.) turned om-wear into high fashion. Though the company began here in Vancouver in 1998, it took a good decade for its name to become synonymous with carefully cut tops, space-age fabric, and yes, yoga pants that can soar to over $100. But Eastern philosophy and stretching aren't the only philosophy linked to the workout togs—shopping bags are printed with the phrase "Who is John Galt?" a reference to the Ayn Rand book *Atlas Shrugged*.

Gourmet Goodies

Ladurée (1141 Robson St., 604/336-3030, www.laduree.fr/en, 10am-9pm Mon.-Sat., 11am-7pm Sun.) is a boutique—one that sells only cookies. The fancy French macarons are made in Europe and imported to Vancouver, and the multiple flavors are a rainbow behind the counter. The entire store feels like the inside of an elaborate birthday cake, and the delicate desserts make great gifts. A salon in back serves meals and sit-down treats; the surprisingly thorough menu features afternoon tea, sandwiches, and frothy desserts.

Gastown and Chinatown
Clothing and Shoes

Welcome to the temple of **John Fluevog** (65 Water St., 604/688-6228, www.fluevog.com, 10am-7pm Mon.-Wed. and Sat., 10am-8pm Thurs.-Fri., noon-6pm Sun.), the shoe line's flagship store and workshop. The funky footwear is popular among celebrities (the brand is quick to point out that Madonna showed off a pair in her movie *Truth or Dare*). Fluevog, who began the store in Vancouver, still personally designs each shoe style in the open space of the second-story workshop, itself topped with multicolor glass skylights. Shoes often show off his sense of humor—one sole reports that it repels water, acid, and Satan.

The streets of Gastown are lined in high-end boutiques, but **Community Thrift and Vintage Frock Shoppe** (311 Carrall St., 604/682-8535, www.communitythriftandvintage.ca, 11am-7pm Mon.-Sat., noon-5pm Sun.) has markedly different stock—yet a similar look, with racks positioned artfully around a light-filled space. The shop calls its wares vintage clothing at thrift-shop prices. Most notably, it employs residents from the Downtown Eastside neighborhood, a poor area that directly borders the rejuvenated commercial center of Gastown, and donates all proceeds to charities that address local housing needs. There's also a unisex shop at 11 West Hastings Street.

The Chinatown street where boutique **Charlie & Lee** (223 Union St., 604/558-3030, www.charlieandlee.com, 11am-6pm Mon.-Sat., noon-5pm Sun.) sits is removed from the bustle of Gastown, but the fashion is no less up to date. Clothing pieces represent small designers from around the globe, but most are a casual retro style that would seem at home in Portland or Brooklyn—imagine a $90 chambray skinny tie. A dark den holds the menswear in the back, decorated with an arty axe on the wall.

Leatherworker **Erin Templeton** (511 Carrall St., 604/682-2451, www.erintempleton.com, 11am-5pm Mon.-Tues., 11am-6pm Wed.-Sat.) likes to work with recycled leather pieces, turning them into simple, bold bags and wallets, often in bright colors. She also sells vintage clothing out of her store and studio, located on a grubby corner of Chinatown.

Gift and Home

The good news is that **Secret Location** (1 Water St., 604/685-0090, www.secretlocation.ca, 11am-6pm Mon.-Sat., 11am-5pm Sun.) isn't as hard to locate as its name suggests. The real secret is what the real mission is here. A "concept" store out front has gifts and clothing in a wide space marked by tall concrete pillars and a pale wood floor.

You can be forgiven for thinking you took a wrong turn and ended up in Portland. No, you're just at **Old Faithful**

Shop (320 W Cordova St., 778/327-9376, www.oldfaithfulshop.com, 11am-7pm Mon.-Fri., 10am-7pm Sat., 11am-6pm Sun.), a home store that sells arty watering cans, artisanal relish, and retro canvas laundry carts (perfect for re-creating scenes from *Annie!*). The brick walls hark back to the owner's original inspiration, the general stores owned by his grandparents.

Gourmet Goodies

Save On Meats (43 W Hastings St., 604/569-3568, www.saveonmeats.ca, 10am-7pm Mon.-Thurs., 8am-10pm Fri.-Sat., 8am-7pm Sun.) isn't just a butcher shop—now it's a phenomenon, thanks to a reality show called *Gastown Gamble*. The owners reopened the once-shuttered neighborhood institution, saving the space from becoming a high end condo, and relit the neon sign featuring a flying pig. Besides a long deli case full of raw meat, the spot also features a diner, cooking classes, and a sandwich counter. A token program is meant to address the number of hungry or itinerant people in the neighborhood. The $2.25 tokens, handed out individually or by the store's community partners, can be redeemed for hot breakfast sandwiches throughout the day, and a new clothing token system with $5 tokens was just launched.

Yaletown
Gift and Home

The shelves at **Örling & Wu** (28 Water St., 604/568-6718, www.orlingandwu.com, 10am-6pm Mon.-Wed., 10am-7pm Thurs.-Sat., 11am-6pm Sun.) carry plates, clocks, glassware, and pillows from around the world, including Scandinavia and New York City. Many pieces represent a vintage look, and they're doing their part to bring wallpaper back into fashion.

Health and Beauty

Though not nearly as extensive as makeup emporium Sephora, **BeautyMark** (1268 Pacific Blvd., 604/642-2294, www.beautymark.ca, 10am-7pm Mon.-Sat., noon-5pm Sun.) excels at the lotions-and-lipstick trade while adding nail services and a smattering of hats and clothing in one corner. A more wide-ranging selection is on the store's website, but the bright shop on the edge of Yaletown offers personal consultations from staff, who like to hand out samples of recommended products.

Granville Island
Arts and Crafts

Yes, you can wear the scarves made and sold at **Alarte Silks** (1369 Railspur Alley, 778/370-4304, www.alartesilks.com, 10am-6pm Mon.-Sat., 11am-6pm Sun.), but as the gallery-like space suggests, they're works of art. The pieces are painted by artist Izabela Sauer, whose textile work has won awards and who splits her time between the South Pacific and the Granville studio. Her Nuno collection includes Japanese-style felting, while the Shibori are creased into folds. None are cheap, but the wild-faced ceramic heads used as display mannequins are worth a peek even if you're not buying.

The Craft Council of British Columbia operates the show **Crafthouse** (1386 Cartwright St., 604/687-7270, www.craftcouncilbc.ca, 10am-6pm daily), and getting a piece on the shelves takes more than having a price sticker. Local artists must pass a Standards of Quality Jury, which judges the craftsmanship and picks product lines for the shop. Pieces include one-of-a-kind ceramic works, jewelry, and even cards, and staff members are adept at spelling out an artist's biography to interested shoppers.

Gift and Home

It doesn't matter if you already have a vacuum cleaner designed by NASA. The **Granville Island Broom Company** (1406 Old Bridge St., 604/629-1141, www.broomcompany.com, 10am-6pm daily) is a must-see on a trip around Granville

Island. It's like entering the Wicked Witch of the West's fantasy closet, where broomcorn (a kind of sorghum) is handcrafted in a traditional Shaker style. Handles are made of eucalyptus, birch, or even locally forged iron. The sisters show off their broom making and even sell doll-like figures made from broom heads. They know you're not actually going to clean with these works of art.

Walking into **Ainsworth Custom Design** (1243 Cartwright St., 604/682-8838, www.ainsworthcustomdesign.com, 10am-6pm Mon. and Fri., noon-6pm Sat., noon-5pm Sun.) is like entering a birthday party already in full swing—brightly colored art pieces, wall hangings, and paper goods are for sale, all made by local Vancouver artists.

Rhinoceros Accessories (1551 Johnston St., No. 102, 604/684-3448, www.rhinostore.ca, 10am-6pm daily) is even more of an assault on the senses. The gift shop is crammed with handpainted glassware, holiday decorations, and knickknacks. The store has been on the island for more than three decades, even opening a Gastown outpost in recent years. It's the kind of place where you go to buy a gift for someone you don't know too well.

Kids' Stuff
Though smaller than the food-and-arts Public Market on Granville Island, the nearby **Kids Market** (1496 Cartwright St., 604/689-8447, www.kidsmarket. ca, 10am-6pm daily) feels as big to the under-12 set. Two floors of 25 shops in an old factory building include a magic store, a kite and puppets emporium, and a kids-only hair salon where kids can get a trim while sitting in a Thomas the Tank Engine chair. Yes, kids only.

North Vancouver
Gourmet Goodies
Located near where the SeaBus lands in North Vancouver, **Lonsdale Quay Market** (Lonsdale Ave. and Carrie Cates Ct.,

604/985-6261, www.lonsdalequay.com, 9am-7pm daily) features individual shops hawking spices, candy treats, and flowers, plus full-service restaurants and cafés. There are also gifts of the scarf, jewelry, and handbag variety in the space, which opened during Expo '86. Climb to the top of the stairs in the Q Tower—literally a platform topped by a giant letter Q—for views of the city.

Sports and Recreation

Parks
Portside Park
Follow Main Street all the way to the end, over the railroad tracks, and around a big curve to reach the waterfront **Portside Park** (101 E Waterfront Rd., http://vancouver.ca, dawn-dusk daily). The rocky beach has some of the best people-watching in the city, plus two playgrounds and a spray park for kids. The view takes in the more industrial side of Vancouver's waterfront plus the towering mountains behind Burrard Inlet. The full name is CRAB Park at Portside, CRAB standing for Create a Real Available Beach, the neighborhood group that supported the formation of the park. There's no crabbing to be done here, but a large lawn hosts arts performances in the summer.

Queen Elizabeth Park
Located a few kilometers south of downtown, **Queen Elizabeth Park** (4600 Cambie St., 604/873-7000, http://vancouver.ca) is one of the city's prettiest plots of land. Its peak, the 500-foot Little Mountain, is the highest spot in the city of Vancouver. It contains a garden built in a former quarry, sculptures, a rose garden, and an arboretum full of 1,500 trees from across the country. There's a pitch-and-putt golf course full of par-3 golf holes, tennis courts, and a lawn bowling area. The **Bloedel Conservatory** (33rd Ave. between Cambie and Main Sts.,

10am-8pm daily summer, 10am-5pm daily winter, $6.50 adults, $4.35 seniors and children 13-18, $3.15 children 3-12, children under 3 free) opened in 1969. This geodesic dome is full of exotic birds, like macaws and African parrots, tropical plants, and a koi fish pond. Next door is the **Dancing Waters Fountain** with 70 jets of water.

Beaches

The city's most popular beach is **English Bay Beach** (Beach Ave. between Gilford and Bidwell Sts., http://vancouver.ca), located southeast of Stanley Park and across from a busy neighborhood full of bars and shops. The beach has a long strip of sand with two volleyball courts (11:30am-8:30pm May-Sept.), lifeguards (May-Sept.), and a swimming dock with a slide. There are kayak rentals and a fenced off-leash dog park (Lagoon Dr., 7am-9pm). On New Year's Day, the Vancouver Polar Bear Swim Club takes a chilly dip in the water here. It started in 1920 with 10 brave souls and now more than 2,000 people take part. Washrooms, pay parking, and an outpost of the **Cactus Club Café** (1790 Beach Ave., 604/681-2582, www.cactusclubcafe.com, 11am-midnight Sun.-Thurs., 11am-1am Fri.-Sat., $23-40) are available.

The view from **Spanish Banks Beach Park** (4801 NW Marine Dr., 604/257-8400, http://vancouver.ca) is amazing. Where else can you sit in the sun on the sand and see snowcapped mountains and a cityscape? Spanish Banks East stretches toward Tolmie Street, offering volleyball courts and lifeguards (May-Sept.). Larger Spanish Banks West is designated as a "quiet beach" without stereos or other amplified sound. The park is located in Westside, between Kitsilano and the University of British Columbia. From downtown Vancouver, cross the Burrard or Granville Bridges and follow West 4th Avenue west to NW Marine Drive. Turn right onto NW Marine Drive and follow it for 1.8 kilometers (1.1 miles) to the park. Parking is free.

Biking

Some of the best cycling in the city is inside **Stanley Park** (604/257-8531, http://vancouver.ca), but there are other places to pedal. Follow a seaside bike ride from **Vanier Park** (1000 Chestnut St., Kitsilano, http://vancouver.ca) along Kitsilano Beach, then on West 3rd Avenue until the road meets NW Marine Drive. Follow the bike lane to Spanish Banks Beach Park (4801 NW Marine Dr.) less than 6 kilometers (4 miles), or all the way to the Museum of Anthropology for a 9.6-kilometer (6-mile) cycle.

For mountain biking, try the North Shore's **Mount Seymour CBC Trail** (1700 Mount Seymour Rd., North Vancouver, 604/986-2261, www.mountseymour.com). It's not easy, but it is very popular and has a shuttle ($5) hauling bikes between endpoints of the trail.

Bike Rentals

To rent a bike near Stanley Park, head to the giant **Spokes Bicycle Rental** (1798 W Georgia St., 604/688-5141, www.spokesbicyclerentals.com, 8am-9pm daily summer, 9am-6:30pm daily winter, $7.82-10.48 per hour), where a well-oiled rental machine quickly gets tourists on a bike and headed toward the park on an easy cruiser and with a helmet and basket. The shop has existed in some form since 1938, so they know how to see Vancouver by bike.

For more specialized mountain bikes, try North Vancouver's **Endless Biking** (101-1467 Crown St., North Vancouver, 604/985-2519, www.endlessbiking.com/rentals, 9am-6pm daily summer, 10am-4pm daily fall, by appointment in winter, $35-65 for 4 hours). They have full suspension and hardtail bikes, and have packages that include pads, helmet, gloves, and armor—and maps. They also offer guided tours on North Shore trails.

Day Trip to Whistler

Whistler isn't named for the slow "I'm impressed" whistle visitors make when they finally arrive at the mountain resort town; it got its moniker from the marmots that live in the rocks and make distinctive whistling sounds. But it's undeniably impressive, with some of the best skiing in the country and a town full of restaurants, shops, and après-ski spots. From Vancouver, it's an easy 90-minute drive north to Whistler, about 120 kilometers (75 miles) via Highway 99, known as the Sea to Sky Highway.

Winter

Skiers can attack one of two mountains, **Whistler** or **Blackcomb** (4545 Blackcomb Way, 604/967-8950, www.whistlerblackcomb.com, two-day tickets: $176-206 adults, $147-181 seniors and children 13-18, $81-104 children 7-12, children under 7 free). The mountains have a combined 37 total lifts, including four gondolas. The longest run is more than 11 kilometers (7 miles) of cruising. This is, simply, some of the best skiing on the planet. The two are connected by the **Peak 2 Peak Gondola** (www.whistlerblackcomb.com, $53 adults, $45 seniors and children 13-18, $28 children 7-12, children under 7 free). This wonder of modern aerial transportation travels more than 4 kilometers (2.5 miles) across a valley and creek, at times more than half a kilometer up in the sky.

Whistler also offers Nordic skiing from its **Whistler Olympic Park** (5 Callaghan Valley Rd., 604/964-0060, www.whistlerolympicpark.com, Nordic skiing: $24 adults, $14 children 7-18) with 27 trails for cross-country skiers and snowshoers. For a chance to try bobsled or skeleton luge racing, the **Whistler Sliding Center** (4910 Glacier Ln., 604/964-0040, www.whistlerslidingcentre.com, 9am-5pm daily, rides $179, walking tours $10) has a 1,450-meter track and allows the public to experience a ride where the Olympic athletes once sped. You'll be going much slower than the gold medal athletes, of course, but at speeds of up to 130 miles per hour, it'll feel fast enough.

Summer

Use the ski lifts for **hiking** in the summer, including a Peak 2 Peak ride. The **Whistler Mountain Bike Park** (866/218-9690, http://bike.whistlerblackcomb.com, $69 adults, $61 seniors and children 13-18, $39 children 5-12) is open May-October. The park uses some of the lifts and includes beginner, intermediate, and incredibly scary, gnarly, expert-only trails. An indoor bike arena called the Air Dome is available for practice (3 hours for $22).

Food and Accommodations

The fare at **Rimrock Café and Oyster Bar** (2117 Whistler Rd., 604/932-5565, http://rimrockcafe.com, 5:30pm-9:30pm daily, $35-52) is among the best in Whistler; especially delectable are the scallops and well-blended classic cocktails. Central Whistler Village has no shortage of eateries, but **Mongolie Grill** (4295 Blackcomb Way, 604/938-9416, www.mongoliegrill.com, 11:30am-10pm daily, $18-36) offers a hands-on experience. Guests select their favorite meats, vegetables, and sauces from a large buffet and then watch as the chef stir-fries the concoction on a giant grill. Payment is by the gram.

Après-ski is a big scene, with drinks, music, and crowds in the early evening; try **Garibaldi Lift Company** (4165 Springs Ln., 604/905-2220, www.whistlerblackcomb.com, 11am-1am daily, $16-17) to be in the middle of it all.

Staying in Whistler is not a cheap endeavor, but **Hosteling International—Whistler** (1035 Legacy Way, 778/328-2220, www.hihostels.ca, $33-40 shared rooms, $95-110 private rooms) offers one alternative. The beautiful building resembles a boutique hotel, with sleek bunks, modern fireplaces, and outdoor picnic areas. On the opposite end of the spectrum, the standout **Fairmont Chateau Whistler** (4599 Chateau Blvd., 604/938-8000, www.fairmont.com, $699-1,200) has all the grandeur of a European castle in the Alps, plus a heated pool, spa, and wedding chapel. To get out of the bustle, try the **Nita Lake Lodge** (2131 Lake Placid Rd., 604/966-5700, www.nitalakelodge.com, $359-1,100) across the highway, still close enough to walk to lifts but peaceful with its cozy spa and restaurant.

Hiking
Grouse Grind

Distance: 2.9 kilometers (1.8 miles) one-way
Duration: 2 hours
Elevation gain: 853 meters (2,799 feet)
Effort: strenuous
Trailhead: Skyride Terminal (6400 Nancy Greene Way)

Grouse Grind has to be the city's hardest hike, an unforgiving slog up Grouse Mountain to the ski and recreation area on top. Leave from the Skyride Terminal and purchase a Grind Timer Card to track your time (the $20 ticket comes with free transfer for your bag to the top). The day's best times are logged on the website. It's a rough hike straight uphill, with steps that can exhaust even the most fit of hikers, but the trees offer nice shade for most of it. There are 2,830 stairs to tackle through thick, tall forest. Panting hikers rest on seat-like rocks on the side of the trail. But when you emerge up top, you'll behold vistas of the city sparkling below. Look west to see large freighter ships anchored just off Stanley Park. Hiking downhill isn't allowed for safety reasons, so you'll have to ride the Skyride ($10) back down.

Beacon Hill Trail

Distance: 1 kilometer (0.6 mile) round-trip
Duration: 50 minutes
Elevation gain: 100 feet
Effort: easy
Trailhead: access off Beacon Lane in Lighthouse Park

For an easy ramble, try Lighthouse Park in North Vancouver. The still-functioning lighthouse that gives the park its name dates back to the 1870s, and the park's trails wind next to cliffs and through forest. A short hike leads uphill on the Beacon Hill Trail to the lighthouse viewpoint and the knolls looking over Burrard Inlet and Howe Sound.

If you'd like to wander more, take a map at the trailhead to see the large network of trails—though don't worry too much about getting lost on this peninsula—and meander from one to the other, past first-growth Douglas fir trees. Routes head to coves and exposed points that offer more ocean views.

Food

This close to the Pacific Ocean it's not surprising that seafood has a firm hold in the Vancouver culinary scene. What *is* surprising is the huge variety (besides fish and clams), and that some of the most notable cuisine in town has Asian roots. As with the rest of the Northwest, local ingredients are highly coveted.

You can't go more than a few blocks in Vancouver, or any Canadian city for that matter, without coming across a **Tim Hortons** (www.timhortons.com). The doughnut and coffee chain is named for an NHL player who played professional hockey for 22 seasons and is known to have invented the slap shot. The restaurant he started is credited with inventing the apple fritter. Today Tim Hortons has more than 3,500 locations in Canada and sells fast-service coffee, doughnuts, and sandwiches, including breakfast sandwiches, and outside urban areas, many locations have drive-through service. The name Tim Hortons has become a cultural trademark, and while the fare may not be exciting cuisine, it is quintessentially Canadian.

Downtown
Canadian

Pretty much the entire menu at ★ **Smoke's Poutinerie** (942 Granville St., 604/669-2873, www.smokespoutinerie.com, 11am-11pm Mon.-Tues., 11am-3am Wed.-Thurs., 11am-4am Fri.-Sun., $7-10) is Canada's favorite dish, poutine. The counter-service spot has locations from Saskatchewan to Nova Scotia, and has even snuck down into the States. The menu has 30 combinations alone, plus a create-your-own option. The fry base is made from Canadian potatoes that are soaked, rinsed, and fried in canola oil (no trans fats, so it's almost healthy—yeah, right). They're seasoned before adding toppings, including gravy that comes in vegetarian, peppercorn, and signature Quebec styles; the cheese curds also hail from Quebec. Then come the extra toppings, like chipotle pulled pork, sautéed mushrooms, Italian sausage, caramelized onions—combine all four for the terrifying Hogtown poutine dish. Vegetable versions use vegetable gravy, and the meat averse can try the Rainbow poutine with sriracha. The space is ideal for food late at night, with stools, bright red lights, and takeout options.

The dining room at **Hawksworth** (801 W Georgia St., 604/673-7000, hawksworthrestaurant.com, 6:30am-10pm Mon.-Fri., 7am-10pm Sat.-Sun., $44-57) in the Rosewood Hotel Georgia is gleamingly white, but it's not oppressively fancy; locals gather beneath stark modern art pieces and give the restaurant a lively buzz. Head chef and namesake David Hawksworth is a celebrated Canadian chef, and his plates are as artistic as the walls. Lamb saddle is crusted with licorice, duck breast comes with a foie gras au jus, and every serving has its colorful toppings and garnishes placed just so. The same group also opened **Nightingale** (1017 W. Hastings St., 604/695-9500, https://hawknightingale. com, 11am-midnight daily, $15-28), a more casual dining spot downtown, to serve wood-fired pizzas and house-made pastas. That space is airier than the more formal Hawksworth, with bird motifs in a cavernous two-story space. The many seating options make it easy to have just the meal—casual, businesslike, or celebratory—that will fit your day. Don't miss the long list of vegetable dishes; they're not simple sides to be ignored.

It's not uncommon to see a line outside **Twisted Fork Bistro** (1147 Granville St., 604/568-0749, www.thetwistedfork. ca, 8am-3pm daily, $16.50) on weekend mornings, but here brunch happens every day, in a prix fixe mode. The frittatas, scrambles, and Benedicts are worth the queue, not to mention the six mimosa-like sparkling morning cocktails and more intense "hair of the dog" concoctions. The bistro has a French influence, but one need not know terms more complicated than "pâté" and "confit" to understand the menu. The wine and beer lists are pointedly local, including only British Columbia small wineries and microbreweries. Tables are smaller than the artwork on the deep red walls, and there isn't much seating in the narrow restaurant—so if you're in line for brunch, say yes to a counter seat.

Meat eaters shouldn't despair, **Botanist** (1038 Canada Pl., 604/695-5500, www. botanistrestaurant.com, 6:30am-10:30am, 11:30am-2pm, and 5pm-10pm Mon.-Fri.; 7am-2pm and 5pm-10pm Sat.-Sun., $22-38) doesn't only serve vegetables, even though its name calls to mind a greenery-only gardener. Located in the Fairmont Pacific Rim, a hotel inspired by the countries around the Pacific Ocean, the restaurant isn't an Asian spot but rather a local-first Canadian eatery serving picturesque fish, bird, and meat with a number of local vegetables. Tables sit under a trellis that holds dozens of local plants growing along it, and the champagne menu is extensive.

Asian

There are several Japanese Guu outposts around the city, but **Guu Garden** (888 Nelson St., 604/899-0855, www.guu-izakaya.com, 11:30am-2:30pm and 5:30pm-midnight Mon.-Thurs., 11:30am-2:30pm and 5:30pm-12:30am Fri., noon-3pm and 5:30pm-12:30am Sat., noon-3pm and 5:30pm-midnight Sun., $20-30) specializes in *oden*, a kind of Japanese hot pot that has roots in food cart cuisine but gets an upscale treatment here. The space has wood floors and ceilings, a small rock garden with a fountain out one side, and some outdoor seating. The menu also has *izakaya* classics and "carbohydrates":

Poutine: Canada's National Dish

The gourmands of Canada would probably insist that the national dish is some variety of carefully prepared fish, and coffee fiends would point to Tim Hortons coffee. But poutine is probably the best-recognized, unofficial national dish of Canada. It originated in Quebec but is easily found throughout all the provinces.

All poutine needs is three things: French fries, gravy, and cheese curds. (The latter are sometimes called "squeaky cheese" and are made without whey.)

High-end restaurants will add pork belly or beef brisket, while others make it with mushroom gravy and different variations.

In downtown Vancouver, **Smoke's Poutinerie** (page 105) has a version that will match almost any palate. At **The Flying Pig** (page 111) the dish is served with pulled pork. The treat also comes in lowbrow versions at the drive-through: The Burger King chain in Canada serves a fast-food version of poutine, and Canadian chain Harvey's dishes up some with their skin-on French fries.

FOOD

kimchi bibimbap and sushi dishes. The sake and *shochu* lists are matched by frozen cocktail specials and drinks made with lychee liqueur and Asian beers. "Guuing may be addictive" or "Guu is guuu'd" reads the chopstick packaging, and chopsticks don't lie.

★ **Hapa Izakaya** (909 W Cordova St., 604/420-4272, www.hapaizakaya.com, 11:30am-midnight Mon.-Fri., 5pm-midnight Sat.-Sun., $10-16) embraces the Japanese style of *izakaya*, a bar with bites. There are currently two Vancouver locations serving hot and cold tapas, plus a small smattering of rice and noodle dishes. The mini chain garners national awards and has been credited with helping popularize the restaurant style. The ultramodern decor of the downtown restaurant, in shades of tan and black, plus outdoor seating and plenty of sharable dishes attract a young and trendy crowd. The food is well regarded, but the scene and people-watching is even better. Reservations are recommended, and the happy hour (5pm-6pm daily and 9pm-close Sun.-Thurs.) has great deals.

Gastown and Chinatown
Canadian

The popular ★ **Café Medina** (556 Beatty St., 604/879-3114, www.medinacafe. com, 8am-3pm Mon.-Fri., 9am-3pm Sat.-Sun., $12-19), located in a dark building

with a black iron gate on the border of Chinatown, is surprisingly light and airy inside, with small tables and a few counter seats. The bistro has Belgian and Australian roots, which means venison burgers and Moroccan lamb-and-beef meatballs, plus handheld waffles covered in chocolate, pistachio rosewater, or berries. Brunch usually means a line, but you can fight hunger with drinks and waffles while you wait. Later in the day, wander next door to the **Dirty Apron Cooking School and Delicatessen** (540 Beatty St., 10:30am-6pm Mon.-Fri., 10:30am-5pm Sat.-Sun., $8.50-19), from the same owners, which offers cooking classes and has a store full of sandwiches, salads, and cheeses, plus canned goods and sauces. Courses teach cooking in French, Italian, seafood, or other styles, or for couples, singles, or kids.

Asian

The chic ★ **Bao Bei** (163 Keefer St., 604/688-0876, www.bao-bei.ca, 5:30pm-midnight Tues.-Sat., 5:30pm-10pm Sun., $14-25) has quickly become the place to see and be seen in Chinatown, an upscale brasserie that lives up to its name, which translates to "precious." Tables can be hard to come by on weekend evenings and particularly during the night market that invades Keefer Street during the summer. Tables are small and the lighting is low, barely enough to see the flowered wallpaper on one side and, on the other, the real knives and cleavers mounted on the wall, then painted over so they look like relief art. Culinary influences come from around China—Taiwan, the Sichuan province, and Shanghai—and the menu is largely made up of what they call "petits plats Chinois," sharable plates of salad and meat dishes. The "kick ass house fried rice" lives up to its name, and the octopus salad is a great fresh palate cleanser before the flavorful crispy pork belly. Reservations aren't taken, but it's easier to get a table now that it's been open a few years.

The unassuming **Harvest Community Foods** (243 Union St., 604/682-8851, ww.harvestunion.ca, 11am-8pm Mon.-Fri., 10am-7pm Sat.-Sun., $10-12) is so into fresh fruits and veggies, they operate a farm-share program out of the store, delivering boxes of produce to one-time or season-long members. For anyone not interested in hauling around a box of zucchini, there are hot Asian soups like udon and ramen, with ingredients rotating with the freshest crops of the week. Order from the counter in the small space and try to score one of the tables, or head outside to a sidewalk seat during warm months.

No one quite knew what to make of **Kissa Tanto** (263 E Pender St., 778/379-8078, www.kissatanto.com, 5:30pm-midnight Tues.-Sat., $18-46), an Italian-Japanese fusion restaurant in a small 2nd-floor space on an otherwise unremarkable block of Chinatown. But it was from the founder of Bao Bei, so it was no surprise when the unusual food began garnering rave reviews. Some single dishes combine both flavors—the chef's own lineage traces back to the two countries—like a lasagna with a miso béchamel sauce. The crudo is deservedly famous, and the fun interior recalls a 1930s club or train station. Reservations are necessary unless you want to show

Hawksworth restaurant

up midafternoon to wait for a table with other hopeful diners.

Coffee

The very popular **Revolver** (325 Cambie St., 604/558-4444, 7:30am-6pm Mon.-Sat., $3-5) is all about the coffee, offering every variety of coffee preparation to java nerds drawn to the subtleties of the bean; you can even get a single coffee type prepared in three different ways to compare them. There isn't much to eat, just a small selection of pastries, but the energetic buzz from inside the brick-walled space comes from more than the caffeine.

The warm and darling ★ **Finch's Tea and Coffee House** (353 W Pender St., 604/899-4040, www.finchteahouse. com, 9am-5pm Mon.-Fri., 11am-4pm Sat., $5-9) is the perfect corner spot to relax over a cup of tea—or spend the day reading while you subsist on sandwiches and coffee (though don't rely on wireless access). The menu at the coffee joint is written on little chalkboards above the counter, and leafy plants hang from the ceiling. Baguettes are topped with cheese, prosciutto, avocado, and free-range egg salad, and drinks include coffee, teas, and Italian sodas—everything delicate enough to match the cozy spot. A small table up by the window provides a great view of the Vancouver street, just beyond the white curtains.

You can smell **Nelson the Seagull** (315 Carrall St., 604/681-5776, www.nelson-theseagull.com, 8am-5pm Mon.-Fri., 9am-5pm Sat.-Sun., $5-12) before you get inside—the maddening aroma of bread wafts out to the street. Just "bread and coffee," announces the café, but they do a little more, dishing up salads, breakfast, and fresh-squeezed juices from the open kitchen. Breads and pastries are the real attraction, but it's not unusual for the bakery to sell out completely in the afternoon—so don't show up at closing with a baguette craving.

Irish

Despite its very Irish name, **Irish Heather** (212 Carrall St., 604/688-9779, www. irishheather.com, 11:30am-midnight Sun.-Thurs., 11:30am-2am Fri.-Sat., $15-20) promises no green beer and no leprechauns. Its prime Gastown location makes it a kind of anchor for a collection of bars and restaurants owned by Sean Heather (who also created Shebeen Whiskey House and others). The menu has classic Irish dishes like soda bread and steak-and-ale pie, but it's more an upscale eatery than a beery pub. One side of the brick-walled restaurant has a 40-foot communal table that hosts a regular Long Table Series several nights a week with a prix fixe menu and a social atmosphere. Be sure to run to the loo, even if you haven't downed too many beer cocktails—famous quotes are beautifully displayed on the bathroom doors, so you can get a little culture even as you wait.

Southern

The breakfasts at **Deacon's Corner** (101

Chinatown's Night Market

For years, Vancouver's Chinatown has hosted a **night market** (www. vancouver-chinatown.com) in the streets, allowing vendors to hawk arts, crafts, and food once the summer sun had set. But in 2013, the organizing committee decided that the market needed fresh blood, especially to differentiate the Vancouver version from the large night market in the nearby city of Richmond.

New acts and activities were brought in to the market stage: hip-hop karaoke, Chinatown Outdoor Cinema, and a Street Fighter II tournament. A Chinatown Night Market Ping Pong Club was formed. Food trucks park next to the stalls run by Chinatown businesses. The old standbys—booths selling socks, for instance—are still there, but crowds also gather for dim sum to go, art installations, and pieces of art.

The night market takes place on Keefer Street between Main Street and Columbia Street, 6pm-11pm every Friday, Saturday, and Sunday, May-September—and it happens regardless of the weather.

Main St., 604/684-1555, www.deaconscorner.ca, 8am-6pm Mon.-Fri., 9am-6pm Sat., 9am-5pm Sun., $8-14) are big and a little greasy, in a diner that resolutely rejects the hip, ecofriendly look so popular in modern Vancouver. It's meant to evoke a Manitoba truck stop: red walls, pies on pie stands, and stools in front of a long counter. These are the Southern-inspired dishes you use to treat a hangover or ravenous stomach: buttermilk pancakes served with pulled pork, chicken-fried steak, and eggs Benedict with truffle hollandaise sauce. Hash browns are seasoned and fried to a perfect brown. But what does all that have to do with a Canadian truck stop? Well, there are grits mixed with maple syrup, of course. Though breakfast is a highlight, there's also a lunch menu with the same philosophy—lots of flavor, lots of cheese, not a lot of delicacy.

The Canadians sure do like food from the American South. Gastown's **Peckinpah** (2 Water St., 604/681-5411, www.peckinpahbbq.com, 11:30am-11pm Sun.-Thurs., 11:30am-1am Fri.-Sat., $11-30) is dedicated to eastern North Carolina-style barbecue, even though its wood-fixed decor and cattle-skull logo recall Texas. (Oh, and it's named for the California director known for his Texas cowboy films.) But don't linger over issues of authenticity. Peckinpah is located on a central corner of Gastown in a classic old red building that gets possibly more foot traffic than any spot in the city. Juicy ribs and mounds of coleslaw come in baskets lined with red-and-white wax paper, and the bourbon list is almost longer than the rest of the menu. Sauces include Carolina-style chili vinegar and a house mild sauce. The four-person banquet is almost $100. Lunch specials and occasional pig roasts are also offered.

Yaletown
Canadian

The rotisserie at ★ **Homer Street Café and Bar** (898 Homer St., 604/428 4299, www.homerstreetcafebar.com, 11:30am-2:30pm and 5pm-10pm Mon.-Thurs., 11:30am-2:30pm and 5pm-11pm Fri., 10:30am-3pm and 5pm-midnight Sat., 10:30am-3pm Sun., $18-42) always has quarter, half, and whole chickens, along with the day's featured meat (beef, fish, lamb, or pork). Nothing's wasted—the chicken drippings flavor the roasted potatoes. The space, which spreads along the 1st floor of two historical buildings, was all kinds of factories before it became this chic Gastown spot. It's now farmhouse chic, decorated with delicately weathered fixtures and a black-and-white tile floor. It's a buzzy spot (the bar and multiple seating areas fill with Vancouver scenesters), but the eats are richer than those usually found in a destination dining spot. Before you leave, be sure to peek into the cockiest room in the place, the private dining area with reclaimed factory windows and row after row of rooster paintings.

Despite the name, **The Flying Pig** (1168 Hamilton St., 604/568-1344, www.theflyingpigvan.com, 11am-midnight Mon.-Fri., 10am-midnight Sat.-Sun., $21-36) by no means restricts its focus to pork. Entrées are sometimes served on wood planks and are as likely to include halibut, chicken, or veal, plus a bone marrow cheesy bread so rich the menu describes it as "OMG." Inside are bright red brick walls, glowing white barstools, and a young and attentive staff.

Seafood

It's clear that **Blue Water Cafe** (1095 Hamilton St., 604/688-8078, www.bluewatercafe.net, 4:30pm-1am daily, $17-44) serves seafood. From the name to the big plates of oysters being delivered to the blue water painting on the wall, it's no secret. But the massive restaurant is big enough to convince you that it serves all the seafood in Vancouver, especially in summer months when the outdoor seats on Yaletown's warehouse-like patio level are full. It's the first place people think of when considering fish dishes in the city. Its menu is crammed with sturgeon, sablefish, lingcod, and more. The raw bar serves sashimi and *nigiri* as well as familiar rolls. The two live tanks have lobster, clam, sea urchins, and the local delicacy geoduck (pronounced "gooey duck"), a large, slightly rubbery clam that's no challenge to most palates. While there may be individual dishes around the city that can beat Blue Water in terms of flavor, the breadth and sheer size of the joint keep it on top of the city's seafood dining scene.

Granville Island
Canadian

Edible Canada (1596 Johnston St., 604/662-3606, www.ediblecanada.com,

10am-10pm Mon.-Fri., 9am-10pm Sat.-Sun., $18-32) doesn't sound great at first, billing itself as a "culinary tourism company." But besides a retail shop and tour base, it's a restaurant with excellent outdoor seating on Granville Island and a menu that makes the most of its proximity to the Granville Market. Fraser Valley-raised meats and mussels from Salt Spring Island are served alongside duck fat fries and greens—plus a shot of whiskey is on the sides menu. Though it would be easy to make a restaurant in this location a tourist trap, there's real thought in the preparation and service, and it's not a bad place to get a quick survey of the area's cuisine. Lines move quickly.

West Side
Canadian

Though just across the bridge from downtown proper, **Farmer's Apprentice** (1535 W 6th Ave., 604/620-2070, https://farmersapprentice.ca, 5:30pm-10pm Mon., 11am-2pm and 5:30pm-10pm Tues.-Sun., $43-58) is a world away, a mimimalist space that almost looks like someone's crowded apartment. But here the menu is the star, changing nightly and served prix fixe. Both a vegetarian and an omnivore version are offered, but each focuses on what's fresh that day, and very little meat is used even on the latter.

The man behind **Fable Kitchen** (1944 W 4th Ave., 604/732-1322, www.fablekitchen.ca, 11:30am-2pm and 5pm-10pm Mon.-Fri., 10am-2pm and 5pm-10pm Sat.-Sun., $22-32) is something of a legend in Vancouver, having appeared on the TV cooking competition *Top Chef Canada*. He actually came up with the restaurant's concept and name while on the show. In a space decorated with reclaimed wood and exposed brick walls, the kitchen delivers sandwiches and salads for lunch and simple pleasures at dinner: steelhead trout, duck breast, and squash gnocchi. Despite its TV roots, the

Vij's Takes Over the World

When Vikram Vij and his wife Meeru Dhalwala started Vij's, a modest little Indian restaurant removed from downtown Vancouver's busy streets, they could never have imagined what it has become. Waits top two hours, and the *New York Times* called it "among the finest Indian restaurants in the world." Vij's first 14-seat diner opened in 1994, right around the same time he married Dhalwala. Eventually the restaurant began winning awards and moved to a (slightly) larger location. Food Network chefs began stopping by, and lines got longer and longer.

Vancouver locals have a strategy for Vij's—show up a little after 5pm, which gets you about 30 people back in line when the restaurant opens at 5:30pm, tell the hostess you want the second seating, and spend the next 1.5 hours noshing on free appetizers and sipping drinks from the bar. You'll get a table at an ideal dinner time, around 7pm.

Though Vij originated the recipes, it was Dhalwala who eventually took over the kitchen. Vij likes to wander the dining room every night. In 2016 the restaurant moved to a new space close by, expanding its seating capacity—but waits remain for the lamb popsicles and the rest of the menu.

Within Vancouver, there are ways to get Vij-inspired food besides waiting in line. There's **Rangoli** (1488 W 11th Ave., 604/736-5711, www.vijsrangoli.ca, 11am-midnight daily, $10-21) next door to the old restaurant, with a much shorter wait and lunch service. Menu items don't replicate what's served at Vij's but still represent a wide swath of Indian cuisine: curries, grilled fish, and spicy pulled pork. The market inside Rangoli has frozen packaged curries and chicken in Vij's masala, plus chutneys, spices, and rice pudding. And if getting out to the South Granville neighborhood is too much, track down Vij's food truck **Railway Express** (604/639-3335, www.vijsrailway-express.com, $9-12), which pops up on downtown streets and at farmers markets and serves yet another Indian fusion menu with choices like butter chicken and curried squash.

restaurant has a warm vibe. Desserts are good and brunch is even better.

Across from a Tim Hortons and a liquor store, **Jethro's Fine Grub** (3420 Dunbar St., 604/569-3441, www.jethros-finegrub.com, 8am-4pm daily, $8-14) certainly captures the college vibe, making it a good stop for breakfast or lunch on the way to or from the University of British Columbia. Breakfast dishes are indulgent, with French toast made with chocolate-chip banana bread, apple cobbler, or Nutella; lunch includes sandwiches of the messy kind—a catfish po'boy, a Denver melt.

Asian

People speak in reverent tones when they speak of ★ **Vij's** (3106 Cambie St., 604/736-6664, http://vijsrestaurant.ca, 5:30pm-10:30pm daily, $24-35). It's the kind of can't-miss meal you plan an entire night—or trip—around. The restaurant is in a fairly residential neighborhood south of downtown, but the line for the first serving at the Indian restaurant forms well before 5pm, and it's not unusual to find a two-hour wait for a table. What's more, it's not unusual to find diners happily waiting those two hours, getting cocktails or chai from Vij's tiny bar and snacks passed by the waitstaff.

Can dinner at Vij's really be worth all that trouble? In a word, absolutely. The space is fairly plain and diners aren't necessarily dressed in finery, but the food is tender, flavorful, mouthwatering Indian, inspired by all regions of the country. Dishes rotate seasonally, but the lamb popsicles (meat, not dessert) in fenugreek cream curry are a standby—the tender meat alone is worth the wait.

Order some for the table, then add pork tenderloin, goat, or grilled fish. The restaurant makes its own ghee (clarified butter) and yogurt, and roasts and grinds its own spices.

North Vancouver
Canadian
Don't think too much of the name of the bistro **Burgoo** (3 Lonsdale Ave., 604/904-0933, www.burgoo.ca, 11am-10pm Mon.-Wed., 11am-11pm Thurs.-Sat., $10-18)? The owners dug the name out of a library book about stews (and a burgoo stew with lamb is even on the menu). The low-key restaurant has four locations across the city; this one is close to Lonsdale Quay in the busiest part of North Vancouver and right next to where the SeaBus docks. The menu is heavy on soups and salads, daily drink specials, and comfort dishes from around the world like jambalaya, ratatouille, and beef bourguignon. Biscuits ordered on the side are made with white cheddar and parsley.

The District Brasserie (13 Lonsdale Ave., 778/338-4938, www.thedistrictsocial.com, 3pm-11pm daily, $14-19), also near Lonsdale Quay, offers charcuterie, soups, and sharable frites in a variety of preparations, including an Amsterdam-inspired version with peanut sauce, mayo, and onions. Bigger plates include meats, mussels, and hearty burgers. The smallish restaurant fills quickly, so reservations are recommended; a small patio outside seats about 20 people.

Seafood
Although the "sea" section of the menu at **The Beachhouse Restaurant** (150 25th St., 604/922-1414, www.thebeachhouserestaurant.ca, 11:30am-10pm Mon.-Thurs., 11:30am-11pm Fri., 11am-11pm Sat., 11am-10pm Sun., $18-39) is longer than the "land" list, it's not totally a seafood restaurant. You can score a roast chicken or Angus beef filet if you're not up for a lobster roll or halibut from the Haida Gwaii (off the north coast of the province). The location at Dundrave Pier, however, is all about the water. Look across to Stanley Park or as far out as Vancouver Island. The patio is heated, so it doesn't shut down at the first sign of fall.

From its perch on the hills that rise in North Vancouver, **Salmon House on the Hill** (2229 Folkestone Way, 604/926-3212, www.salmonhouse.com, 5pm-9:30pm Mon.-Thurs., 5pm-10pm Fri., 10:30am-2:30pm and 5pm-10pm Sat., 10:30am-2:30pm and 5pm-9:30pm Sun., $29-45) has amazing views, including a look at the well-lit downtown once the sun goes down. It's been open for more than 40 years. The menu leans heavily toward seafood, like grilled sable fish with Thai curry potatoes and lobster tagliatelle pasta, but also has bison from the Peace River region and grilled lamb.

Accommodations

Downtown Vancouver has plenty of hotel rooms, partially thanks to the 2010 Olympics. Many midpriced hotels line Granville Street, which cuts through the city but can be a rowdy thoroughfare after dark. The Coal Harbor waterfront features shining towers with killer mountain views and is directly next to the cruise ships that depart for Alaska, while Yaletown properties tend to be fashionably reworked older buildings.

Downtown
Under $150
The stuffed bear and bar in the lobby of **SameSun Backpacker Hostel** (1018 Granville St., 604/682-8226, www.samesun.com, $38-51 dorms, $120-180 private rooms) says a lot about the place—on the looser and louder end of the spectrum. Breakfast, wireless Internet, and access to a Netflix-enabled TV comes with an overnight stay, and the hostel sells local sporting event tickets and advertises ski trips to Whistler.

Though **Hosteling International Vancouver Central** (1025 Granville St., 604/685-5335, www.hihostels.ca, $44-55 dorms, $114-160 private rooms) is right in the middle of bustling Granville Street, it retains a quaint charm with flower boxes in the windows. Stays include a free breakfast (the scones are particularly good) and free wireless Internet access. The kitchen has limited facilities: toaster yes, stove no. Both dorm beds and private rooms are available—some even have their own bathrooms. For a quieter stay, the **Hosteling International Vancouver Downtown** (1114 Burnaby St., 778/328.2220, www.hihostels.ca, $41-47 dorms, $108-173 private rooms) is located on a much quieter residential street and offers a roof deck and complete kitchen facilities, but the building has a distinct institutional vibe.

$150-250

The motor lodge past of the ★ **Burrard Hotel** (1100 Burrard St., 604/681-2331, http://theburrard.com, $149-389) is evident in the retro styling (stone walls in the lobby, yellow and blue hotel room doors). Cars are hidden below a central garden, where a courtyard area has seating, a big tree, and a giant Jenga game. Brooklyn Cruiser bicycles are available for guests to use for free, and the rooms themselves triumph in style even though they suffer from mid-20th-century standards for hotel room size.

Art is around every corner at ★ **Listel Hotel** (1300 Robson St., 604/684-8461, www.thelistelhotel.com, $220-407)— sometimes it's crouching next to the front desk, as is the case with a series of bright red statues. The boutique hotel is partnered with the Buschlen Mowatt Fine Art Gallery, which places more than $2 million worth of art around the building, including in individual rooms. Museum of Anthropology pieces also pop up around the property, and solar panels provide the power. For all the striking modern art, rooms have a surprisingly classic feel,

but the unusual touches, like blood-red shower curtains, add personality to a space that could otherwise feel corporate.

The **Sylvia Hotel** (1154 Gilford St., 604/681-9321, www.sylviahotel.com, $169-289) harks back to a time of seaside retreats, when this eight-story building was the only thing standing on the English Bay beachfront. Much of the 1912 building is being swallowed by ivy that creeps up the brick facade, only adding to the charm. Inside, that charm and the killer views make up for the cramped rooms and basic amenities. The lobby has puzzling medieval touches—a coat of arms, a stained-glass window—but it's hard to wish a modern renovation on such a singular and affordable waterfront hotel. Select rooms and suites have kitchens.

There's a simplicity to the **Kingston Hotel Bed and Breakfast** (757 Richards St., 604/684-9024, www.kingstonhotel-vancouver.com, $149-179 shared bath, $235-295 private bath), where rooms come with a single bed, a double bed, or two single beds; the latter come with private bath, and the former without. Furnishings are dated and floral, and the building dates back to 1910 but doesn't feel particularly historical. The fireplace lounge features a small but pretty rock chimney, and a continental breakfast is free. The location is central but not too loud. It's a good choice when on a budget.

Find a whole lotta blue at the **Blue Horizon Hotel** (1225 Robson St., 604/688-1411, www.bluehorizonhotel.com, $169-219), from the tiles in the lobby to the waters of the indoor swimming pool. With 214 rooms spread over 31 stories, the hotel is an impressive tower on Robson, especially because all the rooms have private balconies. Wireless Internet is free, parking is only $15 (not bad for downtown Vancouver), and the pool is joined by a whirlpool and sauna in the fitness center. The on-site **Abode Restaurant** (1223 Robson St., www.aboderestaurant.ca, 6:30am-10pm Sun.-Fri.,

6:30am-10:30pm Sat.) serves breakfast, coffee, and cocktails as well as meals. The hotel shows some signs of age, but the location and amenities make up for it, and the price is a good deal.

Over $250

Close to some of the city's biggest and buzziest hotels, **The Loden** (1177 Melville St., 604/669-5060, www.theloden.com, $425-570) is tucked sideways on an unobtrusive block. The boutique hotel has high-end design touches, like giant tubs and sliding doors that open the space between bathroom and bedroom, and select rooms have patios next to a tiny water feature. Bikes are available for use, and two British taxi vehicles drive guests anywhere in the downtown core.

Although many hotels with the Fairmont name are historical properties—like the castle-shaped Fairmont Hotel Vancouver just a few blocks away—the ★ **Fairmont Pacific Rim** (1038 Canada Pl., 877/900-5350, www.fairmont.com, $594-738) is thoroughly modern, a luxury hotel with all the amenities (spa, rooftop pool, etc.). The decor is inspired by the Pacific Rim, and is mostly contemporary clean lines in neutral colors. Bathrooms on the north side of the hotel face the grassy roof of the convention center across the street, not to mention the striking North Vancouver mountains across the water. **The Lobby Lounge** (10am-1:30am Mon.-Sat., 10am-11pm Sun.) downstairs, with its fire element and high-end cocktails, attracts a buzzy, well-dressed crowd. The hotel is popular with celebrities, and a few luxury automobiles are usually parked outside by the valet stand. Got a lot of cash burning a hole in your pocket? The Chairman's Suite, inspired by a Balinese villa, is a two-story unit with two living rooms, a kitchen, a butler's pantry, and a rooftop patio—for only $10,000 per night.

from top to bottom: Pinnacle Hotel at the Pier; Bao Bei in Chinatown; Nightingale restaurant.

Though the exterior of the ★ **Shangri-La Hotel** (1128 W Georgia St., 604/689-1120, www.shangri-la.com, $475-755) is a glassy tower much like the rest of Vancouver, it feels like a trip to Asia thanks to the lion statues outside and large art pieces inside. Rooms are decked out with luxury trappings—fine sheets and furnishings in warm, muted tones—and the spa has ultra-large rooms with private showers, an ideal spot for total relaxation when paired with the outdoor pool.

Yaletown
$150-250

The exterior is white at the **Moda Hotel** (900 Seymour St., 604/683-4251, www.modahotel.ca, $129-199), but interior walls are apt to be black or even deep red, a calming design touch that nevertheless recalls the giant Staples store just across the street. Small bathrooms notwithstanding, this is the closest to a budget stay as you'll find this close to the tony blocks of Yaletown, complete with free wireless Internet and dog friendliness. Junior rooms have showers only and are as small as 150 square feet, while suites top out at 900 square feet.

The suites at **Rosedale on Robson** (838 Hamilton St., 604/689-8033, www.rosedaleonrobson.com, $149-249) fill up quickly—and the 200-plus rooms are all suites with galley kitchens, living rooms, and big windows. Amenities include an indoor pool and steam room and an outdoor garden terrace. Its proximity to the arenas that host football and hockey games inspire ticket packages offered by the hotel.

Over $250

The ★ **Opus Hotel** (322 Davie St., 604/642-6787, http://vancouver.opushotel.com, $380-456) has a signature scent, and rooms are designed around a series of imaginary guests (are you a Dede, a Pierre, or a Billy?). Still, the hotel isn't as loopy as its most notable touches, though very much on trend with solid-color walls, in-room iPads, and original artwork. Some rooms offer the use of a local cell phone with an unlimited data plan during the guest's stay. The central Yaletown location doesn't do anything to detract from the hip vibe of the hotel. It racks up awards, as does the Northern Italian eatery next to the lobby, **La Pentola della Quercia** (350 Davie St., 604/642-0557, www.lapentola.ca, 7am-10:30pm Mon.-Wed., 7am-11pm Thurs., 7am-midnight Fri.-Sat., 7am-10pm Sun., $9-18 breakfast, $12-19 lunch, $19-32 dinner).

Granville Island
Over $250

Playing on Granville Island can fill an entire day or weekend. Staying there makes it a lot easier to enjoy the Public Market, boat rides, and shopping. The **Granville Island Hotel** (1253 Johnston St., 604/683-7373, www.granvilleislandhotel.com, $250-380) is the only place to stay in the tiny neighborhood and offers luxury amenities and waterfront views. Downstairs, the **Dockside Restaurant** (604/685-7070, www.docksidevancouver.com, 7am-10pm daily, $11-19 breakfast, $14-29 lunch, $26-37 dinner) is, as it sounds, a few feet away from the sailboats and yachts parked in False Creek. A 50-foot aquarium runs along the side of the kitchen, and a number of fireplaces warm the restaurant. Bikes are available to rent from the hotel, and the health center has a small hot tub covered by a glass ceiling.

North Vancouver
Under $150

Just across Vancouver Harbour from downtown, **Grouse Inn** (1633 Capilano Rd., 604/988-7101, www.grouseinn.com, $105-225) is, like this North Vancouver neighborhood, a lot quieter. Its position near Highway 1 and Capilano Road gives travelers quick access to suspension-bridge or skiing day trips and lets anyone skip some traffic on the way to Whistler or the Victoria ferry at Horseshoe Bay. Standard rooms are clean but with few frills, and suites with sofa beds and kitchens are appealing to families.

Over $250
The **Pinnacle Hotel at the Pier** (138 Victory Ship Way, 604/986-7437, www.pinnaclepierhotel.com, $259-439) prominently faces downtown Vancouver, but you won't envy those across the harbor. Rooms have crisp linens, marble bathrooms, and cushy robes; the gym facilities include a swimming pool with a water view. The **Lobby Restaurant** (604/973-8000, www.pinnaclepierhotel.com, 6:30am-10pm Mon.-Fri., 7am-10pm Sat.-Sun., $8-16 breakfast, $9-19 lunch, $16-34 dinner) serves afternoon tea, complete with double Devonshire cream and finger sandwiches. And if all the peace and quiet is too much to bear, downtown is just a SeaBus ride away, as the passenger ferry docks nearby.

Information and Services

Visitor Information
Located just across from Canada Place's big white sails, **Tourism Vancouver Visitor Centre** (200 Burrard St., 604/683-2000, www.tourismvancouver.com, 9am-5pm daily) is staffed with city experts who speak multiple languages and can hand out free maps and sightseeing ideas. The center is also where you can buy half-price theatre and sports tickets from Tickets Tonight (www.ticketstonight.ca), a vendor for reduced-price same-day tickets.

Library Square, home of the **Vancouver Public Library** (350 W Georgia St., 604/331-3603, www.vpl.ca, 10am-9pm Mon.-Thurs., 10am-6pm Fri.-Sat., 11am-6pm Sun.), is an entire block in downtown Vancouver. The library has the look of a Roman coliseum, with a curved concourse topped with a roof of glass surrounding one side of the building. Inside, the library offers public lockers and computers with Internet access.

Media and Communications
The **Vancouver Sun** (www.vancouversun.com) broadsheet newspaper is a century old and provides daily news, sports, lifestyle, and arts coverage, but it isn't published on Sundays. It can be purchased from newsstands or newspaper boxes. Two free papers, **Metro** (www.metronews.ca) and **24H** (http://vancouver.24hrs.ca) are available on weekdays, often in boxes near transit stops. They cover news and arts and are meant to be read on a short commute.

For an alternative look at arts and culture, the weekly **Georgia Straight** (www.straight.com) is available in street boxes and has listings for live music along with political and lifestyle stories. The award-winning paper has been in existence since the counterculture 1960s and is proud of its history of being raided by police and hiring Bob Geldof.

Services
The Vancouver **Main Post Office Retail Location** (495 W Georgia St., 866/607-6301, www.canadapost.ca, 9am-4pm Mon.-Fri.) offers stamps and package services.

There are no lockers at the Pacific Central Station, where Greyhound and Amtrak routes depart, but there is a baggage storage check. **C & N Backpackers Hostel** (927 Main St., 604/682-2441, www.cnnbackpackers.com), across the street, may take same-day baggage storage for a fee if they have room.

For urgent health care in the case of a nonemergency, try **Crossroad Clinics Vancouver** (507 W Broadway, 604/568-7229, www.crwalkin.com), though you may have to check if they accept citizens of other countries. In an emergency, call 911 or head to the emergency room at **St. Paul's Hospital** (1081 Burrard St., 604/682-2344, www.providencehealthcare.org).

Getting Around

Vancouver's downtown core is mostly walkable, and taxis are easy to find. The SkyTrain is less useful for tourists, but some trips can be simplified with the light rail trains. Visitors to Vancouver will best experience the city by foot or, for the slightly more daring, on a bike.

Car

Downtown Vancouver can be tricky to navigate because many streets are one-way and lanes through Stanley Park change direction according to the time of day. **Parking** downtown is also a challenge as parking meters accept both coins and credit cards and are connected to a pay-by-phone app (604/909-7275, http://vancouver.ca). Parking rates are $1-6 per hour and active 9am-10pm daily, and rates can change throughout the day. Parking on Granville Island can also be difficult, but some free spots can be used for up to three hours and pay lots offer rates from $3.50 per hour.

Vancouver's streets are crowded during **rush hour** (7am-9am and 4pm-6pm). Especially impacted are the Lions Gate Bridge, which connects Stanley Park and downtown to North Vancouver, and Highway 1, which runs east to west through North Vancouver.

Vancouver has no **toll roads,** but drivers looking to bypass downtown Vancouver on a trip from the U.S. border to Whistler should be aware that the Port Mann Bridge from Coquitlam to Surrey on Highway 1 requires a $3.15 toll for cars (plus an extra fee for vehicles not preregistered with the province's fee system). Drivers in Canada must have a valid driver's license from their home country (or an International Driving Permit for longer periods) and carry insurance.

Car Rental

A number of car rental companies, including **Avis** (604/606-2847, www.avis.

ca) and **Budget** (604/668-7000, www.budget.com), have rental facilities on the ground floor of Vancouver International Airport (3211 Grant McConachie Way, Richmond, 604/207-7077, www.yvr.ca). In downtown Vancouver, car rentals are at **Hertz Rent a Car** (1270 Granville St., 604/606-4711, http://hertz.com) and **Thrifty Car Rental** (413 Seymour St., 604/606-1666, http://thrifty.com). Or try a new kind of car share, **car2go** (855/454-1002, http://vancouver.car2go.com), where very small cars are rented by the minute (gas included) and can be picked up on the streets around the city or at the airport. Advance registration is required because users get a card that opens and activates their rental car.

Taxi

Don't rely on hailing a cab in Vancouver when you need one. Instead, call ahead to **Yellow Cab** (604/681-1111, www.yellowcabonline.com) or **MacLure's Cabs** (604/831-1111, www.maclurescabs.ca). Cabs are usually hybrid vehicles, and all drivers accept credit cards. Rates are $1.84 per kilometer, with an initial $3.20 fee.

RV

If driving an RV into Vancouver, head to West Vancouver's **Capilano River RV Park** (295 Tomahawk Ave., 604/987-4722, www.capilanoriverrvpark.com, $55-82), which has an outdoor pool and hot tub, plus laundry, a rec room, and Wi-Fi throughout the property. It's located just past the Lions Gate Bridge with easy access to both downtown Vancouver and the Capilano Suspension Bridge.

RV rentals are available from **CanaDream** (8223 92 St., Delta, 604/940-2171, www.canadream.com), a $42 cab ride from the airport in the town of Delta. Van campers and motorhomes that can hold up to six people are also available. In the town of Richmond, head to **Westcoast Mountain Campers** (150-11800 Voyageur Way, Richmond, 604/279-0550, www.

wcmcampers.com), which has "vanconversion" rides and motorhomes, and offers transfers from the airport.

Public Transit

Public transportation is operated through **TransLink** (604/953-3333, www.translink.ca) and includes bus, ferry, and light rail options. The bus system, which includes 12 NightBus routes, covers most of the city. The **SeaBus** is a passenger ferry that crosses from downtown to North Vancouver. The **SkyTrain** has three lines, including one that travels from downtown to the airport. Fares on the bus and train are determined by travel zones; there are three within the greater Vancouver area, though single-zone prices apply after 6:30pm everyday and all day on Saturdays and Sundays.

Within the downtown core, you'll only pay single-zone fares ($2.85 adults, $1.80 children 5-13 and seniors). To get to the airport from downtown requires a two-zone fare ($4.10 adults, $2.80 children and seniors). Buses require exact fare in cash. SeaBus and SkyTrain stations have vending machines. Compass Cards can be purchased at London Drug stores or SkyTrain and SeaBus stations, and can be pre-loaded with money. Day passes are also available for $10 ($7.75 for children and seniors) and are good across any TransLink transportation.

Victoria

With its stately old hotels and Parliament Buildings, Vancouver Island's little city may be a dead ringer for Britain, but it's no mere copycat—it's a bustling New World gem.

Vancouver

BC
CAN
USA
WA

70 MI / 113 KM
3 HOURS

★ VICTORIA

26 MI / 42 KM
1.5 HOURS

Port
Angeles

107 MI / 172 KM
3 HOURS

Olympic
National
Park

Seattle

Victoria

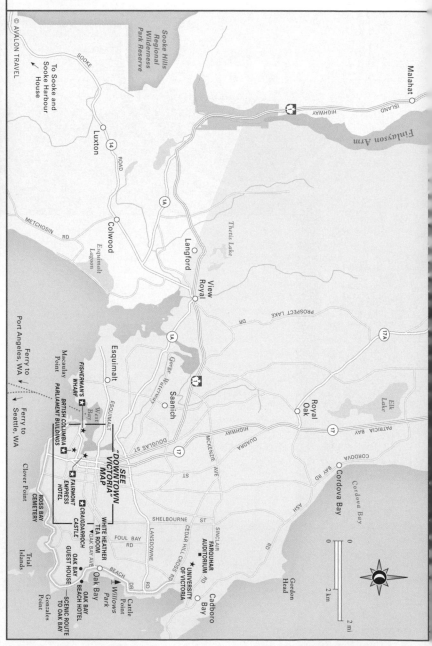

© AVALON TRAVEL

Sooke Hills Regional Wilderness Park Reserve

To Sooke and Sooke Harbour House

Malahat

Finlayson Arm

ISLAND HIGHWAY

Luxton

SOOKE ROAD

14

14

METCHOSIN RD

Colwood

Langford

View Royal

Thetis Lake

PROSPECT LAKE DR

Esquimalt Lagoon

1A

17A

Elk Lake

Royal Oak

17

PATRICIA BAY

Ferry to Port Angeles, WA

Ferry to Seattle, WA

Macaulay Point

FISHERMAN'S WHARF

BRITISH COLUMBIA PARLIAMENT BUILDINGS

West Bay

Esquimalt

Saanich

ESQUIMALT

Gorge Waterway

DOUGLAS ST

17

McKENZIE AVE

QUADRA ST

CORDOVA

BAY RD

ASH

Cordova Bay

Cordova Bay

Clover Point

ROSS BAY CEMETERY

FAIRMONT EMPRESS HOTEL

"SEE DOWNTOWN VICTORIA" MAP

ST

SHELBOURNE ST

SINCLAIR RD

RD

Gordon Head

CRAIGDARROCH CASTLE

WHITE HEATHER TEA ROOM

OAK BAY AVE

FOUL BAY RD

LANSDOWNE

CEDAR HILL CROSS RD

FARQUHAR AUDITORIUM

UNIVERSITY OF VICTORIA

Cattle Point

Trial Islands

OAK BAY GUEST HOUSE

BEACH

DR

Willows Park

Oak Bay

OAK BAY BEACH HOTEL

SCENIC ROUTE TO OAK BAY

Cadboro Bay

Gonzales Point

0

0

2 km

2 mi

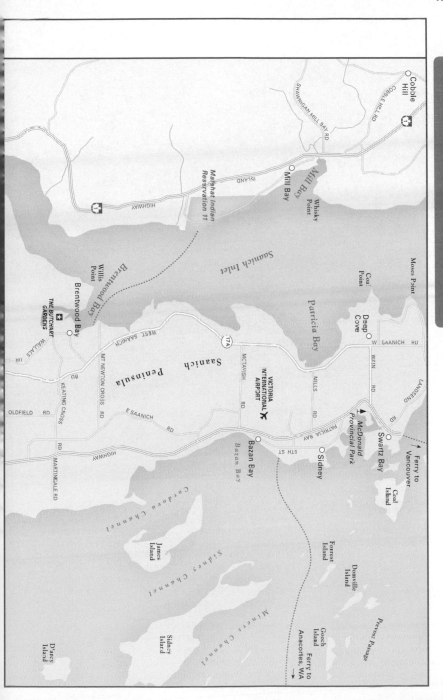

Highlights

★ **Fairmont Empress Hotel:** This old castle of a hotel, located in the center of downtown, is home to a tea service that's worth raising a pinky (page 130).

★ **Fisherman's Wharf:** The wharf's quaint floating homes provide a backdrop to waterfront food stands and great people- and wildlife-watching (page 131).

★ **The Butchart Gardens:** An old quarry was transformed into a world-class garden, and the resulting grounds take hours to fully appreciate (page 133).

★ **British Columbia Parliament Buildings:** Victoria's governmental buildings are one of the city's best architectural displays (page 130).

★ **Craigdarroch Castle:** The home of an industrial baron is now a historical site with dozens of original stained-glass windows (page 132).

The city of Victoria is located at the very southeastern tip of Vancouver Island, a 280-mile bean-shaped landmass of small towns, pointed peaks, and rugged coastline.

Victoria is right across from Washington State's San Juan Island chain and is almost as close to Seattle as it is to Vancouver, but in truth the waterways have provided such a barrier to both that the city has grown its own unique character. The old-world architecture and afternoon tea tradition blends with a bustling harbor and windswept views. Visitors continue to squeeze themselves down narrow Fan Tan Alley in what was once North America's biggest Chinatown.

Although native Canadian tribes have lived in the area for centuries, Victoria's recent history began in 1843 when it became a Hudson's Bay Company trading post, grew as a port during the Fraser Valley gold rush on the mainland, and then gained an international flavor from its position as a busy seaport. As the province of British Columbia was formed, it was named the provincial capital.

As travel by sea diminished in the 20th century, the city of Victoria has lagged behind Vancouver when it comes to skyscrapers, keeping it a smaller, more historical city. Big mansions in Oak Bay and Rockland hark back to the city's boom years. A naval base, university, and fishing fleet regularly infuse the city with new influences. Float planes land every few minutes while ferries connect it to both the United States and the global hub of Vancouver.

And no matter how chilly it gets, there's always a hot cup of tea waiting.

Getting to Victoria

From Seattle

Seaplane

There's no way around it—getting to Victoria takes a while. The fastest route is by seaplane, at less than an hour from Seattle's Lake Union right to Victoria's Inner Harbour on **Kenmore Air** (866/435-9524, www.kenmoreair.com, $155-165). International customs are performed on the Canadian side, where there are none of the long lines that clog the highway border crossings and the large airport passport control. Though some Kenmore flights are seasonal, the Seattle-to-Victoria route is year-round, and despite the planes being small, they can fly through almost all weather, save extreme fog.

Departures from Seattle leave from the Kenmore terminals on Lake Washington (6321 NE 175th St., Kenmore) and Lake Union (950 Westlake Ave. N), in the South Lake Union neighborhood right next to the Museum of History and Industry. The trip includes spectacular vistas of Puget Sound and its wooded islands from above. The pilot may even point out specific towns, mountains, and islands during the flight; ask to sit in the front seat for the best views.

Ferry

The **Victoria Clipper** (800/888-2535, www.clippervacations.com, $95-109 adults, $47.50-54.50 children) is a passenger-only ferry that leaves from downtown Seattle and takes about three hours to reach the terminal in Victoria (254 Belleville St.). The ferry terminal is located on the south side of the Inner Harbour, between the Black Ball Ferry Terminal and Laurel Point Park, and is within easy walking distance of many hotels, including the central Fairmont Empress Hotel, and the Parliament Buildings. Ferry service between Seattle

Best Accommodations

★ **Inn at Laurel Point:** Tucked out of the way and yet still so convenient, the waterfront hotel is a getaway within a vacation town (page 139).

★ **The Magnolia Hotel and Spa:** A modern high-end boutique hotel makes new history rather than relying on an old reputation (page 140).

★ **Fairmont Empress Hotel:** This is one of Canada's classic hotels, still regal in her room presentation and tea service (page 140).

★ **Oak Bay Beach Hotel:** In a not-so-distant neighborhood, a classy old property with ageless glamour beckons (page 141).

and Victoria runs year-round, with 1-2 ferries daily (though occasional blackout dates occur). The views from the boat as it passes through the San Juan Islands are gorgeous. The ride can double as a whale-watching trip when Puget Sound's resident and visiting orcas are visible.

Car Ferry

To take a car from Seattle via a single ferry, there is one option. About 80 miles north of Seattle, the **Washington State Ferry** (888/808-7977, www.wsdot.com/ferries, adults US$19.45, US$9.70 seniors and children, US$54.20-67 vehicle and driver plus surcharge for larger vehicles) is a car ferry that departs from the Anacortes ferry dock for Sidney, BC, 25 kilometers (15.5 miles) north of Victoria. The ferry can take almost three hours to reach Sidney, and not every departure goes all the way to Canada. Besides, it may make as little as one trip a day in the off-season between October and April. International customs is on the Canadian end and can add time to the trip. To get there, drive north on I-5 to exit 230 in Burlington, and then follow Highway 20 to the Anacortes ferry dock, a drive of about an hour and a half. Between the drive and the ferry, your total travel time could be almost five hours. Advance reservations are recommended.

A two-ferry trip involves taking the Washington State Ferry across Puget Sound to the Olympic Peninsula.

From the Olympic Peninsula

From the Kingston ferry dock, where the Edmonds-Kingston ferry arrives, follow Highway 104 across Hood Canal to U.S. 101, about 25 miles total, and then follow U.S. 101 for about 50 miles to Port Angeles. In Port Angeles, head to the ferry dock (101 E Railroad Ave.) for the **Black Ball Ferry** (888/993-3779, www.cohoferry.com, $64 for car and passenger) to Victoria, about a 90-minute ride. The ferry docks right in the Inner Harbour. Reservations are advised and start at $11.

From Vancouver

Two vehicle ferries run between the greater Vancouver area and the Victoria end of Vancouver Island. Reservations are recommended for both routes. The **B.C. Ferry** (888/223-3779, www.bcferries.com, $17.20 adults, $8.60 children 5-12, children under 5 free, $57.50 vehicles, surcharges for fuel and large vehicles) departs Tsawwassen (1 Ferry Causeway, Delta), south of Vancouver, arriving in Swartz Bay north of Victoria. The ferry crossing is about 90 minutes. From Swartz Bay, follow Highway 17 south for 32 kilometers (20 miles) to reach Victoria. Ferry frequency can range from 8 crossings a day to as many as 16.

Another **B.C. Ferry** (888/223-3779, www.bcferries.com, $17.20 adults, $8.60 children 5-12, children under 5 free, $57.50 vehicles, surcharges for fuel and large vehicles) departs from Horseshoe Bay (6750 Keith Rd., West Vancouver),

Best Restaurants

★ **10 Acres:** Everything's local at a farm-to-fork eatery that grows much of its own food (page 136).

★ **Red Fish Blue Fish:** Sure you can eat fish out of an old shipping container, at least when it's from the city's best takeout spot (page 137).

★ **Il Terrazzo Ristorante:** Even if it isn't a special occasion, the brick fireplaces and delectable Italian food by candlelight makes the meal feel notable (page 138).

about 20 kilometers (12 miles) north of downtown Vancouver. The ferry arrives in the town of Nanaimo on Vancouver Island, and the trip takes about 1.7 hours. From Nanaimo, follow Canada Highway 1 south for 115 kilometers (71 miles) to reach Victoria. Ferries run 7-12 times daily in each direction.

Sights

With so much history in every corner of this small city, it's hard to imagine that there's room to make more. The British-inspired architecture and culture is a big draw, but nature gets its day with a famous garden and a bustling harbor.

Downtown
Victoria Harbour

Although First Nations people first used the area for winter villages, **Victoria Harbour** (www.victoriaharbour.org) is now a bustling recreation and business center, with float planes landing in the calm waters that the Hudson's Bay Company found ideal for its Pacific Northwest headquarters. It was the ideal spot for ships to bring supplies when gold prospectors came to Vancouver Island on their way to the Fraser River Valley gold rush. Later, elegant passenger liners departed from Victoria to head across the Pacific. At times it has been a shipbuilding and fishing hub (and both businesses remain active), but now tourism plays a major role. Tiny **Victoria Harbour Ferry**

boats (www.victoriaharbourferry.com) carry passengers across the water, dodging the planes and whale-watching boats, the car ferry from Port Angeles, and the speed passenger ferry from Seattle. The area right in front of the Parliament Buildings and Fairmont Empress Hotel has a tiered walkway, often home to or tisan vendors and buskers—plus the three-sided harbor is one of the most picturesque sights in town.

Royal BC Museum

The building that houses **Royal BC Museum** (675 Belleville St., 250/356-7226, www.royalbcmuseum.bc.ca, 10am-5pm Sun.-Thurs., 10am-10pm Fri.-Sat. summer; 10am-5pm daily winter, $22 adults, $16 seniors, students, and children 6-18, children under 6 free) itself may not have the classic grandeur of the buildings that surround it, but the 1960s-built complex holds impressively ancient artifacts, representing both Vancouver Island's human and natural history. Outside are footprints from a hadrosaur and carnosaur, cast from the original dinosaur impressions in the Peace River Canyon. The 90-foot tower nearby is the **Netherlands Carillon,** whose 62 bells are played live every Sunday by the Provincial Carillonneur.

Inside, the BC Archives hold 200 years of the country's history. In the Royal BC Museum proper, a natural history gallery includes exhibits on the coastal forest, the nearby Fraser River delta, and a giant ice age mammoth. A domed room devoted to

Downtown Victoria

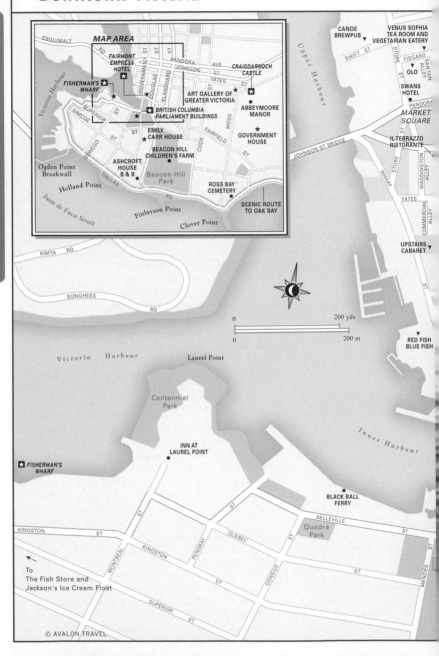

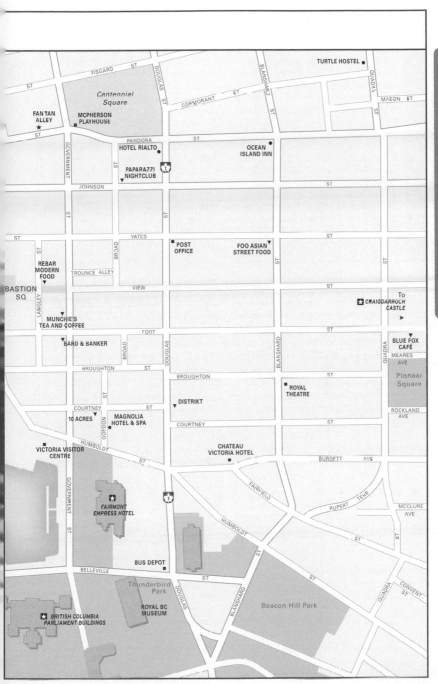

One Day in Victoria

Wake up in one of the city's quaint bed-and-breakfasts, like **Abbeymoore Manor** (page 141), to get a fresh, home-made meal, or grab a bite at the **Blue Fox Cafe** (page 136). Start a day of history at the **Royal BC Museum** (page 127) and peruse the Haida carvings inside. Then walk west on Belleville Street to consider the city's architectural and governmental history during a free tour at the **British Columbia Parliament Buildings** (page 130).

Head across the street for the Afternoon Tea of cucumber sandwiches and scones at the **Fairmont Empress Hotel** (page 130). From the hotel, you can board a shuttle bus for **The Butchart Gardens** (page 133), 35 minutes north of downtown Victoria. Or it's just a 30-minute walk east along Fort Street to **Craigdarroch Castle** (page 132), where you can revel in the city's posh history.

Return downtown and head north up Government Street to the city's old Chinatown. Slip down super-skinny **Fan Tan Alley** (page 132) and imagine life when opium dens instead of clothing stores lined the passageway.

End the day with an Italian meal around the corner at stately **Il Terrazzo Ristorante** (page 138) before strolling the Inner Harbour again at night to see lights reflecting off the water.

---

climate change has computers modeling future scenarios, allowing you to choose your own adventure (or apocalypse). One floor up, the human history gallery holds a hall of totem poles and a collection of Haida carvings in argillite, a black shale found throughout the Haida Gwaii region. More modern exhibits show off a water wheel and cannery replica. Because the museum has so little room for its extensive collection—only 0.01 percent is on display—it hopes to expand in coming years. Visiting exhibitions are devoted to historical and artistic topics, sometimes premiering here before traveling across Canada or internationally.

The museum also boasts the largest IMAX screen in the province, showing educational films and Hollywood flicks on an 85-foot-wide screen.

★ Fairmont Empress Hotel

You don't have to stay at the **Fairmont Empress Hotel** (721 Government St., 800/441-1414, www.fairmont.com) to be impressed by Victoria's centerpiece. More than 800 people a day enter to enjoy Afternoon Tea at the **Lobby Lounge** (11am-6pm daily, $75), a tradition that requires both a reservation and a "casually elegant" dress code. Originally opened in 1908 as the Canadian Pacific Railway's Empress Hotel, it was almost torn down in 1965, when a campaign called "Operation Teacup" saved the hotel with a $4 million renovation. Notable guests have included celebrities, a few ghosts (allegedly, of course), and royals such as King George VI and Queen Elizabeth II.

The hotel has an artist in residence, whose pieces hang in the upper lobby and who often chats with visitors to the gallery. The lobby's design took its inspiration from the hotel's trademark William Edwards china (also sold in the lobby gift shop with the signature Empress Tea blend).

★ British Columbia Parliament Buildings

The **British Columbia Parliament Buildings** (501 Belleville St., 250/387-3046, www.leg.bc.ca, tours 9am-5pm daily summer, 9am-5pm Mon.-Fri. fall-spring, self-guided tours 8:30am-4:30pm Mon.-Fri.) are a reminder that Vancouver may have overtaken Victoria as western Canada's biggest city, but this is still the capital of British Columbia. The blue-domed buildings were designed in the late 19th century by a 25-year-old unknown named Francis Rattenbury. After entering a design competition using a pseudonym, he would go on to design major western Canadian Pacific Railway hotels, including the Empress Hotel and the courthouse that later became the Vancouver Art Gallery. (Rattenbury is a local legend who also honeymooned on the Yukon Gold Rush and died at the hands of his wife's lover.)

The Parliament Buildings were largely made from local rock, brick, and wood. Free tours are held daily in the summer and on weekdays the rest of the year; they depart hourly and are led in both English and French. Besides hearing about the rotunda and statues, guides explain the parliamentary system of government to visitors unfamiliar with its quirks. Costumed actors are sometimes present to supplement the experience (and make for good photo opportunities). At night, more than 3,000 bulbs illuminate the buildings and grounds.

★ Fisherman's Wharf

The **Fisherman's Wharf** (Dallas Rd. and Erie St., 250/383-8326, www.fishermanswharfvictoria.com) area just west of the Inner Harbour isn't the collection of fishing vessels you might expect. Instead, you'll likely find yourself fantasy househunting the floating homes that line the docks. These multicolored dwellings have all the design flair of a landed Craftsman or cottage home, including balconies, roof decks, and landscaping, but with the soothing bob of water as a foundation. Otters and harbor seals are frequent neighborhood visitors.

Several snack joints sell food, including **The Fish Store** (205/383-6462, www.floatingfishstore.com, 11am-9pm daily), **Jackson's Ice Cream Float** (250/858-0052, http://jacksonsicecreamvictoria.com, 11am-dark daily), and **Barb's Fish**

from top to bottom: Fairmont Empress Hotel; Fisherman's Wharf; Craigdarroch Castle.

and Chips (250/384-6515, http://barbsfishandchips.com, 11am-dark daily). Public picnic tables line the docks, and geese and other waterfowl tend to gather, expecting food scraps from the dining throngs.

Emily Carr House

Even though the two-story **Emily Carr House** (207 Government St., 250/383-5843, www.emilycarr.com, 11am-4pm Tues.-Sat., May-Sept., $6.75 adults, $5.75 seniors and students, $4.50 children 6-18, children under 6 free) has all the delicacy of a dollhouse, it was the home of a writer and artist with life-sized impact. Emily Carr, born in 1871, grew up in this house back when it was a farm fairly removed from town. Carr went on to create impressionist paintings depicting First Nations subjects. Her book *Klee Wyck* is an autobiographic collection of stories about Carr and First Nations people. Original artifacts are gathered in one room, and the rest is restored with period-specific accuracy. The house is hung with Carr's work, but also serves as a gallery for new art exhibitions. Two cats, Misty and Whiskers, roam the grounds.

Fan Tan Alley

In Canada's oldest Chinatown, **Fan Tan Alley** (Fisgard St., between Stone St. and Government St.) is possibly the narrowest attraction in the province (in fact, it claims to be the narrowest street in the country). The ultrathin passage makes up in decoration what it lacks in width—old brick walls give way to doors and windows, and signs point to a barber shop and gift stores.

Beacon Hill Park

At one time, **Beacon Hill Park** (100 Cook St., 250/361-0600, www.beaconhillpark. ca) was home to a series of beacons that warned sailors when they were maneuvering onto a dangerous sea ledge. Today the park has trails and ponds and is home to a number of waterfowl including herons and peacocks. It has a putting green

and a children's petting zoo, the **Beacon Hill Children's Farm** (250/381-2532, http://beaconhillchildrensfarm.ca, 10am-5pm daily), which has goat stampedes twice a day. A totem pole towers more than 120 feet high, and in the summer live concerts take place in the park's band shell.

Greater Victoria

The fancy neighborhood of Rockland lies east of the Inner Harbour and southeast of downtown and used to be where the city's richest lived. The architecture today is evidence of the money they had to spend on their mansions. Farther afield is the Saanich Peninsula (the triangle-shaped outcropping of Vancouver Island that has Victoria at its base) with a handful of attractions for visitors, most notably the famous Butchart Gardens.

★ Craigdarroch Castle

No, you've not stumbled into Scotland. **Craigdarroch Castle** (1050 Joan Crescent, Rockland, 250/592-5323, www.thecastle.ca, 9am-7pm daily summer, 10am-4:30pm daily fall-spring, $14.25 adults, $13.25 seniors, $9.25 students 13 and older, $5 children 6-12, children under 6 free) may be Scottish in style, but it's a Canadian "bonanza castle" built in the late 1800s by industrial baron Robert Dunsmuir. The estate has a colorful history of ownership; it was once sold in a raffle and later turned into a military hospital in World War I. Re-creations of its most vital era depend on a single photograph left from the early twentieth century. Visitors are asked to use an automatic shoe cleaner before exploring the four floors of renovated interiors, including a giant collection of 32 original stained-glass windows. The space has appeared in a number of movies, and the live arts use it as a stage in site-specific theatrical events.

Art Gallery of Greater Victoria

The house that holds the **Art Gallery of Greater Victoria** (1040 Moss St.,

Rockland, 250/384-4171, www.aggv. ca, 10am-5pm Tues.-Wed. and Fri.-Sat., 10am-9pm Thurs., $13 adults, $11 students and seniors, $2.50 children 6-17, children under 6 free) is as much a work of art as everything inside. Built in 1889, the mansion was owned by the Spencer family, who needed not one, but two tennis courts. It now houses art collections focusing on Canadian and Asian artists, with permanent displays of books and paintings from Emily Carr. The Asian garden includes a Ming dynasty bell that was a gift to the city in 1903. Drop-in tours are free with admission and are held most weekends.

★ The Butchart Gardens

It's hard to imagine something as beautiful as **The Butchart Gardens** (800 Benvenuto Ave., Brentwood Bay, 250/652-4422, www.butchartgardens.com, daily: 9am-4pm Mar. and Oct., 9am-5pm Apr.-May, 8:45am-6pm June 1-15, 8:45am-10pm June 15-Sept. 2, 8:45am-9pm Sept. 3-15, 8:45am-5pm Sept. 16-30, 9am-3:30pm Nov. and Jan. 7-Feb., 9am-10pm Dec. 1-Jan. 6; $18.35-32.60 adults, $9.20-16.30 children 13-17, $2-3 children 5-12) started as an industrial limestone quarry and cement plant. After the deposits were taken from the area about 24 kilometers (15 miles) north of Victoria, the wife of the quarry owner, Jennie Butchart, brought in soil and turned it into the Sunken Garden. Later she added an Italian, Japanese, Mediterranean, and Rose Garden.

The **Rose Carousel** ($2) sits next to the **Concert Lawn,** which hosts open-air theater and music concerts (June-Sept.) as well as fireworks (Sat. evenings) in summer. In **Butchart Cove,** small boats (the *R.P.* and *Jennie B.* are named for the Butcharts) depart for **tours** ($11.80-18.80) of Tod Inlet. Winter brings fewer blooms but outdoor ice-skating ($3-5) and Christmas displays. The Butchart manor houses the **Coffee Shop** ($13-18), which offers to-go options, and the

Dining Room Restaurant (250/652-4422, ext. 320), which serves an afternoon tea ($35.75), lunch ($19-19), and dinner ($29-41).

To reach The Butchart Gardens from Victoria, take Highway 17 north about 16 kilometers (10 miles), and then take a left at exit 18 onto Keating X Road. Keating X Road becomes Benvenuto Avenue, which leads into The Butchart Gardens. The drive can take up to half an hour. A **BC Transit** bus (250/382-6161, www.bctransit.com, $2.50) departs Victoria at Blanshard Street and Fairfield Road, just east of the Inner Harbour. Bus packages from **CVS Tours** (877/578-5552, www.cvstours.com, $76.20 adults, $73.20 seniors, $55.24 children 12-17, $29.53 children 5-12, children under 5 free) include free hotel pickup, admission to the gardens, and narration from a guide during the bus trip, but you'll be on your own in the gardens; a visit to Victoria Butterfly Gardens follows.

To combine the gardens with something a bit more nautical, **Prince of Whales Whale Watching** (888/383-4884, princeofwhales.com/victoria-tours/the-whales-gardens, $150 adults, $125 youth 13-17, $100 children 5-12, children under 5 free) has a five-hour trip that goes in search of the orca whales that live nearby before docking at the Butchart private dock and offering guests a chance to wander the gardens.

Entertainment and Events

Nightlife

The **Bard & Banker** (1022 Government St., 250/953-9993, www.bardandbanker. com, 11am-1am daily) looks like a posh bank on the outside. The name references Robert Service, a famous Canadian poet who once worked in the building as a bank teller. Inside are five fireplaces, a

50-foot polished bar, a second-level bar, two outdoor patios, and 30 beers on tap. (A fancy beverage system means the wine is also on tap.) The bar hosts live music every night and is incredibly popular; luckily there's enough square footage to handle all the comers.

Although located on the Inner Harbour, **Spinnakers Brewpub** (308 Catherine St., 877/838-2739, www.spinnakers.com, 8am-11pm daily) is out of the way on the north shore. The oldest brewpub in Canada, it serves its own ales and has a daily cask open during the week. The facility also makes malt vinegar.

The patio at **CANOE Brewpub** (450 Swift St., 250/361-1940, 11:30am-11pm Sun.-Wed., 11:30am-midnight Thurs., 11:30am-1am Fri.-Sat.) has waterfront views, and inside there's live music three nights a week. There's no cover, free parking, and kids are welcome at the 1894 brick-lined building until 9pm. The beer is made in house, and tours of the brewery are available for $10, though it's probably best just to experience the local craftsmanship with a Witbier at an outdoor table.

Victoria isn't known for its raging dance scene, but the **Distrikt** (919 Douglas St., 250/383-7137, www.strathconahotel.com, 10pm-2am Fri.-Sat.), located in the Strathcona Hotel, means serious business—it's tucked into the basement and pushes the bottle service scene during custom light shows and guest DJs.

Meanwhile **Upstairs Cabaret** (15 Bastion Sq., 250/385-5483, upstairscabaret.ca, 11am-3am Tues.-Thurs., 10am-2am Fri.-Sat.) has a dance floor for Top 40 and hip-hop music, plus a stage for local DJs and live music on Thursday nights.

Best known for its cheap drinks, **Paparazzi Nightclub** (642 Johnson St., 250/388-0505, www.paparazzinightclub.com, 4pm-2am daily) is gay friendly and popular by virtue of having little competition. Monday is karaoke night.

The Arts

The 1914 **McPherson Playhouse** (3 Centennial Sq., 888/717-6121, www.rmts.bc.ca/mcpherson) hosts family and music concerts amid beautiful interiors that were refurbished in the mid-20th century. Larger and closer to the Inner Harbour, the older **Royal Theatre** (805 Broughton St., 888/717-6121, www.rmts.bc.ca/royaltheatre) was built in 1913 and is home to classical groups like the **Pacific Opera Victoria** (250/385-0222, http://pov.bc.ca) and the **Victoria Symphony** (250/385-6515, www.victoriasymphony.ca), which is almost as old as the theater. The orchestral group hosts the annual Victoria Symphony Splash in the Inner Harbour in the summer and also performs at the **UVic Farquhar Auditorium** (University Centre, University of Victoria, 250/721-8480, www.uvic.ca/auditorium).

Festivals and Events

As home of the country's oldest Chinatown, Victoria is the ideal place to celebrate **Chinese New Year** (Feb.). A parade typically winds its way through Chinatown's narrow streets while local venues hold music or performance events. And because it's Victoria, look for specials at Chinatown's teahouses—there's no occasion in town that can't be celebrated with tea.

The **Victoria Highland Games and Celtic Festival** (www.victoriahighlandgames.com, May) has been running for more than 150 years, most likely because the pastime of watching people throw heavy logs or play bagpipes while wearing a kilt is timeless. More than 25,000 people attend the Celtic culture fest, which also includes a tartan parade and a pub crawl.

After running for more than a quarter century, **Victoria Symphony Splash** (250/385-6515, www.victoriasymphony.ca, Aug.) has established itself as a cornerstone summer event in town. On an August evening, the Victoria Symphony plays on a floating stage in the Inner Harbour, allowing attendees to sit around the harbor or listen from boats and kayaks on the water.

The midsummer **Victoria Fringe Theatre Festival** (250/590-6291, www.victoriafringe.com, Aug.-Sept.) turns the city into a stage, putting on alternative theater productions. Shows aren't judged, and participating theaters are picked by lottery. Plus, tickets are cheap and revenue goes back to the artists.

Originally **Art of the Cocktail** (250/389-0444, www.artofthecocktail.ca, Oct.) was meant to simply support the Victoria Film Festival, but it grew into an October event unto itself, a three-day series of tastings, demonstrations, workshops, and meals featuring craft mixology. The Grand Tasting includes dozens and dozens of spirits, and best cocktail awards are bestowed.

Now 10 years old, the music festival **Rifflandia** (778/433-4743, http://rifflandia.com, Aug.-Sept.) invites indie and quirky musical artists to a stadium in Victoria, featuring a nighttime festival called Electric Avenue.

Shopping

Books

The stately **Munro's Books** (1108 Government St., 250/382-2464, www.munrobooks.com, 9am-9pm Mon.-Wed., 9am 9:30pm Thurs.-Sat., 9:30am-6pm Sun.) has tons of literary cred, or at least literary adjacency—it was founded by the Nobel Prize-winning writer Alice Munro and her first husband. The neoclassical building that now holds the bookstore was originally owned by the Royal Bank of Canada and is a cathedral to books, with intricate, tall ceilings. After celebrating 50 years in business, the store is still going strong, though it hasn't been directly associated with Munro in decades.

Clothing and Accessories

The clothing sold at the flagship store for **Smoking Lily** (1713 Government St., 250/382-5459, www.smokinglily.com, 10am-6:30pm Mon.-Thurs. and Sat., 10am-7pm Fri., noon-5pm Sun.) is sewn and silk-screened locally, often with local materials. The store is located in a historical building it shares with a Buddhist temple. Items for sale include silk scarves, T-shirts, unique dresses, and handbags made from unusual materials like maps.

At one time you could purchase opium or gamble in the dens off Fan Tan Alley; now you can find Doc Martens and other punk fashions at **Heart's Content** (18 Fan Tan Alley, 250/380-1234, http://heartscontentvictoria.ca, 11am-5:30pm daily) or Buddhist dharma charms at **Whirled Arts** (3 Fan Tan Alley, 250/386-2787, 10am-6pm daily).

There's something about Victoria that encourages whimsy, so it's no wonder the impractical headwear at **Roberta's Hats** (1318 Government St., 250/384-2778, www.robertashats.com, 10am-5:30pm Mon.-Sat., 11am-5pm Sun.) are so popular. The cute shop carries everything from boaters to bowlers, and it can even suggest what to select based on your face and body shape.

Gourmet Goodies

Located in Chinatown, **Silk Road Tea** (1624 Government St., 250/382-0006, www.silkroadteastore.com, 10am-6pm Mon.-Wed., 10am-8pm Thurs.-Sat., 11am-5pm Sun.) goes further than the pastry-heavy afternoon tea rituals at nearby hotels and restaurants. The store sells Chinese tea blends and has a tea-tasting bar. The crisp, spacious destination is run by an owner who's been dubbed "Canada's Queen of Tea"—she even designed a teacup that won awards. Bath and body items are also for sale, and a spa is located in the store. Check the calendar for workshops, like the oh-so-educational free Sunday class on pairing tea with chocolate.

Sports and Recreation

Beaches

Although much of Victoria is on the water, there aren't many beaches. One exception is found in **Willows Beach** (Dalhousie St. and Beach Dr., www.oakbay.ca), which has a sandy beach on Oak Bay. It doesn't really have waves to speak of, just calm, lapping ripples in the very cold Haro Strait water. Changing rooms and picnic tables are available in the park, plus lawns and a children's play area. The neighborhood around the beach is residential, so the sand and walkway is often filled with locals.

Kayaking

Kelp Reef Kayaking Adventures (12 Erie St., 250/386-7333, www.kelpreef. com, $65-130) leads paddlers among the protected bays of Victoria or out of the Inner Harbour to visit kelp forests and view wildlife such as otters, herons, and eagles. Boats launch seasonally from Fisherman's Wharf, and trips depart in the morning, midday, or evening and last 2-3 hours. Morning trips include a picnic and the kayak-through snack options on Fisherman's Wharf.

Daily trips from **Victoria Kayak** (1006 Wharf St., 250/216-5646, www.victoriakayak.com, $59-149) explore the harbor, while the summer-sunset paddle ends at a pub for warm-up drinks. The outfitter also rents single and double kayaks (2 hours, $40-50), and the nighttime tour is ideal for spotting river otters.

Whale-Watching

Eagle Wing Tours (Fisherman's Wharf, 800/708-9488, www.eaglewingtours.com, $80-135) offers whale-watching tours that last 3-3.5 hours. The peak whale-watching season is May-October. An onboard naturalist will point out orcas and can sometimes even tell if they're from the resident killer whale pods that call the Strait of Juan de Fuca home. Bring warm clothing, binoculars, and sunscreen.

Food

The old Chinatown contributes a strong Asian culinary scene, while seafood is served up fast and fresh at Fisherman's Wharf.

Canadian

The bright colors of the **Blue Fox Cafe** (919 Fort St., 250/380-1683, www.thebluefoxcafe.com, 7:30am-4pm Mon.-Fri., 8am-3pm Sat.-Sun., $8-14) will wake you up if the menu doesn't—even the brick walls are covered in vivid art. The all-day breakfast is best paired with mango peach mimosas or the Bloody Caesar drink, a Canadian classic that's like a Bloody Mary made with Clamato juice. Sure, burgers, sandwiches, and other lunch items are on the menu, but it's hard to pass up the Moroccan chicken eggs Benedict or Apple Charlotte French Toast. While several Mexican-inspired dishes appear, the menu also has a touch of old Britain with bubble and squeak, a dish made with potato and vegetables.

The dishes at **Olo** (509 Fisgard St., 250/590-8795, www.olorestaurant.com, 5pm-10pm Sun.-Thurs., 5pm-11pm Fri.-Sat., $19-35) are aggressively local, and its name is too—it comes from the Chinook jargon, a language used by First Nations people. (Fittingly, it means "hungry.") The farm-to-table Canadian fare leans heavily on vegetables, and one of the two prix fixe options ($45-55) is all-vegetarian. Still, there's plenty of meat, including ling cod, duck, and chicken. The farmhouse-style decor gives the restaurant a relaxed vibe, but it's one of the better dinners in Victoria.

Local ingredients are aggressively promoted at ★ **10 Acres** (611 Courtney St., 250/220-8008, www.bonrouge.ca, 11am-midnight Sun.-Thurs., 11am-1am Fri.-Sat., $19-32), which has its own farm to supply seasonal produce. The restaurant has a heated courtyard with an outdoor fireplace and metal art hanging above the

The Tea Tradition

Tea isn't a drink in Victoria, it's a meal. Famously served at the Fairmont Empress Hotel, Afternoon Tea is very different from High Tea (a dinner meal for the working classes). The tradition was started by the Duchess of Bedford in the early 19th century as a filler meal between lunch and dinner, and it incorporated the invention by the Earl of Sandwich—a filling spread between two pieces of bread.

The **Fairmont Empress Afternoon Tea** (721 Government St., 800/441-1414, www.fairmont.com/empress-victoria, 11am-6pm daily, $75) is served in the Lobby Lounge, on tables made from the original wood floor, to almost 100,000 people per year. The pattern on the tea china was first used in Victoria during a visit by Queen Elizabeth. The tea itself is a proprietary blend that includes leaves from Kenya, Tanzania, South India, Assam, Sri Lanka, and China—and the experience comes with a free sample to take home. Bites come on a multilevel tray filled with cucumber sandwiches, scones, and shortbread. A dress code must be followed—hey, the waiters are wearing bow ties. Reservations for the mini-meal are recommended.

However, the Empress isn't the only tea game in town. **Murchie's Tea and Coffee** (1110 Government St., 250/383-3112, www.murchies.com, 7:30am-6pm Mon.-Sat., 8am-6pm Sun. $2-9) as a company dates back to 1894, but now has free wireless Internet and cheap scones. In Chinatown, **Venus Sophia Tea Room and Vegetarian Eatery** (540 Fisgard St., 250/590-3953, www.venussophia. com, 11am-6pm Wed.-Sun., $22-35) does a modern vegan or vegetarian twist on Afternoon Tea. **The White Heather Tea Room** (1885 Oak Bay Ave., 250/595-8020, www.whiteheather-tearoom.com, 10am-5pm Tues.-Sat., $23-68) in Oak Bay has sconewiches with pepper jelly and lots of homey charm. **The Butchart Gardens** (800 Benvenuto Ave., Brentwood Bay, 250/652-4422, www.butchartgardens. com, Apr.-Sept., $35.75) also offers a version.

diners, with rustic touches and wooden-block tables inside, a big change from when the place used to be painted red and called Bon Rouge. Daily lunch specials are often available, but all dishes usually feature something local, be it mussels or mushrooms. The free-range rotisserie chicken, served with pan-drip potatoes, is only offered during a short window in the dinner service.

Seafood

Try quoting some Dr. Seuss while you're in line at ★ **Red Fish Blue Fish** (1006 Wharf St., 250/298-6877, www.redfish-bluefish.com, 11am-9pm daily Feb.-Nov., $11-24), located in an old cargo container on a pier in the Inner Harbour. The fish-and-chip standbys are here in halibut, cod, or salmon, plus fish sandwiches like an "RFBF BLT" made with smoked albacore tuna belly and scallop burger. There's also spicy fish poutine and grilled oysters, and a number of creative sauces to flavor any dish. Counter seating is an option, but most people take food to go. Note that the restaurant operates seasonally, but if the weather's bad it may not open.

The Fish Store (1 Dallas Rd., 250/383-6462, www.floatingfishstore.com, 11am-9pm daily, $11-24) on Fisherman's Wharf is subject to the weather, which can affect its opening hours year-round. It processes fresh catch and will pack fresh seafood to go, but most people come for the ready-made food. The fish-and-chips come with homemade tartar sauce. Oysters come by the piece or by the dozen, fresh from local waters and a buck each in the late afternoon. Wait a little longer for steamed crab, which is picked from the live tank before being prepared. Around the Fisherman's Wharf area are picnic tables, shared by a few food stands, and geese and other waterfowl tend to gather, expecting food scraps from the dining throngs. Also try **Barb's Fish and Chips** (1 Dallas Rd., http://barbsfishandchips.com, 11am-dark daily Mar.-Oct., $11-24) for a classic take on one of the city's signature dishes: crisp-fried cod, sockeye, or halibut.

Asian

The theme at **Foo Food** (769 Yates St., 250/383-3111, www.foofood.ca, 11:30am-10pm Mon.-Sat., 11:30am-9pm Sun., $8-14) is "Asian street food," meaning it's inspired by a quick-serve stall despite being an actual brick-and-mortar restaurant. The chef once led the kitchen in Australia's Cambodian embassy and now pulls from around Southeast Asia and the subcontinent. The limited menu is printed on blackboards above the kitchen: banh mi, ramen soup, fried rice made with fresh pineapple, and butter chicken. Seating is on stools or available to go, and the Inner Harbour is not far for those who'd like to sit and watch the boats and seaplanes.

French

Though much of Victoria salutes the very British roots of British Columbia, plus the deep First Nations culture that formed the region, **Brasserie L'ecole** (1715 Government St., 250/475-6260, http://lecole.ca, 5:30pm-11pm Tues.-Sat., $18-38) connects to Canada's French heritage. Red walls surround an intimate dining room whose wall mirrors do little to expand the space; expect to be cozy. The food is flavorful and the menu crammed with classics like French onion soup, mussels in a thick broth, and duck confit. Lines can form for the candlelit tables—no reservations taken—but that just leaves more time to think up excuses to order the crème brûlée.

Italian

Access ★ **Il Terrazzo Ristorante** (555 Johnson St., 250/361-0028, www.

ilterrazzo.com, 11:30am-3pm and 5pm-9pm Mon.-Fri., 5pm-9pm Sat.-Sun., $16-42) from Waddington Alley downtown, and enter a covered courtyard that's more brick than anything else; it has six brick fireplaces around the dining area. The classic Northern Italian fare includes braised veal shank and a lamb dish, a wood oven roasts meats and pizza, and the pastas are homemade. The spot is incredibly popular, so the din of all the excited diners can be overwhelming, sometimes even ruining the romantic ambience.

Vegetarian

Inspired by a juice bar in Seattle, the chef behind **Rebar Modern Food** (50 Bastion Sq., 250/361-9223, www.rebarmodernfood.com, 11:30am-9pm Mon.-Fri., 9:30am-9pm Sat., 9:30am-8pm Sun., $13-21) is a full-fledged vegetarian restaurant with fresh salads and almond-vegetable burgers. A few fish-based dishes are served but no other meat, and several of the dishes are vegan. Juices and smoothies are made from local ingredients, including fruits and vegetables. The decor is aggressively funky, including an Elvis sculpture and copper jelly molds, and the walls are a stark chartreuse.

Accommodations

Downtown
Under $150
The cheerful, yellow house that holds **Turtle Hostel** (1608 Quadra St., 250/381-3210, www.turtlehostel.ca, $29-30 dorms, $38-62 private rooms) is several blocks inland from the Inner Harbour, but it's still walkable to Victoria's tourist attractions. Several small and midsized rooms have double beds, and dorm rooms have up to 10 bunks and bright murals on the walls. All share bathrooms. The hotel provides bed linens and towels. There's a fee for nearby parking.

Only a few blocks from Turtle Hostel

but a little closer to the water is **Ocean Island Inn Hostel** (791 Pandora Ave., 888/888-4180, www.oceanisland.com, $35-43 dorms, $54-73 rooms with shared bath, $125-140 rooms with private bath), located in a utilitarian but large historical building. The rooms have the usual bright-wall hostel cheeriness, and dorms are both co-ed and single sex. Private rooms are barely big enough for the double beds; others have a pair of bunk beds. The shared kitchen is open 24 hours, and it offers laundry facilities. The hostel is decorated in Indonesian art. The hostel's lounge offers live music, along with open mic and quiz nights.

The rooms at the **Ashcroft House Bed and Breakfast** (670 Battery St., 250/385-4632, www.ashcrofthousebandb.com, $129-199) are in an 1898 house built by a globe-trotting Brit—inside the hotel, look for a photo of him on an elephant. The five rooms, some with fireplaces, have some classic touches but mostly bright, modern decor; some even have stark yellow walls. Breakfast is a grand procession of fresh scones, crepes, omelets, and pancakes. The James Bay location is a short walk from the Inner Harbour, close to Beacon Hill Park and the waterfront right on the Strait of Juan de Fuca.

$150-250

The downtown **Hotel Rialto** (653 Pandora Ave., 250/383-4157, www.hotelrialto.ca, $189-249) has a slight Italian theme, with fresco walls and marble touches, but rooms are sleek and modern. Bathrooms have heated floors, and rooms include plush linens. Some rooms have street noise from busy Douglas Street. To encourage sustainable environmental practices, the hotel gives a $10 restaurant credit for giving up maid service during a stay.

The **Swans Hotel** (506 Pandora Ave., 250/361-3310, www.swanshotel.com, $145-255) has only 30 units, all with full kitchens and homey touches like full couches and houseplants. Outside the 1913 building, a former warehouse, it's just as green, with flower boxes lining the glassed-off sunroom and a roof terrace with more greenery overlooking the city. Some rooms are located directly above the 1st-floor pub—home to nightly live music—and are not for light sleepers; other units are two stories. Bigger rooms have two bedrooms, and the penthouse has three levels, six balconies, and a wood-burning fireplace. The property also holds a brewery, bistro, and beer and wine shop. The hotel's name, the story goes, comes from the building's former "ugly duckling" status before it emerged with all the hospitality businesses.

Not quite as castle-like as the Empress Hotel located just adjacent, **Chateau Victoria Hotel** (740 Burdett Ave., 250/382-4221, www.chateauvictoria. com, $219-305) still has a great central location. Standard "traditional" rooms are located on the lower floors and are adequate, but not luxurious. Suites feature balconies and multiple flat-screen TVs, and a few include kitchens complete with a stove and an oven. Not all rooms have spectacular views though—some simply overlook the parking lot. The in-house bar, **Clive's Classic Lounge** (250/361-5684, www.clivesclassiclounge. com, 11:30am-midnight Mon.-Wed., 11:30am-1am Thurs.-Fri., 5pm-1am Sat., 5pm-midnight Sun.), focuses on classic and creative cocktails. It earned a nomination for World's Best Hotel Bar from the drinking expo Tales of the Cocktail.

Over $250

The ★ **Inn at Laurel Point** (680 Montreal St., 250/386-8721, www.laurelpoint.com, $274-324) is not only located right on Victoria's Inner Harbour, it has its own tiny peninsula. Surrounded by Laurel Point Park, it's a 10-minute walk from the center of town and has a Japanese garden on the grounds—one that doesn't allow cell-phone use. The structure has two wings, the original Laurel wing of rooms with private balconies, and the newer Erickson wing with recently reno-vated suites. There's a small indoor pool and a collection of art pieces from Native American tribes and international cultures. The on-site restaurant, **Aura** (250/414-6739, www.aurarestaurant.ca, 7am-10pm daily) has a Pacific Rim menu, an outdoor patio and water views, and a monthly Sunday morning brunch with live music.

★ **The Magnolia Hotel and Spa** (623 Courtney St., 250/381-0999, www.magnoliahotel.com, $219-429) is a re-furbished deluxe hotel decked out in muted grays and creams. Some rooms have harbor views (as far across as the Parliament Buildings) and fireplaces or balconies. Bathrooms have big tubs and marble floors. The spacious on-site spa offers the usual massages, facials, and scrubs. The on-site **Catalano Restaurant & Cicchetti Bar** (250/480-1824, lunch and dinner daily, brunch Sat.-Sun.) has a Mediterranean angle and serves tapas-like dishes. All parking is valet, and

breakfast is included (both hot and cold items).

The ★ **Fairmont Empress Hotel** (721 Government St., 800/441-1414, www.fairmont.com, $499-899) is more than a fancy hotel—it's the center of Victoria. Opened in 1908 and designed by Francis Rattenbury, the same person behind the Parliament Buildings, it's where royalty stays when they visit British Columbia. The stone-and-brick structure is built in what's called Chateau style, and the steep roofs, turrets, gables, and ivy-colored exterior are certainly castle-like. A major renovation in the 1980s added an indoor swimming pool. Shortly after the hotel's centennial, honeybee hives were added to make honey that's served at the hotel's famous Afternoon Tea. The 477 rooms are all slightly different, owing to the age of the building and various re-models and additions. Rooms look out at the city, the harbor, or the Inner Harbour. Some furnishings are fussy—flowered curtains, antique-style furniture—but

Fairmont Empress Hotel

consistently high-end. The hotel has a spa as well as several restaurants, including **Q at the Empress** (6:30am-11am, 11:30am-2:30pm, 5:30pm-9:30pm) and the **Lobby Lounge** for tea (11am-6pm daily).

Greater Victoria
Under $150

Oak Bay, about 5 kilometers (3 miles) east of the Inner Harbour, is a quiet, mostly residential neighborhood with a few choice accommodations. The **Oak Bay Guest House** (1052 Newport Ave., Oak Bay, 250/598-3812, www.oakbayguesthouse.com, $109-210) has been a hotel of some kind since 1922. Some of the nine rooms have dated four-poster beds while others have more cozy flowered curtains and simple beds. Not all rooms have tubs, but all have some kind of private bathroom, even if it is located across the hall. The bed-and-breakfast is the only one in the area, and the owners like to compare their hotel to *Fawlty Towers*. Breakfasts are a three-course affair, and the guesthouse is walking distance from the short commercial strip in Oak Bay.

$150-250

Abbeymoore Manor (1470 Rockland Ave., Rockland, 250/370-1470, www.abbeymoore.com, $149-259) is a few kilometers from the Inner Harbour, but close to Craigdarroch Castle and across the street from public gardens and the lieutenant governor's mansion. The bed-and-breakfast has a large porch and 2nd-floor balcony. The 1912 house is decorated in classic Victorian style, but rooms have flat-screen TVs, cable, and DVDs. Some have fold-out couches. Gourmet breakfasts are served in a sunny dining room. Some rooms have claw-foot tubs, deluxe showerheads, or gas fireplaces.

Over $250

★ **Oak Bay Beach Hotel** (1175 Beach Dr., Oak Bay, 250/598-4556, www.oakbaybeachhotel.com, $312-869) is located in an area that used to be a seaside retreat and home to many Brits. The hotel overlooks the water, and a series of pools and hot tubs sit right next to the rocky shore. Some rooms have fireplaces, and all have oversized tubs and heated floors in the bathrooms. The vast on-site amenities include a spa offering diamond-dust facials and a Rolls Royce and driver available for pickups at the seaplane docks. This is the kind of hotel that can get you a tee time at an exclusive local course. The **Snug Pub** (11am-midnight Sun.-Wed., 11am-1am Thurs.-Sat.) serves beer and wine amid carefully salvaged wood beams and light fixtures, while the **David Foster Theatre** pairs dinner with a show ($30 theatre tickets support a local charitable foundation).

It's a 40-kilometer (25-mile) drive to **Sooke Harbour House** (528 Whiffin Spit Rd., Sooke, 250/642-3421, www.sookeharbourhouse.com, $329-525), located on the south shore of Vancouver Island. Rooms feature wood-burning fireplaces, jetted tubs, and private balconies or terraces; each comes complete with a complementary bottle of port. The hotel also has an art gallery, gardens filled with hundreds of edible plants, and a restaurant with a 2,000-bottle wine cellar. The views stretch across the strait to Washington State and the Olympic Mountains. The area is very quiet and secluded, even quainter than the town of Victoria.

Information and Services

Visitor Information

The **Victoria Visitor Centre** (812 Wharf St., 800/663-3883, www.tourismvictoria. com, 8:30am-8:30pm daily May-Sept., 9am-5pm daily Sept.-Apr.) is located right on the Inner Harbour. Maps are available, and the staff can recommend tours and accommodations, and they also tweet recommendations on Twitter (@victoriavisitor).

Media and Communications

The newspaper tradition in Victoria goes back to 1858, and today's *Times Colonist* (www.timescolonist.com, Tues.-Sun.) is a combination of two of the city's longtime papers. For music and event listings, visit the website of the weekly-turned-monthly *Monday Magazine* (www.mondaymag.com).

Services

Victoria's main post office is the downtown **Canada Post** (709 Yates St., 9am-5pm Mon.-Fri.), which offers stamps and international shipping services.

The Victoria **Greyhound** station (721 Douglas St., 250/388-5248, www.greyhound.ca, 7am-8pm daily) has no luggage lockers, but ticketed passengers can store a piece of luggage for 24 hours.

In the case of a medical emergency, call 911. Emergency rooms are located at **Royal Jubilee Hospital** (1952 Bay St., 250/370-8000, www.viha.ca), east of downtown, and at **Victoria General Hospital** (1 Hospital Way, 250/727-4212, www.viha.ca), northwest of the Inner Harbour.

Getting Around

Car

A car can be helpful reaching some neighborhoods or attractions, or if coming into town by way of the road rather than by air or water. However, the streets around the Inner Harbour and the bulk of Victoria's main attractions are small and narrow, and most hotels and restaurants are within walking distance.

Rush hour isn't as intense here as in, say, Vancouver. Highway 1 and Route 17 (known as Douglas Street and Blanchard Street downtown, respectively) are busy in the morning and late afternoon on weekdays. Street **parking** (8am-6pm Mon.-Sat.) is available, and pay stations accept credit cards. Some stores offer coupons for an hour of free parking to the five city-run parking garages downtown, which otherwise require fees at all times.

Drivers in Canada must have a valid driver's license from their home country (or an International Driving Permit for longer periods) and carry insurance.

Car Rental

A rental car may be useful for travel to Oak Bay, The Butchart Gardens, or the Vancouver ferries. Downtown outposts for **Budget Car and Truck Rental** (757 Douglas St., 800/668-9833, www.budgetvictoria.com, 7am-7pm daily) and **Avis** (1001 Douglas St., 250/386-8468, www. avis.com, 7:30am-6pm Mon.-Fri., 8am-4pm Sat., 9am-4pm Sun.) are walkable from the Inner Harbour where the Port Angeles ferry and Seattle float plane flights arrive. Slightly farther away, **Island Rent-A-Car** (850 Johnson St., 250/384-4881, http://islandrentacar.ca,

9am-6pm Mon.-Sat., 10am-5pm Sun.) offers lower rates, but imposes more rules.

Taxi

The **Victoria Taxi** (250/383-7111, http://victoriataxi.com) cars are bright green, and the company offers an app that will hail cabs. **Yellow Cab of Victoria** (250/381-2222, www.yellowcabvictoria.com) vehicles are the more expected color. Both companies pride themselves on using hybrid vehicles. Rates within Victoria are $1.88 per kilometer with an initial $3.30 charge.

RV

Travel by RV is not ideal unless a trip to other destinations on Vancouver Island is in the cards. Otherwise, renting in Vancouver or Port Angeles is preferable. RV rentals are available at **RV Rent Victoria** (250/812-4610, www.rvrentvictoria.com, $735-910 per week). RVers can park their rig at **Fort Victoria RV Park** (340 Island Hwy., 250/479-8112, www.

fortvictoria.ca, $50), about 7.25 kilometers (4.5 miles) from downtown.

Public Transit

Victoria Harbour Ferry and **H2O Water Taxi** (250/708-0201, www.victoriaharbourferry.com) provide service around the Inner Harbour, Upper Harbour, and Outer Harbour. The water taxi has 11 stops, including Fisherman's Wharf and the Empress Hotel. Pay the captain of the tiny, passenger-only vessel ($6, more for trips outside the Inner Harbour), or purchase a 10-hop card for $51. The company also offers a 45-minute harbor tour ($26 adults, $24 seniors and students, $14 children 13 and under), and the fleet performs a coordinated 20-minute "ballet" on the Inner Harbour waters at 10:45am Sunday mornings (May-Sept.), a 20-year tradition.

For ground service, look to **BC Transit** (250/382-6161, www.bctransit.com, $2.50 adults, children under 6 free, $5 day pass) for regional service around Victoria, Sidney, and Sooke.

Olympic Peninsula

Just across the water from Seattle, the remote Olympic Peninsula has its own mystique, with a thick rain forest, a wild coast, and gritty towns.

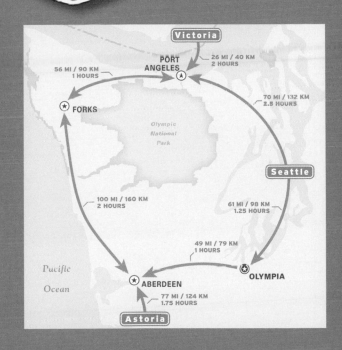

Victoria

PORT ANGELES

26 MI / 40 KM
2 HOURS

56 MI / 90 KM
1 HOURS

70 MI / 132 KM
2.5 HOURS

FORKS

Olympic National Park

Seattle

100 MI / 160 KM
2 HOURS

61 MI / 98 KM
1.25 HOURS

49 MI / 79 KM
1 HOURS

Pacific Ocean

ABERDEEN

OLYMPIA

77 MI / 124 KM
1.75 HOURS

Astoria

Olympic Peninsula

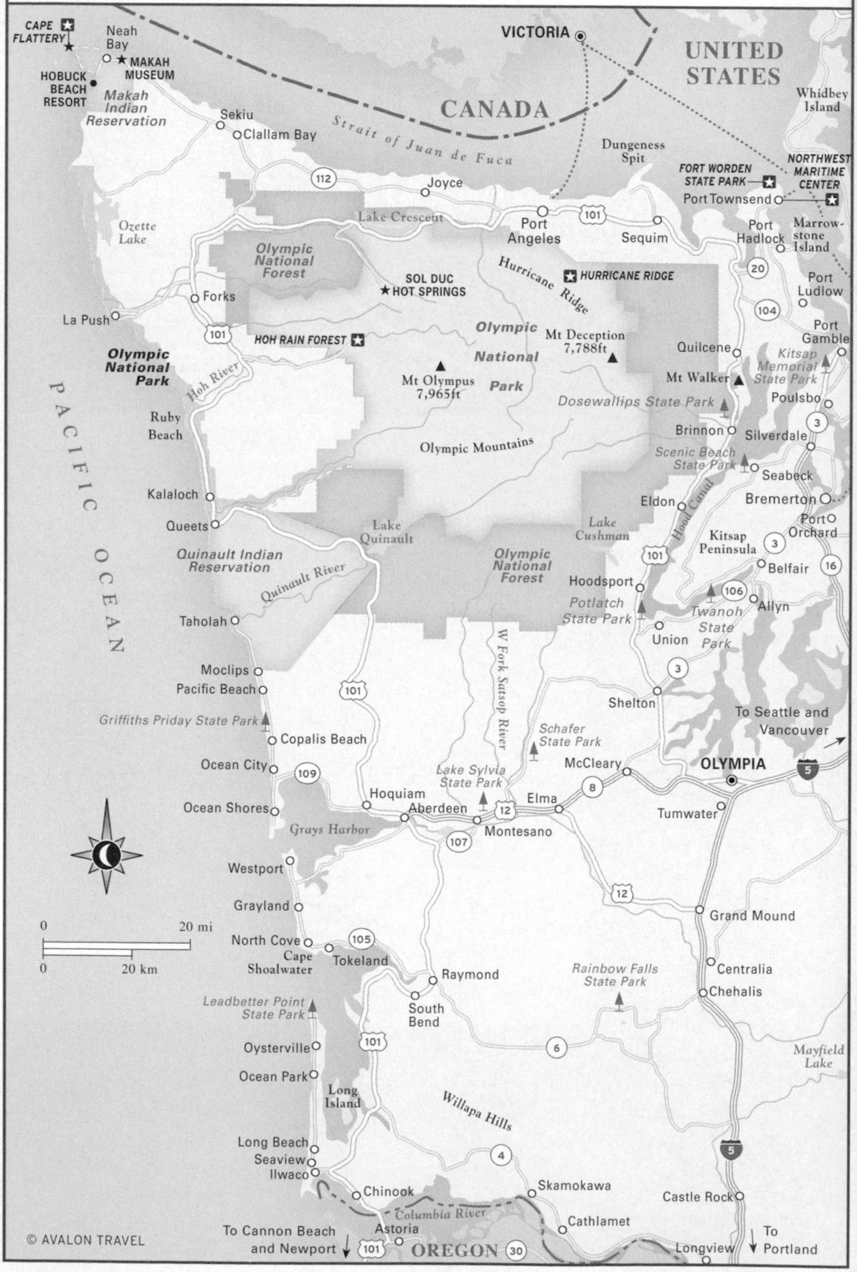

CAPE FLATTERY ★
Neah Bay
★ MAKAH MUSEUM
HOBUCK BEACH RESORT
Makah Indian Reservation
Sekiu
Clallam Bay
112
Joyce
VICTORIA
UNITED STATES
CANADA
Strait of Juan de Fuca
Dungeness Spit
Whidbey Island
FORT WORDEN STATE PARK ★
NORTHWEST MARITIME CENTER
Port Townsend
Ozette Lake
Lake Crescent
Port Angeles
101
Sequim
Port Hadlock
Marrow-stone Island
20
Olympic National Forest
SOL DUC HOT SPRINGS ★
Hurricane Ridge
★ HURRICANE RIDGE
Port Ludlow
104
Port Gamble
Forks
HOH RAIN FOREST ★
Olympic
Mt Deception 7,788ft
Quilcene
Kitsap Memorial State Park
La Push
101
National
Mt Walker ▲
Poulsbo
3
Olympic National Park
Hoh River
Mt Olympus 7,965ft ▲
Park
Dosewallips State Park
Brinnon
Silverdale
Ruby Beach
Olympic Mountains
Scenic Beach State Park
Seabeck
Kalaloch
Eldon
Bremerton
Port Orchard
Queets
Lake Quinault
Lake Cushman
Kitsap Peninsula
3
Belfair
16
Quinault Indian Reservation
Quinault River
Olympic National Forest
Hoodsport
101
106
Twanoh State Park
Allyn
Taholah
Potlatch State Park
Union
Moclips
W Fork Satsop River
Shelton
3
To Seattle and Vancouver
Pacific Beach
101
Schafer State Park
OLYMPIA
Griffiths Priday State Park ▲
Copalis Beach
Lake Sylvia State Park
McCleary
8
5
Ocean City
109
Hoquiam
Aberdeen
12
Elma
Ocean Shores
Grays Harbor
107
Montesano
Tumwater
Westport
Grayland
12
Grand Mound
North Cove
105
Centralia
Cape Shoalwater
Tokeland
Raymond
Rainbow Falls State Park
Chehalis
Leadbetter Point State Park ▲
South Bend
Mayfield Lake
Oysterville
101
6
Ocean Park
Long Island
Willapa Hills
Long Beach
Seaview
Ilwaco
4
Chinook
Skamokawa
Castle Rock
Columbia River
Cathlamet
To Cannon Beach and Newport
101
Astoria
OREGON
30
To Portland
Longview

PACIFIC OCEAN

0   20 mi
0   20 km

© AVALON TRAVEL

Highlights

★ **Fort Worden State Park:** The military campus turned state park boasts beaches, a lighthouse, old battlements, and historical houses (page 151).

★ **Northwest Maritime Center:** All things boat-related are taught, made, and celebrated at the home of the Wooden Boat Festival (page 153).

★ **Hurricane Ridge:** This alpine meadow overlooking the peaks of the Olympic Mountains is home base in Olympic National Park (page 166).

★ **Hoh Rain Forest:** More than 12 feet of rain fall on this stretch of old-growth forest, home to herds of Roosevelt elk (page 174).

★ **Cape Flattery:** Welcome to the edge of the world, where a rugged point of land meets the Pacific Ocean (page 178).

Best Accommodations

★ **Palace Hotel:** Quaint from its striped awning to its brothel past, this is a perfect downtown hotel for a Victorian seaport (page 157).

★ **Lake Crescent Lodge:** An old-fashioned, wood-sided lakeside hotel offers cozy individual cottages and boat rentals (page 172).

★ **Lake Quinault Lodge:** This woodsy retreat measures its rainfall in feet, not inches, and offers plenty of relaxing options regardless (page 176).

★ **Hobuck Beach Resort:** If you're willing to make the drive to the outer end of the peninsula, you'll be rewarded with waterfront cabins, a broad beach, and outdoor fire pits (page 178).

★ **Kalaloch Lodge:** Sitting where the Pacific Ocean pounds the wild coastline, this national park property provides an ideal mix of forest and beach setting (page 183).

You can't drive across the Olympic Peninsula—a mountain range is in the way. Here the route circles instead, caught between the shoreline and the slopes.

The rectangular peninsula is more than just trees and shore. Historical Port Townsend has a preserved military base with killer views and a Victorian downtown embellished with art galleries. In industrial Port Angeles, ships come from faraway ports, making their first stops on the continent in a harbor hugged by the delicate sand spit of Ediz Hook.

Past the sparkling waters of Lake Crescent is an area that survived the *Twilight* boom. Anglers and loggers share their modest little town of Forks with vampire fans and werewolf groupies. And just off the main roads, each separated by pristine, wild beaches, the Native American reservations of the Makah, Quileute, Hoh, and Quinault tribes marry ancient tradition with modern economies.

At the tip of the Olympic Peninsula sits Cape Flattery, the very corner of the

country and the most northwestern point of the contiguous United States. Stand above the craggy cliffs, where the brutal waves of the Pacific roll in endlessly from the mist.

A temperate rain forest and herds of elk are even farther south, as is the gritty hometown of grunge legend Kurt Cobain, where he wrote songs under a grotty bridge. Take your time on the peninsula's large loop, and don't forget to stop for the hot springs, the majestic old hotels, and—if you see him—Bigfoot.

Getting to the Olympic Peninsula

From Victoria
40 kilometers, 2 hours

The **Black Ball Ferry Line** (www.cohoferry.com, $18.50 adults, $9.25 children 5-11, children 4 and under free, $64 for car and driver, $11-16 reservation fee) departs Victoria Harbor 2-4 times daily. (Ferry reservations are available online.) The 90-minute cruise crosses the Strait of Juan de Fuca arriving in **Port Angeles.**

After taking the ferry to Port Angeles, follow **U.S. 101** west for 56 miles. This is the road that traces three sides of the Olympic Peninsula—west, north, and

Best Restaurants

★ **Chimacum Café:** It's pie time at a classic, unchanging diner on the road to Port Townsend (page 156).

★ **Elevated Ice Cream Co.:** Though it started in an old elevator, this dessert joint has expanded to a spacious parlor and outdoor patio (page 157).

★ **Next Door Gastropub:** A friendly, local bar straddles the divide between neighborhood joint and sophisticated eatery (page 163).

★ **Bread Peddler:** Indulge in the capital city's best spot for bready snacks and meals (page 190).

★ **Waterstreet Café:** A fine-dining destination focuses on the best seafood of Puget Sound (page 190).

east—in an upside-down U. Speeds slow as the road hugs the south shore of Lake Crescent, so take care through the tight turns.

From Seattle
70 miles, 2-2.5 hours
One big thing stands between the urban bustle of Seattle and the Olympic Peninsula—Puget Sound. Cross it by ferry at Edmonds, about 15 miles north of downtown Seattle. Take **I-5** north to exit 177, following **Highway 104** and signs for the Kingston ferry. Check departure times for the **Washington State Ferries** (888/808-7977, www.wsdot. wa.gov, $8.20 adults, $4.10 children 6-18, children 5 and under free, $18.20 for car and driver). Plan to arrive a half hour or even a full hour early—long lines lead to lengthy waits, especially on summer weekends.

After the 30-minute crossing, continue west on Highway 104 across the Hood Canal Bridge, and then turn right on Highway 19 through Beaver Valley. The road merges into Highway 20 right before reaching Port Townsend. Without traffic on the Hood Canal Bridge, it's about a 35-mile, 50-minute drive from the ferry dock to Port Townsend.

The drive from Port Townsend to **Port Angeles** takes about an hour. From Port Townsend, follow Highway 20 south for 13 miles to the base of Discovery Bay. At the junction with U.S. 101, turn right and follow U.S. 101 west for 33 miles.

Stopping in Port Gamble
Did you take a wrong turn and end up in bucolic New England? No, but it sure feels like it in Port Gamble, where meticulously trimmed lawns and blinding-white picket fences evoke the cleanest town in Maine—on purpose. The founders of the Puget Mill Company, a timber outfit, wanted to re-create their birthplace from back East on this turn of Highway 104 on the tip of the Kitsap Peninsula. The town was founded in 1853 and is accordingly Victorian in style.

Although the sawmill has closed, the town is a national historic landmark and home to almost 1,000 people. An annual ghost-hunting conference is held in October, all the better to explore the spirits haunting the old buildings. Year-round, more corporeal visitors can explore the exterior of **St. Paul's Church** (31899 Hwy. 104, 360/297-8074, www. portgambleweddings.com) from 1879, fronted by a gray-and-white steeple and stained-glass windows. It copies a house of worship in East Machias, Maine.

Among the antiques shops and day spa are several craft-oriented stores, including **The Artful Ewe** (32180 Rainier Ave. NE, 360/643-0183, www.theartfulewe. com, 10am-5pm Fri.-Sun.), a warm yarn shop stocked with soft skeins of wool.

Two Days on the Olympic Peninsula

If you're taking the ferry from Seattle, start this itinerary in Port Townsend. Ferrying from Victoria, the trip picks up in Port Angeles (a one-hour drive west of Port Townsend).

Day 1

In **Port Townsend,** start with breakfast at **The Blue Moose Café** (page 156). Afterward, it's just a short drive east on Sims Way to downtown. Appreciate the Victorian architecture and then tour the wooden boats at the **Northwest Maritime Center** (page 153). Drive 2 miles north on Jackson Street to **Fort Worden State Park** (page 151) and explore the former military site's abandoned old battlements.

From Port Townsend, it's an hour drive west on Highway 20 to U.S. 101 and the coastal city of **Port Angeles.** The Victoria ferry lands here, and the town is a suitable gateway for excursions into the Hurricane Ridge area of **Olympic National Park** (page 165). Chow down at **Next Door Gastropub** (page 163), and then drive 17 miles south on Heart O' the Hills Road to the **Hurricane Ridge Visitor Center** (page 168). Enjoy a short hike before driving back to Port Angeles; turn east on U.S. 101 to Lake Crescent and spend the night at the park's **Lake Crescent Lodge** (page 172).

Day 2

From Lake Crescent Drive, it's a 40-minute drive south on U.S. 101 to Forks. Grab a coffee or a sack lunch at **Forks Coffee Shop** (page 180) and follow La Push Road 15 miles west to the town of the same name. Hike the **Second Beach Trail** (page 181) and enjoy your lunch with views of the sea stacks.

Return to Forks and head 30 miles south on U.S. 101 to explore the southern sections of Olympic National Park. Turn east on Upper Hoh Road to reach the **Hoh Rain Forest Visitor Center** (page 174), home to the famous Olympic rain forest. Or stay on U.S. 101 and drive 68 miles south to **Lake Quinault** (page 175) for nature walks and epic trees. **Kalaloch** (page 183), 30 miles south of Forks, provides a nice beach detour along the way.

From Lake Quinault, it's a straight shot south on U.S. 101 for 44 miles to **Aberdeen** (page 184). In Aberdeen, you have two options: Head inland via Highway 8 for 50 miles to Olympia and I-5, returning to either **Seattle** or **Portland** (see page 185); or continue 70 miles south on U.S. 101 to Astoria, Oregon, and explore the **Oregon Coast** (see page 186).

The proprietor is often spinning or winding yarn in the corner on a large wooden wheel.

In the back of the **Port Gamble General Store** (32400 Rainier Ave. NE, 360/297-7636, www.portgamblegeneralstore.com, 10am-3pm Mon. and Wed.-Thurs., 8am-4pm Fri.-Sun.) is a café open for breakfast and lunch. Instead of biscuits, they pour sausage or mushroom gravy over Native American fry bread, and weekend specialties include lemon ricotta pancakes. Lunch dishes source from Beecher's Cheese in Seattle and other local purveyors.

From the Oregon Coast
185 miles, 3.5 hours

From Astoria, follow U.S. 101 north through rural southeastern Washington, passing the east side of Willapa Bay. U.S. 101 reaches the industrial towns of Aberdeen and Hoquiam in about 77 miles, and then passes through forest, an Indian reservation, and part of Olympic National Park before reaching Forks in 100 miles (or about two hours). The total drive will take a little less than four hours, most of it on narrow two-lane highways.

Port Townsend

The Victorian seaport of Port Townsend is pretty as a picture, with a waterfront central street stacked with ornate, historical buildings. Ferries glide into a dock that bookends one end of town, while a massive wooden boat center stands on the other. The town was founded before Seattle. Its location on the northeast corner of the peninsula was considered key, and at one point it was expected to become the state capital. (It didn't, losing out to Olympia.)

The thriving port was busy with the timber trade, and the U.S. military built fortifications, which they called Fort Worden, at the nearby point. But the town became known for something else in the early 20th century—it was one of the biggest centers for shanghaied sailors on the West Coast, where inebriated crewmen could wake up to find themselves on a slow boat to anywhere in the world.

Although the town suffered in the Great Depression, the pulp and paper mill just south of the city helped sustain the area. The smell of pulp is still in the air as you approach the city of almost 10,000.

Sights
★ Fort Worden State Park
At one time the parade grounds of **Fort Worden** (200 Battery Way, 360/344-4400, www.parks.wa.gov/fortworden, 8:30am-dusk, $10 parking) were used by marching soldiers; now they're perfect kite-flying fields. The 434-acre state park includes rows of old military housing, now used as conference buildings and vacation rentals.

Two miles of shore line the park, with the red-roofed **Port Wilson Lighthouse** located among the driftwood. The **Port Townsend Marine Science Center** (360/385-5582, www.ptmsc.org, 11am-5pm Wed.-Mon. summer, noon-5pm

Fri.-Sun. fall-spring, $5 adults, $3 children 6-17, children 5 and under free) sits on a pier among the waves, with a natural history offshoot back on shore. Although trails cross parts of the park, the old battlements are the most exciting places to wander. The concrete **Battery Kinzie** held two 12-inch disappearing guns 1910-1943, ready for a possible attack from the west. Plenty of metal ladders, short tunnels, and dark bunkers remain. The **Commanding Officer's Quarters** (noon-5pm daily May-Sept., noon-5pm Sat.-Sun. Oct.-Nov. and Mar.-Apr., $6 adults, $5 seniors, $1 children 3-12) is a museum that focuses on the military history of the area, as well as the creation of the nearby national park.

Even though Fort Worden never saw military action, its claim to fame came later when the film *An Officer and a Gentleman* starring Richard Gere was largely filmed on its grounds in 1981.

Jefferson County Historical Society
The Jefferson County Historical Society runs several historical sites around town. Right on the town's main street, in the old city hall built in 1892, is the **Jefferson Museum of Art and History** (540 Water St., 360/385-1003, www.jchsmuseum.org, 11am-4pm daily, $6 adults, $5 seniors, $1 children), which uses the courtroom and fire hall spaces. It's a classic small-town history museum, with a nine-minute video introduction to the area and exhibits that represent both the peninsula's Native American history and its more recent settlement. There's also a section about the Chinese settlers in early Port Townsend. An art gallery hosts exhibitions by local artists or by theme, and the city's old jail cells remain, teaching visitors about crime and sin throughout the city's history.

The historical society also runs the **Rothschild House** (Franklin and Taylor Sts., 360/385-1003, www.jchsmuseum.org, 11am-4pm daily May-Sept., $6 adults, $5 seniors, $1 children 3-12) a

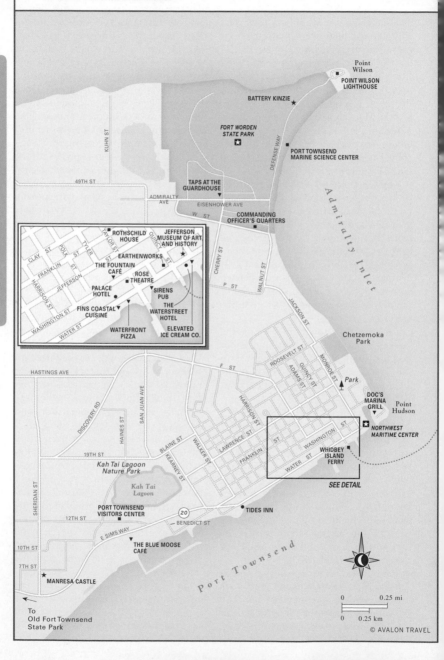

Port Townsend

Point Wilson

POINT WILSON LIGHTHOUSE

BATTERY KINZIE

FORT WORDEN STATE PARK

PORT TOWNSEND MARINE SCIENCE CENTER

DEFENSE WAY

Admiralty Inlet

TAPS AT THE GUARDHOUSE

ADMIRALTY AVE

EISENHOWER AVE

W ST

COMMANDING OFFICER'S QUARTERS

KUHN ST

49TH ST

ROTHSCHILD HOUSE

JEFFERSON MUSEUM OF ART AND HISTORY

CLAY ST
POLK ST
TYLER ST
TAYLOR ST
QUINCY ST
ADAMS ST

EARTHENWORKS

THE FOUNTAIN CAFÉ

FRANKLIN ST

ROSE THEATRE

PALACE HOTEL

JEFFERSON ST

HARRISON ST

SIRENS PUB

FINS COASTAL CUISINE

THE WATERSTREET HOTEL

WASHINGTON ST

WATER ST

WATERFRONT PIZZA

ELEVATED ICE CREAM CO.

CHERRY ST

P ST

WALNUT ST

JACKSON ST

Chetzemoka Park

HASTINGS AVE

F ST

ROOSEVELT ST

MONROE ST

Park

DOC'S MARINA GRILL

Point Hudson

NORTHWEST MARITIME CENTER

DISCOVERY RD

HAINES ST

SAN JUAN AVE

BLAINE ST

WALKER ST

LAWRENCE ST

HARRISON ST

ADAMS ST

QUINCY ST

ST

WASHINGTON ST

WHIDBEY ISLAND FERRY

19TH ST

Kah Tai Lagoon Nature Park

KEARNEY ST

FRANKLIN ST

WATER ST

SEE DETAIL

Kah Tai Lagoon

SHERIDAN ST

PORT TOWNSEND VISITORS CENTER

12TH ST

20

BENEDICT ST

TIDES INN

E SIMS WAY

10TH ST

THE BLUE MOOSE CAFÉ

7TH ST

MANRESA CASTLE

Port Townsend

To Old Fort Townsend State Park

0   0.25 mi

0   0.25 km

© AVALON TRAVEL

few blocks away, named for the local family that owned it. D. C. H. Rothschild, Bavarian-born and known as "The Baron," settled in Port Townsend in 1858 and started a mercantile. The Rothschilds made few changes to the structure before donating it, so the historical house has no re-creations or reproductions and no electricity. Rooms are left just as they were used, and the house displays artifacts from the family.

★ Northwest Maritime Center

For boat builders and fans of anything seaworthy, the **Northwest Maritime Center** (431 Water St., 360/385-3628, www.nwmaritime.org, 10am-5pm daily, free) is like Mecca. The facility was built in 2009 and is home to the Wooden Boat Foundation, which runs the hugely popular annual Wooden Boat Festival in September. The waterfront complex includes a boat shop where visitors can watch craft being made and interact with the artisans at work, while the Chandlery shop sells nautical gifts and the pulls, knobs, and flags one needs to kit out a sailboat.

Classes are held in a marine simulator in the building's Pilothouse, which also boasts views of the area waterfront. More than 1,600 people contributed to the fundraising that made the center possible, as evidenced by the compass rose outside made from engraved paving stones.

Sports and Recreation
Parks and Beaches

The lovely **Chetzemoka Park** (900 Jackson St., www.ptguide.com) is named for the Klallam leader who assisted white settlers in communicating with local tribes. The park sits on a hill overlooking the Strait of Juan de Fuca, with flower gardens to wander and excellent trees for climbing. There is a playground, and the park has beach access. It was the city's first park, made by volunteers in 1904. Hop on a swing for one of the best views in town.

Biking

The best-known bike trail in town is the **Larry Scott Memorial Trail** (www.ptguide. com), which travels from Port Townsend to the Four Corners area near Discover Bay. It is also the first section of the still-evolving **Olympic Discovery Trail** (www. olympicdiscoverytrail.com), which winds 130 miles from Port Townsend to the Pacific Ocean, crossing the entire peninsula. (For now about half of the trail miles are completed, with the rest on the busy highway.) The **Larry Scott Trail** is about 8 miles long and begins at the Boat Haven Marina (2601 Washington St.). Park near the restroom in the boat yard, or find more parking across the main road at a park-and-ride lot near the Safeway. The paved trail goes along the waterfront and then west; after 4 miles it turns south at Cape George Trailhead (Cape George and Crutcher Rd.). The next several miles of trail, to Four Corners, are still under construction.

There are also 12 miles of bike trails in **Fort Worden** (200 Battery Way, 360/344-4400, www.parks.wa.gov/fortworden), which make for an easy mountain-biking day. Park at the parade grounds and bike west, looking for dirt roads that head right from the main road.

The downtown **PT Cyclery** (252 Tyler St., 360/385-6470, www.ptcyclery.com, 9am-6pm Mon.-Sat. summer, noon-6pm Tues.-Sat. winter) rents mountain and road bikes ($7 per hour), plus tandem bikes and child trailers. They have maps and information about local mountain biking.

The Broken Spoke (630 Water St., 360/379-1295, http://thebrokenspokept. blogspot.com, 9am-6pm Mon.-Sat., 11am-4pm Sun. summer; 10am-6pm Mon.-Sat., 11am-4pm Sun. winter) also does rentals (half day $20-35) and has a repair shop in case you actually end up with a broken spoke. Both stores offer free lock and helmet rental with their bikes.

Kayaking

Located near the water inside Fort Worden, **Port Townsend Paddlesports** (Harbor Defense Way, Fort Worden State Park, 360/379-3608, www.ptpaddle-sports.com, 9am-5pm daily June-Sept.) rents kayaks and stand-up paddleboards ($35-45 per two hours), as well as bikes. It also has wetsuit rentals for the very cold days. Reservations are recommended, but walk-up rentals are also available noon-4pm. It also leads kayak tours ($50-110 adults, $39-69 children) of the waterfront area near Fort Worden or beyond to North Beach and Bird Island; specialty tours require a reservation.

Entertainment and Events
Bars and Clubs

Sirens Pub (823 Water St., 360/379-1100, www.sirenspub.com, noon-2am daily) has 11 microbrews on tap, but the beer isn't usually the most interesting draw at this downtown bar. Live music takes the form of a Tuesday bluegrass night, an open mic night, karaoke, and dance music following live shows on weekends. A deck out back overlooks the water and ferry dock, while brick walls and dark trim dim the interior. Food features a local twist on pub fare—fried oysters, crab cakes, and steamed clams, plus burgers, pasta, and pizzas. Look for the bar's sign on the main drag, Water Street, then head up a long staircase to this locals' hangout.

Don't be alarmed by the jail cells at Fort Worden's **Taps at the Guardhouse** (300 Eisenhower Ave., 360/344-4400, fortworden.org/eat-here, 1pm-10pm daily): You haven't had so much to drink that you ended up in the pokey. This was formerly used by military law enforcement, and the historical aspects are well preserved. The bar's menu features hearty bites that go well with local beers and nicely crafted cocktails. Sit outside to get a view of the bustle of the fort, but leave time to explore the interior that dates back to 1904.

a bunker at Fort Worden State Park

Though the small town of Chimacum used to be little more than a crossroads on the way to Port Townsend, a slew of new attractions has made it worth stopping for. **Finnriver Cidery** (124 Center Rd, 360/339-8478, www.finnriver.com, Mon.-Thurs. noon-6pm, Fri.-Sat. noon-9pm, Sun. 10am-9pm), built on the site of an old dairy, has a tasting room featuring a wide selection of apple-based drinks, including habanero cider and a dry-hopped favorite. A wood-fired oven bakes pizzas for the long tables of drinkers, and orchard views and horseshoes make it feel more like a family picnic spot.

Cinema

Only a few drive-in movie theaters are left in the state, making the **Wheel-In Motor Movie** (210 Theatre Rd., 360/385-0859, 7:45pm Wed.-Sun., $9 adults, $7 children 6-12, children 5 and under free), in operation since 1953, a special place to see a flick. A sign out front reads "Howdy Pardner"; drive in and park on the open

field. The screen is surrounded by a thick forest of evergreen trees, which means double features are uninterrupted by excess light. A snack bar serves the requisite hot dogs and nachos.

The historical **Rose Theatre** (235 Taylor St., 360/385-1089, http://rosetheatre.com) was originally a vaudeville house in 1908 until it closed. It was then a variety of stores before reopening in 1992, when the original murals and tintile ceiling were restored. Now it's a cinema showing independent movies, filmed arts performances, and cult classic films. The **Starlight Room** (http://rosetheatre.com), above the Silverwater Café next door, has cocktails, beer, wine, antipasti, desserts, and popcorn.

Festivals and Events

The **Strange Brewfest** (American Legion Hall, 209 Monroe St., 360/385-3454, www.strangebrewfestpt.com, Jan.) is dedicated to all the weird ways you can make beer—with fruit, chocolate, coffee, and even odder ingredients. Many beers are specially made for the event, and winners can be picks like a tomato beer, peanut butter beer, or a salami beer. Entertainment during the event includes costume contests and circus performers. It's also a music festival with an eclectic lineup of funk and soul music.

Centrum (223 Battery Way, Fort Worden State Park, 360/385-3102, www.centrum.org), an arts organization based in Fort Worden, hosts the **Festival of American Fiddle Tunes and Jazz Port Townsend** (July), **Port Townsend Acoustic Blues Festival** (Aug.), and **Olympic Music Festival** (Aug.-Sept.)

The **Wooden Boat Festival** (360/385-3628, www.woodenboat.org, Sept.) is a Port Townsend tradition that stretches back more than 40 years. The festival, centered at the Northwest Maritime Center (431 Water St.), includes demonstrations and hundreds of wooden boats on display—this is where boat enthusiasts come to celebrate their craft. Guests can buy single-day or multiday tickets. Boats are open for tours, and boat builders demonstrate everything from caulking to decorating to how to hold a chef's dinner at sea; other talks are about the history and nature of local waterways. Posters for the annual festival are a popular collector's item, so expect to see past versions around town.

The **Great Port Townsend Kinetic Sculpture Race** (www.ptkineticrace.org, Oct.) is something between an art festival and a drag race. Entrants make bizarre moving structures that are human-powered, then drivers (called "kineticnauts") race them on a course over road, water, sand, mud, or other surfaces. Bribes are encouraged in the voting process—one motto is "cheating is not a right, but a privilege." The biggest winner is the Mediocrity Award, for the vehicle that scores right in the middle. The races are held all over, but Port Townsend's version is one of the wildest, and organizers are proud of its grassroots, noncorporate history. The race begins at City Hall (250 Madison St.).

Shopping

The Northwest Man (901 Water St., 360/385-6734, http://theclotheshorseporttownsend.wordpress.com, 10am-5:30pm daily) is an emporium of all things manly, at least the flannel stuff. Besides shirts and hats, the best finds are Pendleton blankets made of stiff, durable wool woven in patterns inspired by Native American designs (they've been made in the Northwest for more than 100 years).

When you're ready to dress like a pirate, head to **World's End** (1020 Water St., 360/379-6906, www.worldsendporttownsend.com, 10am-6pm daily), where almost every piece of clothing for sale is in black-and-white stripes. Steampunk-style jewelry and frilly cuffs complete the nautical look, and there's even a photo of Johnny Depp from the *Pirates of the Caribbean* movies for inspiration.

In a town of galleries, **Earthenworks** (702 Water St., 360/385-0328, www.earthenworksgallery.com, 10am-5:30pm daily) is both the best known and arguably the best. The airy store displays Northwest arts and crafts, including metalwork, ceramics, wood pieces, and paintings.

Chefs or anyone who has fun in the kitchen will find treasures at home decor store **The Green Eyeshade** (720 Water St., 360/385-3838, 10am-6pm daily), which specializes in gifts to be given with a chuckle: a mason jar cocktail shaker, or a weathered wall sign that reads "I Love You More Than Cheese."

Food

The menu at **The Fountain Café** (920 Washington St., 360/385-1364, hwww.fountaincafept.com, 11:30am-3pm and 5pm-9pm Sun.-Thurs., 11:30am-3pm and 5pm-9:30pm Fri.-Sat., $15-36) includes touches of Italian pastas and Moroccan chicken, but the saffron-yellow walls and red stools suggest a Southwestern cheeriness. In a small space that exudes Boho chic, the eatery draws locals as much as tourists willing to make the very small detour off the main drag.

Finding **The Blue Moose Café** (311 Haines Pl., 360/385-7339, 6:30am-2pm Mon.-Fri., 7am-2pm Sat.-Sun., $8-15, cash only) means venturing into Port Townsend's busy marina, where fishing boats are being cleaned and sailboats are lifted into dry docks by giant hoists. Inside the cramped quarters are mostly locals, happy to share a table when the breakfast crowd overwhelms the tiny establishment. A breakfast burrito is enough for two meals, but that could be the friendly chatter that fills you up, too.

Classic country diner ★ **Chimacum Café** (9253 Rhody Dr., Chimacum, 360/732-4631, 6am-8pm Sun.-Thurs., 6am-9pm Fri.-Sat., $6-12) is a great place to stop just outside of Port Townsend—just look at the back of the menu: There you'll find a long list of homemade pies. If the café has the seasonal wild blackberry, it's a can't-miss—a sweet dream served a la mode.

At one time **Doc's Marina Grill** (141 Hudson St., 360/344-3627, https://doc-sgrill.com, 11am-11pm daily, $13-32) housed nurses on Point Hudson, the very end of town and right on the waterfront. Now the restaurant dishes up halibut, rockfish tacos, and half-pound burgers and has plenty of outdoor seating. It's a bit of an awkward walk from downtown, as you'll stroll through parking lots around the harbor, though it's physically not far; there are plenty of sailboat docks to pass along the way.

Pick your (tasty) poison: Downstairs at **Waterfront Pizza** (951 Water St., 360/385-6629, 11am-8pm daily, $8.50-32) is a crowded counter selling slices loaded with toppings, easy to carry out to the piers that extend into Puget Sound nearby. As befits a small-town pizzeria, the staff is jovial, if perhaps raucous at times. Up a narrow staircase on the 2nd floor is the pizzeria's full-service restaurant, where the sourdough-crust pizzas can be topped with homemade Italian sausage.

Where there are piers, sailboats, and a parade of tourists, there will be an old-fashioned ice cream parlor. Fortunately, ★ **Elevated Ice Cream Co.** (631 Water St., 360/385-1156, www.elevatedicecream.com, 10am-9pm Sun.-Thurs., 10am-10pm Fri.-Sat., $4) is as uplifting as it was when it began in the 1970s in an antique elevator. Homemade flavors like cardamom and maple walnut are served by the ounce, not by the scoop. Request "jimmies," a house specialty: The scooper will dunk your cone in sprinkles before handing it over.

Accommodations
Under $150
The ★ **Palace Hotel** (1004 Water St., 360/385-0773, www.palacehotelpt.com, $99-159) is every bit the dollhouse inside that it looks to be from the street. The

most convenient hotel in town is a block from the ferry terminal and right on the main drag, in a building constructed in 1889 by a retired sea captain. Both inside and out, it's decorated in bright, sometimes clashing colors—perhaps a nod to its life as a brothel in the early 20th century. Rooms are more sedate, with wrought-iron beds, and guests share bathrooms with claw-foot tubs. Plenty of froufrou decorates the hotel, but it doesn't get too precious. Thank the endless staircases and landings, hallway turns, and chandeliers—one almost suspects a secret passageway could be found in the old hotel's bones.

Head inside the Pacific Traditions Gallery to find **The Waterstreet Hotel** (635 Water St., 360/385-5467, www.waterstreethotelporttownsend.com, $50-175). The inn's front desk is within the art space, with the well-hidden rooms in the two floors above. Smaller rooms share baths, while suites have full kitchens, and one suite can sleep up to six. The vibe is much of the same Victorian hodgepodge that's everywhere in Port Townsend, but the unlabeled location helps it feel calmer, and some rooms have water views.

If you're looking to stay in a castle, you won't find many opportunities beyond **Manresa Castle** (651 Cleveland St., 360/385-5750, www.manresacastle.com, $101-245) in this corner of the world. The cream stone and pointed tower are Prussian in style, after the birthplace of the building's first owner and the town's first mayor. It sits atop a hill south of town, less out of place than it would be in any other Northwest town. Each hotel room has Victorian touches like a brass bedframe or highly ornate living room furniture. A chapel, which dates back to when Jesuits owned the property, is now a café that serves breakfast.

$150-200
How proud is **Tides Inn** (1807 Water St., 360/385-0595, www.tides-inn.com,

$109-299) of its scene in the 1980s flick *An Officer and a Gentleman*? Very—the movie poster is still above the reception desk, even though the place barely resembles the roadside motel it was 30 years ago. Now, larger suites make up most of the inn, with balconies that face the very top of Puget Sound and a rocky beach. Inside furnishings are either plain or oddly ornate (and really quite ugly), but the sprinkling of private whirlpool tubs in select rooms forgives all manner of sins.

Over $250

There's hardly any town to speak of around **Inn at Port Ludlow** (1 Heron Rd., Port Ludlow, 360/437-7000, www.port-ludlowresort.com/inn, $260-350), though the rural area is certainly populated. The small bay is a popular boat harbor at the tip of Hood Canal, and the resort itself is connected to an 18-hole golf course. The Fireside restaurant in the hotel's base is centered around a large stone hearth, but all rooms have gas fireplaces of their own—not to mention whirlpool tubs.

Almost every type of accommodation is available at **Fort Worden** (200 Battery Way, 360/344-4434, www.parks.wa.gov/fortworden). The Officer's Row ($449-849) houses many duplexes with servant's quarters and fireplaces; rentable units have as many as six bedrooms, and kitchens are fully stocked. Also all built before 1915, the Non-Commissioned Officer houses ($249-370) have full kitchens and 2-4 bedrooms. Then there are more unusual rentals, like Alexander's Castle ($359), a Scottish-style brick tower from 1883 that's now a one-bedroom rental. Blissful Vista house ($359) has two bedrooms, a fireplace, and a remote location with a view.

Camping

Fort Worden (360/344-4431, www.parks.

from top to bottom: Chetzemoka Park; Manresa Castle; Port Townsend ferry dock.

Island Hopping

To Whidbey Island

The **Washington State Ferry** (206/464-6400, www.wsdot.wa.gov, $3.25 adults, $1.60 seniors and youth, $0.50 bicycle surcharge, $13.40 cars) boats, with their signature white-and-green color scheme, are a common and picturesque sight on the Port Townsend waterfront. The ferry leaves from the downtown terminal (1301 Water St.) and travels a short 30 minutes to Keystone (1400 Hwy. 20, Coupeville) on Whidbey Island. RVs and trailers must have reservations for the ferry, and it's recommended for cars.

On Whidbey, the terminal is close to **Fort Casey** (S Engle Rd., 360/678-4519, www.parks.wa.gov/parks, $10 parking), a park with concrete ruins, trails, the 1903 Admiralty Head Lighthouse, and guided tours of the gun batteries on weekends in summer. There is also a **campground** (888/226-7688, https://washington. goingtocamp.com) with 21 tent sites ($12-31) and 14 RV sites ($30-42).

To San Juan Island

The passenger boat **Puget Sound Express** (227 Jackson St., 360/385-5288, www.pugetsoundexpress.com, $103.50 adults, $65 children 2-10, $15 bicycles) is a kind of private ferry service between Port Townsend and Friday Harbor on San Juan Island. The once-daily service leaves at 9am and returns at 5pm (May-Sept. only) and includes the boat ride and two hours in the quaint town of Friday Harbor. The company also runs a four-hour **whale-watching tour** ($95 adults, $65 children 2-10) from Port Townsend, multiday tours, and special Christmas trips to Seattle.

---

wa.gov, open year-round) has two campgrounds. The **Beach Campground** ($31-39) is near the old battery ruins and the Port Townsend Marine Science Center; it has 50 full-service RV sites in an open field. The **Upper Campground** ($29-35), with only 30 water and electric sites, is in a forested area. Reservations are recommended for both. There are also five walk-in primitive sites ($12) and one for boat-in campers ($12).

Information and Services

The **Port Townsend Visitors Center** (2409 Jefferson St., 360/385-2722, www.visitjeffersoncountywa.com, 9am-5pm Mon.-Fri., 10am-4pm Sat.-Sun.) has brochures and maps of Port Townsend, as well as information on the entire Quimper Peninsula, this particular bump of the larger Olympic Peninsula.

Getting There

Port Townsend sits on the northeast tip of the Olympic Peninsula, abutting Puget Sound. It is 47 miles east of Port Angeles (and the ferry to Victoria, BC) via U.S. 101 and a three-hour drive (with no ferry crossings) west from Seattle via I-5 and U.S. 101. Olympia lies 98 miles directly south on U.S. 101.

Sequim

Sequim (pronounced "skwim") sits almost halfway between Port Townsend and Port Angeles and is a mostly residential area. It's notable for its acres of lavender fields and the long Dungeness Spit reaching out into the Strait of Juan de Fuca.

Dungeness National Wildlife Refuge

The Dungeness Spit is a 5.5-mile stretch of sand that reaches out into the Strait of Juan de Fuca; it's been part of the **Dungeness National Wildlife Refuge** (Voice of America Rd. and Park Rd., 360/457-8451, www.fws.gov/washington-maritime/dungeness, $3 parking) since 1915. The beach here doesn't allow pets, Frisbees, or kites because they disturb the birds and harbor seals protected here. Fish, migrating birds, shellfish, and seals can be found throughout the protected area, and the black brant bird is present in especially high numbers in April. The spit itself grows every year due to sand build-up and is the longest of its kind in the country.

It's possible to hike the spit out to near the end where the **New Dungeness Lightstation** (http://dungeness.com/lighthouse) alerts passing boats. The 11-mile round-trip hike should be carefully planned with tides, though it's always passable. Daily tours of the lighthouse are available.

The nearby county park, **Dungeness Recreation Area** (554 Voice of America Rd. W, 360/683-5847, www.clallam.net), has a one-mile bluff hiking trail, picnic areas, and **camping** in 64 sites (tents $25, hike-in/bike-in $7). There are no utility hookups, but there are showers.

Lavender Farms

Sequim calls itself the lavender capital of the world because the plant grows almost as well here as it does in the south of France. A number of farms offer tours, you-pick gathering, plant sales, and lavender products. **Oliver's Lavender Farm** (82 Cameron Acres Ln., 360/681-3789, www.oliverslavender.com, 10am-5pm daily June-Sept.) has manicured gardens and a quaint gazebo. **CreekSide Lavender Farm** (1141 Cays Rd., 888/881-6055, www.lavenderconnection.com, summer only) sells lavender essential oil and other bath and home products. **Nelson's Duck Pond and Lavender Farm** (73 Humble Hill Rd., 360/681-7727, www.nelsonsduckpond.com, 10am-5pm Thurs.-Sun. May-Sept., 10am-5pm Thurs.-Mon. Oct.-Apr.) has a small pond and a wide selection of lavender products. The **Lavender Festival** (www.lavenderfestival.com, July) takes place in town with a street fair and farm tours. A cycling event, the **Tour de Lavender** (http://tourdelavender.wordpress.com, Aug.) encourages visitors to

bike between farms; a more intense long-distance ride is from the Kingston ferry terminal.

Food

A plate of Dungeness silver oysters feels like the most appropriate dish at **Dockside Grill** (2577 W Sequim Bay Rd., 360/683-7510, www.docksidegrill-sequim.com, 11:30am-3pm and 4pm-9pm Wed.-Sun. Apr.-Oct., 11:30am-3pm and 4pm-8pm Wed.-Sun. Nov.-Mar, $17-24), given that the windows face the marina and gray-blue waters of Sequim Bay. The seafood is local, including halibut and salmon, and dishes are classic—shrimp and grits, prawns in white wine and butter. A surprising number of vegan options are also on offer. Reservations might be helpful when the warm summer evenings fill the small dining room.

Get ready to confess at **Blondie's Plate** (134 S 2nd Ave., 360/683-2233, www.blondiesplate.com, 4pm-9pm Sun.-Thurs., 4pm-10pm Fri.-Sat., $11-40), an eatery that occupies an 1896 Episcopalian church. The arched windows may scream sermon, but the interior feels more like an upscale diner, with midcentury accents and striking light fixtures. The menu leans heavily on local clams, market vegetables, and salmon. Dishes tend toward the hearty and warm, including risotto and buttermilk fried chicken, and there are significant discounts during happy hour (4pm-5pm). Many items are vegetarian, gluten-free, or dairy-free.

Everything on the menu at **Nourish Sequim** (101 Provence View Ln., 360/797-1480, www.nourishsequim.com, 11:30am-9pm Wed.-Sat., 11am-9pm Sun., $16-28) is gluten-free, and everything down to the condiments is made in-house to ensure there's no contamination. Flavors in the seasonal menu tend to be lighter, with a number of salads on offer and pastas paired with local fish—though there is a tasty burger, too. Brunch includes garbanzo flour crepes and farm-egg Benedicts. The restaurant is located on a farm that dates back to 1880; many of the herbs and produce are grown just feet away. Guests are invited to walk the gardens, including the lavender patch—the spot claims to be the oldest herb farm in the state.

Accommodations

Although part of a chain, the **Holiday Inn Express Hotel and Suites** (1441 E Washington St., 877/859-5095, www.ihg.com, $258-296) has neat, modern rooms, some with kitchenettes. There's a pool and free access to the hot breakfast bar. The rooftop is lined with solar panels, and the outdoor patio has tables, strings of lights, and a nice view of the hillside.

The **Juan de Fuca Cottages** (182 Marine Dr., 360/683-4433, www.juandefuca.com, rooms $210-350, cottages $300-360) are located right on the Strait of Juan de Fuca, and some units have views of the Dungeness Spit and its lighthouse. Kayaks, bicycles, and snowshoes are available to rent. Rooms in the main beach house have fold-out sleeper sofas and one has a rock fireplace, plus they're close to the beach. The Dungeness Bay Lodge rooms are slightly farther inland and have whirlpool tubs and electric fireplaces. Cottages are scattered around the property, and some have outdoor patios. Most units have kitchens, though a few just have mini-fridges and microwaves.

Nelson's Duck Pond and Lavender Farm (73 Humble Hill Rd., 360/681-7727, www.nelsonsduckpond.com, $225-275 for two nights) also has a rental cabin in a red barn that sleeps four, with a full bath, kitchen, and access to the you-pick lavender field. Check-in comes with a lemon lavender pound cake.

Getting There

Sequim is located on U.S. 101 about 17 miles east of Port Angeles; it is a 31-mile drive from Port Townsend. Take Highway 20 for 13 miles from Port Townsend to Discovery Bay, where it meets U.S. 101. Take U.S. 101 west for 18 miles to Sequim.

Port Angeles

If Port Townsend is a Victorian dollhouse turned into a town, then Port Angeles is the backyard tool house reimagined as a small coastal city. The long Ediz Hook protects a harbor that was a center of business long before Europeans settled here—Klallam tribes have used it for thousands of years. The peninsula's booming logging trade led to shipping facilities and pulp mills near the harbor, though recent years have seen a decline in the city's industrial health.

But still, everything in town has a job to do: The Coho ferry departs for Victoria in Canada, and signs in downtown stores welcome the crews of large barges by name. The town is also home to the headquarters for Olympic National Park, and the road that leads to its largest visitors center, at Hurricane Ridge, starts in the middle of the gritty downtown.

Sights
Ediz Hook

Accessing the three-mile **Ediz Hook** means a trip through the downtown lumber mills, which have seen a flurry of sales and management changes in recent decades. The public is allowed to drive about two-thirds of the way out, but the U.S. Coast Guard lays claim to the end of the spit. Like the Dungeness Spit in Sequim, the Ediz Hook is a narrow path into the massive waterway that borders the top of the Olympic Peninsula, though here you get a much better glimpse of the region's industrial life. The rocks and driftwood that made up the edges of the hook make a good platform for shore-based whale-watching or simply counting the ships that pass through the Strait of Juan de Fuca. At dusk, look back at land to see the lights of Port Angeles reflected in the water, a sharp contrast to the Olympic Mountains that rise steeply behind them.

Port Angeles

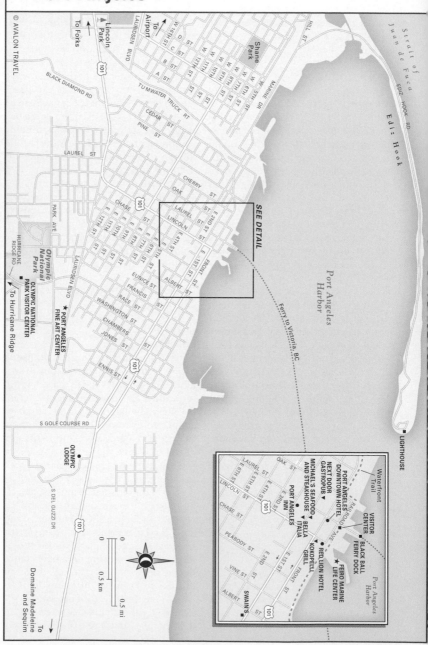

© AVALON TRAVEL

Feiro Marine Life Center

Located next to Hollywood Beach on the Port Angeles waterfront, **Feiro Marine Life Center** (315 N Lincoln St., 360/417-6254, www.feiromarinelifecenter.org, 10am-5pm daily summer, noon-4pm daily winter, $5 adults, $3 children 3-17, children under 3 free) has touch tanks full of marine critters and staff to show you how to touch an anemone or starfish without causing any damage. But it's not just about the colorful sea creatures—there are also wet and dry displays about the very important plant life from the area and microscopes to view slides. Small children will enjoy getting the tide pool experience without having to balance on slippery rocks.

Port Angeles Fine Arts Center

The **Port Angeles Fine Arts Center** (1203 E Lauridsen Blvd., 360/457-3532, www.pafac.org, 11am-5pm Thurs.-Sun. spring-fall, 10am-4pm Thurs.-Sun. winter, free) is a small contemporary art museum started by a painter and philanthropist married to a newspaper publisher. It's located in a midcentury house with a curved side that sits on a hill in Port Angeles, giving visitors great views from the gallery. The Webster's Woods area outside includes a five-acre sculpture park with works by dozens of Northwest artists carefully placed within the trees.

Shopping

If you can't find it at **Swain's** (602 E 1st St., 360/452-2357, www.swainsinc.com, 8am-9pm Mon.-Sat., 9am-6pm Sun.), you probably don't need it in Port Angeles. The general store is a hometown staple, the kind of place where high school students sell cookies as a fundraiser out front. Aisles upon aisles stock piles of blue jeans, rolls of socks, and home goods—think of this as the local, proto-Wal-Mart. Local salmon and halibut catches are listed near the hunting bow displays, and there's plenty of camo, but the shoe selection also includes practical, high-end styles alongside hip waders and hiking boots. The store also has an extensive gardening section.

Food

The Southwestern influence at **Kokopelli Grill** (203 E Front St., 360/457-6040, www.kokopelli-grill.com, 11am-9pm Mon.-Thurs., 11am-10pm Fri.-Sat., 2pm-8pm Sun., $15-35) isn't overwhelming, as the menu still features dishes decidedly not desertlike, such as smoked salmon chowder and Louisiana bayou shrimp and grits. The wall of wine racks and the purple walls, on the other hand, seem to suggest an Italian vineyard theme. But the restaurant is a well-decorated dinner spot that doesn't skimp on portion size—burgers are a real two-handed workout.

The all-underground **Michael's Seafood and Steakhouse** (117B E 1st St., 360/417-6929, www.michaelsdining.com, 4pm-10pm daily, $25-50) has the feel of a wine cellar—which would make its patrons, sitting in quiet booths celebrating big events, the shelved wine. But it's very happy wine in the town's only fine-dining location. Chef's specials include a ceviche made of bay shrimp and geoduck (pronounced "gooey duck"), a giant local mollusk that can live more than 150 years.

Even though the town has its share of grubby taverns, ★ **Next Door Gastropub** (113 W 1st St., Ste. A, 360/504-2613, www.nextdoorgastropub.com, 11am-11pm Mon.-Thurs., 11am-midnight Fri.-Sat., 10am-10pm Sun., $9-30) is a bar with a restaurant feel. A blackboard lists microbrew specials, there's a small outdoor patio, and Sundays feature live music. A night-owl menu includes a build-your-own-french-fries platter.

Downtown's **Bella Italia** (118 E 1st St., 360/457-5442, www.bellaitaliapa.com, 4pm-9pm Sun.-Thurs., 4pm-10pm Fri.-Sat., $10-25) features a spread of fresh Italian dishes; some incorporate local Dungeness crab or clams, halibut caught in Neah Bay, or mushrooms from the forests around the Olympic Mountains. Otherwise, the menu covers the Italian basics—veal parmigiana, chicken saltimbocca, and a slate of pizzas and pastas. The wine list has more than 500 wines, including a special house blend of sangiovese. Despite the overwhelming selection, the restaurant still has a family-dining vibe. The logo in the window is a big, bright tomato, which matches the bright red walls inside and the red exterior door.

Accommodations

Colette's Bed and Breakfast (339 Finn Hall Rd., 360/457-9197, www.colettes.com, $195-375) has 10 acres of beautiful gardens that overlook the Strait of Juan de Fuca. The rhododendron plants, when they bloom, are multicolored, and the grounds also include purple thistles and stately cedar trees. The five rooms have water views and private patios, plus jetted tubs and fireplaces. The decor is right between modern and homey, and rooms are fully equipped with modern conveniences (TVs with cable, wireless Internet, and coffeemakers). There are also pillow and blanket menus. The common room has a fireplace and a 40-foot wall of windows. A small fire pit is outdoors. The extensive breakfasts make use of local ingredients whenever possible.

Despite its name, the **Olympic Lodge** (140 S Del Guzzi Dr., 800/600-2993, www.olympiclodge.com, $179-259) isn't a national park property, or even particularly wilderness-like. Located just off U.S. 101, its backside has the best view, facing a golf course. Still, it's the nicest digs in town, with a light-filled lobby with a wood-burning fireplace and an outdoor pool. Rooms are large and decked out in generic but classy suburban hotel style. Some rooms have patios—fortunately facing the links, not the road.

Port Angeles' only large waterfront hotel, the **Red Lion Hotel** (221 N Lincoln St., 360/452-9215, www.redlion.com, $199-239) has retro appeal. The accordion roof and long hallways have a 1970s vibe, though rooms feel more updated and many face Hollywood Beach and the water. With 186 rooms, meeting space, and an outdoor pool, the hotel has a sprawling, substantial feel.

The colorful paintings on the walls of the **Port Angeles Downtown Hotel** (101 E Front St., 360/565-1125, www.portangelesdowntownhotel.com, $60-120) are done by the manager, and the whole property has a European, hostel feel. Rooms are sparsely appointed, most sharing hall bathrooms, located on the 2nd and 3rd floors of a downtown building. A kitchenette apartment is a little larger, while the apartment suite (which tops out at $120 per night in the high season) boasts two queen beds, a bathroom, and a full kitchen, plus enough living-room space to hold a small dance party.

The **Port Angeles Inn** (111 E 2nd St., 360/452-9285, www.portangelesinn.com, $160-195) is a hardy motel just uphill from the town's two main streets, with lattice balconies, striped awnings, and small windows overlooking the water. For all its homeyness—and the flower baskets do have a comfy charm—it's no backup hotel. Rooms book up for summer weekends, with regular customers planning ahead to get their favorite views.

Information and Services

The website for the **Port Angeles Regional Chamber of Commerce and Visitor Center** (121 E Railroad Ave., 360/452-2363, www.portangeles.org) has useful area information on transportation, lodging, and weather. **Port Angeles Underground and Heritage Tours** (360/460-1001, http://portangelesheritagetours.com, 10am and 2pm Mon.-Sat. May-Sept., 10am and 2pm daily Oct.-Apr., $15 adults, $12 seniors and students, $8 children 6-12, children under 6 free) leave from the office. The website for the **Olympic Peninsula Tourism Commission** (www.olympicpeninsula.org/destinations/port-angeles) also has useful information like festival listings and suggested itineraries. The **Olympic National Park Visitor Center** (3002 Mount Angeles Rd., 360/565-3130, www.nps.gov/olym, open daily but hours vary) has information about activities throughout the entire peninsula.

Getting There

Port Angeles is about an hour's drive from Port Townsend. Take Highway 20 about 13 miles southeast to the bottom of Discovery Bay, where it dead-ends. Then turn right onto U.S. 101 and follow it 34 miles to Port Angeles, where the major highway splits into two one-way streets in town. From Forks, take U.S. 101 about 57 miles northeast, winding through a section of Olympic National Park and around Lake Crescent.

Olympic National Park

The highest peak on the peninsula is called Mount Olympus, the mythic home of the gods, and so the mountain range and landmass itself have a mythic name. But Olympic National Park, the approximately one million protected acres that make up much of the peninsula's northern end, contains treasures of an earthly variety. Its three million annual visitors make it one of the top five most-trafficked national parks, coming in just behind big names like Yellowstone and Yosemite.

It took two Roosevelts to make the park: First, Teddy protected lands as a national monument in one of his last acts as president, then Franklin D. Roosevelt began the push to make it a proper park. It's no wonder the elk that roam the lands in herds are known as Roosevelt elk, and the area was almost given the moniker "Elk National Park."

The heart of the mountain range is

from top to bottom: Olympic National Park Visitor Center; Feiro Marine Life Center; sunset in Port Angeles.

accessed only by the hardiest of back-packers and climbers, but the periphery offers plenty of wild experiences, from hiking among marmots at Hurricane Ridge to watching waves crash on the remote beaches.

Visiting the Park

The Olympics owe their mossy, green feel to the rain that gathers here, up to 14 feet a year on the western side. Precipitation is always a possibility, though chances of the sun breaking out are best in July, August, and September. Hurricane Ridge is snow covered through the winter and early spring months yet is often still accessible to brave drivers on weekends.

Visitors Centers

The **Olympic National Park Visitor Center** (3002 Mount Angeles Rd., 360/565-3130, www.nps.gov/olym, open daily but hours vary by season) in Port Angeles is a kind of gateway to the national park, and a good place to stop whether you're going straight up the hills to Hurricane Ridge or continuing on U.S. 101 to one of the other national park locations. The center has videos and exhibits about the area's natural history and early settlers. There are two short nature trails next to the center, and rangers are available to plan hikes or other activities.

Entrances

Olympic National Park has two major components. The Olympic Mountain range and its surrounding foothills make up a giant circle in the heart of the Olympic Peninsula. The second section of the park is a narrow strip along the west coast of the Olympic Peninsula, reaching from Ozette Lake past Kalaloch. The two pieces don't touch, and it's difficult to visit multiple parts of the park in a single day.

The hugely popular **Hurricane Ridge** area, with its visitors center and trail-heads, is 17 miles south of Port Angeles and has the most activities. Cars must carry chains on the road to Hurricane Ridge November 15-April 1, and the road can close in bad weather. The visitors center (360/565-3130, www.nps.gov/olym, free) is open daily in summer, but weekends only the rest of the year and when the road isn't closed to snow.

West of Port Angeles, the area's main thoroughfare, U.S. 101, goes directly along the shores of Lake Crescent and past the **Storm King Ranger Station** (summer only). This is the easiest national park area to visit without going off the main road, though with fewer activities and vistas here. U.S. 101 is open year-round. The Sol Duc area is a 14-mile drive off U.S. 101. The road leaves the highway west of Lake Crescent and is open year-round when there isn't too much snow.

The **Hoh Rain Forest Visitor Center** is southeast of Forks, about an hour's drive from the small town. It is about 18 miles east of U.S. 101, and the road is open year-round. Farther south, Lake Quinault almost touches U.S. 101, about 43 miles north of Aberdeen. Like Lake Crescent, it is very accessible from the main road but doesn't get as deep into the protected lands and mountains; the road is open year-round.

Fee **entrance stations** ($25 per vehicle, $10 per person on foot, bicycle, or motorcycle) are on the roads to Hurricane Ridge, the Hoh Rain Forest, and Sol Duc. The fee is good for seven days at any Olympic National Park entrance. If roads are open but fee stations are unstaffed, payment is still required at the self-pay stations. No entrance fee is required at Lake Crescent or to drive U.S. 101 through the national park.

★ Hurricane Ridge

The vista from Hurricane Ridge, on clear days, is a breathtaking one, with peaks and deep valleys crowding the panorama. The Olympic Mountain range isn't tall, by most standards, topping off just under 8,000 feet, but the uneven terrain makes

167

Olympic National Park

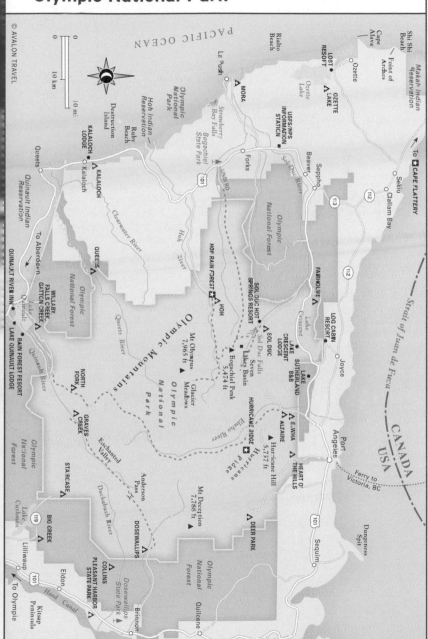

the center of the mountain clump hard to access. This area comes by its name honestly—winds in the exposed meadow near its visitors center top 75 miles per hour, sculpting the snow in the winter and blowing off ball caps in the summer. Numerous trails are accessible from here.

The Hurricane Ridge area is located 17 miles south of Port Angeles on Hurricane Ridge Road. From U.S. 101 in downtown Port Angeles, turn south (away from the water) onto Race Street, which becomes Hurricane Ridge Road. The mountain road is plowed of snow on winter weekends.

Hurricane Ridge Visitor Center

The **Hurricane Ridge Visitor Center** (360/565-3130, www.nps.gov/olym, open year-round, hours vary seasonally) houses exhibits (including a 20-minute orientation film) and a limited snack bar and a gift shop on the lowest level. But the real draw is outdoors, where wildflowers bloom in the alpine meadows in the summer. In their signature wide-brimmed hats, park rangers—part police force, part naturalists, part tour guides—give guided walks and talks about the area.

Hiking
Hurricane Hill
Distance: 3 miles round-trip
Duration: 1.5 hours
Elevation gain: 650 feet
Effort: moderate
Trailhead: Hurricane Ridge Visitor Center
Views of the area get even better from the top of Hurricane Hill, a peak more than 5,700 feet high. From here you can see the broad Strait of Juan de Fuca and the full spread of the Olympic peaks. The entire route is paved, but only the first section is wheelchair accessible.

Big Meadow Trail
Distance: 0.5 mile round-trip
Duration: 20 minutes
Elevation gain: none

Hurricane Ridge

Effort: easy

Trailhead: Hurricane Ridge Visitor Center

The gentle Big Meadow Trail crosses the high-alpine meadows on a paved route. Though it doesn't climb above the parking area, it allows for some new views of the Strait of Juan de Fuca below.

High Ridge Trail

Distance: 0.5 mile round-trip

Duration: 20 minutes

Elevation gain: 200 feet

Effort: easy

Trailhead: Hurricane Ridge Visitor Center

The High Ridge is partially paved, but there's slight elevation gain and a short spur to a viewpoint, where the jagged peaks of the Olympics to the south are visible in sharp relief to the deep valleys that separate them, the bottoms of the deep Vs often lost in thick green trees.

Klahhane Ridge

Distance: 7.6 miles round-trip

Duration: 3 hours

Elevation gain: 1,700 feet

Effort: moderate

Trailhead: Hurricane Ridge Visitor Center

Klahhane Ridge is a more challenging route. Climb 2.8 miles to the Klahhane Switchback Trail, then follow it for 1 mile to Klahhane Ridge. Switchbacks climb through meadows and forest, and even on temperate days can exhaust hikers who don't bring plenty of water. Once on Klahhane Ridge, follow the Lake Angeles Trail for as long as you're comfortable, taking care with the steep drop-offs and taking in views of towering Mount Angeles. Look for maps in the visitors center, since the many trail connections in the area can be confusing.

Winter Sports

In winter, the Hurricane Ridge area is popular with the local crowd, with an average snowfall that tops 400 inches. Skiers from Port Angeles come up on weekends to use **Hurricane Ridge Ski and Snowboard Area** (360/565-3131, www.hurricaneridge.com, $34), one of only three downhill ski areas located in a national park. Two rope tows and one surface lift operate on weekends, with a separate area just for tubing. Downhill and cross-country skis, as well as snowshoes, are available for rent in the visitors center.

Camping

Camping is available in the **Heart O' the Hills** campground (Hurricane Ridge Rd., www.nps.gov/olym, first-come, first-served, $20, year-round), home to 105 sites in old-growth forest and located on the road to Hurricane Ridge. The campground has running water and flush toilets, but no hookups. In summer, rangers lead campfire programs in the amphitheater. When heavy snows hit, campers may have to walk, rather than drive, to campsites. It's located just past the Heart O' the Hills entrance station, about 5 miles from Port Angeles and about 12 miles from the Hurricane Ridge area.

OLYMPIC NATIONAL PARK

Lake Crescent

It's shocking how close the highway gets to the waters of Lake Crescent. It feels like a twitch on the steering wheel would put your car right in the middle of the deep blue, glacier-carved lake. The lake is popular with boaters and divers. This body of water is so deep that measurements are hard to make, but a wrecked 1927 Chevrolet is at the bottom (it takes an experienced diver to go down that far). The lake also has a unique kind of trout, which was isolated in the lake when a landslide blocked it from a nearby lake 7,000 years ago.

Lake Crescent is located right on U.S. 101 about 18 miles west of Port Angeles and about 34 miles east of Forks. The road is on the lake's south shore, passing the Lake Crescent Lodge area, the Storm King Ranger Station, and a boat launch and campground at Fairholme. The Log Cabin Resort is on the north shore.

Storm King Ranger Station

The **Storm King Ranger Station** (www. nps.gov/olym, summer only, hours and days vary) is next to the Lake Crescent Lodge on the lake's south shore, the first right after the highway turnoff and next to the boat launch. It has accessible bathrooms and ranger assistance when open. When it's closed, the front desk at the Lake Crescent Lodge may have useful maps and directions.

Hiking

Marymere Falls Nature Trail

Distance: 1.8 miles round-trip
Duration: 1 hour
Elevation gain: 400 feet
Effort: easy
Trailhead: Storm King Ranger Station next to Lake Crescent

The route travels under U.S. 101 before curving up into old-growth forest. Several other trails branch off from the main route, but junctions are well signed. Just 0.9 mile from the trailhead, it reaches Marymere Falls, a 90-foot drop that can

be viewed from below or from the stairs to the right of the falls. The trail has little elevation gain in the ascent and is one of the easiest, quickest, and most popular day trips in the area. No park fee payment is required.

Mount Storm King

Distance: 4.5 miles round-trip
Duration: 2.5 hours
Elevation gain: 2,000 feet
Effort: moderate
Trailhead: Storm King Ranger Station next to Lake Crescent

This trail begins on the same route as Marymere Falls, then veers east after the trail goes under U.S. 101 and steeply switchbacks up the mountain. The work is worth it; during breaks you can enjoy the lush smell of the damp Olympic greenery. The trail gains a moderate amount of elevation on the grind up, and with exposed ledges, it's not a hike for those new to the outdoors. Two lookouts are near the top, the first with a spectacular view of Lake Crescent.

Sol Duc Falls

Distance: 1.6 miles round-trip
Duration: 1 hour
Elevation gain: 200 feet
Effort: easy
Trailhead: Sol Duc Trailhead at the very end of Sol Duc Hot Springs Road, about a mile past the Sol Duc Hot Springs Resort and the ranger station

The Sol Duc Valley is best known for its hot springs, but the trail to Sol Duc Falls is almost as popular. It's a mostly flat route to the falls, which are wide with many fingers rather than one tall pillar. There are viewing areas and an old shelter. It's a quick walk but a significant 12-mile drive from the highway and requires a park entrance fee. A longer loop can be made by starting at the Sol Duc Hot Springs Resort and taking the Lover's Lane Trail along the Sol Duc River to the Sol Duc Falls, then crossing at the bridge there and returning along the north side of the river for a 6-mile loop.

Waterfall Wanders

Where there's a rain forest and mountains, there are waterfalls. Hundreds of water features are scattered throughout the peninsula. Some are located near the road, while others are accessible only to the hardiest hikers. Of the 23 waterfalls in the greater Olympic Peninsula, the following provide a nice detour on your road trip. Visit www.olympicpeninsula-waterfalltrail.com/map for a complete map and details.

Lake Crescent

* **Marymere Falls:** Just 0.9 mile down the Marymere Falls Nature Trail (page 170), this 90-foot drop can be viewed from below or from the stairs to the right of the falls.

* **Sol Duc Falls.** It's a 12-mile drive to the trail to Sol Duc Falls (page 170), a 0.8-mile walk to a cascading waterfall.

Neah Bay and Ozette Lake

* **Beaver Falls:** This block of falls, about 20 feet wide, is just a few feet off the road on Highway 113 (2 miles from Sappho) heading south on the way to Forks.

Hoh Rain Forest

* **Mineral Creek Falls:** The Hoh River Trail (page 174) starts at the Hoh Rain Forest Visitor Center and runs a full 18 miles to the Blue Glacier. This tall, skinny waterfall is only 2.8 miles from the trailhead, on the left side of the trail.

Lake Quinault

* **Willaby Creek Falls:** The short Quinault Rain Forest Nature Trail (page 176) includes a footbridge across Willaby Creek for a view of the small, multitiered falls.

* **Merriman Falls:** This 40-foot waterfall is just off South Shore Road, 3.5 miles from Gatton Creek Campground (page 176).

* **Bunch Creek Falls:** The 60-foot-long Bunch Creek Falls doesn't fall straight but rather meanders down between rocks. It's just next to Lake Quinault's South Shore Road, 12 miles from where it leaves U.S. 101.

Forks and La Push

* **Strawberry Bay Falls:** On a hike to Third Beach (page 182), turn left once you reach the sand. The 100-foot, very thin stream of water—so small it can disappear completely in summer—is a little more than half a mile south on the beach.

Boating

The 5,000-acre Lake Crescent—so deep it was once fabled to be bottomless—is popular with boaters. It's not unusual to see sailboats next to kayaks and even motorboats. There are boat ramps at Storm King Ranger Station in the middle of the lake, as well as at Fairholme on the west end, and East Beach and Log Cabin Resort on the east end. **Lake Crescent Lodge** (416 Lake Crescent Rd., 360/928-3211, www.olympicnationalparks. com, 9am-4pm daily May-Oct. weather permitting), next to Storm King Ranger Station, rents canoes, single and double kayaks, and rowboats ($20 per hour, $60 per day). **Log Cabin Resort** (3183 East Beach Rd., 888/896-3818, www.olympic-nationalparks.com, 8am-7pm daily May-Sept. weather permitting) rents stand-up paddleboards, single and double kayaks, paddleboats, and canoes ($20 per hour, $60 per day). The **Fairholme Store** on the west end of the lake, just off U.S. 101, rents kayaks, canoes, and rowboats ($10 per hour).

Fishing

Fishing in Lake Crescent is catch-and-release, with a season that lasts June 1-October 31. The lake is home to Beardslee and coastal cutthroat trout. In the 20th century, more than 14.5 million fish were planted in this lake. No license is required, and anglers must use artificial lures with single, barbless hooks. Motorboats are also allowed on the lake. Lake Crescent no longer rents fishing equipment, so guests need to bring their own or stock up in Port Angeles; **Swain's** (602 E 1st St., 360/452-2357, www.swainsinc.com, 8am-9pm Mon.-Sat., 9am-6pm Sun.) is a good resource for outdoor gear.

Food

The **Lake Crescent Lodge Restaurant** (416 Lake Crescent Rd., 360/928-3211, www.olympicnationalparks.com, 7am-10:30am, 11am-2:30pm, and 5pm-9pm daily May-Jan., $15-40) has windows that overlook Lake Crescent. It specializes in fine Washington wines and has dozens of Washington and Oregon vintages on the menu. Dinner entrées include a bison burger and wild salmon cooked on cedar planks. The lavender lemonade is homemade, and desserts use local marionberries.

Because the hot pools are a dozen miles from the main highway and even farther from other restaurants, the **Springs Restaurant** (12076 Sol Duc Hot Springs Rd., 360/327-3583, www.olympicnationalparks.com, 7am-10:30am and 5pm-9pm daily Mar.-Oct., $15-35), at Sol Duc Hot Springs Resort, is popular with both hotel guests and campers. It serves both breakfast and dinner, but a deli out by the hot springs pools has sandwiches, snacks, beer, and wine at lunchtime, and also sells boxed lunches. The restaurant's breakfast features pancakes, omelets, and other hearty dishes, including a Dungeness crab cake Benedict, and dinner includes fresh fish, pork ribs, and a rotating mac-and-cheese special.

Accommodations

Guests gather around the lobby's stone fireplace at ★ **Lake Crescent Lodge** (416 Lake Crescent Rd., 360/928-3211, www.olympicnationalparks.com, rooms $123-238, cottages $292-328), even if they're staying in one of the hotel's cottages. The building was erected in 1916 and is a light gray, wood-paneled building—not a heavy log or stone lodge. A glassed-in sun porch faces the crescent-shaped lake. Some rooms in the historical building share bathrooms, but others have private baths in the Storm King, Marymere, and Pyramid Mountain buildings. None have TVs, all the better to focus on nature. One- and two-bedroom cottages have little porches with wicker chairs, but are lined up in a row—they're private but not secluded. The Roosevelt Fireplace Cabins have fireplaces but still no TVs or telephone. All rooms and cabins are simply decorated, and although many materials are worn, the hotel has a shabby charm.

Across the lake from Lake Crescent Lodge, the **Log Cabin Resort** (3183 East Beach Rd., 888/896-3818, www.olympicnationalparks.com, May-Sept., rooms $164-191, cabins $111-205) is a calmer destination, off the beaten path of U.S. 101. Hotels have been in the spot since 1895, though the current building dates back only to the 1950s. Lodge rooms have private bathrooms and a small outdoor patio, all facing the water (and the mountains beyond). A-frame chalets sleep up to six, while the rougher camper cabins share communal bath facilities but do have electricity. Other rustic cabins date back to the 1920s and have lake views as well as private bathrooms, and some have kitchens. A small general store sells some food, beer and wine, and candy. A restaurant, the **Sunnyside Cafe,** has a breakfast buffet ($13.75 adults, $8.75 children 5-12, children under 5 free), and a lakeside deli offers sandwiches and pizzas, plus laundry facilities.

The heated pools of **Sol Duc Hot Springs Resort** (12076 Sol Duc Hot Springs Rd., 360/327-3583, www.olympic-nationalparks.com, Mar.-Oct., $208-287) are its biggest draw, bringing people up a 12-mile road that traces the Sol Duc River in the north end of the national park. The mineral waters are pumped into round pools used by cabin guests and fee-paying walk-ins; there are also massage services. Besides the natural hot tubs, the accommodations are rather bare, and the "deluxe-style" cabins have dated furniture. The river suite has three bedrooms and better decor. The area waterfalls are noted for their misty beauty, and coho salmon clog the river when they spawn. Several trails leave from the resort area.

Camping

Fairholme Campground (U.S. 101, 27 miles west of Port Angeles, www.nps.gov/olym, May-Sept., $20) is located on the westernmost point of Lake Crescent. The campground has 88 sites and flush toilets but no hookups or showers, and all sites are first-come, first served. A boat launch is here, and a general store sells snacks and candy and rents boats.

The **Sol Duc Campground** (Sol Duc Hot Springs Rd., 12.5 miles from U.S. 101, www.nps.gov/olym, year round, $21-24) is helpful because it's close to the hot springs pools. It offers 82 reservable sites, many along the Sol Duc River, with running water in summer. There are no hookups or showers. In winter, there is no water and only pit toilets, and the road may close in bad weather.

The **Sol Duc Hot Springs Resort Campground** (12076 Sol Duc Hot Springs Rd., 360/327-3583, www.olympicnation-alparks.com, Mar.-Oct., $21-40) is about a quarter mile from Sol Duc Hot Springs Resort. It has 17 sites with water and electric, and the campground accepts reservations.

from top to bottom: Lake Crescent; Neah Bay; Kalaloch.

★ Hoh Rain Forest

Unlike other Olympic National Park spots, there are no sweeping vistas of peaks or the ocean here. The real draw is the trees—many Sitka spruce—and thick forest. The 12-14 feet of rain that falls here annually is the reason the forest feels so rich. When trees die and fall, they become nurse logs to new plants, so it's rare to find any surface that isn't coated in mossy life. Sometimes trees grow in a line, evidence that they all began on the same nurse log.

Come to see one of the most spectacular temperate rain forests in the world and more shades of green than you thought existed. Most travelers stop at the visitors center before hitting the trails or seeing the rushing Hoh River. Keep an eye out for Roosevelt elk, birds, and black bears; about one-tenth of the park's elk live in this river valley.

Located on the western edge of the park, the Hoh Rain Forest is accessible via Upper Hoh Road heading east from U.S. 101. Take U.S. 101 for 13 miles south from Forks and look for national park signs. At the end of the 18-mile road is an 88-site year-round campground, located on the banks of the Hoh River.

Hoh Rain Forest Visitor Center

In the **Hoh Rain Forest Visitor Center** (Upper Hoh Rd., 18 miles from U.S. 101, 360/374-6925, www.nps.gov, daily June-Sept., Fri.-Tues. May-June, hours vary) exhibits explain the complexities of the temperate rain forest, and self-guided nature trails leave from the central location. A small gift shop is here, but no food is sold; picnic tables are outside. The small, low building blends into the thick forest, and even the phone booth is layered with moss and lichen. Cars pass through a fee station before reaching the visitors center.

Hiking
Hall of the Mosses
Distance: 0.8 mile round-trip
Duration: 30 minutes
Elevation gain: 100 feet
Effort: easy
Trailhead: Hoh Rain Forest Visitor Center

Look for information plaques along this short, informational trail, which winds through the giant, moss-covered trees that Olympic National Park is famous for. Elk graze nearby, and the signage tells the story of the forest's complex ecosystem.

Spruce Nature Trail
Distance: 1.2 miles round-trip
Duration: 45 minutes
Elevation gain: 250 feet
Effort: easy
Trailhead: Hoh Rain Forest Visitor Center

Like the Hall of the Mosses trail, this is a short, family-friendly wander through the woods, though it also goes to the Hoh River, an ideal spot to stop for a snack. Wildlife in the area includes bears, but rangers keep tabs on dangerous animals, so it's a safe area.

Hoh River Trail to Glacier Meadows
Distance: up to 35 miles round-trip
Duration: 1 hour-multiple days
Elevation gain: 300-3,700 feet
Effort: moderate
Trailhead: Hoh Rain Forest Visitor Center

This more intense hike goes along the Hoh River all the way to the base of Mount Olympus. Climbers hoping to scale the Olympics' tallest peak often begin here. It's 17.3 miles to Glacier Meadows below the mountain, which is about as far as casual backpackers should go (past that point, special equipment is necessary to go up the Blue Glacier to the summit). Day hikers can follow the trail as far out as they like before turning back. The river is visible after 1 mile, the Mount Tom Creek campsite is 2.3 miles out, and **Mineral Creek Falls** is 2.8 miles out. Five Mile Island, in the Hoh River, is about 5.3 miles from the visitors center, and a picnic shelter is 0.5 mile farther, a good place to turn around for an intense, nearly 12-mile day hike. Fortunately, there's little elevation gain in the first

10 or so miles from the Hoh Rain Forest Visitor Center, so hikers can appreciate the burbling river and giant trees.

Boating

Located outside the national park, **Rainforest Paddlers** (4883 Upper Hoh Rd., 360/374-5254, www.rainforest paddlers.com, May-Oct., $44-79) offers river rafting and kayak trips on the Hoh River. The Hoh is mostly serene, never more than Class II rapids, and guides talk about the area's natural and human history during half- or full-day trips. Wetsuit, helmet, and life jacket rentals are included. They also have kayak rentals ($11 per hour, $29 per day), but customers must have kayak experience. The store is almost 5 miles up Upper Hoh Road, on the way to the Hoh Rain Forest Visitor Center. A shuttle will take renters within 10 miles for $10 per group.

Camping

Right before the visitors center is the **Hoh Campground** (Upper Hoh Rd., 18 miles from U.S. 101, www.nps.gov/olym, $20, year-round) with three loops of 88 sites with no hookups. Sites are in the old-growth forest next to the Hoh River. There's a dumpsite, running water, and storage lockers to keep animals out of food. Like most Olympic National Park campgrounds, reservations are not accepted as sites are first-come, first-served.

Lake Quinault

Located on the edge of Olympic National Park, Lake Quinault is at the intersection of public recreational use, protected forest, and Native American reservation land. The lake sits near where two forks of the Quinault River combine, at the base of the Quinault Valley. It makes a great base for exploring the national park's forests. You can camp anywhere, from a remote, small campground to a lakeside site with amenities and easy access to restaurants. Short trails wind near

the lake, and longer day hikes leave farther up the valley. And best of all, you're never far from U.S. 101.

Lake Quinault is within the lands of the Quinault Indian Nation, which regulates boating and fishing access; the lake has a limited trout fishing season. Permits are required, and the front desk of the Lake Quinault Lodge has more information on what's required at any given time. Swimming is permitted.

Information Stations

Two offices have visitor information on Lake Quinault. On the north side of the lake, the **Quinault Rain Forest Ranger Station** (North Shore Rd., 4 miles from U.S. 101, www.nps.gov/olym, Thurs.-Mon. June-Sept., hours vary) on Kestner Creek has bathrooms, picnic tables, and a ranger available to answer questions. Short interpretive trails leave from the parking lot, including Kestner Homestead Trail and Maple Glade Trail.

On the south shore of the lake is the **Pacific Ranger District-Quinault office** (353 South Shore Rd., 360/288-2525, www.fs.usda.gov, 8am-4:30pm Mon.-Fri., 9am-4pm Sat.-Sun. summer; 8am-4:30pm Mon.-Fri. winter). It's operated by the U.S. Forest Service, not the national park, but staff can answer many questions about driving and hiking in the area.

Hiking
Kestner Homestead Trail
Distance: 1.5 miles round-trip
Duration: 1 hour
Elevation gain: none
Effort: easy
Trailhead: Quinault Rain Forest Ranger Station on North Shore Road

On the north end of the lake, this trail heads up Kestner Creek before reaching the site of the 1889 Kestner-Higley Homestead, where a barn and house still stand. Interpretive signs along the route explain homesteading and pioneer life in the valley. The short hike is rewarding for those who've tired of the endless lush greenery and need a little human history.

Quinault Loop Trail

Distance: 4 miles round-trip
Duration: 2 hours
Elevation gain: 500 feet
Effort: moderate
Trailhead: Rainforest Trail Loop trailhead, 1.3 miles up South Shore Road

Stop in the ranger station for a map of the trails from this trailhead as they can be combined in a number of ways. For a moderate stretch of the legs, go up into the forest past a cedar bog, then back down to the lakeside, past Lake Quinault Lodge, and along the shore back to where you started.

Quinault Rain Forest Nature Trail

Distance: 0.5 mile
Duration: 20 minutes
Elevation gain: 50 feet
Effort: easy
Trailhead: Rainforest Trail Loop trailhead, 1.3 miles up South Shore Road

The trail gives a quick peek into the woods; some, but not all, of the short loop is wheelchair accessible. Walk past the old-growth conifer forest and thick ground cover of ferns that define this part of the Olympics. As you pass the bridge over the South Shore Road, look underneath to where Willaby Creek heads toward the lake. A footbridge across the creek has a view of **Willaby Creek Falls.**

Graves Creek Trail

Distance: 7 miles round-trip
Duration: 3 hours
Elevation gain: 1,500 feet
Effort: moderate
Trailhead: at the end of South Shore Road, past where it turns to gravel (6.2 miles past the bridge that links the North and South Shore Roads)

Get away from the bustle of the lake by heading up the Quinault Valley and along Graves Creek. Switchbacks help make the elevation gain bearable, and a number of (easy) creek crossings keep the path

interesting. When the trail dead-ends into the rushing waterway at 3.5 miles, turn around and head back the way you came.

To skip hiking altogether, head to **Merriman Falls,** a 40-foot waterfall a few feet off the road. It's about 3.5 miles from Gatton Creek Campground on South Shore Road and on the way to the Graves Creek Trailhead.

Accommodations

A rain gauge is painted on the chimney exterior at ★ **Lake Quinault Lodge** (345 South Shore Rd., Quinault, 360/288-2900, www.olympicnationalparks.com, $229-364), its rainbow hues cheerfully marking how many feet of water fell in the previous year. The original 1926 building has steep roofs and Catskill resort charm, with Adirondack chairs dotting the lawn that slopes down to Lake Quinault. An indoor pool and game room entertain guests during real downpours, because the original guest rooms are small. The decor in the main building matches the rustic lodge style of the structure—wood furniture and delicate light fixtures, and some rooms have claw-foot tubs. Fireside, Lakeside, and Boathouse rooms in other buildings have various combinations of views, decks, fireplaces, and more modern furnishings. The **dining room** (www.olympicnationalparks.com, 7:30am-3pm and 5pm-9pm daily spring-summer, 7:30am-11am, 11:30am-2pm, and 5pm-8pm daily fall-winter, $12-36) is named for its most famous guest, Franklin Delano Roosevelt, who dined here less than a year before proposing the lands become a national park. Coincidence? Perhaps it was the lovely view. Today the restaurant serves omelets that use Olympic Mountain mushrooms, hearty burgers, and some seafood dishes.

The Quinault area has several other accommodations that are not national park concessions. The **Quinault River Inn** (8 River Dr., 360/288-2237, www.

quinaultriverinn.com, $159) is just off U.S. 101, right where the Quinault River leaves Lake Quinault. Some rooms have wood-paneled walls and balconies overlooking the river. Most are decorated with vintage-style photography. There is a campfire circle outside, a small fitness center, and an RV campground ($29) that takes reservations.

On the south shore, **Rain Forest Resort** (516 South Shore Rd., 360/288-2535, www.rainforestresort.com, rooms $145-189, cabins $179-245) sits right on the lake with two small buildings with hotel rooms, all with simple furnishings and private bathrooms. Cabins have fireplaces, and some have kitchens as well. The RV campground has 31 sites ($30) with water and electrical hookups, but it does not accept reservations.

Camping

Two campgrounds are located within the Olympic National Park, past Lake Quinault and up the Quinault Valley. **Graves Creek Campground** (South Shore Rd., 19 miles from U.S. 101, www.nps.gov/olym, $20, year-round) is located in temperate rain forest on the South Fork of the Quinault River. The 30 primitive sites (no hookups) are quiet, with restrooms in summer, but no water and only pit toilets in winter. The road to the campground is gravel for the last dozen miles.

North Fork Campground (North Shore Rd., 17 miles from U.S. 101, www.nps.gov/olym, $10, open seasonally) has only 9 sites, no water, and only pit toilets. When it's open, it's a very remote camping spot. The road in is narrow and not recommended for RVs.

Three national forest campgrounds are located on the south shore of Lake Quinault, all about 1 mile from each other. **Willaby Campground** (South Shore Rd., 1.5 miles from U.S. 101, www.fs.usda.gov, $25), **Falls Creek Campground** (South Shore Rd., 3 miles from U.S. 101, www.fs.usda.gov, $25), and **Gatton Creek Campground** (South Shore Rd., 3.5 miles from U.S. 101, www.fs.usda.gov, $20) are all close to area trails and the lakeshore. Willaby and Falls Creek sites have flush toilets, while Gatton Creek has only pit toilets. Combined they offer 50 RV sites (no hookups) and 17 walk-in tent sites. Reservations are not accepted.

Getting There

Lake Quinault is next to U.S. 101, 63 miles south of Forks and 42.5 miles north of Aberdeen. The North Shore Road, which heads east from U.S. 101, leads to the Quinault Rain Forest Ranger Station and then continues on to the North Fork campgrounds in the Quinault Valley via a gravel road. The South Shore Road, which also heads east from U.S. 101 about 2 miles south of North Shore Road, leads to Lake Quinault Lodge and the Olympic National Forest park information station, and then becomes a gravel road that leads up to the Graves Creek Campground. There is a bridge across the Quinault River past where both become gravel roads.

Neah Bay

The community of Neah Bay is so isolated, it's unsurprising that the Makah Indian Reservation town flew under the radar for so long. Situated on a small bay at the state's—and the country's—very northwest tip, this is home to fewer than 1,000 people and was best known to anglers who came to reach the halibut that live just off the coast. But in the late 1990s, the Makah petitioned the U.S. government and International Whaling Commission to allow them to partake in their treaty-granted whaling rights.

When the Makah hunted a gray whale in 1999, their first in 70 years, it became an internationally followed incident, with protesters making the long trek to Neah Bay. The hunt used a combination of traditional methods—including using almost every part of the whale's blubber, oil, and meat—and modern techniques intended to more humanely kill the whale. Despite the attention and legal struggle, the Makah haven't hunted a whale since, outside of a kill not sanctioned by the tribe in 2007.

Besides tribal buildings, the village is home to a U.S. Coast Guard station and a tugboat tasked specifically to respond to oil spills in the remote but crowded shipping lane.

Sights
Makah Museum
Two giant statues welcome visitors to Neah Bay and the Makah Cultural and Research Center. The complex is home to the **Makah Museum** (1880 Bayview Ave., 360/645-2711, http://makahmuseum. com, 10am-5pm daily, $5 adults, $4 students, children 5 and under free), which is home to many of the artifacts discovered at the Lake Ozette site that yielded an archaeological bonanza in 1970. A botanical garden outside grows native plants. The museum store sells crafts from Makah artists as well as the recreation permit ($10) needed to park in any reservation trailhead or beach.

★ Cape Flattery
Just past Neah Bay and up a few miles from the last signs of civilization is the trailhead for **Cape Flattery,** a jagged point where the Pacific Ocean meats the Strait of Juan de Fuca. The 0.75-mile trail is well maintained, with boardwalks and steps over the muddy terrain. Several viewing platforms face the tiny coves and massive sea stacks that make up the point, with the biggest facing Tatoosh Island. The small island just off the coast was once a Makah whaling camp and now has the unmanned Cape Flattery lighthouse, built in 1857. Although wind, rain, and furious waves are common, on clear days whales and otters can be seen in the dark waters.

Food and Accommodations
Even though dining options in Neah Bay are scarce, the **Warm House Restaurant** (900-1099 Bayview Ave., 360/645-2077, 7am-7pm Sun.-Thurs., 7am-8pm Fri.-Sat, $8-15) has harbor and marina views and staples like halibut and burgers. Service is known to be slow, but there aren't many reasons to hurry in this out-of-the-way town.

★ **Hobuck Beach Resort** (2726 Makah Passage, 360/645-2339, www.hobuckbeachresort.com, cabins $150-200) has campsites and RV hookups, but once you've made it to this far-off corner of the world, it's worth staying in the waterfront cabins. Small but solid, some have beautiful views and are fully furnished, all with stoves and fridges. Most have twin bunks or a sleeping loft in addition to a master bedroom. Follow signs from Neah Bay, leaving the main road before it heads out to Cape Flattery. Beach access requires a $15 daily pass.

Getting There
Neah Bay is located at the end of Highway 112, about 71 miles northwest of Port Angeles. From Port Angeles, take U.S. 101 west for about 5 miles to Highway 112 and turn right. Follow Highway 112 west for 65 miles to the small town of Neah Bay. From Forks, drive north on U.S. 101 for about 12 miles, then turn left onto Highway 113. Head north on Highway 113 for 10 miles to where it meets Highway 112; stay straight to follow Highway 112 west for 26.5 miles to Neah Bay.

Ozette Lake

There's a serenity to Ozette Lake, located near the north end of Olympic National Park's coastal strip. The lake is only barely inland, reached by a 21-mile road from Seiku on Highway 112—but the expanse takes well over an hour to travel as it follows a series of rivers toward the ocean. Though remote, the area was once populated by homesteaders, who left traces of buildings that stood more than a century ago. Native American petroglyphs are older signs of civilization. Continue all the way to **Ozette Ranger Station** (Hoko-Ozette Rd., 206/963-2725, www.nps.gov/olym, hours vary but usually daily June-Sept.), 21 miles from Highway 112. The ranger station has bathrooms and picnic areas, and there's a national park fee station.

Hiking
Ozette Triangle/Cape Alava Loop
Distance: 9.5 miles round-trip
Duration: 4.5 hours
Elevation gain: 100 feet
Effort: moderate
Trailhead: Ozette Ranger Station

Though the hike from Ozette to the ocean is time-consuming, it's one of the state's most classic hikes. Before you begin, ask for a handout at the Ozette Ranger Station to spot the Makah petroglyphs on Wedding Rock, and to consult tide charts to avoid being trapped during high tides. Hike three miles on a boardwalk trail (which can be slippery when wet) that hovers above the delicate forest, eventually reaching a wet prairie at a little over two miles; it was once a farm but shows little evidence. Continue to the beach and the roaring Pacific, where at low tide the tide pools teem with life, and sea otters can be spotted in the ocean. Turn left and make your way to Wedding Rock and the Cape Alava archaeological site. A 300-year-old village was unearthed by archaeologists, who found more than 50,000 artifacts, among them longhouses that had been buried in mudslides. A small replica longhouse stands at the site, but most of what was recovered is in the Makah Museum in Neah Bay. Return via the Sand Point Trail, marked on the beach with a large disc.

Fishing
A license is not required to fish in Ozette Lake, but you can only keep yellow perch, largemouth bass, pikeminnow, and bullhead (with no limits) from the last Saturday in April to October 31. Only artificial lures and barbless single-point hooks are permitted. Other fish are catch-and-release. Check the Olympic National Park's fishing regulations (www.nps.gov/olym/fishregs.htm) for any updates and consumption advisories. Boat launches are next to the Ozette Ranger Station and about a mile south of Lost Resort on Hoko-Ozette Road. However, there are no spots to rent fishing gear or boats.

Camping
The national park campground on **Ozette Lake** (Hoko-Ozette Rd., 21 miles from Highway 112, $20, year-round) has only 15 sites and limited bathroom facilities. Spots fill quickly in summer, and some campsites close when water levels rise. It has limited drinking water access and only pit toilets; no RV hookups. All sites are first-come, first-served.

Lost Resort (208660 Hoko-Ozette Rd., 360/963-2899, www.lostresort.net, Feb. 15-Nov. 15, campsites $20, cabins $85), just outside the national park boundary, has more campsites and sells essentials like espresso and breakfast. Cabins are rustic, each with a double bed and bunk bed, linens, and electric stove; showers and bathrooms are attached to the store. The owners claim to have never filled the campground or been forced to turn away campers.

Getting There
Lake Ozette is one of the most remote parts of Olympic National Park. From Port Angeles, it's a two-hour drive. Go west on U.S. 101 for 4.5 miles, then turn right onto Highway 112 West. Follow it for 48.5 miles, sometimes winding along the coast, through the towns of Clallam Bay and Sekiu; 2.3 miles after Sekiu, turn

left onto Hoko-Ozette Road and follow it 21 miles to Ozette Lake.

From Forks, take U.S. 101 north 10 miles and turn left onto Highway 113. Go 10 miles north to where it meets and becomes Highway 112. Stay straight and follow Highway 112 for 10.5 miles to Hoko-Ozette Road; follow it 21 miles to Ozette Lake. For both routes, the last gas station is in Clallam Bay, about 40 miles from Ozette Lake.

Forks

Once upon a time, there was a tiny town that wasn't really on the road to anywhere. It was best known to anglers, campers, and anyone making the full loop of the Olympic Peninsula. Then a tiny book called *Twilight* happened to Forks—the teen vampire romance is set here—and the one-time timber town became the destination for vampire fans the world over.

Twilight mania has largely faded in Forks since the release of the last movie—the films weren't shot here, and you're more likely to see fishing puns on motel reader boards than vampire references. The town remains a useful fuel stop and home base for trips to Neah Bay, La Push, or the western end of the national park.

Sights
Even though mania over Stephenie Meyer's blockbuster book series has mostly died down, its impact on Forks was notable. The town's chamber of commerce website (http://forkswa.com) has an entire section devoted to the phenomenon, including the annual celebration in September, Forever Twilight; head to **Rainforest Arts Center** (11 N. Forks Ave., 360/374-2531, limited hours) for a gallery of costumes and props from the movie, including a motorcycle. Tours used to be offered by various locals, but as the phenomenon has died down, they've ceased. A vacation rental on the road to La Push

has billed itself as the home of a book character, and drivers stop to photograph the red house and prominent sign. Just before the edge of Forks on U.S. 101 is an outdoor firewood stand hawking "Twilight firewood," which, at $5 per bundle, appears to be indistinguishable from other firewood sold at local on-your-honor roadside stands.

Food
The prices at **Sully's Drive-In** (220 S Forks Ave., 360/374-5075, 10:30am-10pm Mon.-Sat., $4) are a throwback to another era, when a deluxe burger could actually come in under $3. The menu is a gut-busting array of chili dogs, fish-and-chips, burgers, and delicious milkshakes, but it's not actually a drive-in, so at least you'll get a few steps of exercise on the way in.

The **Forks Coffee Shop** (241 S Forks Ave., 360/374-6769, www.forkscoffee-shop.com, 5:30am-8pm daily, $5-18) is a basic diner, albeit one with an 18-point stuffed elk head as decor. It has booths and a long lunch counter, and the menu is the kind that calls pancakes "hotcakes." Burgers are only $2.50, and the kitchen will pack sack lunches with sandwiches, fruit, pastries, chips, and candy.

The bright yellow building that houses **Taqueria Santa Ana** (80 Calawah Way, 360/374-3339, 7am-9pm Mon.-Sat., 7am-8pm Sun., $7-15) is a welcoming sight in an often drizzly town, and the no-frills Mexican joint dishes equally bright meals. Breakfasts include loaded Mexican omelets and, sometimes, cinnamon toast specials, while the dinner menu is a broad selection of tacos, tortas, and burritos. Order at the counter and pick a glass-bottled drink to enjoy while you wait.

Head to **Blakeslee's Bar and Grille** (1222 S Forks Ave., 360/374-5003, 11am-11pm Sun.-Thurs, 11am-2am Fri.-Sat., $10-27) on the north end of town for drinks and something fried, but don't expect frills. The building is somewhat blank and overlarge, inside and out, but the place attracts locals who appreciate the full bar, pool table, and social atmosphere.

Accommodations

There's a certain simplicity to the **Forks Motel** (351 S Forks Ave., 360/374-6243, www.forksmotel.com, $95-175). Rooms are small and the TVs are tiny, and the beds aren't winning any comfort awards. But rooms are cheap and plentiful in the property, and some have lovely exposed beam ceilings. The motel even has an outdoor pool for the rare warm, sunny days in Forks.

"Edward Cullen didn't sleep here" reads one of the slogans on the sign for **Olympic Suites Inn** (800 Olympic Dr., 800/262-3433, www.olympicsuitesinn.com, $104-119). (For the uninitiated, he's the *Twilight* vampire.) The collection of suites feels more like a neighborhood apartment complex than a hotel, nestled in thick fir trees just outside Forks. The suites come in one- and two-bedroom sizes and have full kitchens and living rooms. Signs remind guests not to gut fish in the recently renovated units.

The three-story 1916 house that holds the **Miller Tree Inn Bed and Breakfast** (654 E Division St., 360/374-6806, www.millertreeinn.com, $215-275) has a large wraparound porch and a white picket fence. This is the classic bed-and-breakfast experience. Some rooms have gas fireplaces or jetted tubs, and all have TVs. Some rooms have quilts on the wall and some bric-a-brac, but most are more understated. The house has a cat, which is kept out of guest rooms. Although the inn is close to the middle of town, the views are mostly of hillsides and an old barn.

The **Pacific Inn Motel** (352 S Forks Ave., 360/374-9400, www.pacificinnmotel.com, $104-199) is, for the most part, a basic motel in the middle of Forks. Rooms have standard motel furnishings, air-conditioning, wireless Internet, and flat-screen TVs, and there are on-site laundry facilities. A larger suite has

a gas fireplace and a washer and dryer in the room. The motel does have a few *Twilight*-themed rooms with posters, dark linens, and embroidered towels.

Information and Services

The **Forks NPS/USFS Recreation Information Center** (551 S Forks Ave./U.S. 101, 360/374-5877, www.nps.gov/olym, hours vary, closed in winter) has maps and a few exhibits about the local wilderness and the ocean coast. Rangers can answer questions about hikes in the area.

Getting There

Forks is located on U.S. 101, 56.5 miles west of Port Angeles and 107 miles north of Aberdeen.

La Push

West of Forks, the Quileute Indian Reservation at La Push is a very small settlement built at the end of the Quillayute River. The beaches west of Forks may not be named with any imagination, but the stretches of First, Second, and Third Beaches are rugged and beautiful. First Beach is the beach within the town of La Push, and a good viewing spot for drive-up whale-watching. Second and Third Beaches require flat hikes on boardwalk trails to reach secluded shorelines surrounded by headlands and natural rock arches.

Hiking

The epic waves, stately sea stacks, and sandy stretches of La Push's best beaches are accessible only by short hikes.

Second Beach Trail

Distance: 1.4 miles round-trip
Duration: 1 hour
Elevation gain: none
Effort: easy
Trailhead: a small parking lot on La Push Road about 0.75 mile from where the road ends in La Push (past Quileute tribal administration buildings)

Take an easy ramble through the seaside woods to reach the ocean; you'll hear and smell it well before you see the sand. Second Beach is a mile wide with natural rock arches and views of sea stacks inhabited by birds. The walk isn't too taxing, but don't try to cross the headlands to the beaches on either side; tides and crumbling, steep coastline can be dangerous. Instead, return the way you came.

Third Beach Trail

Distance: 3.6 miles round-trip
Duration: 2 hours
Elevation gain: 300 feet
Effort: moderate
Trailhead: 3.8 miles west of where Mora Road branches off La Push Road

A walk on a wide forest trail eventually becomes a careful descent down to the crashing waves; the trail isn't too difficult thanks to roots and rocks that serve as steps, but be ready to have your hands available for balance. The route ends at the mile-long beach between two headlands, covered in driftwood that visitors often pile into forts or makeshift benches. If you'd like to possibly catch a glimpse of small **Strawberry Bay Falls**—so thin it sometimes disappears completely in summer—turn left once you hit the sand; it's a little more than half a mile south on the beach. Swimming isn't recommended on these beaches, where currents can be strong and the waters of the Pacific Ocean are very cold. Expert surfers and sea kayakers take to the waves, but most visitors enjoy the wild views from the sandy and rocky shore.

Surfing

The waves in the entire northwest corner of the state are intense, and the surfing out here isn't anything like the chill, crowded scene on California or Hawaiian beaches. **North By Northwest Surf Company** (902 S Lincoln St., Port Angeles, 360/452-5144, www.nxnwsurf.com, noon-6pm Tues.-Fri., 9am-6pm Sat.-Sun.) is headquartered in Port Angeles but has a summer outpost in La Push, where it offers one-day surf lessons ($70-80 with equipment) along what it calls "the last remaining stretch of true wilderness in the continental U.S." The company also rent surfboards, wetsuits, and other gear ($15-30 per day).

Food and Accommodations

There's not much to the **River's Edge Restaurant** (41 Main St., 360/374-0777, 8am-7pm daily, $10-13) in La Push, but there are generous portions of simple salads, salmon dishes, and steaks. Look for the multicolored totem pole outside. The views are much more spectacular than the food, with windows facing the ocean, sea stacks, and marina.

Even though there's little for tourists in La Push, the **Quileute Oceanside Resort** (330 Ocean Dr., 360/374-5267, www.quileuteoceanside.com, $20 camping, $40 RV sites, $134-189 rooms, $99-299 cabins) has been built into quite the complex, with hotel rooms and cabins just outside the town proper. The 33 deluxe waterfront cabins are the most impressive, with fireplaces, kitchens, and large jetted tubs, some with beach views. The hotel rooms have kitchens or kitchenettes.

The **Mora Campground** (Mora Rd., 3.6 miles from La Push Rd., www.nps.gov/olym, $20), run by Olympic National Park, is just across the Quillayute River mouth, but getting there from La Push means driving 6 miles back up La Push Road to where it meets Mora Road and following that 3 miles to the campground. It has 94 first-come, first-served sites in the forest, some with river views. The campground has an RV dump station (but no hookups) and flush toilets. A ranger station is open intermittently in summer. Rialto Beach is 2 miles farther down Mora Road and just 200 feet from the road via an accessible path. The Hole-in-the-Wall arched rock formation is 1.5 miles north on the beach. Always check tide tables before hiking on the beach so as not to get trapped at high tide.

Getting There
From Forks, head north on U.S. 101 for 1.5 miles and turn left onto La Push Road/Highway 110. Follow La Push Road/Highway 110 for just under 8 miles. Where Mora Road splits from the main road, stay on La Push Road for another 6 miles. The road ends in the small settlement of La Push. First Beach is located at the end of the road at a large parking area.

Stopping Along the Coast
Scenic **Ruby Beach** (U.S. 101, 27 miles south of Forks and 19.5 miles north of Kalaloch) has a free parking area just off the highway and requires a short 300-foot walk down to the shore. With tide pools and many rock formations and sea stacks, it's one of the most picturesque beaches on the coast and makes for a quick stop. The sand is somewhat red in places, but the stretch is breathtaking even without the beach's namesake shade. You can hike 3 miles north along the water to where the Hoh River empties into the ocean.

Kalaloch

Kalaloch, a Quinault word for "good place to land," is a small stop along a long stretch of U.S. 101 that sticks close to the beach. **Kalaloch Ranger Station** (U.S. 101, 34.5 miles south of Forks) is on the inland side of the highway and has a few exhibits about shore wildlife, as well as rangers with area maps and advice about hiking along the beach.

Food
The **Kalaloch Creekside Restaurant** (157151 U.S. 101, 360/962-2271, www. thekalalochlodge.com, 7am-9pm daily, $16-38) in the Kalaloch Lodge has an outdoor patio and views of where Kalaloch Creek meets the Pacific Ocean amid a mess of driftwood. The menu has egg and pancake dishes for breakfast, a salmon burger and flatbread pizzas for lunch, and dinner entrées like Pacific lingcod and grilled salmon with a marionberry port sauce.

Accommodations and Camping
The ★ **Kalaloch Lodge** (157151 U.S. 101, 360/962-2271, www.thekalalochlodge. com, $195-311 rooms, $246-350 cabins)— pronounce it "klay-lock"—sits on a pristine stretch of Pacific coastline, nestled in a small cove. The main lodge has beds with Pendleton blankets, and some have lovely views of Kalaloch Creek and the ocean; others are above the kitchen and face U.S. 101. The larger Becker's Room has a wood-burning fireplace that comes with a bundle of wood. Ten more rooms in the Seacrest Building (located with the property's cabins closer to the bluff above the beach) have private balconies or patios, and some have fireplaces. In between are 40 cabins in two lines on a beachfront bluff. The weathered wood that makes up each cabin's exterior belies the cozy, well-appointed rooms within. Wood fires are stocked with firewood, and each cabin has a kitchenette or kitchen and breakfast table. Neither cabins nor rooms have wireless Internet, TVs, or phones. A single group campsite can hold three small RVs or six tents and has no hookups.

Less than a mile north of the lodge is **Kalaloch Campground** (U.S. 101, 34 miles south of Forks, 877/444-6777, www.recreation.gov, $14-18), one of only two campgrounds in Olympic National Park that takes reservations for summer months (the other is in Sol Duc). Most sites are in the trees close to the beach, but some sites are right up against the bluff. This campground has 170 sites and running water year-round, but no RV hookups.

Getting There
Kalaloch is located right on U.S. 101, 34.5 miles south of Forks and 73 miles

north of Aberdeen. Services are few and far between on the western side of the Olympic Peninsula (the gas station here closed in 2013). The nearest gas station is in Queets, 7 miles south on U.S. 101.

Aberdeen

The twin industrial towns of Aberdeen and Hoquiam sit at the inside tip of Grays Harbor, a bay near Washington's southwestern corner. At one time the Hoquiam River was thick with timber coming to the mills, ships, and trains in the two towns. Now both have seen depressed economic growth, though yacht building in the Westport Shipyards and biodiesel manufacturing still buoy the area.

Sights
Aberdeen Museum of History
There's more to the region than just the roots of Nirvana, according to the **Aberdeen Museum of History** (111 E 3rd St., 360/533-1976, www.aberdeen-museum.org, 10am-5pm Tues.-Sat., noon-4pm Sun., suggested donation $2 adults, $1 students and seniors). Located in an old armory from 1922, the museum has a replica blacksmith shop, a re-created general store, and a museum shop with, yes, Kurt Cobain action figures.

Kurt Cobain Landing
Before fronting Nirvana during the birth of grunge, and long before his suicide rocked the '90s music scene, Kurt Cobain was just a teenager writing lyrics under a Wishkah River bridge in his hometown of Aberdeen. Now the area is a small park known as **Kurt Cobain Landing,** with a guitar sculpture and a sign explaining the site's impact on Cobain and the band—Nirvana's last album is named for the river, where some of the late singer's ashes were spread. There's little parking for the site, which sits at the end of East 2nd Street northeast of downtown, but

it's a pleasantly serene site in the middle of the industrial city.

For more memories of the area's most famous son, see the Aberdeen Museum of History's **Walking Tour of Kurt Cobain's Aberdeen** (www.aberdeen-museum.org/kurt.htm), a self-guided route described online. They note the addresses of where Cobain lived as a baby, where his uncle bought him his first electric guitar, and where a teenaged Kurt Cobain vandalized an alley and got arrested. Most sites don't commemorate Cobain in any way, but the modest buildings are a reminder of how unglamorous the rock star's life was before he hit it big.

Lady Washington
The replica *Lady Washington* is based on a 1787 vessel, the first American ship to land on the West Coast and the first American-flagged vessel to travel to Japan, Hong Kong, and Honolulu. The 1989 version was built in Aberdeen and docks at the **Grays Harbor Historical Seaport Landing** (320 S Newell St., 360/532-8611, www.historicalseaport.org, 4pm-5pm Tues.-Fri, 10am-1pm Sat.-Sun., hours vary seasonally, $3 or by donation) when it isn't out sailing the world—which is often. The 72-foot ship appears in movies and on TV, most notably in *Pirates of the Caribbean* and in a Macklemore video. The ship, along with the similar *Hawaiian Chieftain*, travels around the western coast doing educational programs, scenic sails, and walk-on tours. When the ship is in town, it is also open for walk-on tours.

Food and Accommodations
With few tourist attractions or notable dining options, Aberdeen is likely only an overnight stop for those too tired to make it to Seattle or Tacoma after a Peninsula trip. There's absolutely no pretense in this rough, industrial town, and **Billy's Bar & Grill** (322 Heron St., 360/533-7144, www.billysaberdeen.com, 8am-11pm Mon.-Sat., 7am-9pm Sun., $9-23) is a

straightforward eatery with big burgers, a prime rib dinner, and a busy bar. It's located on a corner in downtown and has a neon "Cocktails" sign outside. The bar is allegedly named for a local serial killer who used to capture naval officers and dispose of their bodies out a chute in the restaurant in the early 1900s. Still, children are welcome during daytime hours.

The **GuestHouse Inn & Suites** (616 W Heron, 360/533-4200, www.guesthousecintl.com, $96-147) is a serviceable hotel that sits right where the Wishkah River meets the bigger Chehalis River—and next to a Wal-Mart. Wi-fi is free, and the inn has a heated indoor pool and hot tub.

A Harbor View Inn (111 W 11th St., 360/533-0433, www.aharborview.com, $139-169) is a bed-and-breakfast in a house built in 1905 that was, before being broken up and enduring a fire, a 30-room palace. It was restored in the 1920s and has since been largely unchanged. Because it's located on a hillside overlooking the Wishkah and Chehalis Rivers, every room has a water view. The five guestrooms also have private baths, TVs, and wireless Internet. Many of the furnishings are antiques, and one room has a claw-foot tub. A sunroom overlooks Grays Harbor where breakfast is served.

Getting There

Aberdeen is located on Grays Harbor, where U.S. 101 meets Highway 12. From Kalaloch, follow U.S. 101 south for 73 miles.

To I-5 via Olympia

The main I-5 artery travels through the middle of Olympia and continues 61 miles north to Seattle or 113.5 miles south to Portland.

from top to bottom: a tree on the beach at Kalaloch; bridge over the Wishkah River in Aberdeen; the Fish Tale Brewpub in Olympia.

To U.S. 101 South and the Oregon Coast

To continue south on the Oregon Coast, stay on U.S. 101 South as it brushes past Willapa Bay. At 54.6 miles after leaving Aberdeen, take a left on Highway 4. Follow Highway 4 south about 5 miles and take a right on Highway 401, which travels 12 miles south to the Astoria Megler Bridge. Take a left to rejoin U.S. 101 south and cross the bridge to Astoria, Oregon. The drive takes about 1.75 hours.

Despite the name, **Cape Disappointment State Park** (Robert Gray Dr., Ilwaco, 360/642-3029, www.parks. wa.gov/parks, 6:30am-dusk daily, $10 parking) is hardly a letdown. The dramatic piece of land juts into the Pacific Ocean at the mouth of the Columbia River on the Washington side, across from Astoria. A lighthouse that dates back to 1856 is one hardworking beacon of light because the river bar is a hairy point along a coastal stretch known as the Graveyard of the Pacific. A second tower, the North Head Lighthouse, is also within the park.

Cape Disappointment State Park offers yurts and cabins for rent ($69). The lighthouse keeper residence includes a two-story Victorian house ($308-437), complete with library. The seaside rental feels ghostly on the foggy, wet nights that are so common on the Pacific coast.

Olympia

Though not the biggest city in Washington—it's much smaller than Seattle—Olympia wields some power as the state capital. Located at the base of the V-shaped Puget Sound, Olympia has the reputation for being a funky little city. The local Evergreen State College promotes alternative education, and signs around town still have the Olympia Beer motto, "It's the Water," even though the brewery has been closed for years.

The town has a sprawling Capitol campus with historical buildings and manicured grounds, a thriving farmers market, and several blocks of downtown shops. The I-5 freeway runs through town, making Olympia a way station between Seattle and Portland.

Sights
Artesian Well

Olympia's offbeat vibe is best captured at the **Artesian Well** (4th Ave. E between Adams St. SE and Jefferson St. SE, www. olympiawa.gov), where water bubbles up from 90 feet underground. For a long time the well was just a metal pipe in a downtown parking lot, and locals stopped by to fill jugs with the crisp, pure water. The flow of water never stops—10 gallons per minute, all free to anyone who wants it. Recently an artist decorated the pipe with a large mosaic and mural, turning it into a piece of art. In 2013 the city council voted to make the spot, now a parking lot between downtown buildings, a city park with bathroom facilities and space for food-truck parking.

Hands On Children's Museum

The **Hands On Children's Museum** (414 Jefferson St. NE, 360/956-0818, www. hocm.org, 10am-5pm Tues.-Sat., 11am-5pm Sun.-Mon., $12.95 adults, $10.95 seniors, children under 2 free), located near the marinas on the northeastern corner of downtown, has play spaces for very young children, each dedicated to nature, construction, arts and crafts, or the ever-exciting emergency vehicles. The Puget Sound display has a microscope and moving crane, and the nature area has a two-story slide. There's also a museum café.

Olympia Farmers Market

The covered **Olympia Farmers Market** (700 N Capitol Way, 360/352-9096, www. olympiafarmersmarket.com, 10am-3pm Thurs.-Sun. Apr.-Oct., 10am-3pm Sat.-Sun. Nov.-Dec.) has rows of stalls selling produce, flowers, and meat, plus crafts

Olympia

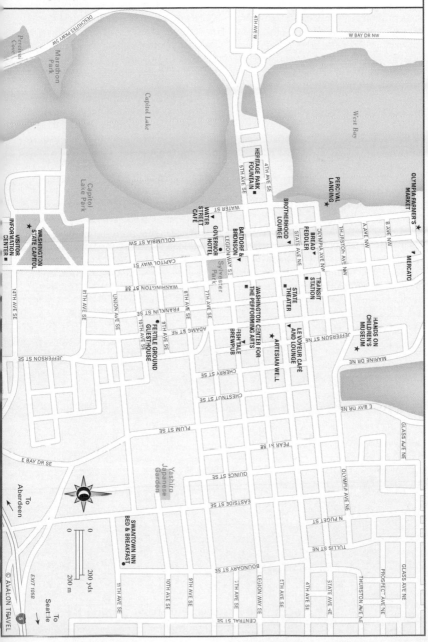

and baked goods. Outside, a stage is used for daily performances in summer, and food stands sell prepared goods. Close to half a million visitors come to the market every year, and in summer the parking lot gets very crowded.

Percival Landing

Percival Landing (Olympia Ave. NW and Columbia St. NW, www.olympi-awa.gov) is a waterfront park named for the old commercial wharf and the family that ran it. Today it has boat docks, a playground, picnic areas, and a board-walk with benches. The nearly mile-long boardwalk follows the marina to where the industrial port begins. Right before it ends, a viewing tower sits near the Olympia Farmers Market.

Washington State Capitol

The dome of the **Washington State Capitol** (Cherry Lane SW and Sid Snyder Ave. SW, 360/902-8880, www.des.wa.gov) is visible from I-5 and much of downtown

since it towers above the rest of the city on a hill. The dome was finished in 1928 and is one of the biggest masonry domes in the world, coming in after the likes of St. Peter's Cathedral and the Florence Duomo. A Tiffany chandelier under the dome's rotunda has 438 pieces and is the largest in the world—weighing in at 10,000 pounds.

Free guided tours begin hourly at the Tour Information Desk, just inside the main entrance doors of the domed Legislative Building. The **Visitor Information Center** (103 Sid Snyder Ave., 360/704-7544, www.visitolympia. com, 10am-5pm Mon.-Fri., summer only 10am-4pm Sat., free) has maps and tourist information.

The campus around the dome includes a sunken garden and a 50-foot Tivoli Fountain, a replica of the famous one in Copenhagen, Denmark. Sculptures and memorials populate the grounds, and a trail leads down a steep hill to Capitol Lake and downtown. The trail circles

Washington State Capitol

1.5 miles around Capitol Lake, and it's a short walk to the **Heritage Park Fountain** (330 5th Ave. SW) with jets erupting from the ground.

Parking is available along Water St. SW, along the diagonal roads that cross the main lawn, or in lots throughout the campus.

Entertainment and Events

The **State Theater** (202 4th Ave. E, 360/786-0151, www.harlequinproductions.org) was once a grand downtown movie theater. But it was an abandoned dollar-movie house when Harlequin Productions (a local theater troupe) bought it and restored it to former glory. The group puts on original plays and classic theater pieces, plus an annual 1940s- or 1950s-themed Christmas show and the occasional rock musical version of a Shakespeare play.

Downtown's biggest performance venue is the **Washington Center for the Performing Arts** (512 Washington St. SE, 360/753-8585, www.washingtoncenter. org), which has a facade with 1924 pieces but an all-modern interior. It hosts visiting classical, jazz, blues, and pop musical acts, along with comedy shows, lecturers, and film screenings.

The **Brotherhood Lounge** (119 Capitol Way N, 360/352-4153, www.thebrotherhoodlounge.com, 3pm-2am daily, cash only) is so named because the space used to be home to labor unions. A large sign still reads "Labor Temple" outside. Now the popular bar has shuffleboard and pool, an outdoor patio, and a photo booth. Draft beers are mostly local. Sometimes aerialists and trapeze artists perform, other times a movie is playing in the bar, and DJs play on some weekend nights.

Once upon a time, the city was known for Olympia Beer (which is still produced, but brewed elsewhere); now the city's biggest beer export is Fish Tale organic ales from Fish Brewing, located in an old knitting factory with a brightly painted mural on its facade. Across the street is its **Fish Tale Brewpub** (515 Jefferson St. SE, 360/943-3650, www.fishbrewing.com, 11am-10pm Mon.-Thurs., 11am-midnight Fri., 9am-midnight Sat., 9am-10pm Sun.), also with murals on the exterior, and with 14 beer and cider taps plus a menu of oyster shooters, fish-and-chips, burgers, salads, and desserts. It has outdoor seating in the summer and occasional live music performances.

The menu at **Le Voyeur Café and Lounge** (404 E 4th Ave., 360/943-5710, www.voyeurolympia.com, 11am-2am daily) is a double of itself, because every sandwich, salad, and entrée has a vegan counterpart. Bottled beers come from around the world. The space has red walls and funky, colorful decor. Most nights it hosts live music, often without a cover.

Food

The **McMenamins Spar Café** (114 4th Ave. E, 360/357-6444, www.mcmenamins. com/spar, 7am-midnight Sun.-Thurs.,

7am-1am Fri.-Sat., $12-25) was a classic downtown diner with logging paraphernalia on the walls until it was purchased by the McMenamins, a Portland-based company known for historical restoration. What was once a cigar counter is now a large seating area, but its history remains on the walls. The beer brewed on-site uses artesian well water, and the menu boasts pub classics like burgers, pizza, and salads.

The ★ **Bread Peddler** (222 Capitol Way N, 360/352-1175, www.breadpeddler.com, 7am-5pm daily, $8-12) opened in Olympia when a French chef decided the town needed a bakery like those in his home country—and he wasn't afraid to write the menu in French. Patrons order at a counter before sitting with a croque Madame, salad, cheese puff, or other delectable pastry. The café is sunny and busy, with just a few chairs next to the bakery counter, but expands into adjacent spaces that include a bistro section with more and bigger tables for breakfast and lunch, and a white-walled creperie next door.

Although the coffee roastery for **Batdorf & Bronson** (516 S Capitol Way, 360/786-6717, www.batdorfcoffee.com, 6:30am-6pm Mon.-Fri., 7am-6pm Sat.-Sun.) is next to the farmers market and offers tasting tours, the homegrown company sells its drinks at a coffeehouse downtown. There's a fireplace and couches, plus free wireless Internet. The vibe is more personable than a chain coffeehouse, but more adult than a college meet-up spot.

An old American Legion hall next to Capitol Lake is now ★ **Waterstreet Café** (610 Water St. SW, 360/709-9090, www.waterstreetcafeandbar.com, 10:30am-2pm and 4:30pm-9pm Sun.-Thurs., 10:30am-2pm and 4:30pm-midnight Fri.-Sat., $16-30), an Italian restaurant with some of the finest plates in town. The menu includes fish dishes, chutneys, and combinations like scallops with pulled pork. Brunch is daily. The restaurant is dark inside, despite the fireplace and light touch to the furniture and art pieces, but a large outdoor patio has views of the lake.

The feel of **Gardner's** (111 Thurston Ave. NW, 360/786-8466, gardnersrestaurant.com, 5pm-10pm daily, $22-36) is so classic it's strange that it only dates to the 1980s, not the establishment of statehood. It offers fine dining, complete with scallop dishes and a daily rack of lamb preparation. Even the cocktails are classics, from martinis to Manhattans, and the dark wood ceilings give the space the proper solemnity.

Since the fresh vegetable stands of the farmers market are just across the street from **Mercato** (111 Market St., 360/528-3663, http://ramblinrestaurants.com, 11am-9pm daily, $14-26), it's no wonder so many of its Italian dishes feature fresh produce. The menu is filled with accessible but well-crafted pastas and pizzas, and weekdays feature a special three-course chef's menu. Outdoor seating is popular in the summer, but the large interior keeps wait times down.

Accommodations

The downtown **Governor Hotel** (621 Capitol Way S, 360/352-7700, www.olympiagovernorhotel.com, $119-219) is located between the commercial district and the Capitol campus and easily walkable to both. Long a serviceable if unflashy hotel, it recently was reborn as a boutique-style property with modern and retro-style furnishings, bold flashes of color, large flat-screen TVs, and luxury down comforters and showerheads. The hotel hasn't completely shaken its dated exterior, but the location is very convenient, and some rooms overlook Capitol Lake and have private balconies.

The **Swantown Inn Bed & Breakfast** (1431 11th Ave. SE, 877/753-9123, www.swantowninn.com, $179-249) is located in a bold Victorian house east of downtown. It's not within walking distance of shops and restaurants but is in a quiet residential neighborhood. The 1887 mansion has four guest rooms decorated in dark, ornate wallpapers and draperies and all with private baths. One room has a two-person jetted tub. A day spa in the attic offers massages and antique foot soak tubs.

More than a bed-and-breakfast, **Fertile Ground Guesthouse** (311 9th Ave. SE, 360/352-2428, www.fertileground.org, $95-110) is a garden and tool-share site and a place for chickens to hang out in a coop next to rows of vegetables. A sauna handmade from cedar and redwood sits next to the 100-year-old house located downtown. A shared bathroom has wood floors, claw-foot tubs, and bubble bath. One of the three rooms has a private bath, while a dormitory room offers three beds and a bathroom. Room rentals come with breakfast.

Getting There

To reach Olympia from Aberdeen, take U.S. 12 (which crosses U.S. 101 in downtown Aberdeen) east for 21.5 miles until it becomes Highway 8 in Elma (no turns necessary). Follow Highway 8 east for 23 miles where it again changes names (no turns), becoming U.S. 101. From this point, continue 7.5 miles east on U.S. 101 to I-5; take I-5 North and exit almost immediately at exit 105 and follow signs for Olympia. The drive takes about an hour when there's no traffic coming into Olympia.

The local **Amtrak** station (6600 Yelm Hwy. SE, www.amtrak.com, 8:15am-9:30pm daily) isn't actually in Olympia; it's outside the suburb of Lacey on Yelm Highway. There's no ticket office, just a kiosk and an enclosed waiting area. Six trains depart daily for Seattle ($14-44) and six trains daily for Portland ($20-61). **Intercity Transit** bus route 64 (Olympia Transit Center, 222 State Ave. NE, 360/786-1881, www.intercitytransit.com, $1.25 adults and children 6-18, children under 6 free) goes from downtown Olympia to the Amtrak station, a 42-minute trip.

Oregon Coast

The long, straight sands of the Oregon Coast are a point of pride to Oregonians. Beaches are clean and open to everyone, so no private landowner can hoard the savage beauty of the Pacific.

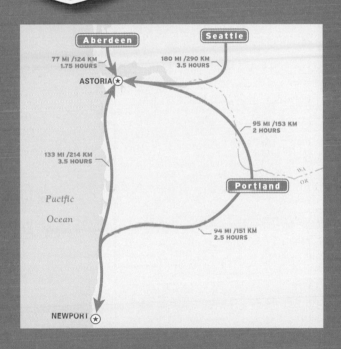

Aberdeen

Seattle

77 MI /124 KM
1.75 HOURS

180 MI /290 KM
3.5 HOURS

ASTORIA ★

95 MI /153 KM
2 HOURS

133 MI /214 KM
3.5 HOURS

Pacific
Ocean

Portland

94 MI /151 KM
2.5 HOURS

NEWPORT ★

Oregon Coast: North

Oregon Coast: South

Highlights

★ **Fort Clatsop:** Lewis and Clark finished their epic journey here, where they were greeted by local Native Americans (page 200).

★ **Haystack Rock:** This unofficial symbol of the Oregon Coast is at Cannon Beach, where the photogenic rock also serves as a bird sanctuary (page 204).

★ **Tillamook Cheese Factory:** The warehouse of cheese offers views of giant cheese-making and packaging floors, plus endless free samples (page 212).

★ **Oregon Coast Aquarium:** Local sea life is represented well in this giant park with touch tanks and feeding shows (page 222).

★ **Yaquina Head Lighthouse:** Oregon's tallest lighthouse sits nestled within a protected wildlife area (page 224).

★ **Heceta Head Lighthouse:** One of the prettiest lighthouses on the Oregon Coast has something most don't—a bed-and-breakfast inside the keeper's house (page 229).

★ **Oregon Dunes National Recreation Area:** The sandy hills that guard Oregon's beaches also serve as an outdoor playground for dune buggies (page 232).

Best Accommodations

★ **The Surfsand Resort:** Enjoy a classic beach vacation at this well-equipped and central accommodation (page 207).

★ **Inn at Manzanita:** Charm is behind every garden corner at this romantic retreat (page 211).

★ **Inn at Spanish Head:** Find true luxury at a full-on resort that cascades down beachfront bluffs (page 218).

★ **Sylvia Beach Hotel:** This bright blue, old-fashioned beach hotel is perfect for a bookish holiday (page 226).

★ **Overleaf Lodge & Spa:** Waves crash below a waterfront getaway with spacious rooms (page 229).

Y ou'll want to stay inside for storm-watching in the windy winter months, but that's why they made fireplaces, hot tubs, and warm clam chowder.

Come summer, the kites come out and the sandcastles emerge.

Lighthouses out here are hardy and necessary—shipwrecks still dot the coastline.

Every town has a slightly different feel along U.S. 101, which traces the coastline from border to border. In historical Astoria at the mouth of the Columbia River, barges still inch up the waterway. Seaside is the carnival town with the beachside promenade, whereas Cannon Beach is a sedate sandcastle-on-the-beach area. Manzanita is cute and quirky, and Tillamook is the inland town with the great cheese tradition.

Pacific City is an out-of-the-way hamlet with an oversized brewery, and Lincoln City has hotels and the world's shortest river. Tiny Depoe Bay is so close to the ocean it almost falls in. That's one reason it sees the most whales. Newport is a big town with big lighthouses, a working waterfront, and a renowned aquarium. Yachats is an unassuming bend in the road, while Florence is a genteel little town near the rolling coastal dunes.

Of course, there are constants along the entire northern half of the Oregon Coast—you'll find saltwater taffy and clam chowder almost everywhere, and wildlife pops up in tide pools and along sandstone cliffs the whole way.

Getting to the Oregon Coast

Driving from Portland
95 miles, 2 hours

From downtown Portland, head west on **U.S. 26,** also known as the Sunset Highway. U.S. 26 intersects U.S. 101 in about 75 miles, between Cannon Beach and Seaside. Follow U.S. 101 north for 20 miles to reach Astoria. Alternately, take I-5 north for 46 miles to Longview, and then follow U.S. 30 west for 50 miles to Astoria. Both routes take just under 2 hours.

Driving from Seattle
180 miles, 3.5 hours

Although **I-5** is often a colorless drive south from Seattle, it's the fastest route to the Oregon Coast. Leave the interstate at exit 36A in the town of Longview, where Highway 432 travels west. After 2 miles, turn left onto Oregon Way/Highway 433, which immediately crosses the Columbia River into Oregon. Once on the Oregon side, merge onto U.S. 30 heading west to

Best Restaurants

★ **Stephanie Inn Dining Room:** Enjoy fine dining in the round, on white tablecloths and inside one of the coast's best hotels (page 206).

★ **Newmans at 988:** Inside a twee house are some of Cannon Beach's best plates (page 206).

★ **Big Wave Cafe:** Start with casual seafood, end with desserts made in-house (page 210).

★ **Pelican Pub & Brewery:** Here's a big beachfront brewery with sunset views and plenty on tap (page 215).

★ **Restaurant Beck:** Find fine dining with local ingredients just outside Depoe Bay (page 220).

★ **Saffron Salmon:** A cozy dockside favorite has water views and a bright dining room (page 225).

★ **Waterfront Depot:** This cute local's favorite offers a bistro menu and good cocktails (page 231).

Astoria. The drive can be as short as 3.25 hours, but I-5 traffic usually lengthens the trip.

Driving from the Olympic Peninsula

77-185 miles, 1.75–3.5 hours

From Forks, **U.S. 101** continues south for 185 miles through rural southwest Washington to Astoria, Oregon. It's 77 miles from the town of Aberdeen to Astoria. The road sideswipes **Willapa Bay,** known for its oysters, and the long, skinny **Long Beach Peninsula,** which is dotted with the beach towns of Seaview, Long Beach, and Ocean Park.

By Air, Train, or Bus

The Oregon Coast is served by **Portland International Airport** (PDX, 7000 NE Airport Way, Portland, 503/460-4234, www.pdx.com). The **Eugene Airport** (EUG, 28801 Douglas Dr., Eugene, 541/682-5544, www.eugene-or.gov) has flights to Portland, Seattle, and Los Angeles. To reach the Oregon Coast from Eugene, drive south on Highway 99 for 1.5 miles to Highway 569. Take Highway 569 west, and when it dead-ends 3.5 miles later, turn right onto Highway 126. Follow Highway 126 west for 55.5 miles to Florence.

Amtrak trains stop at Portland, Salem, Albany, and Eugene along the I-5 Oregon corridor; however, no train service goes to the coast.

Greyhound (800/231-2222, www.greyhound.com) runs bus service on some sections of U.S. 101, such as from Astoria (900 Marine Dr., 503/861-7433, 7:30am-6pm Mon.-Fri., 7am-6pm Sat.-Sun.) to Cannon Beach (187 E Madison St., 503/436-2623).

Astoria

Sitting at the meeting point between a mighty river and a massive ocean, this historical little town lives and breathes its seagoing heritage. It was named for John Jacob Astor, the fur-trading magnate, whose company founded Fort Astoria only a few years after the Lewis and Clark Expedition hit the Pacific Ocean at nearby Fort Clatsop. Today the town retains many of its early 20th-century buildings and sits as an anchor at the top of the Oregon Coast.

Sights
Astoria Column

From its position at Astoria's highest point, Coxcomb Hill, the 125-foot **Astoria Column** (1 Coxcomb Dr., 503/325-2963, www.astoriacolumn.org, dawn-dusk, $5

One Day on the Oregon Coast

Start the day in Astoria, at the end of the Columbia River and among classic Victorian houses. Wake up at the **Cannery Pier Hotel** (page 202) under the **Astoria-Megler Bridge** (page 198). Learn a little about the area's history at the **Columbia River Maritime Museum** (page 198) or the **Flavel House Museum** (page 199), or just start driving south on U.S. 101 to hit the beaches.

No shore visit is complete without a stop to see **Haystack Rock** (page 204), and the best place to park is in Cannon Beach, just south at **Tolovana Beach Recreation Site** (page 204). After poking through some tide pools, hop back on U.S. 101 and continue driving 40 miles south past **Oswald West State Park** (page 208) and on to Tillamook for a stop at the **Tillamook Cheese Factory** (page 212). Those cheese samples will have to tide you over until lunch at **Pelican Pub & Brewery** (page 215) in Pacific City, 25 miles south.

Back on U.S. 101, drive south for 35 miles through Lincoln City. Then slow down in Depoe Bay to see the smallest harbor in the world. In 10 miles, exit U.S. 101 at NW Lighthouse Drive (north of Newport) and follow it west to see **Yaquina Head Lighthouse** (page 224), the tallest lighthouse in the state.

It's only 5 more miles to Newport, where you can visit the **Oregon Coast Aquarium** (page 222) to see a giant Pacific octopus and puffins. If you feel like some pan-Asian cuisine, walk over to **Noodle Café** (page 226). Or cross the Yaquina Bay Bridge to dine with a bay view at **Saffron Salmon** (page 225).

From Newport, it's 50 miles south on U.S. 101 to Florence to watch the sun set from **Oregon Dunes National Recreation Area** (page 232). End the day with a drink at **Waterfront Depot** (page 231) before heading to a bed at the **River House Inn** (page 231), located a short walk away under Florence's bridge.

per vehicle) has the best view in the city. An Italian American artist was hired to mimic an Italian bas-relief technique that matches the column's inspiration, Trajan's Column in Rome. Images of the area's history spiral the pillar, starting with early Native American settlements and ending with the arrival of the railroad to Astoria. During World War II, the site was a base for a blimp squadron. The sea air is rough on the mural, but a major restoration, costing almost a million dollars, was completed in 2015. Today visitors can climb to a viewing platform at its top to see the Astoria-Megler Bridge, Cape Disappointment, and the Pacific Ocean—if the weather is clear enough, of course.

Astoria-Megler Bridge

At just over 4 miles long, the **Astoria-Megler Bridge** is an impressive expanse. It carries U.S. 101 from Oregon to Washington at the mouth of the Columbia and was the last link completed of the first California-to-Washington route. Winds at the mouth of the Columbia can get as high as 150 miles per hour during storms, but the views from the middle are well worth the pummeling felt by cars and cyclists (no pedestrians allowed).

Columbia River Maritime Museum

The **Columbia River Maritime Museum** (1792 Marine Dr., 503/325-2323, www.crmm.org, 9:30am-5pm daily, $14 adults, $12 seniors, $5 children, children under 6 free) preserves the seagoing and river travel history of Astoria with a museum and research library. Pilot boats and relics from area shipwrecks are a reminder of just how deadly the Columbia Bar has been to sailors. Out back, tethered to a dock, is the lightship *Columbia,* the last of five ships with that name to serve as a

Astoria and Vicinity

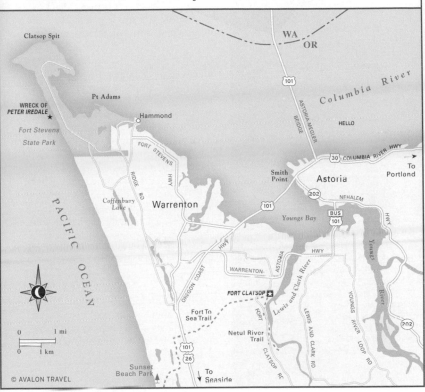

floating lighthouse. Climb aboard to see the officer's quarters and radio room, and the mess hall where off duty crew hung out while stationed just five miles off the mouth of the river. Inside, films play at the museum's 3D digital theater. Next door is the **Barbey Maritime Center,** housed in a renovated 1925 railroad depot, offering wooden boat building classes and workshops in nature illustration.

Flavel House Museum

Being a bar pilot, or a captain who guides ships across the mouth of the Columbia River, has been a well-paying gig for more than a century—that's one reason Captain George Flavel had such a fancy house. Today the Victorian mansion known as the **Flavel House Museum** (Duane and 8th Sts., 503/325-2203, www. cumtux.org, 10am-5pm daily May-Sept., 11am-4pm daily Oct.-Apr., $6 adults, $5 seniors and students, $2 children 6-17, children under 6 free) is part of the Clatsop County Historical Society. The steep roof, wraparound porch, and octagonal tower—so Captain Flavel could keep an eye on boat traffic—are all touches from the Queen Anne architectural style. The roof and verandas still have original wrought-iron casting. Tours include the six fireplaces, music room, library, housekeeping areas, and the carriage house.

★ Fort Clatsop

As part of the Lewis and Clark National Historical Park, **Fort Clatsop** (92343 Fort Clatsop Rd., 503/861-2471, ext. 214, www. nps.gov/lewi, 9am-6pm daily mid-June-Labor Day, 9am-5pm daily Labor Day-mid-June, $5 adults, children 15 and under free) represents the winter camp of the two famous explorers. Sent by President Thomas Jefferson to explore the Louisiana Purchase and Pacific Coast in 1804, Meriwether Lewis and William Clark started from near St. Louis and traveled to this spot close to where the Columbia River meets the Pacific Ocean. They wintered here before heading back east. Today the spot includes a replica of the old fort and an exhibit hall. In the summer season (mid-June-Labor Day), ranger-led programs and costumed rangers bring the old Oregon to life on a daily basis.

From Astoria, drive 3.5 miles south on U.S. 101. Turn left onto Marllin Drive (or U.S. 101 Business) and follow Marllin Drive for about 0.5 mile. When the road dead-ends, turn left and stay on U.S. 101 Business for 2 miles. Turn right onto Fort Clatsop Road to reach the park.

Parks and Beaches
Fort Stevens State Park

In the past, the head of the Columbia River was an important military center. Today **Fort Stevens State Park** (100 Peter Iredale Rd., Hammond, 503/861-1671, www.oregonstateparks.org, $5 per vehicle) is a recreational area that embraces evidence of its past. It has overgrown military structures, miles of beach (including the wreck of the steel ship *Peter Iredale*), and swimming areas and picnic tables at Coffenbury Lake.

To reach the park from Astoria, take U.S. 101 for 4.5 miles south, and then turn right on East Harbor Street. After a little more than a mile, turn left onto SW

from top to bottom: Columbia River Maritime Museum; Fort Clatsop; Flavel House Museum.

9th Street in Warrenton. Drive 1 mile and turn right into NW Ridge Road. Follow NW Ridge Road for 2 miles, then turn left into the park.

Food

Like the Cannery Pier Hotel next door, the **Bridgewater Bistro** (20 Basin St., 503/325-6777, www.bridgewaterbistro. com, 11:30am-11pm Mon.-Sat., 10:30am-11pm Sun., $15-35) makes the most of its waterfront location in an old boatyard—most tables have river views. The fare is definitely inspired by the water, with salmon, oysters, and fish-and-chips, but includes plenty of steak, duck, and chicken for stubborn landlubbers. Gluten-free options abound, and live jazz bands play on weekend nights.

Plenty of humor is on tap at **Fort George Brewery and Public House** (1483 Duane St., 503/325-7468, www.fortgeorgebrewery.com, 11am-11pm Mon.-Thurs., 11am-midnight Fri.-Sat., noon-11pm Sun., $10-18). They claim the coffee-flavored Working Girl Porter was brewed because the brewers were "looking for a good reason to drink beer in the morning." The public house sits in an old service station building and offers a variety of regular and seasonal beers on tap. Big baskets of fries—made from organic potatoes, of course—and house-made sausages are popular favorites. On weekends be sure to take a tour (1pm or 4pm) of the brewery either before or after eating.

The bar at **Silver Salmon Grille** (1105 Commercial St., 503/338-6640, http://silversalmongrille.com, 11am-10pm daily, $10-20 lunch, $19-33 dinner) is more than 130 years old and made from Scottish wood that had to be shipped on a boat around the world. The restaurant serves well-prepared seafood, oysters, and clam chowder.

The **Columbian Cafe** (1114 Marine Dr., 503/325-2233, www.columbianvoodoo.com, 8am-2pm Mon.-Fri, 9am-2pm Sat.-Sun., $15-20, cash only) is more than just an eatery, though there's plenty of

vegetarian fare and seafood in the funky red café. The Voodoo Room event space is known for readings and music performances, while the Columbian Theater movie house, run by the same company, makes it an action-filled stop.

Just across the street from the Columbia River Maritime Museum, **Bowpicker Fish & Chips** (1634 Duane St., 503/791-2942, www.bowpicker.com, 11am-6pm Wed.-Sun. weather permitting, $9-11, cash only) is run out of a red-and-white gillnet boat called the *Columbia*. Lines stretch down the platform built next to the boat, now on a trailer in a gravel parking lot. You come here for one thing—the albacore tuna, fried to a delicate crisp, and a pile of steak fries. About the only choice you have is between tartar sauce and vinegar, or whether you want to split with a friend.

Accommodations
Under $150

The lobby of the renovated **Commodore Hotel** (258 14th St., 503/325-4747, www. commodoreastoria.com, $88-208) is a little bit hip, with a painted-on fireplace and sleek benches, and a little bit maritime in its braided-rope hangings. The building began its hotel history in the 1920s but then closed in the 1960s before reopening in the 21st century. Even where space is tight in the guest rooms, there's design—wall-to-ceiling modernist paintings over the beds stand in for headboards and canopies. Cabin rooms share the hall bathrooms, but rooms are stocked with flashlights for midnight walks to the facilities; suites have their own bathrooms.

Fort Stevens State Park (100 Peter Iredale Rd., Hammond, 503/861-1671, www.oregonstateparks.org, $56 yurts, $100 cabins) offers yurts and cabins for rent.

$150-250

The **Astoria Riverwalk Inn** (400 Industry St., 503/325-2013, http://riverwalkastoria.

com, $158-194) is located near the Cannery Pier and Astoria-Megler Bridge. This straightforward hotel may have older furnishings, but the waffle bar and balconies overlooking the water make up for it.

A relic of the 1920s is **Hotel Elliot** (357 12th St., 503/325-2222, www.hotelelliott.com, $189-289), whose 32 rooms include a variety of suites. Many rooms have fireplaces, and all have goose down pillows and heated bathroom floor tiles. In the suites, amenities include Jacuzzi tubs and, in the presidential suite, a two-story apartment with full kitchen and piano. The rooftop terrace has a view of the Columbia River and is accessible to all guests whenever it isn't booked for private events.

Over $250
The **Cannery Pier Hotel** (10 Basin St., 503/325-4996, www.cannerypierhotel.com, $309-399) isn't exactly ostentatious, but its position under the Astoria-Megler Bridge, right on the Columbia River, makes it an oft-photographed site. The industrial shape evokes the cannery that once stood on these pilings, but guests don't rough it—every room has a balcony with a river view, a fireplace, and a dining table, and wine and lox are served every evening in the lobby. Retro bicycles are free for guests to use along the riverfront.

Getting There
To reach Astoria from Seaside, drive north on U.S. 101 for a little less than 17 miles. The last mile includes a beautiful drive across Youngs Bay, with views of the Columbia River.

Seaside

While Astoria is crammed with history and Cannon Beach has amazing beaches, Seaside is a quintessential beach town. This is where you find saltwater taffy and arcade games and a history of beauty

pageants (the Miss Oregon Pageant happens here). It may not be the fanciest stop on the coast, but Seaside still has classic appeal.

Sights
Promenade
The seaside **Promenade** (Ave. U to 12th Ave.) is a century-old, 8,000-foot-long boardwalk right on Seaside Beach—that's 1.5 miles of flat, paved walking surface. At a turnaround at the end of Broadway is a Lewis and Clark memorial. In August, the Hood to Coast relay ends here. The 200-mile race begins in the mountains and is the longest relay race in the world.

Seaside Carousel
The **Seaside Carousel** (300 Broadway St., 503/738-6728, www.seasidecarouselmall.com, 9am-9:30pm daily summer, hours vary fall, winter, and spring, $2.50) isn't quite as old as it looks. It has a classic carnival look but was built in 1990. Many of the seats are made to resemble animals like rabbits, cats, and bears. The mall that surrounds the indoor carousel was built on the site of an old dance hall. Shops include a hat store and a candy spot, one of many places to find bin after bin of saltwater taffy.

For something more historical, try the bumper cars at **Interstate Amusement** (110 Broadway St., $0.50-1.25), where you can ride in the classic cars, play 10 holes of putt-putt golf, and eat a corndog. It's "open whenever there is a crowd."

Shopping
Saltwater taffy is sold everywhere on the Oregon Coast, but **Phillip's Candies** (217 Broadway St., 503/738-5402, www.phillipscandies.com, 10am-9pm Sun.-Thurs., 10am-10pm Fri.-Sat.) has a particularly delicious array, including a lime saltwater variety alongside the usual vanilla, strawberry, and peppermint. The store has been around since the 19th century, and there's a classic simplicity to the fudge flavors and lollipops.

Food

Tsunami Sandwich Company (11 Broadway St., 503/738-5427, opens 11am "most days," www.tsunamisandwiches. com, $8-14) is close to the beach and an easy place to grab food for a picnic. Tsunami bypasses the Oregon chowder competition by serving Ivar's clam chowder from Seattle, but the chili is homemade, and the ice cream is from Tillamook. Be forewarned when asking for extra meat—the MegaTsunami uses a full pound of pastrami. The store has a corner marked "Tsunami Info Zone" with maps of evacuation zones and a mural of the Lewis and Clark memorial just outside being dwarfed by a giant wave. Ask about the storm-watching tours led by the store's owner.

Accommodations

Some rooms at the **Sandy Cove Inn** (241 Ave. U, 503/738-7473, www.sandycove-inn.net, $169-199) have special themes— a Monopoly room has a game board painted on the wall, and a vintage game room has classic games as decor. The inn is a few blocks from the south end of the Promenade in a fairly residential neighborhood, a good 10 minutes by foot to Broadway. But the cozy motel shows off a calmer side of Seaside, and service is attentive.

True to its name, **The Inn at the Prom** (341 S Promenade, 800/507-2714, www. innatprom.com, $169-249) is right on the beach so waterfront rooms have an unobstructed view of the water. Rooms have two-person jetted tubs and fireplaces, while others have full kitchens or kitchenettes; some rooms can feel crowded with the giant pillow-top beds and foldout sofas. The small hotel is dwarfed by some of the bigger properties nearby, but the property is updated and has nice amenities. A gas barbecue is

from top to bottom: Haystack Rock; Seaside Carousel; Ecola State Park.

available for guest use along with chairs and beach toys outside.

Getting There

Seaside is about 17 miles south of Astoria on U.S. 101. From U.S. 101, take a right on Broadway, and then cross the Necanicum River to immediately reach downtown and the Promenade (watch for one-way streets). From the south, Seaside is 9 miles from Cannon Beach. From Portland, take U.S. 26 (a.k.a. the Sunset Highway) east from Portland. Turn right when U.S. 26 dead-ends into U.S. 101, 4 miles south of Seaside.

Cannon Beach

The big rock in the middle of this sandy stretch is one of the most photographed landmarks in the state. This is the kind of beach Oregon has become famous for, with soft, dense sand, scattered rocks, and enough wind for a good kite flight. Inches inland is shopping, a thriving small-town theater, and fine seafood dining.

Sights
★ Haystack Rock

Guess what shape **Haystack Rock** (near S Hemlock and Pacific Sts.) is? Yep, the 235-foot basalt monolith is wide at the bottom and slightly pointed on top, one of the biggest and most recognizable rocks on Oregon's coast. If you visit just one section of the state's stretches of coastal sand, this should be it; the photo opportunities are classics. Tide pools around its base teem with sand dollars and anemones. When the tide is at its lowest, beach access to the rock is possible; however, would-be climbers should stay off the nesting refuge, populated by tufted puffins and other birds (and high tides still sometimes strand people on the rock). Around sunset, groups often make beach fires from piles of driftwood to stay warm in the chilly maritime air.

Parks and Beaches

These parks—listed from north to south along U.S. 101—are the best places to access the beach.

Ecola State Park

On Tillamook Head between Cannon Beach and Seaside is **Ecola State Park** (Ecola State Park Rd., 503/436-2844, www.oregonstateparks.org, $5 per vehicle), protecting a bluff with killer views and picnic spots. William Clark, of the Lewis and Clark Expedition, sang its praises in his journal when he passed the area while looking for a beached whale. Trails wind through the waterfront area, and you can see the ghostly, abandoned Tillamook Rock Light just offshore. Just over a mile away on a small basalt rock, it got the nickname "Terrible Tilly"—not only was it incredibly difficult to build, but an English vessel was shipwrecked right next to the lighthouse just days before it was lit for the first time. The expensive lighthouse was deactivated in the 1950s, and it is now privately owned as a repository for human ashes.

Haystack Hill State Park

Haystack Rock is one of the coast's most popular destinations, but **Haystack Hill State Park** (E Chena St. and S Hemlock St.) is seldom visited, even by locals. The state park is located between U.S. 101 and the beach, right across from Haystack Rock. Trails lead to an excellent viewpoint, the trees are thick, and it can feel like you've found an island of wilderness in the middle of residential Cannon Beach.

Tolovana Beach Recreation Site

Tolovana Beach Recreation Site (W Warren Way and S Hemlock St., 503/436-2844, www.oregonstateparks.org) is the best place to access the sand in Cannon Beach. Less than a mile south of Haystack Rock, the wayside offers lots of parking—though hardly enough on busy summer weekends—and a ramp down the short

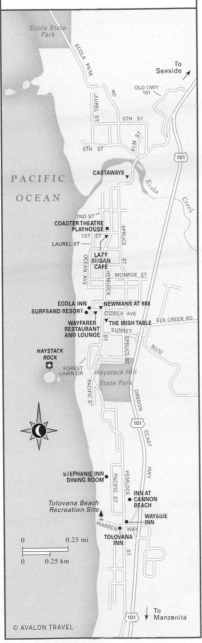

Cannon Beach

Ecola State Park

To Seaside

OLD HWY 101

AUREL ST

ECOLA PARK RD

6TH ST

5TH ST

4TH ST

101

PACIFIC

OCEAN

CASTAWAYS

Ecola Creek

2ND ST
COASTER THEATRE
PLAYHOUSE
1ST ST

LAUREL ST

OCEAN AVE

SPRUCE ST

LAZY SUSAN CAFE

HEMLOCK ST

MONROE ST

ECOLA INN
SURFSAND RESORT

NEWMANS AT 988

GOWER AVE

WAYFARER RESTAURANT AND LOUNGE

THE IRISH TABLE

SUNSET ST

SPRUCE ST

ELK CREEK RD

SPRUCE ST BLVD

HAYSTACK ROCK

FOREST LAWN DR

PACIFIC ST

Haystack Hill State Park

OREGON COAST HWY

101

STEPHANIE INN
DINING ROOM

Tolovana Beach Recreation Site

PACIFIC ST

HEMLOCK ST

INN AT CANNON BEACH

WAYSIDE INN

WARREN WAY

WAY

TOLOVANA INN

ST

0   0.25 mi

0   0.25 km

To Manzanita

101

© AVALON TRAVEL

---

bluff to the beach. It also has a bathroom and a small playground. **Mo's** (195 W Warren Way, 503/436-1111, www.moschowder.com, 11am-8pm Sun.-Thurs., 11am-9pm Fri.-Sat., $7-17), across the parking lot, is good for meals, but most of the other businesses here are hotels. On the beach, look for tufted puffins, a common sight since they nest on Haystack Rock. Several of the streets between Tolovana and Haystack Rock are named for Alaskan Rivers—Matanuska, Susitna, Chisana—but Tolovana gets its name from a hot springs in the Alaskan interior.

Arcadia Beach State Recreation Site

South of Tolovana Beach is **Arcadia Beach State Recreation Site** (U.S. 101 near S Park Ave., 503/368-3575, www.oregonstateparks.org), with access to a mile-long beach between Hug Point and Humbug Point. At low tide, you can pass Humbug Point and continue another 0.5 mile north to Silver Point. There are sandstone cliffs to the east. The parking area has picnic tables and bathrooms.

Hug Point State Recreation Site

At **Hug Point State Recreation Site** (U.S. 101 near Hug Point Rd., 503/368-3575, www.oregonstateparks.org) are traces of the old stagecoach road that followed the Oregon Coast. The area is named for the point where the trail hugged the rocks to get around a headland. The beach has access to sandstone cliffs, small caves, and a waterfall. There are picnic tables and a bathroom at the parking lot.

Entertainment and Events

Although the town is chock-full of second homes and vacation rentals, a small-town theater scene is thriving at the **Coaster Theatre Playhouse** (108 N Hemlock St., 503/436-1242, www.coastertheatre.com, $20-25). The onetime roller rink now has a stage for classic musicals and popular Christmas shows, a warm entertainment option on the common rainy days on the Oregon Coast.

Food

Sure, the decor at **Lazy Susan Café** (126 N Hemlock St., 503/436-2816, www.lazy-susan-cafe.com, 8am-3pm Wed.-Mon. spring-summer, 8am-2:30pm Wed.-Mon. fall-winter, $7-14) is warm, with antiques on shelves, wood-paneled walls, and laminated tablecloths, but one sign does read, "Be Nice or Leave." The breakfast and lunch spot specializes in quiches and salads, but most exciting are the marionberry scones that are bigger than the plates.

Located in a swanky hotel on a quiet strip of beach, ★ **Stephanie Inn Dining Room** (2740 S Pacific St., 503/436-2221, www.stephanie-inn.com, 5:30pm-9pm daily, $33-50) goes for the immersive dining experience. Unlike most of the hotel rooms in the building, the dining room doesn't even face the ocean. The focus instead is the four-course menu that changes each night, often featuring local seafood paired with Washington and Oregon wines. Reservations are required, and meals aren't rushed.

Despite being just feet from the Pacific Ocean, ★ **Newmans at 988** (988 S Hemlock St., 503/436-1151, www.newmansat988.com, 5pm-9pm daily July-Oct., 5pm-9pm Tues.-Sun. Oct.-June, $24-39) specializes in French-Italian cuisine, most notably food from the Piedmont and Genoa areas—like lobster ravioli, chicken marsala pasta, and duck breast. White tablecloths and fresh single roses add elegance to the small space, which is decorated with stained-glass pieces. Reservations are necessary because there are only a handful of tables and the chef-owner boasts a good local reputation, with multiple James Beard House appearances to his name.

Although the cuisine at **The Irish Table** (1235 S Hemlock St., 503/436-0708, www.theirishtablerestaurant.com, 5:30pm-9pm Fri.-Tues., $15-37) is appropriately inspired by the Emerald Isle, it isn't soda

Cannon Beach

bread and potatoes—think lamb stew or chicken pasties, plus mussels, a cheese board, and salads. The beer and whiskey selection may be the most Irish thing about the spot. The space is a café and coffee roaster during the day, and it gets crowded at night; call ahead to get on the waitlist.

With a menu crammed with jambalaya and jerk chicken, **Castaways** (316 Fir St., 503/436-4444, 5pm-9pm Wed.-Sun., $20-33) evokes beach cultures around the world, not just Oregon's cold and windy ones. Cajun flavors meet popular mai tais, but yes—there is also a rich seafood chowder. The bright walls compete with the colors on the plate.

Accommodations
Under $150
The simplest rooms at **Ecola Inn** (1164 Ecola Ct., 503/436-2457, www.ecolainn.com, $127-145) have little more than standard beds and a few seaside decorations—paintings of seashells and such—but the waterfront location in front of Haystack Rock is the real appeal. The property is family run and almost 75 years old with 13 rooms; all have full kitchens, and some have fireplaces. The hotel closes in the dead of winter, save a short holiday season. Rooms rent by the night and week, and it's rare for any to be available in the summer season, but the hotel posts cancellations online.

The **Tolovana Inn** (3400 S Hemlock St., 503/436-2211, www.tolovanainn. com) is set right next to Tolovana Beach State Park, and most rooms ($129-149) with ocean views look out at the sand, not the parking lot. An indoor saltwater pool, spa, and sauna provide options for when the wind blows too hard. Suites ($229-409) include large kitchens, and the hotel provides a shuttle to other parts of Cannon Beach.

$150-250
★ **The Surfsand Resort** (148 W Gower Ave., 503/436-2274, www.surfsand.com, $129-369), just north of Haystack Rock, has full or partial ocean views from every room. It's the kind of place you don't want to leave, with soaking tubs in some rooms and two-head walk-in showers in others, and large patios and cabana service at the beach. Weekends include a hosted ice cream social and weenie roast at a beach bonfire. The nearby restaurant, **Wayfarer Restaurant and Lounge** (1190 Pacific Dr., 503/436-1108, 8am-9pm daily), specializes in local sea specialties, like a hot Dungeness crab sandwich topped with Tillamook cheddar.

Wayside Inn (3339 S Hemlock St., 503/436-1577, www.thewayside-inn. com, $159-259) offers rooms with gas fireplaces, and some rooms have decks with views of the state park. Suites include kitchenettes, and the inn has an indoor pool and a hot tub.

Over $250
Although not directly on the water, the

Inn at Cannon Beach (3215 S Hemlock St., 503/436-9085, www.innatcannonbeach. com, $259-299) has a cozy garden, pond, and trellises outside the room doors—and the beach is only a block away. It makes for a quiet stay in rooms decorated in warm, earthy tones and fireplaces. A breakfast buffet serves yogurt, waffles, and other simple eats.

Getting There

Cannon Beach is a short drive from Seaside, only 9 miles south on U.S. 101. Elin Avenue "exits" off 101 lead to Cannon Beach: The Sunset Boulevard turnoff goes to the more commercial north end of town, and Warren Beach Road heads straight to Tolovana Beach south of Haystack Rock. From the south, reach Cannon Beach by following U.S. 101 for 14.5 miles from Manzanita.

To reach Cannon Beach from Portland, take U.S. 26, also called the Sunset Highway, east from downtown Portland. U.S. 26 hits U.S. 101 about 4 miles north of Cannon Beach; take a left and start looking for Cannon Beach signs.

Manzanita

The small town of Manzanita may be the most casually chic town on the Oregon Coast, its small commercial area dotted with boutiques and higher-end hotels. And yet the dining, while good, is mostly casual. The town is sandwiched between Neahkahnie Mountain and Nehalem Bay and is a favorite site for posh second homes. Of course, it's still the Oregon Coast, so the town is quaint and fairly unassuming. U.S. 101 only brushes the side of the town, so don't miss the turnoff, right next to a tight bend in the highway.

Parks and Beaches

The 4-mile sand spit of **Nehalem Bay State Park** (9500 Sandpiper Ln., 503/986-0707, www.oregonstateparks.org, $5 per vehicle) keeps the park isolated. The dunes and shore pines—planted to secure the sand—surround day-use areas, a playground, and a campground. The beaches are popular for people hunting for washed-up treasure from cargo ships and from the area's former beeswax industry.

Oswald West State Park (U.S. 101 near milepost 39, 503/368-3575, www. oregonstateparks.org, free) is located about 4.5 miles north of Manzanita. U.S. 101 cuts right through it, and there are a few parking areas directly on the main road. It's a heavily wooded park but with beach access, about a half mile from the road, that's very popular with surfers. A bridge crosses Short Sand Creek just before the beach. The park protects 13 miles of coastline and many groves of western red cedar, western hemlock, and Sitka spruce trees. Recent tree falls, including one tree 11 feet in diameter, worried officials enough that overnight camping is no longer permitted in the park.

Hiking
Neahkahnie Mountain Trail
Distance: 3 miles round-trip
Duration: 2 hours
Elevation gain: 900 feet
Effort: moderate
Trailhead: Use the South Neahkahnie Mountain Trailhead, located up a short road between mileposts 41 and 42 on U.S. 101.

The Neahkahnie Mountain Trail, just north of Manzanita and inside Oswald West State Park, is one of the most popular on the Oregon Coast, with views of headlands and the waves far below. From the southern trailhead, you'll hike up switchbacks and past a radio facility to the top of Neahkahnie Mountain, at 1,600 feet, and find breathtaking vistas. Keep an eye peeled, as rumor has it Spanish sailors stashed riches nearby (but don't dig—the rumors are persistent enough that digging for treasure is prohibited in the area). From the summit, return the way you came; though the trail does continue, it ends up at the North Neahkahnie Mountain Trailhead, and you'd need to walk south on U.S. 101 for a mile, a hazardous proposition, to reach your starting point.

Shopping

The beach may require nothing more than a bathing suit and a warm sweat-shirt, but **Syzygy** (447 Laneda Ave., 503/368-7573, www.syzygymanzanita.com, 10am-5pm daily) can outfit shoppers for most occasions. The walls of this small-town boutique are different vivid colors. Their clothes are just as bright, and many are the kind of funky pieces that serve as both wardrobe staple and vacation souvenir. There are also high-end rain boots and raincoats. Home decor, while limited, is rarely along the beachy, seashell-and-anchor spectrum, tending more toward cheery paintings and mirrors.

Salt and Paper (411 Laneda Ave., 503/368-7887, 9am-6pm daily) is located in a house with worn wooden siding and behind a picket fence and vine-covered arbor—about as charming as a seaside cottage gets. The wares for sale have just as much charm. The front porch is crowded with flowerpots and hanging decorations, birdbaths and patio furniture. Inside are stationery and art supplies, plus the ubiquitous saltwater taffy.

Dogs are popular companions along the Oregon Coast. Many hotels accommodate pooches and even shower them with special gifts. The store **Four Paws on the Beach** (144 Laneda Ave., 503/368-3436, www.fourpawsonthebeach.com, 10am-5pm daily) specializes in spoiling canines and sells organic and specialty dog food, collars and leashes, plus gifts for pet owners. And, even more a gift for humans are the doggie costumes with

from top to bottom: Lazy Susan Café in Cannon Beach; Tillamook Air Museum; Cannon Beach's Coaster Theatre Playhouse.

skirts and headpieces. Better in concept, perhaps, than execution.

Food

Manzanita's central **Manzanita Coffee Co.** (60 Laneda Ave., 503/368-2233, 7am-9pm daily) serves the only thing better than a beach latte—doughnuts and ice cream. The doughnuts, croissants, and apple fritters are big and doughy, and the Tillamook ice cream case is a popular destination on sunny beach days. The bench outside is helpful because lines go out the door on weekends and in summer.

Only the **San Dune Pub** (127 Laneda Ave., 503/368-5080, www.sandune-pub.com, 11:30am-10pm Mon.-Sat., 11:30am-9pm Sun., $7-16) would describe its location in relation to the nearest popular surf spot (Oswald West State Park, 10 miles away), rather than the town of Manzanita. The redbrick pub has 17 beers on tap and TVs playing big sports games. There's an outdoor patio for when it's warm and a wood-burning fireplace indoors for when it's not. More than a dozen kinds of burgers are on the menu, and fries can be covered in Tillamook cheese. Food is simple but well prepared—solid pub fare. The pub hosts live music on weekends, and it's popular with locals, surfer or not.

The small dining area at **Marzano's Pizza** (60 Laneda Ave., 503/368-3663, www.marzanospizza.com, 4pm-8:30pm Sun.-Tues. and Thurs., 4pm-9pm Fri.-Sat., $12-29) is nowhere near big enough for all the people who come for its bubbly pizza. The offerings are straightforward—pizza, calzones, and salads—and toppings are the usual combination of vegetables and meat, though the restaurant does make its own sausage. The most popular pizza is a roasted vegetable concoction, served only until they run out of fresh veggies. No alcohol is served in the restaurant, but it is available to go, and many families come for the takeout.

The ★ **Big Wave Cafe** (822 Laneda Ave., 503/368-9283, www.oregonsbig-wavecafe.com, 8am-8pm Sun.-Thurs., 8am-9pm Fri.-Sat., $8-21) is a casual restaurant specializing in simple seafood preparations. A blackboard notes where every kind of seafood was caught. Salads, burgers, and gourmet sandwiches round out the menu. And since the chef's wife is a pastry chef, desserts are house-made; the manager is their son. The interior is casual but the food is some of the best in town.

Accommodations
Under $150

Spindrift Inn (114 Laneda Ave., 503/368-1001, www.spindrift-inn.com, $109-225) is a cheery motel in the middle of Manzanita, its yellow shingle sides complementing white brick and blue trim. It was built in 1946, and though the interiors used to have all the lace touches and flowered bedspreads of eras past, recent renovations have added solid-color palettes and updated window treatments to the TVs and wireless Internet. Some rooms have kitchenettes and a sleeper sofa. The location is convenient, only a few blocks from the ocean but close to Manzanita's eateries. It doesn't offer late check-in, so get to the front desk by 8pm. Some rooms are pet friendly, and the inn has an interior flower garden.

The name doesn't lie—the **Sunset Surf Motel** (248 Ocean Rd., 503/368-5224, www.sunsetsurfocean.com, $85-169) gets a dead-on view of both the waves and the sunsets, though a road does pass between the motel and the beach. Still, the lawn and picnic tables and heated outdoor pool pretty up the view. Balconies run along the waterfront side of the motel, but you can still see the water from most rooms. Some rooms have gas fireplaces or nearly full kitchens. The 40 rooms are newly updated but still have a small-town charm. It's as nice as motels get.

It's not a misspelling: It's the **San Dune Inn** (428 Dorcas Ln., 503/368-5163, www.

sandune-inn-manzanita.com, $135-155), not the Sand Dune Inn. Located just a block off the main street in Manzanita, the 14-room hotel is run by a British hotelier at a laid-back pace. About half the rooms are simple one-room units, while the others have separate bedrooms and full kitchens. The amenities are pretty bare bones, with no fancy TVs or DVD players, but there is a guest grilling area and beach chairs for the short walk to the sand—plus Frisbees, volleyballs, and bikes. Many rooms are pet friendly. Even though the rooms have some head-scratching design combinations, the service is friendly and personal.

$150-250
The ★ **Inn at Manzanita** (67 Laneda Ave., 503/368-6754, www.innatmanzanita.com, $179-225) is less a hotel than a collection of 13 small getaways. Each room has a private deck, double jetted tub, and fireplace, and the grounds are carefully maintained to give a sense of privacy between the trees and shrubbery. Many rooms have vaulted ceilings and hardwood floors. Although at one time the hotel only accepted families with children in certain rooms, policies have changed—but it still has the feel of a romantic retreat. (Walkways and trails on the hotel grounds are a little too delicate for rowdy children.) The beach is only a block away, and the stores and restaurants of Manzanita are right across the street.

Over $250
Despite just six units at **Coast Cabins** (635 Laneda Ave., 800/435-1269, www.coast-cabins.com, $225-495), four have hot tubs and all have full kitchens or kitchenettes. Some have personal dry saunas and steam showers, and some have private barbecues. All are close to the cozy communal fire pit. A gym is on the property, and the **Spa Manzanita** (144 Laneda Ave., 503/368-4777, www.spamanzanita.com) is nearby, offering face and body treatments. The complex also includes an art gallery, which features contemporary art from Northwest artists. There are plenty of luxury touches, from granite countertops to featherbeds to teak lounge chairs, and lots of privacy.

Camping
The large campground at **Nehalem Bay State Park** (9500 Sandpiper Ln., 503/986-0707, www.oregonstateparks.org) includes 265 electrical and water sites ($29), 18 rentable yurts ($45-55), walk-in sites for hikers and bikers ($6), and hot showers. Got a private plane and no place to pitch a tent? There is also a 2,400-foot airstrip and dedicated fly-in sites ($11).

Getting There
Manzanita is situated on U.S. 101, 15 miles south of Cannon Beach and 27 miles north of Tillamook.

Tillamook

The name is synonymous with cheese, and the rich countryside is a peek at the rich farming heritage of the state. The town is also home to the biggest wooden structure in the world, which was constructed to hold blimps in World War II. What's striking about Tillamook is how different it feels from the wind-blown seaside towns to the north and south. It's only just inland, on sloughs at the base of Tillamook Bay, but it might as well be the center of Oregon.

Sights
Tillamook Air Museum
The wooden hangar that holds the **Tillamook Air Museum** (6030 Hangar Rd., 503/842-1130, www.tillamookair.com, 10am-5pm daily, $9.75 adults, $8.75 seniors, $6.50 children 6-17, $2.50 children under 6) is gargantuan for a reason—it was built to hold a fleet of blimps for the U.S. Navy in World War II. The space encloses seven acres, and

the ceiling is 15 stories high. Inside are flight and war artifacts, rooms devoted to helium and engines, and dozens of aircraft. The Mini-Guppy parked outside, a fat plane built by Boeing, once carried NASA spacecraft. Even with enough exhibits to fill a few hours, the museum only takes up a small part of its massive hangar home.

★ Tillamook Cheese Factory

A million people every year trek to the **Tillamook Cheese Factory** (4175 U.S. 101, 503/815-1300, www.tillamook.com, 8am-6pm daily Labor Day to mid-June, 8am-8pm daily mid-June to Labor Day, free), drawn from all corners with the promise of free cheese. Samples include small bits of Tillamook's signature cheddar and varieties like pepper jack, plus squeaky cheese curds. Just as popular an attraction is the ice cream stand selling cheap scoops of Tillamook ice cream. The factory also has views of the cheese

production floors and the bright copper and silver equipment where production lines run around the clock. The most famous business on the coast, Tillamook is actually a cooperative; Tillamook County Creamery Association is owned by the farmers that provide the cream for cheese making, and has been for more than 100 years.

Tillamook's famous blue-and-white building is undergoing renovations until the summer of 2018, but there's a temporary visitors center until then, with an ice cream stand and free cheese samples, of course.

Tillamook County Pioneer Museum

The **Tillamook County Pioneer Museum** (2106 2nd St., 503/842-4553, www.tcpm.org, 10am-4pm Tues.-Sun., $4 adults, $3 seniors, $1 children 10-17, children under 10 free) endeavors to preserve the area's history beyond its cheese accomplishments. It's located

Tillamook Cheese Factory

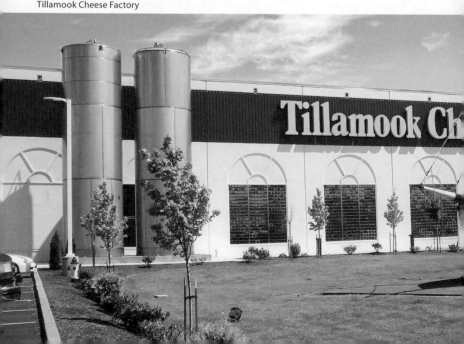

in an old courthouse downtown, a dignified building in a rather well-worn town. The museum's 45,000-item collection includes remnants from prehistoric times, relics from when Tillamook tribes lived in the area, and thousands of photographs of the farming and tourism roots of the area. The place has an old-timey feel to it, and exhibits are quaint but fascinating—stuffed and mounted animals on one floor and Civil War artifacts on the next. A case shows off the glass floats that sometimes appear on Oregon beaches, some from the other side of the Pacific.

Food and Accommodations

The specials at **Blue Moon Café** (2014 2nd St., 503/354-5444, 9:30am-3:30pm Mon.-Fri., $10-14) are scrawled on a whiteboard—burgers, pizzas, and various shrimp and oyster dishes. The baked goods at the small eatery include homemade scones and pies, often using local

MORNING STAR

marionberries and huckleberries. Greasy, hot sandwiches come with chips and a friendly attitude. It's also a good coffee shop with various mixed beverages and espresso milkshakes. The smell of grease hangs in the air, but at least it's tasty grease.

The town isn't known for luxury accommodations, but the **Ashley Inn of Tillamook** (1722 Makinster Rd., 503/842-7599, www.ashleyinntillamook.com, $125-170) has some of the best rooms available. There's an indoor saltwater pool, a hot tub, and a sauna, and the complimentary breakfast includes hot entrées. Some rooms have sofa beds, and all regular beds have memory-foam mattresses. The location is convenient, and the RV parking lot has 20 water and electrical hookups.

The **Shilo Inn Suites Hotel** (2515 N Main St., 503/842-7971, www.shiloinns.com, $134-164), located on the Wilson River in the middle of town, is a straightforward hotel with a small indoor swimming pool, steam room, and hot tub. Some rooms have kitchenettes, and all are good-sized, but the furniture hasn't been updated in a while. Still, it's a decent stopping place. The attached restaurant is a greasy spoon with a bacon-wrapped hot dog and deep-fried onion rings on the menu.

Getting There

Tillamook is located on U.S. 101, about 40 miles south of Cannon Beach and 44 miles north of Lincoln City. To venture inland, take Highway 6 east from Tillamook to where it intersects with U.S. 26 to reach Portland.

Side Trip: Three Capes Loop

The 50-mile Three Capes Loop is a scenic detour with stops at particularly beautiful points on the coast.

Start: Tillamook, inland on U.S. 101

CAPE MEARES: 14 MILES

In Tillamook, drive west on Highway 131 (this is called 3rd Street in town) and follow it northwest for 13.5 miles to **Cape Meares Lighthouse** (503/842-2244, Cape Meares, www.capemeareslighthouse.org, 11am-4pm Mon.-Thurs., 11am-6pm Fri.-Sun., closed 2pm-2:30pm daily, May-Sept., free). The short, squat lighthouse was built in 1889 and features a Fresnel lens. A short trail passes by interpretive signs, viewpoints, and the Octopus Tree, a 250-year-old Sitka spruce with limbs that bend at right angles.

Leaving the park, follow Bayshore Drive south for 2.5 miles to Oceanside, where the road becomes Cape Meares Loop. Turn right on Pacific Avenue and stop for a snack at **Roseanna's Café** (1490 Pacific Ave. NW, 503/842-7351, http://roseannascafe.com, 11am-8pm Mon. and Thurs.-Fri., 10am-8pm Sat.-Sun., $9-32), located in a century-old wooden building, with plenty of seafood to match the waterfront location. After lunch, continue walking north along Pacific Avenue to explore **Oceanside Beach State Recreation Site** (1790-1798 Rosenberg Loop, 503/842-3182, www.oregonstateparks.org, year-round). Walk up the beach and look for a tunnel in the rocks that leads to the next beach, the aptly named Tunnel Beach (only accessible at low tide).

CAPE LOOKOUT: 8 MILES

From Oceanside, follow Highway 131 south for 2.5 miles to the town of Netarts. Turn right on Netarts Bay Drive and follow it for 8 miles to **Cape Lookout State Park** (11645 Whiskey Creek Rd., 503/842-4981, www.oregonstateparks.org, $5 per vehicle). The park lies on a sand spit with quick beach access and more than 8 miles of trails as well as yurts ($44), a cabin ($88), and campsites ($21-29).

CAPE KIWANDA: 12 MILES

Leaving Netarts, follow Cape Lookout Road south for a little more than 3 miles. Turn right onto Sandlake Road and drive 8 miles to **Cape Kiwanda State Natural Area** (Hungry Harbor Rd. and McPhillips Dr., 503/842-3182, www.oregonstateparks.org), where **Pelican Pub & Brewery** (33180 Cape Kiwanda Dr., 503/965-7007, pelicanbrewing.com, 8am-10pm Sun.-Thurs., 8am-11pm Fri.-Sat., $12-24) marks your final stop on this detour. Grab a cream ale or an IPA and enjoy it on one of the patio tables outside. The microbrewery also serves yummy burgers, seafood, and pizza (in case your lunch has worn off).

End: Tillamook (25 miles) or Lincoln City (20 miles)

To complete the loop, return to U.S. 101 by taking Cape Kiwanda Drive south for 1 mile. Turn left onto Pacific Avenue, and then make an immediate right onto Brooten Road, just after the bridge. Follow Brooten Road for 2.5 miles to U.S. 101. Take U.S. 101 north for 25 miles back to Tillamook, or drive south for 20 miles to Lincoln City to continue exploring the coast.

Pacific City

Tucked away off the main road, Pacific City is a nice place to take it slow. The town's biggest attraction is a pub and brewery, plus the beach that's just steps away.

Sights
Cape Kiwanda

Call it the second most famous big rock on the Oregon Coast. Of course, the giant formation is called Haystack Rock, just like the one in Cannon Beach, so the area is better known as **Cape Kiwanda State**

Natural Area (Hungry Harbor Rd. and McPhillips Dr., 503/842-3182, www.oregonstateparks.org, free). This rock is removed from the coast, but the cape has a large beach and is close to where small boats head into the Pacific to fish. It's a good beach for kite flying and beach walks. North past the headland, the beach quickly peters out at high tide, so head south for a long walk since the sand continues all the way down to Bob Straub State Park, where the Nestucca River empties into the Pacific.

Shopping
Pacific City Gallery (35350 Brooten Rd., 503/965-7181, 11am-4pm Thurs.-Sun.) isn't on the beach but across the river near the Pacific City Inn. The building has a wide porch that faces the highway. Inside it has, unsurprisingly, seascapes and glass-float art, plus woodcarvings, glass sculptures, and jewelry. The walls are crowded with pieces by Pacific Northwest artists. They also sell prints.

Food
The ★ **Pelican Pub & Brewery** (33180 Cape Kiwanda Dr., 503/965-7007, pelicanbrewing.com, 8am-10pm Sun.-Thurs., 8am-11pm Fri.-Sat., $12-24) is the real reason to leave the main road to travel up to Pacific City. It's so close to the beach that the outdoor patio tables are practically in the surf. The microbrewery was opened in 1996 and has a full slate of beers—a cream ale, an IPA, and the Imperial Pelican Ale. Four rounds of seasonal beers rotate through. The pub serves seafood entrées, burgers, and pizzas loaded with local shrimp, cheese, and veggies. The menus point out beer pairings, and a number of dishes actually use the beer itself to batter the onion rings or flavor the brownie sundae.

The other beach food in town is at **Doryland Pizza** (33315 Cape Kiwanda Dr., 503/965-6299, www.capekiwandarvresort.com, 11:30am-9pm daily, $8-10), next to and owned by an RV park. The dining room is crowded and lines form at the order window. The pizza is thick, cheesy, and bubbly, and the menu also has sandwiches, pasta, and a salad bar; there's a long line of local beer taps. Kids kill time waiting for pizza with arcade games.

Accommodations
The simple, small **Pacific City Inn** (35280 Brooten Rd., 503/965-6464, www.pacificcityinn.com, $117-195) has only 16 rooms, but it's a friendly little motel in a very quiet town. It even has a bistro with a wine and martini bar and room service. Some rooms have kitchenettes, and laundry is on the premises. The rooms have the kind of dated motel style one would expect from an out-of-the-way motel—some rooms even have fold-down Murphy beds. The cheery bistro has white tablecloths and a farmhouse vibe. The gardens behind the hotel have picnic tables and well-tended flowerbeds.

The massive **Inn at Cape Kiwanda** (33105 Cape Kiwanda Dr., 888/965-7001, www.yourlittlebeachtown.com/inn, $349-389) is a big building for modest Pacific City—all its rooms (most with balconies) face the ocean across the street and the Pelican Pub. The rooms have cushy-bed, leather-furniture luxury, even though the views of the ocean also include the Pelican parking lot. The lobby has a fireplace and comfy chairs, and the hotel has a mini spa. Bike rentals are available, and it's a good area for safe cycling. Some rooms have two-person jetted tubs, and all have gas fireplaces.

Camping
The **Cape Kiwanda RV Resort** (33305 Cape Kiwanda Dr., 503/965-6230, www.capekiwandarvresort.com, $37 tent sites, $51-55 RV sites, $77-175 cabins) is across the street from the Cape Kiwanda beach and has more amenities than the usual RV spot. It's been around since 1969 and eventually took over a nearby Doryman's

Fish Company building. There are 107 sites with full hookups as well as two dozen cabins and cottages, though only the deluxe cabins come with linens. There are also 10 tent sites next to the trees. The complex has an indoor clubhouse with a heated pool, spa, and exercise room. The Marketplace near the road has a deli with hot prepared meals and a grocery store. The seafood market has fresh fish from the Pacific City dory fleet, and they smoke their own fish and oysters. The gift shop sells bathing suits. Outdoors is a playground and horseshoe pit. This really isn't roughing it—free wireless Internet is available. Reservations are recommended.

Getting There

Unlike most towns on the Oregon Coast, Pacific City isn't on U.S. 101. Reach the small town by leaving U.S. 101 at 25 miles south of Tillamook or 20 miles north of Lincoln City. Take a left on Brooten Road and follow it 2.5 miles to the town of Pacific City. To reach the beach and Pelican Pub, keep going across the Nestucca River and take the first right onto Cape Kiwanda Drive. Cape Kiwanda State Natural Area is about a mile ahead on the left.

Lincoln City

Lincoln City is one of the biggest cities on this stretch of coast. It has hotels and restaurants for visitors, plus some of the bigger collections of fast-food restaurants and outlet stores. The town stretches down the coast, past the inland water bodies of Siletz Bay and Devil's Lake, because it was once a collection of smaller towns: Taft, Oceanlake, Delake, Nelscott, and Cutler City. They voted to become Lincoln City by a very small margin, and the resulting town was almost called Surfland. Wave riders do come to the area, but it's a cold, rough ocean out there—more visitors appreciate the

coast by crabbing, building bonfires on the beach, or flying a kite.

Parks and Beaches

Devil's Lake State Recreation Area

The **Devil's Lake State Recreation Area** (1452 NE 6th Dr., 541/994-2002, www.oregonstateparks.org) is nearly in the middle of downtown Lincoln City and has some of the most accessible green and camping space on the coast. The park stretches over both the northwest and southwest sides of the lake, with lots of residences lining its shores, but it's also home to birds like loons, cormorants, and even bald eagles.

D River State Park

The Pacific Ocean is a nearly endless body of water, but the **D River State Park** (SE 1st St. and U.S. 101, 541/994-7341, www.oregonstateparks.org), which connects Devils Lake to the Pacific, is a mere 120 feet long at high tide. It has appeared in the *Guinness Book of World Records* as the shortest river in the world. A group in Great Falls, Montana, started a competition with Oregon, claiming their river was the shortest, and eventually *Guinness* stopped listing the record. The four-acre park—basically just a parking lot next to the mini waterway—is the base for some of Lincoln City's kite festivals.

Lincoln City Beach

There are a number of spots to access the **Lincoln City Beach,** a stretch with a good amount of driftwood. Try the end of NW 26th Street, near NW Inlet Avenue, next to the Pelican Shores Inn. There's a bathroom and steps down to the beach, plus a handful of parking spots next to a stone wall. To drive on the sand itself, follow NE 15th Street to the end.

Gleneden Beach State Recreation Site

Even though much of the waterfront south of Lincoln City has steep bluffs, **Gleneden Beach State Recreation Site**

(Wesler St. and Raymond Ave., 541/265-4560, www.oregonstateparks.org, free) has a paved walkway down to the sand. The surfing spot is also popular with seals, which pop up among the waves. The beach entrance includes picnic tables and a bathroom.

Hiking
Drift Creek Suspension Bridge

Distance: 3 miles round-trip
Duration: 1.5 hours
Elevation gain: 550 feet
Effort: moderate
Trailhead: Forest Road 17
Directions: The site is about 10 miles inland from Lincoln City. Take Drift Creek Road east, then make a right on South Drift Creek Road and a left on Forest Road 17. It's about 10 miles down the road to the trailhead.

It's only a short hike to the Drift Creek Suspension Bridge (www.fs.usda.gov), a 240-foot long bridge that passes over 75-foot Drift Creek Falls. The materials had to be brought to the site via helicopter, and the bridge crosses about 100 feet above the creek and waterfall below. The hike goes downhill in the first half, then back uphill. A picnic table is near the bridge for a forest lunch, a perfect stop before returning the way you came.

Entertainment and Events

The local **Theatre West** (3536 SE U.S. 101, 541/994-5663, www.theatrewest.com, $8-12) turned an old auditorium into a warm community theater, and since the 1980s it has brought in locals onstage, some with experience on Broadway. Productions tend toward comedy, and many are original productions. The low building right on U.S. 101 has a bright blue roof. Reservations must be made by phone.

The brisk winds on the Oregon Coast mean it's not the best for sunbathing, but it's one of the best kite-flying spots in the world. Lincoln City hosts one of the biggest Northwest kite events. The **Summer Kite Festival** (D River State Park, www.oregoncoast.org/summer-kite-festival) is held on the beach in June; the **Fall Kite Festival** (D River State Park, www.oregoncoast.org/fall-kite-festival) is in October. Performers launch show kites and do tricks, sometimes with dozens of kites tied together. They also include kite-making clinics and kids' parades, and an open area is for free kite flying—if you can handle the possible line tangles.

Food

There's a whole dog pound at the **Beach Dog Café** (6042 U.S. 101, 541/996-3647, 7am-2:30pm Wed.-Sun., $7-13, cash only), framed in pictures on the wall—row after row after row of illustrations and photos of pooches. The restaurant serves breakfast and lunch, but the first meal of the day gets the most play here, including French toast, pancakes, elaborate eggs, and potato dishes. More than a dozen hot dogs are on the menu, from a Chicago dog with mustard and relish to a "hot diggity dog" with sriracha sauce. Waits can get lengthy for the homey spot since it has few tables and is the go-to joint for many of the city's tourists—for good reason.

The windows at **The Bay House** (5911 SW U.S. 101, 541/996-3222, www.thebayhouse.org, 5:30pm-10pm Wed.-Sun., $26-44) face the water, in a building that's housed one eatery or another since 1937. It's now one of the finer dining establishments in town, serving dinner only in careful, artistic preparations. The menu is short, with a handful of fish, pasta, and meat entrées, but the tasting menu ($79) is a good mix of locally sourced bites, paired with Oregon wines ($29). Sunsets from the dining room are gorgeous.

The breaded and fried cod with fries at **J's Fish and Chips** (1800 SW U.S. 101, 541/994-4445, 11:30am-7pm Mon.-Thurs., 11:30am-9pm Fri.-Sat. 11:30am-4:30pm Sun., $7-12) is the star, but the restaurant's fish tacos are also popular—plus the halibut, prawns, rockfish, and other sea creatures listed on the blackboard. Order at the counter when you come in, then snag a table once your order is ready. The clam chowder isn't necessarily a standout, but it's good for anyone who doesn't like soups that are too fishy. Like any good fish-and-chips joint, J's serves food in flimsy baskets lined with waxy paper and with sides of slaw and creamy tartar sauce.

Most entrées at the **Blackfish Café** (2733 U.S. 101, 541/996-1007, www.blackfishcafe.com, 11:30am-3pm and 5pm-11pm Wed.-Mon., $13-26) are some kind of seafood: local rockfish or Pacific swordfish, or a cioppino made from a collection of shellfish. The vibe is homey, not too fancy, but the dinners themselves have more preparation than the casual surroundings. Many dishes use locally sourced ingredients. The most popular desserts are the homemade Ding Dongs, chocolate pastries topped with a berry sauce and whipped cream—much better than the kind you can buy at a gas station.

Accommodations
Under $150

Siletz Bay Lodge (1012 SW 51st St., 541/996-6111, www.siletzbaylodgelincolncity.com, $138-158) is located right on Siletz Bay, a giant tidal marsh that is a wildlife refuge for waterfowl and small aquatic mammals. Many rooms have balconies, and all have views of the bay and ocean. But the hotel does, in places, seem stuck in the past: flowered bedspreads, generic wall art, and no air-conditioning, which can be a pain in the warmest summer months. The free continental breakfast is limited but includes some hot items. There's a hot tub and the nearby beach, perfect for evening bonfires.

The wood-sided **Looking Glass Inn** (861 SW 51st St., 541/996-3996, www.lookingglass-inn.com, $114-159) is the classic beach hotel. Some rooms have jetted tubs and fireplaces, and it's right on the water. Laundry facilities are available to guests, along with an outdoor picnic table and grill. Hoping to catch some crab for your dinner? There's an outdoor

crab-cooking station. Some suites have kitchens, and pet-friendly packages include dog bowls, towels, treats, and waste bags. Some of the furniture is dated, but the hotel's location on the north end of Siletz Bay is nearly unbeatable.

The waterfront **Pelican Shores Inn** (2645 NW Inlet Ave., 541/994-2134, www.pelicanshores.com, $109-199) is practically on the sand, so the ground-floor rooms on the ocean have patios overlooking the waves. The indoor pool has an angled glass ceiling, so it feels something like swimming in a greenhouse. The hotel is somewhat small, with only 33 rooms, decorated with Pelican Shores life preservers. Some suites have a small kitchen or sleeper sofa; all have at least a refrigerator and microwave. The inn has a free continental breakfast. The cheapest rooms don't have a view.

The multicolored **Ashley Inn and Suites** (3430 U.S. 101, 541/996-7500, www.ashleyinnlincolncity.com, $89-164) is a few blocks from the beach, but closer than most highway-side hotels. The lobby often smells of chocolate chip cookies (not as a tease, but as a freebie for guests). Some spa rooms have large two-person jetted tubs. The beds all have downy pillows and comfortable mattresses, and the somber decor is more subdued than the starfish-and-buoy motels that populate the Oregon Coast. Couches and multi-room suites are available.

$150-250

All 120 rooms at the ★ **Inn at Spanish Head** (4009 U.S. 101, 541/996-2161, www.spanishhead.com, $205-225) have ocean views. Many have kitchens and balconies, and all can access the pool, saunas, and spa. The outdoor heated pool almost has better views than the rooms themselves. The 10 stories are like a giant flight of stairs right on the beach, though the inland side, oddly, has a northern Italian vibe with its red roof and arches. Rooms and furnishings are adequate but not luxurious.

The three-floor **Inn at Wecoma** (2945 U.S. 101, 541/994-2984, www.innatwecoma.com, $148-219) is convenient to the highway but several blocks from the ocean. Some rooms have fireplaces or balconies, and there's an indoor pool and hot tub. The hotel rents bicycles, and the outdoor recreation area has grills and shuffleboard. The decor is modern and less beachy than some other hotels in the area. The free breakfast includes hot items like pancakes and biscuits and gravy.

Over $250
In a town of beachfront motels, **Salishan Spa & Golf Resort** (7760 U.S. 101, 541/764-3600, www.salishan.com, $259-289) is a different kind of beast—a golf and spa resort. Some rooms have sleeper sofas and fireplaces. The spa has whirlpools and saunas, and the resort has a large pool, tennis courts, and five restaurants, including a casual grill and a lounge with live music performances and balcony. Outdoors, play on the bocce courts or jungle gym, or stay inside with the video games in the entertainment center. For anyone who can't handle the regular golf links, try the 18-hole putting course. Although it's on the inland side of U.S. 101, many rooms have views of the south end of Siletz Bay.

Camping
At **Devil's Lake State Recreation Area** (1452 NE 6th Dr., 800/452-5687, www.reserveamerica.com) are 50 tent sites ($21), several walk-in sites for hikers and bikers ($6), and 25 RV sites with full hookups ($29-31). The flush toilets and hot showers mean that you barely have to rough it. The park also has 10 yurts ($45) available to rent—though you'll need your own bedding. Any campsite, yurt, or boat moorage spot ($10) can be reserved online. This is an especially good destination for campers looking for disabled access because the trail to the lake has a hard surface, and two campsites and two yurts are ADA accessible.

Getting There
Lincoln City is about 44 miles south of Tillamook and 25 miles north of Newport, an easy drive on U.S. 101 from either starting point. The closest connection to Portland is Highway 18, which heads east from U.S. 101 at the small town of Otis. The Salmon River Highway, as Highway 18 is known, passes through the town of McMinnville before slogging through Portland suburbs as Highway 99 West. The drive from Lincoln City to Portland is about two hours under the best traffic conditions, but delays are common.

Depoe Bay

Just how tiny is little Depoe Bay? Signs proudly claim its little harbor is the world's smallest. The town also promotes itself as a whale-watching mecca, though it's also a good spot to wander a short downtown stretch within view of the ocean.

Whale-Watching
The state-run **Whale Watching Center** (119 SW U.S. 101, 541/765-3304, www.oregonstateparks.org, 10am-4pm daily Memorial Day-Labor Day, 10am-4pm Wed.-Sun. Labor Day-Memorial Day, free) is informational, with whalebones and maps spread around the seafront space and binoculars for public use. Volunteers are on hand during busy times to explain where and when to see whales. The most popular animals are the gray whales whose migrations pass the spot twice a year, once in spring and once in winter, but the only times that whales aren't commonly seen in the area are November-early December and mid-January to mid-March. Other species seen include humpback, blue, and sperm whales, as well as orcas. Maps show the best shore spots for whale-watching. A whiteboard also tracks how many whales have been spotted that day, month, and year.

If peering through binoculars on land doesn't score you a whale sighting, head to the seas. **Whale Research EcoExcursions** (Ellingson St. and U.S. 101, 541/912-6734, www.oregonwhales.com, $40 adults, $32 children 2-12) advertises that its trips are done with a marine biologist, Carrie Newell, on board. Trips leave from the **Whale, Sealife & Shark Museum** (www.oregonwhales.com, 10am-4pm daily summer, 10am-4pm Fri.-Sun. winter, $5 adults, $3 children 4-12, children under 4 free), a cramped private museum whose exhibits—a crowded wall of shark jaws, models of seabirds—are best viewed only on the rainiest of days, or in conjunction with one of the trips. But Newell has been known to show off the body of a shark caught in the area in the parking lot. Her whale-watching trips are crammed with info, and they have a high sighting success rate.

The Whale's Tail (270 Coast Guard Dr., 541/921-1323, www.whalestaildepoebay.com, Mar.-Sept., $30-40) was one of the first to perform approved whale-watching trips in Zodiac boats on the Oregon Coast. There are no stairs to access the boats, so it's a better choice for anyone with mobility issues (call for information). Look for the yellow signs for Dockside Charters. The boat only carries six passengers, so trips are intimate. They claim that they get fewer seasick riders because of the smaller boat's low center of gravity and lack of diesel fumes.

Food

★ **Restaurant Beck** (541/765-3220, www.restaurantbeck.com, 5pm-10pm daily, Wed.-Sun. only winter, $18-34), a fine-dining spot located in the Whale Cove Inn, is one of the best spots to eat on the coast, with breathtaking views of Whale Cove and an outdoor patio. Dishes are made from locally sourced ingredients by a chef—he prefers local fish and game meats like wild boar and duck—recognized by the James Beard Foundation. The beer and wine lists include some

the coast at Depoe Bay

local standouts. Reservations are highly recommended.

Don't begrudge the name at **Gracie's Sea Hag** (58 U.S. 101, 541/765-2734, www. theseahag.com, 7am-9:30pm daily, $19-26)—the eatery and staff are anything but hag-like, and the joint's central location makes it one of the most popular spots in town. The lengthy menu has a little bit of everything, from shrimp cocktail to steak sandwiches to prime rib with Yorkshire pudding on Saturday nights. Gracie, the spot's namesake, still appears behind the bar. There's a bar and live music, but the feel is that of a very casual, small-town family restaurant. The menu includes a nine-ounce filet mignon, but this kind of joint calls for the fish-and-chips, or maybe the combination plate of deep-fried local seafood catches.

Accommodations

The **Whale Cove Inn** (2345 U.S. 101, 541/765-4300, www.whalecoveinn.com, suites $455-795) feels separate from

everything else on the busy Oregon Coast. It's just north of Rocky Point State Park, south of Depoe Bay, and has a fairly unassuming edifice on the road. On the other side, however, the hotel looks down on Whale Cove, and inside the lobby is a large vertical water feature. It's a boutique hotel with a luxury feel and amenities, so the few rooms (only nine) are priced much higher than other hotels in the area. Beds are comfortable memory foam, and all rooms have fireplaces and bay views. They also have private balconies with personal outdoor Jacuzzis. A premier suite has three bedrooms. The Whale Cove Inn is where to stay when money's no object and privacy and luxury are desired.

Getting There

Depoe Bay is about halfway between Lincoln City and Newport on U.S. 101, and about 12 miles from both. The town is located directly on the water, and a narrow bridge over the bay entrance goes through the middle of town. Parking on the main drag—since it's both the busy U.S. 101 and the town's busiest commercial street—can be difficult to find, but there are small lots and street parking uphill.

Otter Rock

The town of Otter Rock, 5 miles south of Depoe Bay, has **Mo's West** (122 1st St., 541/765-2442, www.moschowder. com, 11am-8pm daily, $9-12), one of the smallest outposts of the chain—there since 1972—and with a great view. It's the most charming way to take in a bowl of Mo's chowder. Next door, the **Flying Dutchman Winery** (915 1st St., 541/765-2553, www.dutchmanwinery.com, 11am-6pm daily June-Sept., 11am-5pm daily Oct.-May, $5) has regular tastings of their boutique wines. Of course, the grapes are grown inland, as they wouldn't thrive on this salty, windy coast.

Devil's Punch Bowl State Natural Area

You just know that the Devil would spike the punch. At **Devil's Punch Bowl State Natural Area** (851 1st St., 541/265-4560, www.oregonstateparks.org, free), a giant rock formation near the shore, the water churns in and out like a good frothy punch being stirred. It was formed when the roofs of some sea caves collapsed and water continued to dig out a space in the rock. There are tide pools just north of the formation. Catch a view from the end of the road in the small town of Otter Rock, 8 miles north of Newport and accessed from Otter Creek Loop just off U.S. 101. Picnic tables, fire pits, and restroom facilities can be found on the bluff above.

Beverly Beach State Park

Seven miles north of Newport, **Beverly Beach State Park** (NE Beverly Dr. and U.S. 101, 541/265-9278, www.oregonstateparks.org) is one of the most popular parks in the area. Parking is on the inland side of U.S. 101, but a walkway travels under and to the wide sandy beach. A visitors center has registration information for the campground as well as a small store. **Camping** is available in tent ($21), full hookup ($29-31), and hike-in ($6) sites, as well as group sites ($78). The yurts ($45-55) can be reserved online as well. There are play structures and picnic facilities.

Newport

One of the biggest towns on the Oregon Coast, Newport still retains a working waterfront that is as productive as it is touristy.

Sights
Hatfield Marine Science Center
Less massive than the nearby aquarium, the **Hatfield Marine Science Center** (2030 SE Marine Science Dr., 541/867-0100, www.hmsc.oregonstate.edu, 10am-5pm daily Memorial Day-Labor Day, 10am-4pm Thurs.-Mon. Labor Day-Memorial Day, $5 suggested donation) is still a sizable sea-themed destination, albeit one that's more popular with the younger set. The building was originally a marine laboratory for Oregon State University and still hosts marine research of all kinds. A visitors center takes education to a direct level with touch tanks, water displays, and a resident octopus, plus tours of scientific research equipment (submarines) parked outside. Just how different is the center from the Oregon Coast Aquarium? It's been known to offer free events in which a biologist performs a necropsy on a river otter to explain how the animals live (and die)— you won't find that at more conventional science centers.

★ Oregon Coast Aquarium
The massive **Oregon Coast Aquarium** (2820 SE Ferry Slip Rd., 541/867-3474, www.aquarium.org, 10am-6pm daily May-Sept., 10am-5pm daily Sept.-May, $22.95 adults, $19.95 seniors and children 13-17, $14.95 children 3-12, children under 3 free) is one of the most popular attractions on the Oregon Coast. At one time it was the home of the killer whale that played the title role in *Free Willy*. Now it has exhibits devoted to every kind of marine environment, especially the rocky and sandy shores of Oregon. Find a giant Pacific octopus, a massive creature that can be shy—look carefully in the dark corners of the tank. The harbor seal and sea lion exhibits allow for seated spectators at educational presentations, and the aviary provides an open-air space for birds like tufted puffins and horned puffins. An underwater tunnel goes through a deepwater tank for peeks at sharks. Look for the daily feeding schedule to catch the sea otters getting a snack. Then get your own at the new Ferry Slip Café inside (admission is not necessary to eat there).

Newport

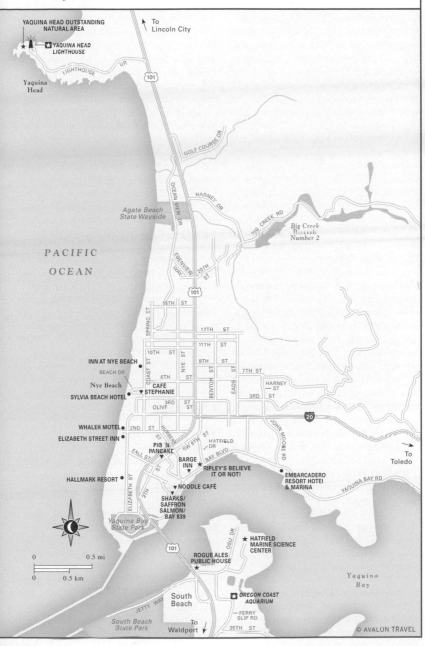

YAQUINA HEAD OUTSTANDING NATURAL AREA

★ YAQUINA HEAD LIGHTHOUSE

Yaquina Head

LIGHTHOUSE DR

101

To Lincoln City

GOLF COURSE DR

OCEAN VIEW DR

HARNEY DR

Agate Beach State Wayside

BIG CREEK RD

Big Creek Reservoir Number 2

PACIFIC OCEAN

EBBENVIEW WAY

20TH ST

101

15TH ST

12TH ST

SPRING ST

11TH ST

10TH ST

COAST ST

8TH ST

7TH ST

INN AT NYE BEACH

BEACH DR

Nye Beach

CAFÉ STEPHANIE

SYLVIA BEACH HOTEL

6TH ST

NYE ST

BENTON ST

EADS

HARNEY ST

3RD ST

3RD OLIVE ST ST

WHALER MOTEL

2ND ST

HURBERT ST

JOHN MOORE RD

20

ELIZABETH STREET INN

PIG 'N PANCAKE

SW 6TH ST

HATFIELD DR

BARGE INN

BAY BLVD

RIPLEY'S BELIEVE IT OR NOT!

FALL ST

EMBARCADERO RESORT HOTEL & MARINA

HALLMARK RESORT

NOODLE CAFÉ

YAQUINA BAY RD

SHARKS/ SAFFRON SALMON/ BAY 839

ELIZABETH ST

9TH ST

Yaquina Bay State Park

OSU DR

HATFIELD MARINE SCIENCE CENTER

101

ROGUE ALES PUBLIC HOUSE

Yaquina Bay

0   0.5 mi

0   0.5 km

South Beach

OREGON COAST AQUARIUM

JETTY WAY

To Waldport

FERRY SLIP RD

35TH ST

South Beach State Park

To Toledo

© AVALON TRAVEL

Ripley's Believe It or Not!

One of more than three dozen outposts of its kind, **Ripley's Believe It or Not!** (250 SW Bay Blvd., 541/265-2206, www. marinersquare.com, 10am-7pm daily July-Aug., 10am-5pm daily June and Sept., 11am-5pm Oct.-May, $14 adults, $8 children 5-12, children under 5 free) has weird and wonderful attractions for anyone not wowed by a giant Pacific octopus or massive lighthouse. Named for the father of the circus sideshow, the museum displays shrunken heads and mummies along with a hall of mirrors and a wax museum that re-creates pop culture figures like Yoda and the cast of *M*A*S*H*. The Undersea Gardens is a more scientific look at the weird and wonderful, with dive shows and illuminated anemones.

Rogue Ales Brewery

It isn't really Oregon until you're tossing back a brew. The **Rogue Ales Brewery** (2320 OSU Dr., 541/867-3664, www. rogue.com, 11am-9pm Sun.-Thurs., 11am-10pm Fri.-Sat.) sits on the same industrial bayfront as the Oregon Coast Aquarium and the Hatfield Marine Science Center. Rogue Ales was founded in the 1980s and has become one of the state's most popular breweries. Space for the brewery was sold by Mohava Niemi, the founder of Mo's, who stipulated that a photo of her naked in a tub remained in the brewpub—and that the brewery give back to locals. It's been so successful that it has tasting rooms and "meeting hall" brewpubs throughout the Northwest, even as far away as San Francisco. It's also famous for its Dead Guy Ale, Chocolate Stout, and pale ale flavored with juniper berries. **Tours** of the brewpub, with its two stories, 40 taps, and Yaquina Bay view, are at 3pm daily.

★ Yaquina Head Lighthouse

Oregon's tallest lighthouse is the prime attraction at the **Yaquina Head Outstanding Natural Area** (750 NW Lighthouse Dr., 541/574-3100, www.blm. gov, park 7am-sunset daily, interpretive center 10am-5pm daily, $7 per vehicle), a headland that's been carefully protected and managed for the sake of wildlife and the historical structure. After paying the entrance fee, drive to the **Interpretive Center;** it contains lots of history, including a giant re-creation of the French-made lighthouse lens.

Built in 1872, the still-working **Yaquina Head Lighthouse** stands 93 feet tall. You can go inside the lighthouse on **ranger-led tours** (daily July-Sept., weather permitting Feb.-June, free), which involve lots of stair-climbing and last about 45 minutes. Space is limited on crowded summer days, so visit the website or call in advance for reservations (877/444-6777, www.recreation.gov, reservation fee applies). Same-day tickets are available on a first-come, first-served basis and can only be reserved in person at the Interpretive Center. From the lighthouse, you can see islands just offshore where birds gather, sometimes more than 65,000 common murres, Brandt's cormorants, and various gulls. Pelicans, bald eagles, and turkey vultures soar by. Look for gray whales in the water beyond. A 0.5-mile walking trail leads around the headland and to the top of Salal Hill, with great views up and down the coast.

Yaquina Bay Lighthouse

Not to be confused with its larger cousin, this lighthouse at **Yaquina Bay State Recreation Site** (1100-1198 SW 9th St., 541/265-5679, www.oregonstateparks. org, year-round, free) is more like a combination of a historical home and a lighthouse. Located in the middle of Newport at the mouth of the Yaquina River, it's the oldest structure in town. An older structure was built in 1871 and decommissioned only three years later when the much bigger Yaquina Head Lighthouse was built. Then it served as a Coast Guard station. Today the living quarters re-create life on the coast a century ago. The surrounding park area has beach access, picnic facilities, and viewpoints.

Parks and Beaches

Three miles south of Newport is **South Beach State Park** (S Beach State Park Rd. and U.S. 101, 800/551-6949, www.oregonstateparks.org), which has views up to Newport's big Yaquina Bay Bridge. Grassy dunes lead down to the beach, and the park is nearly 500 acres. A bike path winds through the park, interpretive programs and guided hikes are held daily in summer, and kayak tours sometimes explore the inland waterways of the area, but visit the campground's hospitality center for schedule information.

Food

There are five **Pig 'n Pancake** (810 SW Alder St., 541/265-9065, www.pignpancake.com, 6am-3pm daily, $8-18) restaurants along the Oregon Coast. All serve the kind of casual family fare that a beach weekend deserves—chowder, burgers, and of course, pancakes and bacon. The chain is still family owned and run. The pancakes come in buttermilk, Swedish, sourdough, and French batter varieties. The restaurant is housed in a building that used to be Newport's city hall, built in the 1920s in a vaguely art deco style. The side now has a pig painting in front of Newport's bridge. Inside are booths, tables, and counter seats, with busy waitresses trying to keep up and waiting patrons browsing the gift shop for postcards and souvenirs.

Newport's bayfront is a strange mix of restaurants, stores, and working waterfront, so a fine meal might be right next to a machine sorting fresh-caught shrimp. In the center is **Rogue Ales Public House** (748 SW Bay Blvd., 541/265-3188, www.rogue.com, 11am-1am Sun.-Thurs., 11am-1am Fri.-Sat., $8-16), sister to the brewery that sits across the bay. This used to be the brewery itself, until it moved in 1992, but this spot is a full-on restaurant with a pool room called the Crustacean Station. There are 35 beers on tap and a menu of beer-friendly dishes like spinach and artichoke dip or Kobe beef meatballs stuffed with Oregon blue cheese. Kobe beef burgers come topped with local Applewood-smoked bacon or local oyster mushrooms. The lengthy offerings also include seafood, pizzas, tacos, and root beer floats, but as the menu points out, no beluga caviar or foie gras—so don't even ask. Brewery tours are not offered, but the rowdy, friendly restaurant does like to offer "free bathroom tours," even though the loos aren't anything special.

This close to the working fisheries, there has to be a greasy, slightly grungy place to grab a beer and a burger. The **Barge Inn** (358 SW Bay Blvd., 541/265-0051, 7am-9pm Sun.-Thurs., 7am-10pm Fri.-Sat., $5-8) is that local joint. The burger menu is on a Pepsi-themed readerboard above the bar, and two bar-to-ceiling poles (which might block your menu view) are labeled "North" and "South." The building is shaped like a barn and labeled "tavern," though a sign above the bar notes it's home to "winos, dingbats & riffraff." It looks like a generic dive bar from the front, with its pool tables and jukebox, but inside it's friendlier—and a little less boozy—than it first appears.

The salmon dinner at ★ **Saffron Salmon** (859 SW Bay Blvd., 541/265-8921, www.saffronsalmon.com, 5pm-8:30pm Mon.-Tues. and Thurs., 11:30am-2:30pm and 5pm-8:30pm Fri.-Sun., $14-34) isn't actually cooked with saffron, but the spicy seafood stew does include it; the wild salmon is paired with vegetables and basil-pine nut butter. The restaurant serves some of the finest meals available on the bayfront section of Newport, with views of fishing boats as they return and unload, and seals frolicking in the bay. The waiter may even be able to point out which ships catch the crab that appears on the table. The pier location has a modern, updated look, but the windows provide the best decoration.

Look for the bright yellow exterior of **Café Stephanie** (411 NW Coast St., 541/265-8082, 7:30am-2pm daily, $5-12), a good beacon when hangovers hit on the salty coast. Breakfasts are legendary and indulgent, from vanilla cinnamon French toast to a "potato tornado" topped with sour cream. Everything is refreshingly cheap and filling, and decorative painted tentacles grace the walls inside. The space is small, so there can be waits on weekends, and there's limited outdoor seating.

The bayfront's **Noodle Café** (837 SW Bay Blvd., 541/574-6688, www.noodle-cafenewport.com, 11am-2:30pm and 4:30pm-9pm Mon.-Tues. and Thurs.-Sat., noon-2:30pm Sun., $11-16) is just a small restaurant, but it's popular with locals up and down the coast. With its bright green exterior, it's hard to miss, and it backs up to the water and an outdoor picnic table area. Stormy days on the coast are a perfect fit for the pho noodle soup, udon, or spicy seafood broth, while those occasional sunny days are better for wraps made of chicken or shrimp tempura. The Asian menu has a wide range of classics, like stir-fry and bulgogi, plus homemade dumplings—actually most items are made from scratch, and it shows.

Accommodations
$150-250

The darling ★ **Sylvia Beach Hotel** (267 NW Cliff St., 541/265-5428, www.sylviabeachhotel.com, $135-275) is a cozy, bookish treasure in a town of big hotels. It's a blue four-story house on a bluff overlooking the beach, and much quieter than the usual beach motel. There are no TVs in the rooms, no wireless Internet, no telephones; but there is a resident cat and a library. Each room is named for an author or book, so the Colette room has a French feel and the Hemingway room has goofy animal heads mounted above the bed. The bedframe in the retro-futuristic Jules Verne room has sprockets and gears.

Yaquina Head Lighthouse

For all the book influences, the library is more a relaxing space than a book depository, but with puzzles and games. Dinner is family style in the **Tables of Content Restaurant** (seatings at 7pm daily summer, 6pm Sun.-Thurs. and 7pm Fri.-Sat. winter, $28); reservations are required. Saturday stays require a two-night purchase, and single guests receive a $10 discount. The stairs are steep, and there's no elevator.

The giant block of the **Elizabeth Street Inn** (232 SW Elizabeth St., 541/265-9400, www.elizabethstreetinn.com, $220-230) is situated to maximize the ocean views from every private balcony. All rooms have fireplaces, and the inn has a heated indoor pool with ocean views. Rooms have updated decor and plush robes for lounging in front of the fire, and once the weather turns chilly, the hotel serves smoked salmon chowder in the lobby. The free breakfast includes hot items such as eggs and waffles. From its top-of-the-bluff location, it's a very short walk down to the beach.

The **Whaler Motel** (155 SW Elizabeth St., 541/265-9261, www.whalernewport.com, $154-204) has an indoor pool, but the ocean views from every room all the way up to Yaquina Head Lighthouse are more impressive. Rooms have a traditional motel feel—flowered bedspreads and dated furniture, but some have gas fireplaces or sleeper sofas. All have private balconies, and the hotel is largely pet friendly. The free breakfast is limited, though popcorn is available in the lobby. The hotel also rents beach houses.

The sloping roofs of the **Embarcadero Resort Hotel and Marina** (1000 SE Bay Blvd., 541/265-8521, www.embarcadero-resort.com, $109-239) are shaped so that every unit has a view of the harbor and the boats just outside. Located inside Yaquina Bay, it's got calmer waters outside and an indoor swimming pool. Standard rooms have flat-screen TVs and comfortable, if mismatched, furniture, and specialty suites are decorated by theme, so the Lady Ruth suite resembles the inside of a boat, and the Sail Away suite has anchors and ship's wheels everywhere. Many rooms have jetted tubs. With views of the bay and Yaquina Bay Bridge, and stained-glass windows, the on-site **Waterfront Grille** serves breakfast, lunch, and dinner in a dining room, plus a special prime rib dinner on weekends. Boaters can park their boats just outside, and one section of dock is reserved for crabbing, right next to the crab cookers. But be warned, the seals also know that this is a crab spot, and they like to steal.

Over $250

Nye Beach is just north of Yaquina Bay in Newport, one of the more central neighborhoods in town. **Inn at Nye Beach** (729 NW Coast St., 541/265-2477, www.innatnyebeach.com, $250-276) bills itself as a boutique hotel, not a beachside motel, offering perks like rain showerheads in the bathrooms, free tea service and French press coffeemakers, and sleek linens and decor. Some rooms have fireplaces or Jacuzzi tubs; a two-bedroom kids' suite has a room with bunk beds. Wine and fresh cookies are served in the lobby, and breakfast is available with room service (fee). The wood-shingle sides of the hotel have that classic beach look, making this is a romantic escape right on the water but still close to town.

Like many hotels on the coast, **Hallmark Resort** (744 SW Elizabeth St., 888/448-4449, www.hallmarkinns.com, $256-399, two-night minimum stay) is a big, blocky building angled right at the water so every room has a private waterfront balcony. Some rooms have fireplaces and two-person tubs, and the hotel has an indoor saltwater pool, a spa, and a sauna. Partial-view rooms are cheaper and still have a taste of the ocean, but not the panorama that larger, more expensive rooms offer. Other suites have lofts or additional rooms for groups and families; two-night minimums may apply. There's an on-site restaurant, **Georgie's Beachside Grill** (541/265-9800, www.georgiesbeachsidegrill.com, 7:30am-10pm Mon.-Sat., 7:30am-9pm Sun.), with casual dining and excellent views.

Camping

South Beach State Park (S Beach State Park Rd. and U.S. 101, 800/551-6949, www.oregonstateparks.org) offers camping in tents ($17-21), RV sites with electrical hookups ($29), and hike-in sites ($6), as well as yurts ($45-55). Amenities include restrooms, showers, picnic tables, and an RV dump station.

Getting There

Newport lies on U.S. 101, 24 miles north of Yachats and about 13 miles south of Depoe Bay. From Newport, U.S. 20 provides access inland to I-5. At U.S. 101, follow U.S. 20 east for 50 miles to Corvallis. Turn right onto Highway 34 and follow it for 10 miles to I-5.

Yachats

Pronounce this small coastal town "Yah-hots," not "yachts." It's little more than a populated bend in the road, but its placement between Florence and Newport makes it a convenient overnight stop.

Food

The busy, quaint **Green Salmon Coffee Shop** (220 U.S. 101, 541/547-3077, www.thegreensalmon.com, 7:30am-2:30pm Tues.-Sun., $5-10) is a worthwhile stop, even if Yachats doesn't end up demanding any more of your time. The little red building is right in the middle of town. The menus of the expanded coffee shop are written on blackboards that take up nearly an entire wall; order at a counter before trying to score a table. Pastries are made in-house, and the berry toast is topped with local blackberries. Breakfast sandwiches are hot and layered with local eggs and veggies. The shop roasts its own coffee and is dedicated to using fair trade and sustainably grown ingredients. Even if you have no time to eat at the table, it's the best place for a hot coffee and gooey Danish.

The warm feeling that radiates throughout **Yachats Brewing and Farmstore** (348 U.S. 101, 541/547-3884, http://yachatsbrewing.com, 11:30am-8pm Mon.-Thurs., 11:30am-9pm Fri.-Sat., 10am-4pm Sun., $11-17) might be from all the gleaming blond Douglas fir wood that lines the wall and bar, which came from an old locomotive shop in Portland. Or it could come from the drinks pouring from the 30 taps—beers from the brewer, along with kombucha, mead, and ginger beer. The food menu is equally local, featuring pork belly cooked on alder planks and salads topped with locally grown nuts.

Accommodations

The retro feel of the **Yachats Inn** (331 U.S. 101, 541/547-3456, www.yachatsinn.com, $94-150) extends outside, where small decks have Adirondack chairs facing the ocean. Kitchens in the suites are limited, but there is outdoor space and a pond in the middle of the property. Regular rooms have dated furnishings, but some of the original suites have gas or wood fireplaces or even a woodstove. The inn also has a small indoor pool and hot tub. Stairs lead down to the beach, and the hotel is close to the center of Yachats.

Deane's Oceanfront Lodge (7365 U.S. 101, 541/547-3321, www.deaneslodge. com, $94-139), about 3.5 miles north of Yachats, isn't particularly near anything. Look either direction on the highway from the turnoff, and you'll see mostly driveways and mailboxes for private residences, not more hotels and eateries. For being only just off the busiest road in the region, it's a remarkably quiet motel, and fairly cheap. Indoors, the rooms have whitewashed cedar walls, adding to the seaside look, and oceanfront rooms have patios with grills and picnic tables. Some have fireplaces, and showers are retro glass-block style. Stairs on the back of the property lead directly to the beach, and the hotel is very pet friendly. Amenities here don't get much fancier than the puzzles in the lobby, but it's the epitome of a quiet waterfront hotel.

Just north of Yachats, ★ **Overleaf Lodge & Spa** (280 Overleaf Lodge Ln., 800/338-0507, www.overleaflodge.com, $221-429) is one of the only true luxury destinations in the area. Some rooms have jetted tubs overlooking the water and balconies with ocean views. Other rooms have patios. The spa has a soaking pool with ocean views and a hot tub, plus steam rooms and saunas—all included for guests. The spa also offers massage and facial services. The included breakfast is a healthy buffet with hot items, too. A trail leads into the center of Yachats, which isn't far from the hotel.

Getting There

Yachats is 25 miles north of Florence and south of Newport on U.S. 101.

Florence

Just slightly inland, Florence is protected from the ocean by a solid line of sand dunes. The old downtown is situated on the Suislaw River, crossed by the 1936 Suislaw River Bridge. Fishing boats leave from the river marina every day, though the town is more geared toward tourism these days, thanks especially to the Three Rivers Casino with golf, slots, lodging, and dining. Restaurants line the historical Bay Street, and more hotels sit along U.S. 101 both north and south of the river.

Sights
Cape Perpetua

Leave U.S. 101 about 2 miles south of Yachats to visit the **Cape Perpetua Visitor Center** (2400 U.S. 101, 541/547-3289, www.fs.usda.gov, 9:30am-4pm daily summer, 10am-4pm daily fall and spring, 10am-4pm Thurs.-Mon. winter, $5 per vehicle), a nature interpretive site located up above the highway and overlooking one of the area's little capes. Rangers lead guided walks and informational sessions in the building while a bookstore sells postcards and souvenirs. Visit during special Whale Watch weekends, or go explore the tide pools to see what lives among the rocks. A number of short trails leave from the center.

★ Heceta Head Lighthouse

The **Heceta Head Lighthouse** (U.S. 101, 0.5 mile north of the Sea Lion Caves, near mile marker 178, www.oregonstateparks. org, $5 per vehicle) isn't the biggest lighthouse on the Pacific Northwest coast, but it's one of the prettiest, and it has something most don't—a bed-and-breakfast inside the keeper's house. It also has one of the strongest lights, in the 56-foot tower built in 1894. Its light can be seen 21 miles from shore. The lighthouse is named after a Spanish navigator who came to the coast in the 18th century. A parking area leads to a sandy beach, viewpoint, and tide pools, but the trail to the lighthouse itself is short. Free tours of both the keeper's house and the lighthouse are available in summer, and a gift shop is in the old generator room.

Sea Lion Caves

The **Sea Lion Caves** (91560 U.S. 101, 541/547-3111, www.sealioncaves.com, 9am-7pm daily, $14 adults, $13 seniors, $8 children 5-12, children under 5 free) are a natural formation, but it takes a trip through a heavily marketed tourist attraction to get to them. The cliff-front building leads visitors downhill to an elevator that goes 200 feet down through solid rock to a giant sea cave, 12 stories high inside, favored by sea lions. It's the largest sea grotto in the country (and claims to be the largest sea cave in the world) and an impressive sight even when the brown Steller sea lions are basking on the basalt rocks inside. The shop upstairs is crammed with beach souvenirs and tchotchkes, and tour buses stop often and can crowd the lines. But the elevator is large, and there are viewpoints on top if you have to wait. The sea lion statue outside is a good spot for photos.

Old Town Park

The tiny **Old Town Park** (Laurel St. and Bay St., www.ci.florence.or.us/public-works/old-town-park), located just off the main Bay Street in downtown Florence, has a cute small gazebo and overlooks that provide great views of the river and bridge. It's where to polish off an ice cream cone after dinner, when the docks up and down the river illuminate the water. Picnic tables and benches face the old pilings from when a ferry was needed to cross the river.

Hiking
Devil's Churn
Distance: 2.2 miles round-trip
Duration: 1.5 hours
Elevation gain: 360 feet
Effort: easy
Trailhead: Cape Perpetua Visitor Center

Take the time to wander to the water side of U.S. 101 from the visitors center, turning south just after crossing the highway for a quick loop along the jagged coastline on what's called the Captain Cook trail. When you return to the highway, follow the trail north and out a small promontory overlooking Devil's Churn. You'll look down on black rocks and the crashing waves that beat them endlessly. The loop here is called the Trail of the Restless Waters, and indeed the ocean never seems very calm in this tight chasm. Return the way you came to reach the visitors center.

Hobbit Trail
Distance: 1 mile round-trip
Duration: 45 minutes
Elevation gain: 200 feet
Effort: moderate
Trailhead: U.S. 101, near milepost 177
Directions: Look for a turnoff and a small sign for the valley trail, and then cross the highway to find the trailhead.

There are easier ways to get to the beach, but the Hobbit Trail is an almost magical route to the sand. The trailhead leaves from U.S. 101; parking is on the inland side of the road, but the trail begins on the ocean side. Immediately past the trailhead, the trail splits: Head right and wander about half a mile to the waterfront. It's called the Hobbit Trail because of the peculiar tree shapes, twisted by the wind and with a trail dug out deep between the gnarled roots. It looks like something out of a fantasy novel. Walk between mossy limbs to the secluded sandy beach, but remember that you have an uphill hike to get back to the car.

Shopping

Outside the **Wood Wizard Gallery** (1431 Bay St., 541/997-4500, www.woodwizardgallery.com, 11am-6pm Tues.-Sun.) stands a wizard painting with two holes for faces—it's the kind of cheesy photoop you can't pass up. There's a touch of kitsch to the wooden wares inside, like the carved flutes and chainsaw art, which are blocks of wood carved into surprisingly delicate animal figures using a bulky power tool. Dozens of bears made by a local chainsaw carver are here. Some of the furniture is beautiful but hard to pack during a long trip. More portable are the delicate wooden watches.

Food

The charming ★ **Waterfront Depot** (1252 Bay St., 541/902-9100, www.thewaterfrontdepot.com, 4pm-10pm daily, $11-20) is the best eatery for miles. It's not too fancy but nice enough to feel like a reward after a long day of play. The building was the Mapleton Train Station, moved to this spot next to the Siuslaw River Bridge; it's decorated with photos of old movie stars and chic mirrors. The outdoor dining area is used in summer, and the small dining space indoors can mean a wait on busy weekends. The bartenders make some of their own mixings, and a bar seat can mean a friendly chat from locals and visitors sitting there, too. The food is mostly American—surf and turf, pasta jambalaya—with hints of global influence, like lamb riblets in a New Zealand style or toasted onion-battered green beans in a Thai style. The owner's Southeast Asian roots are celebrated every week with Singapore chicken curry night.

Traveler's Cove (1362 Bay St., 541/997-6845, 9am-9pm daily, $8-14) bills itself as a family restaurant, but there's a welcoming hometown bar feel to the neon-lit joint with a menu of burgers, salads, and tacos. On weekends, there's live music and dancing in the bar. The patio out back is known as the Margarita Deck, the perfect spot for a cold drink when the sun is shining. The food is saucy and unremarkable, but the salsa is homemade, the vibe is good, and there's rarely a wait.

The big, bustling **Bridgewater Fish House** (1297 Bay St., 541/997-1133, www.bridgewaterfishhouse.com, 11am-10pm Wed.-Mon. summer, 11am-9pm Wed.-Mon. winter, $17-36) is located on the main street in downtown Florence, and the menu celebrates every kind of seafood—tiger prawns, scallops, salmon, and lobster. The whole Dungeness crab is served with melted butter. The building is historical, dating back to 1901, but the interior of the restaurant is modern. The Zebra Lounge cocktail bar has a horseshoe bar and a separate menu, including an early-bird dinner for $17, plus complicated cocktails.

Everything's local at **Homegrown Public House** (294 Lauren St., 541/997-4886, www.homegrownpub.com, 11am-8pm Tues.-Thurs., 11am-9pm Fri.-Sat., $11-21), from the food to the owner. The fish-and-chips is from the water and soil nearby, and even the salad has a taste of the landscape with its fiddlehead ferns on top. A connected deli makes good sandwiches to-go for adventures, and the pub's tap house is small but carefully curated.

Accommodations

The **River House Inn** (1202 Bay St., 541/997-3933, www.riverhouseflorence.com, $129-199) is located right on the Siuslaw River, close to the small, historical waterfront downtown area of Florence. Cheaper rooms don't have a view, but some riverfront rooms have private spa tubs. The complimentary breakfast is underwhelming, and better eateries are within walking distance. The decor is up to date, making up for the somewhat small rooms. The location, however, can't be beat.

Across the river, facing downtown Florence, **Best Western Plus Pier Point**

Inn (85625 U.S. 101, 800/435-6736, www.
bwpierpointinn.com, $215-275) sits on a
bluff above the water. All rooms have
views, and sunsets or fog over downtown Florence can be very picturesque.
The rooms are updated and comfortable, and some suites have a full kitchen.
A heated indoor swimming pool offers
views across the river, spa, and sauna.
The **Bay View Restaurant and Bar** (3pm-
10pm daily) serves American dishes and
local beers, and on Saturday night the
bar hosts karaoke. Breakfast includes a
staffed omelet bar.

The Victorian keeper's house at **Heceta
Head Lighthouse** (U.S. 101, near mile
marker 178, 866/547-3696, www.hece-
talighthouse.com, $215-410) has a bed-
and-breakfast with six rooms (some with
a shared bath) that includes a seven-
course breakfast using local meats, produce, and cheeses. Those staying at the
bed-and-breakfast can drive in through
a separate entrance; directions are given
when reservations are made.

Camping
The **Cape Perpetua Campground**
(Cummins Peak Rd., 877/444-6777, www.
reserveamerica.com, May-Sept., $24),
just north of the Cape Perpetua Visitor
Center, has 37 wooded campsites, but no
electrical hookups. Amenities include
water, a picnic area, and flush toilets.

Getting There
Florence is 50 miles south of Newport
along U.S. 101, or just 25 miles south
from Yachats. To reach I-5 inland (and
continue on to Portland or return to
Seattle), take Highway 126 east for 60
miles to Eugene and I-5. It takes about 1.5
hours of driving through rural Oregon
hills to reach Eugene.

★ Oregon Dunes National Recreation Area
The sand dunes lining the Oregon Coast
aren't just a handy place to store sandcas-
tle materials. Dunes provide a buffer between beach and land that keeps erosion

Oregon Dunes National Recreation Area

at bay. They're also a great place to play. The **Oregon Dunes National Recreation Area** (South Jetty Rd. and U.S. 101, www.fs.usda.gov) is a 40-mile-long protected area with spots for hiking, paddling, and OHVs (off-highway vehicles), better known as dune buggies. The closest access point to Florence is at South Jetty Road, which passes several OHV staging areas—look to the left to see a slope like a ski hill where motorists play—before turning and passing several spots for beach access. At the north end of the road is a fishing and crabbing dock, far from where the motorized vehicles are allowed.

The **Oregon Dunes Visitor Information and Interpretive Center** (855 U.S. 101, Reedsport, 541/271-6000, 8am-4pm Mon.-Fri., free) is 23 miles farther south in the town of Reedsport, and has exhibits, restrooms, and a gift shop. If you didn't pack your own OHV, do a sand dunes tour with **Sand Dunes Frontier** (83960 U.S. 101, 541/997-3544, www.sanddunesfrontier.com, tours $14-35).

They drive around in big purple buggies that resemble trucks, and smaller, more agile vehicles. They'll be as daring as the passengers can tolerate, spinning down the sands. Rentals are available on-site from **Torex ATV Rentals** (541/997-5363, www.torexatvrentals.com, 9am-6pm daily, $50-265 per hour). And as for the most famous dunes, those in the science fiction book *Dune*? They were inspired by these very hills on the Oregon Coast.

Getting There

The Oregon Dunes National Recreation Area is located south of Florence along U.S. 101. To access the South Jetty Dune, follow U.S. 101 south for 2 miles to South Jetty Road. Turn right (west) and follow the road, which becomes Sand Dunes Road as it begins to run parallel to the shore. A number of parking areas provide access to the sand.

To return to I-5 and continue to Portland, drive north on U.S. 101 for 2 miles and turn right (east) on Highway 126. Drive 55.5 miles east through rural Oregon; then turn north onto Highway 569. Follow Highway 569 northeast for 9.5 miles to I-5. From this point, it's 110 miles north to Portland. The drive from the coast to I-5 is windy and slow to navigate in the dark, but it maximizes your time on the interstate. It's also possible to reach I-5 from Newport by driving north for 49 miles, then turning right (east) onto U.S. 20, a more traveled east-west route. Follow U.S. 20 east for 50 miles to Corvallis, and then turn right on Highway 34. Highway 34 reaches I-5 in 10 miles.

Portland

It's easy to be charmed by Portland's relaxed and idiosyncratic vibe, with its elaborate doughnuts, waterfront parks, endless bike lanes, and ecofriendly practices.

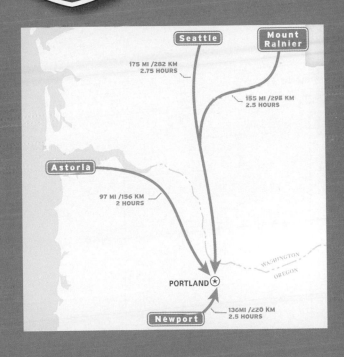

Seattle
175 MI /282 KM
2.75 HOURS

Mount Rainier
155 MI /298 KM
2.5 HOURS

Astoria
97 MI /156 KM
2 HOURS

WASHINGTON
OREGON

PORTLAND ★

Newport
136 MI /220 KM
2.5 HOURS

Portland

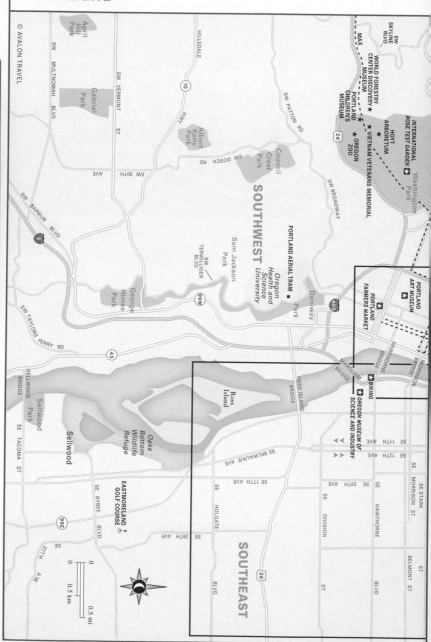

© AVALON TRAVEL

SOUTHWEST

SOUTHEAST

April Hill Park

Gabriel Park

Albert Kelly Park

Council Crest Park

George Himes Park

Sam Jackson Park

Oregon Health and Science University

PORTLAND AERIAL TRAM

SW SKYLINE BLVD

WORLD FORESTRY CENTER DISCOVERY MUSEUM

PORTLAND CHILDREN'S MUSEUM

VIETNAM VETERANS MEMORIAL

INTERNATIONAL ROSE TEST GARDEN

HOYT ARBORETUM

OREGON ZOO

Washington Park

MAX

PORTLAND ART MUSEUM

PORTLAND FARMERS MARKET

OREGON MUSEUM OF SCIENCE AND INDUSTRY

BIKING

Ross Island

Oaks Bottom Wildlife Refuge

Sellwood Park

Sellwood

EASTMORELAND GOLF COURSE

HILLSDALE

SW MULTNOMAH BLVD

SW VERMONT ST

SW BARBUR BLVD

SW TAYLORS FERRY RD

SW 30TH AVE

SW DOSCH RD

SW PATTON RD

SW BROADWAY

SW TERWILLIGER BLVD

Dunlway

SELLWOOD BRIDGE

SELLWOOD BRIDGE

SE TACOMA ST

SE BYBEE BLVD

SE 28TH AVE

SE 17TH AVE

SE MILWAUKIE AVE

SE 20TH AVE

ROSS ISLAND BRIDGE

MARQUAM BRIDGE

HAWTHORNE BRIDGE

MORRISON BRIDGE

SE 11TH AVE

SE 12TH AVE

SE MORRISON ST

SE STARK ST

HAWTHORNE BLVD

SE DIVISION ST

SE HOLGATE BLVD

BELMONT ST

10

26

405

5

99W

99E

43

26

0   0.5 mi

0   0.5 km

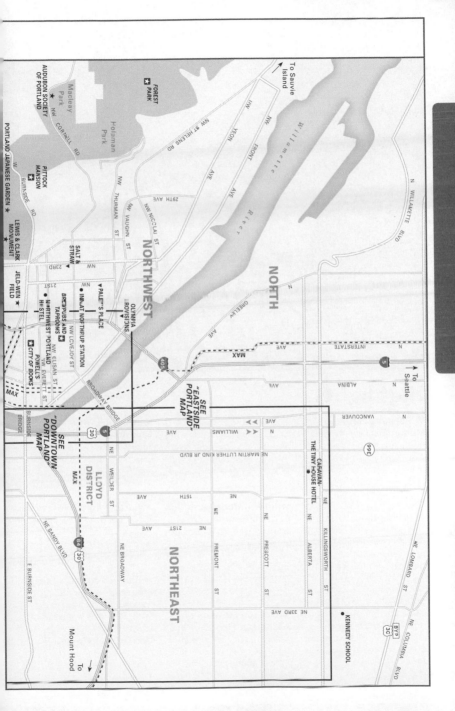

AUDUBON SOCIETY OF PORTLAND

FOREST PARK

Macleay Park

Holman Park

PORTLAND JAPANESE GARDEN ★

PITTOCK MANSION

NW CORNELL RD

NW BURNSIDE RD

LEWIS & CLARK MONUMENT ★

JELD-WEN FIELD ★

NW THURMAN ST

NW VAUGHN ST

NW NICOLAI ST

NW 29TH AVE

NW ST HELENS RD

NW YEON AVE

NW FRONT AVE

To Sauvie Island

Willamette River

NORTH

NORTHWEST

SALT & STRAW

NW 23RD

NW 21ST

● INN AT NORTHRUP STATION ◆

▼ PALEY'S PLACE

BREWPUBS AND TAPROOMS ◆
NORTHWEST PORTLAND ● HI HOSTEL

NW NORTHRUP STATION
NW LOVEJOY ST

OLYMPIA PROVISIONS ▼

NW ELISAN ST
NW EVERETT ST

POWELL'S ● ★ CITY OF BOOKS

MAX

BURNSIDE BRIDGE

BROADWAY BRIDGE

405

30 5

GREELEY AVE

INTERSTATE AVE

MAX

ALBINA AVE

N

To Seattle

5

SEE "EASTSIDE PORTLAND" MAP

SEE "DOWNTOWN PORTLAND" MAP

VANCOUVER AVE

WILLIAMS AVE

N ▶▶
◀◀ AVE

NE MARTIN LUTHER KING JR BLVD

CARAVAN–THE TINY HOUSE HOTEL

366

LLOYD DISTRICT

MAX

NE WEIDLER ST

NE 15TH AVE

NE 21ST AVE

NE BROADWAY

84 30

NE SANDY BLVD

NORTHEAST

NE FREMONT ST

NE PRESCOTT ST

NE ALBERTA ST

NE KILLINGSWORTH ST

NE 33RD AVE

● KENNEDY SCHOOL

NE LOMBARD ST

BYP 30

NE COLUMBIA BLVD

E BURNSIDE ST

To Mount Hood

Highlights

★ **Portland Farmers Market:** Get overwhelmed by endless fresh produce, high-quality crafts, and ready-to-eat meals (page 243).

★ **Portland Art Museum:** This expansive yet accessible art collection emphasizes Native American and Northwest art (page 243).

★ **Powell's City of Books:** Portland's renowned bookstore fills a city block with more than a million volumes of new and used books (page 248).

★ **Pittock Mansion:** One of the city's best views comes from a stately old home with one very weird shower (page 249).

★ **International Rose Test Garden:** The acres of roses astound even those without green thumbs. The grassy amphitheater is an ideal resting spot after a busy day on Portland streets (page 251).

★ **Oregon Museum of Science and Industry:** The hands-on science museum and its submarine aren't just for kids, though you'll feel like one by the end of a full day (page 251).

★ **Brewpubs and Taprooms:** Beer is the signature quaff of Portland, perhaps the country's capital of craft brewing (page 256).

★ **Forest Park:** More than 80 miles of trails await in one of the largest city forests in the country (page 269).

★ **Biking:** Portland is a city where human-powered propulsion is encouraged and celebrated. Two-wheeled activity is as popular with locals as visitors (page 270).

Located on the Willamette River, Portland offers a wealth of nature—Forest Park has miles of trails, while cinder cone volcanoes lie within the city limits.

Downtown is crowded with food carts, independent boutiques, and live music venues, and the small blocks make the streets highly walkable. Driving alternatives—from streetcars to bicycles to aerial tram—can be found everywhere.

Although downtown is a condensed area of shopping and dining, other Portland neighborhoods are equally welcoming. Out on Alberta, Hawthorne, or Division streets, you'll find more of the independent eateries and stores that give the city its reputation for great finds. Locals are friendly and, more often than not, transplants themselves—visitors who came to Portland, loved the way of life here, and never left.

The city doesn't want for nicknames: Rose City, Stumptown, Portlandia (the city where "hipsters go to retire"). Sure, everyone teases the city for its earnest, hipster weirdness—but to tease Portland is to love it.

Getting to Portland

Driving from Seattle
175 miles, 2.75 hours

From Seattle, **I-5** travels southbound directly to Portland, but that doesn't mean it's a quick trip. The 175-mile journey on I-5 can be driven in just under 3 hours when there isn't traffic, but that occurrence is rare. Usually you can expect a crowded freeway, which can make for a drive closer to 3-3.5 hours, especially during weekday rush hours (7:30am-9am and 3:30pm-6:30pm). Other sticky

sections include I-5 through Tacoma (35 miles south) and near Joint Base Lewis-McChord (15 miles south of Tacoma), where thousands of military personnel commute to work. Past Olympia (about 20 miles farther south), traffic tends to thin, as do roadside services, though you're never more than a few exits from a gas station.

From Centralia, I-5 passes the Cowlitz River and the towns of Kelso and Longview before sliding up to the Columbia River, which marks the border between Washington and Oregon. Once the freeway crosses the Columbia River, the city of Portland emerges immediately on the Oregon side, and downtown is another eight miles south on I-5. To reach downtown Portland, take exit 300 B and follow signs for Morrison Street. You'll cross the Morrison Bridge, ending up on Washington Street, a one-way street that heads west through downtown.

Stopping in Centralia
Just before the town of Centralia, about 79 miles south of Seattle, the **Great Wolf Lodge Grand Mound** (20500 Old Hwy. 99 SW, Centralia, 800/640-9653, www.greatwolf.com, $429-459) emerges on the right side of the freeway. The hotel and water park, part of a national chain, is a favorite destination for families. The enclosed water park, available only to hotel guests, has a four-story interactive tree house and a six-story funnel slide, among other water features, plus inter active games and play structures outside the pool. All rooms are suites. There's not much in the area around the hotel, but the water games are the real attraction.

Driving from the Oregon Coast
80-136 miles 1.5-2.5 hours

Three state routes link the Oregon Coast inland to I-5. From **Astoria** (97 miles, 2 hours), take U.S. 30 east along the Columbia River. You can stay on U.S. 30 within Oregon when the road bends south and heads to Portland, though

Best Accommodations

★ **Crystal Hotel:** Come for the central location, stay for the colorful murals and underground soaking pool (page 282).

★ **Hotel Lucia:** A wide photography collection in the lobby reflects the hotel's classy, quiet vibe (page 282).

★ **Heathman Hotel:** The costumed bellhop and lovely library are just some of the charming touches at this boutique hotel (page 284).

★ **Jupiter Hotel:** All the cool kids hang at this motel-style indie hotel next to a popular music venue (page 286).

★ **Kennedy School:** Stay and play in this converted elementary building with quirky decor, a movie theater, an outdoor hot pool, a restaurant, and bars (page 286).

you'll be passing through rural country and small towns. A faster route is to leave U.S. 30 at Longview, Washington. About 47 miles east of Astoria, take Highway 433 north across the Lewis and Clark Bridge into Washington. Then follow Highway 432 East to I-5 South. From this bend, I-5 runs 45 miles south to Portland.

From **Cannon Beach** (80 miles, 1.5 hours), take U.S. 26 (a.k.a. the Sunset Highway) southeast to Portland. The route can get twisty close to the shoreline. Closer to Portland the suburban sprawl can make for slow going.

From **Newport** (136 miles, 2.5 hours), take U.S. 20 east for about 63 miles to the towns of Corvallis and Albany, where it meets up with I-5. From Albany, follow I-5 north for 70 miles to Portland.

By Air, Train, or Bus
Air
The flight between **Seattle-Tacoma International Airport** (SEA, 17801 International Blvd., 206/787-5388 or 800/544-1965, www.portseattle.org/seatac) and **Portland International Airport** (PDX, 7000 NE Airport Way, 503/460-4234, www.pdx.com) is only about 45 minutes long, so you'll spend more time at the airport than in the air. United Airlines (www.united.com) and Alaska Airlines (www.alaskaair.com) have several daily departures.

The Portland airport is located in the northeast corner of the city. Make your way downtown by taxi (about $36), or take the **MAX Light Rail** (503/238-7433, www.trimet.org, $2.50 adults), a trip that's less than 40 minutes.

Train
Amtrak (800/872-7245, www.amtrak.com, $26-54) has five departures to Portland daily, with most trips just under four hours. The *Cascades* route departs King Street Station (303 S Jackson St.) in Seattle's Pioneer Square neighborhood and stops near Sea-Tac Airport (SEA, 17801 International Blvd., 206/787-5388 or 800/544-1965, www.portseattle.org/sea-tac). The route continues through Tacoma, Olympia, Centralia, Kelso-Longview, and Vancouver (Washington, just across the river from Portland) on its way to **Portland's Union Station** (800 NW 6th Ave.). Train cars have wireless Internet access available, and a snack bar sells sandwiches and snacks. You can check baggage as well. Reservations are required.

Bus
BoltBus (877/265-8287, www.boltbus.com) offers service between Seattle and Portland, with up to eight trips daily, each lasting about 3.5 hours. Prices range $17-28 for a one-way trip ($1 fares are advertised but only a few are available each

Best Restaurants

★ **Tasty N Alder:** Brunch is worth the wait at this buzzing downtown eatery (page 274).

★ **Voodoo Doughnut:** Find surprising doughnut options at one of the city's biggest food attractions (page 276).

★ **Castagna and Café Castagna :** A fine-dining restaurant and more casual bistro sit side by side, both overseen by a star chef (page 278).

★ **Pok Pok:** The spicy wings are the star, but the entire Southeast Asian menu bursts with flavor (page 279).

★ **Ava Gene's:** Handmade pastas and local vegetables unite for some of the city's very best plates (page 279).

★ **Por Que No?:** Try one of the city's classic counter-style eateries, where there's as much flair as flavor (page 279).

★ **Tusk:** Middle Eastern flavors get the local, seasonal treatment at a bright white favorite (page 280).

★ **Gravy:** Breakfast doesn't get more overwhelming than with these delicious, diner-sized portions (page 281).

trip). Wireless Internet access is available. Buses depart the Seattle station (5th Ave. S at S King St.) and arrive in Portland at SW Salmon Street between 5th and 6th Avenues. Advance online reservations are highly encouraged.

Bus service is also available through **Greyhound Lines** (800/231-2222, www. greyhound.com), which offers about three departures daily and costs $19-36. The Seattle station is at 503 S Royal Brougham Way (206/628-5526, 7am-12:30am), and the Portland station is at 550 NW 6th Avenue (503/243-2361, 5:45am-11pm).

Sights

The people-watching on the streets of Portland is almost enough entertainment for a weekend trip—you'll see tattoos, outlandish outfits, and perhaps a double-decker unicycle if you hang outside Powell's long enough. But for all its street theater, the city doesn't skimp on organized, institutionalized culture. Its museums are robust, and its gardens show off Portland's international sides, right down to its forest of roses.

Navigating Portland isn't difficult, even though there seem to be bridges everywhere. The Willamette River separates the east from the west side, and Burnside Street divides the city into its south and north sides, while North Williams Avenue separates North from Northeast Portland.

Downtown

The city's densest area of activity is located south of West Burnside Street, a major thoroughfare that nevertheless is lined with restaurants and small shops. One-way streets are the norm, with many of the area's tiny blocks dedicated to parks (or food trucks). Park once and wander on foot. It's much easier to enjoy downtown's quaint bustle when you're not worried about driving the wrong way.

South Park Blocks

The **South Park Blocks** (SW Park Ave. from Salmon St. to Jackson St., www. portlandoregon.gov) is a long promenade with sculptures, lampposts, trees, and small gardens that leads right through downtown. Major attractions like the Portland Art Museum and the Oregon Historical Society Museum now face the

Two Days in Portland

Despite being the biggest city in Oregon, Portland is compact and can be explored in a few days—though it would take years to get to every delectable bite, brew, and boutique.

Day 1

Start the day downtown with a bite at **Kenny and Zuke's Delicatessen** (page 275), where omelets come with pastrami or lox and sour cream. Head east along SW Stark Street, then turn south to continue on SW 9th Avenue. At SW Salmon Street, the road becomes SW Park Avenue as you enter the **South Park Blocks** (page 241). Stop at the **Portland Art Museum** (page 243) to peruse the striking sculptures, or cross the park to visit the **Oregon Historical Society Museum** (page 243) for some hands-on history. If it's Saturday, wander through the produce booths at the **Portland Farmers Market** (page 243), located at the south end.

At lunchtime, walk back up SW 9th Avenue to hit up the **food carts** (page 275) near Alder Street. Work off your meal browsing the numerous aisles at **Powell's City of Books** (page 248).

From Powell's, it's possible to take TriMet bus no. 20 to **Forest Park** (page 269) to see the **Pittock Mansion** (page 249) before it closes for the day, or drive instead to avoid the 0.5-mile walk uphill from the bus stop. With a car, it's just a short drive back down West Burnside to find **Washington Park** (page 250), where the **International Rose Test Garden** (page 251) offers a free ramble through every color of petal imaginable.

At dinner time, return downtown for Peruvian tapas at **Andina** (page 277) in the Pearl District. If you still have energy (you probably won't!), walk five blocks south to take in a show at the **Crystal Ballroom** (page 261).

Day 2

Venture across the Willamette River to explore Portland's east side. For breakfast downtown, forget nutrition and brave the line at **Voodoo Doughnut** (page 276); it's okay, you're going to work off those carbs. Rent a bike from **Waterfront Bicycles** (page 272) near **Tom McCall Waterfront Park** (page 270), and then ride north, passing under the Morrison and Burnside Bridges, to cross the Steel Bridge. Once across the Willamette, head south on the **Eastbank Esplanade** (page 270). Remember your bike lock, because you'll want to park your wheels at the **Oregon Museum of Science and Industry** (page 251). The indoor play space and outdoor submarine tour are just fun enough that you'll forget it's educational. Or for a longer pedal, continue south on the **Springwater Corridor** (page 270) for about 12 miles from the Ross Island Bridge through neighborhoods, meadows, and parks to **Powell Butte State Park** (page 271).

For lunch, bike 2 miles east on SE Division and, if you have the patience, wait for a lunch table at **Pok Pok** (page 279) to indulge in bites you'd find at a Bangkok street cart. If the line's too long, head north to SE Hawthorne for tacos and delicious margaritas at **Por Que No?** (page 279). On the ride back across Hawthorne Bridge, stop at **Lucky Labrador Brewing Company** (page 258) and enjoy a local pint on the patio.

Still not beat? Stay eastside and see an indie band play at **Doug Fir Lounge** (page 261); the venue serves dinner too, and the **Jupiter Hotel** (page 286) is right next door when you need to crash.

park, and the large Portland Farmers Market is held at the south end, close to Portland State University. The park is 12 blocks long, and artwork includes a peace memorial made of granite pillars and a bronze statue of Theodore Roosevelt on horseback, decked out as he was when he charged San Juan Hill. The Portland Parks department has a walking tour of the blocks on their website (www.portlandoregon.gov), along with a map of all the trees.

★ Portland Farmers Market

Forget what you think you know about farmers markets. The **Portland Farmers Market** (SW Park Ave. and SW Montgomery St., 503/241-0032, www. portlandfarmersmarket.org, 8:30am-2pm Sat. Mar.-Oct., 9am-2pm Sat. Nov.-Dec.) is bigger, greener, and busier than what you've experienced before. Blocks of individual stands are set up just outside Portland State University for the city's biggest market, though smaller versions pop up almost every day around town during the summer. Vendors sell produce, crafts, fresh cheeses, meats, nuts, chocolate, and herbs, all in a crowded throng that hums with the energy of a Middle Eastern souk marketplace. Companies with serious brick-and-mortar locations, like Pine State Biscuits and Lauretta Jean's, started here, and many still maintain their market stalls. Locals stock their larders with trips to the market, but there are as many opportunities for immediate gratification, like a peach farm that sells fruit by the pound or individually grilled and topped with balsamic vinegar and huckleberries. The one thing that's hard to find: trash cans. The green-minded waste system requires the venders to use recyclable or compostable packaging, and the market has reduced its waste footprint by 75 percent in recent years.

Oregon Historical Society Museum

Just across the park from the art museum, the **Oregon Historical Society Museum** (1200 SW Park Ave., 503/222-1741, www. ohs.org, 10am-5pm Mon.-Sat., noon-5pm Sun., $11 adults, $9 students over 18 and seniors, $5 children 6-18, children under 6 free) specializes in exhibits that are just a little more family friendly. After all, you don't normally find a rusty Ford truck or a 19th-century explorer's tent in an art museum. Exhibits explore the area's geologic and cultural history, as well as specific periods like the battleship *Oregon*'s role in the Spanish-American War or

Japanese American soldiers in World War II. Even the stairway shows off Portland's literally colorful history with a pink-and-white surfboard and a neon sign from the old Fox Theatre. Don't miss the *Oregon Voices* exhibit, which includes a full-scale mockup of a MAX light rail car and endless interactive displays devoted to the inspiring and sometimes gritty stories of Portland locals. The museum also houses the infamous penny that helped decide the city's name—had it landed differently, you'd be standing in Boston, Oregon, right now.

★ Portland Art Museum

Founded in the 19th century, the **Portland Art Museum** (1219 SW Park Ave., 503/226-2811, www.portlandartmuseum.org, 10am-5pm Tues. Wed. and Sat.-Sun., 10am-8pm Thurs.-Fri., $20 adults, $17 seniors and college students, children under 17 free) claims to be the oldest museum in the Pacific Northwest—one of the oldest in the country even. Although it has traveling exhibits, like a roomful of bicycles hung like sculptures or art from the Louvre, it dedicates 90 percent of its gallery space to the permanent collection. That includes a Vincent van Gogh painting and more than 5,000 prehistoric and historical Native American objects. The complex includes a modern and contemporary art center and a film center, which shows festival, student, and art films. And the art isn't kept from the elements—besides the outdoor sculptures, the 4th-floor gallery is dotted with skylights to show off contemporary works by artists that hail from the Northwest. On most days, including twice on Saturdays, a curator or special guest leads tours of the museum (free with museum admission).

Central Library

For a gallery of exhibits about the city, visit the **Central Library** (801 SW 10th Ave., 503/988-5123, www.multcolib.org, 10am-8pm Mon., noon-8pm Tues.-Wed.,

Downtown Portland

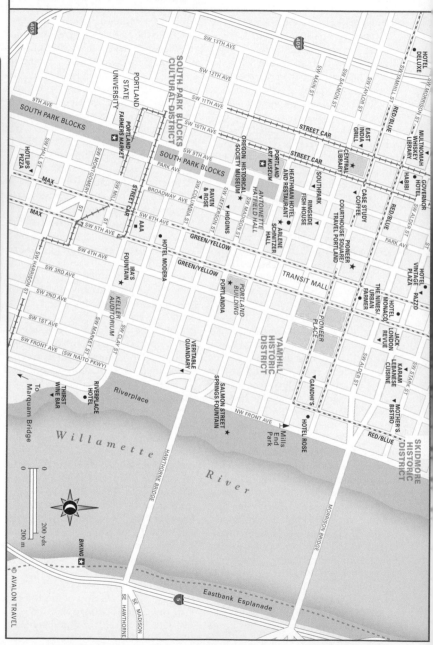

SW 13TH AVE
SW 12TH AVE
SW 11TH AVE
SW 10TH AVE
SW 9TH AVE
PARK AVE
BROADWAY AVE
SW 6TH AVE
SW 5TH AVE
SW 4TH AVE
SW 3RD AVE
SW 2ND AVE
SW 1ST AVE
SW FRONT AVE (SW NAITO PKWY)

SW MORRISON ST
SW YAMHILL ST
SW TAYLOR ST
SW SALMON ST
SW MAIN ST
SW MADISON ST
SW JEFFERSON ST
SW COLUMBIA ST
SW CLAY ST
SW MARKET ST
SW MILL ST
SW MONTGOMERY ST
SW HALL ST
SW HARRISON ST

9TH AVE
SOUTH PARK BLOCKS
SOUTH PARK BLOCKS CULTURAL DISTRICT
SOUTH PARK BLOCKS

PORTLAND STATE UNIVERSITY
PORTLAND FARMERS MARKET

HOTLIPS PIZZA
MAX
MAX
STREET CAR

STREET CAR
STREET CAR

GREEN/YELLOW
GREEN/YELLOW
TRANSIT MALL

RED/BLUE
RED/BLUE
RED/BLUE

HOTEL DELUXE
MULTNOMAH WHISKEY LIBRARY
GOVERNOR HOTEL, HABIBI
EAST INDIA GRILL
CENTRAL LIBRARY
CASE STUDY COFFEE
PIONEER COURTHOUSE SQUARE
TRAVEL PORTLAND
PARK AVE
HOTEL VINTAGE PLAZA
PAZZO
THE NINES/ URBAN FARMER
HOTEL MONACO/ LONDON REVUE
JACK
KARAM LEBANESE CUISINE
MOTHER'S BISTRO
SKIDMORE HISTORIC DISTRICT

OREGON HISTORICAL SOCIETY MUSEUM
PORTLAND ART MUSEUM
HEATHMAN HOTEL AND RESTAURANT
ANTOINETTE
HATFIELD HALL
SOUTHPARK
RINGSIDE FISH HOUSE
ARLENE SCHNITZER HALL
RAVEN & ROSE
HIGGINS
AAA
HOTEL MODERA
IRA'S FOUNTAIN
PORTLANDIA
PORTLAND BUILDING
VERITABLE QUANDARY
KELLER AUDITORIUM
PIONEER PLACE
YAMHILL HISTORIC DISTRICT
GANDHI'S

RIVERPLACE HOTEL
THIRST WINE BAR
To Marquam Bridge
Riverplace
SALMON STREET SPRINGS FOUNTAIN
Mills End Park
HOTEL ROSE
NW FRONT AVE

Willamette River

BIKING
HAWTHORNE BRIDGE
SE HAWTHORNE
SE MADISON
Eastbank Esplanade
MORRISON BRIDGE

0 200 yds
0 200 m

© AVALON TRAVEL

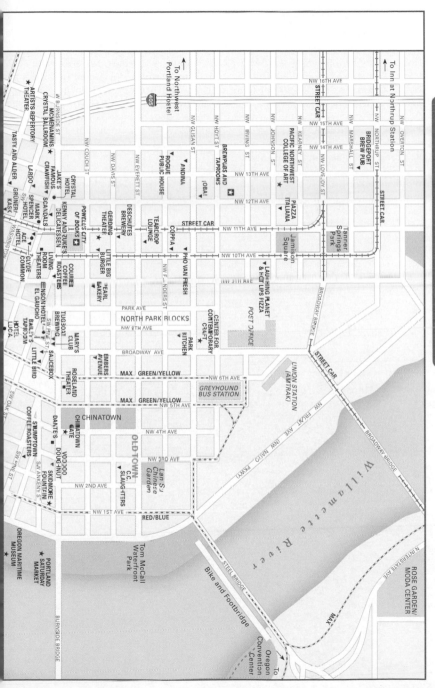

10am-6pm Thurs.-Sat., 10am-5pm Sun.). Part of the Multnomah County Library system, this 1913 building holds three floors of books, including the Beverly Cleary Children's Library and a garden eco-roof, visible on free 20-minute tours booked at the front desk.

Pioneer Courthouse Square

If Portland has a central meeting place, it's probably **Pioneer Courthouse Square** (701 SW 6th Ave., 503/223-1613, www. thesquarepdx.org). The plaza sits on a block originally purchased by a shoe-maker in 1849—he paid just $24 and a pair of boots for the land. It later held a schoolhouse and the Portland Hotel. Then eventually it was donated by the Meier & Frank Company to become a public square and was named for the courthouse on one side. The square now holds a fountain and sculptures of horses and a man holding an umbrella, and a signpost points the way to Mecca,

Times Square, and other far-off destina-tions. Brick steps provide plenty of seat-ing in the square. The Weather Machine is a doohickey on a post that, every noon, predicts the weather by presenting small figurines out of the top and playing a mu-sical fanfare. The square is also home to a number of concerts, and on Mondays in summer it hosts a branch of the Portland Farmers Market.

Portland Building

The 15-story **Portland Building** (1120 SW 5th Ave., 503/823-4000) is a simple mu-nicipal office building, but its striking architecture has made it notable since it opened in 1982. The architect is Michael Graves, now more famous than he was when he won the design competition for the project. The boxy building, with its small square windows, blue glass, and stark color combinations, is known as one of the first postmodern buildings in the country. Which is not to say that it's

Pioneer Courthouse Square

a beloved structure—it has been named one of the "World's Ugliest Buildings" by *Travel + Leisure* magazine and is generally hated.

Mill Ends Park

Before you get lost in the giant forest preserve of Forest Park (or in the blocks of shopping downtown), visit tiny, ridiculous **Mill Ends Park** (SW Naito Pkwy. and Taylor St., www.portlandoregon.gov). It's only two feet in diameter, located in a concrete median on SW Naito Parkway near the waterfront. The park was started by Dick Fagan, a journalist at the *Oregon Journal,* who could see the hole from his office window back in the 1940s. In his column, he called it the world's smallest park (and claimed leprechauns lived there); it became an official city park on St. Patrick's Day in 1976. The small circle of dirt is usually home to a small clump of greenery, but it has been known to feature a miniature swimming pool and little statues. At one point a tiny Ferris wheel was installed—using a full-size crane.

Oregon Maritime Museum

The **Oregon Maritime Museum** (SW Naito Pkwy. at Pine St., 503/224-7724, www.oregonmaritimemuseum.org, 11am-4pm Wed. and Fri.-Sat., $7 adults, $5 seniors, $4 students 13-18, $3 children 6-12, children under 6 free) is located on the river on the sternwheeler tug *Portland* moored next to Tom McCall Waterfront Park. The boat has a giant paddlewheel and looks something like a Mississippi riverboat. The last of its kind still operating in the country, it's been the home of the museum for more than a decade. Sometimes it even takes cruises for special events, traveling to the mouth of the Columbia. Museum visitors should explore the boat first and then check out the exhibits that touch on Oregon shipbuilding, the warships that have visited the area, and local underwater diving. The boat also holds a library of maritime history and a gift store. It's moored on the river at the foot of Pine Street. Look for a ramp with a blue awning.

Portland Saturday Market

Less overwhelming than the farmers market—but only slightly—the **Portland Saturday Market** (2 SW Naito Pkwy., 503/241-4188, www.portlandsaturday-market.com, 10am-5pm Sat., 11am-4:30pm Sun. Mar.-Dec.) is an open-air collection of artisans and craftspeople, billed as the biggest such market in the world. Located in Tom McCall Waterfront Park on the Willamette River, just south of the Burnside Bridge and Ankeny Plaza across the road, it hosts 750,000 shoppers every year. Jewelry, clothing, and woodworks are popular crafts, but the market's directory includes a whole host of crafts that defy categorization, like a fire-starting survival tool and kinetic sculptures. Folk, jazz, and international music acts perform, and the info booth will issue parking validation

or a free TriMet transit ticket for purchases over $25. (Oh, and yes, it's open on Sundays despite its name.)

Pearl District and Northwest

Once a gritty industrial area, the Pearl District got its moniker only recently, when a local business owner wanted to convey the hip reinvention that had taken over the old warehouses and railroad yard. Sitting just north of the downtown core, it has become known for its art galleries and cobblestone streets, with breweries and restaurants tucked into old warehouses. Gus Van Sant used the neighborhood as a gritty backdrop for his 1989 indie flick *Drugstore Cowboy*. Now it's home to Powell's Books and high-end shopping.

Even though the Northwest District is best known for its residential blocks and shopping along NW 23rd Avenue, it is also the gateway to the city's wildest quarter and legendary parks. Besides a startling amount of natural beauty, the area also has a singular pop culture claim to fame—the creator of *The Simpsons,* Matt Groening, is a Portland native who named many of his characters after street names in the area, such as Flanders, Quimby, and Kearney.

★ Powell's City of Books

If you think you've seen big bookstores before, you haven't traveled the byways of **Powell's City of Books** (1005 W Burnside St., 800/878-7323, www.powells. com, 9am-11pm daily). More than a million volumes fill the store, which takes up an entire block on the site of an old car-repair shop. It's open every day of the year, and color-coded signs direct newbies through the rooms and rooms of tall bookshelves. New and used books share shelf space, along with some branded T-shirts and small gifts. A café sits near the romance section (grab a coffee, sneak a peek).

Powell's buys used books and offers cash or store credit. At one time the

bookstore bought 7,000 volumes from author Anne Rice's personal library, some signed or with personal annotations; they're marked as such but sold like any other. Readings and other events occur daily, often one after another, and feature major writers passing through Portland.

Center for Contemporary Art and Culture

When the Museum of Contemporary Craft in the Pearl District closed in 2016, it was a major blow to Portland's vibrant art scene; it had been one of the oldest museums of its kind. Fortunately, the **Center for Contemporary Art and Culture** (511 NW Broadway, 503/226-4391, http://ccac.pnca.edu, 11am-6pm Thurs.-Sun., free) at the nearby Pacific Northwest College of Art took over the collection, and now plans a digitization project for all the holdings. The center has regular exhibits focusing on Northwest art, and one major exhibition in 2018 will cover the cataloging process of the old museum's artifacts.

Lan Su Chinese Garden

The Ming Dynasty gets a showpiece in the middle of the Pearl District at the **Lan Su Chinese Garden** (239 NW Everett St., 503/228-8131, www.lansugarden.org, 10am-7pm daily Mar.-Oct., 10am-4pm daily Nov.-Feb., $10 adults, $9 seniors, $7 college students and youth 6-18, children under 6 free), built by designers from Suzhou, Portland's Chinese sister city, in 2000. The walled botanic garden surrounds pavilions and an artificial lake, and often hosts Chinese holiday celebrations. Plants are mostly native to China, including collections of magnolia, rhododendron, and bamboo. Tea is almost as prevalent as the greenery, with a teahouse located in the central Tower of Cosmic Reflections run by the Portland-based company The Tao of Tea. Events around the history of tea, or its connection to poetry or meditation, are held regularly, along with free sessions of tai chi, Chinese *Go,* qigong, and calligraphy.

Chinatown Gate

The **Chinatown Gate** (NW 4th Ave. and Burnside St.) marks the entrance to Portland's Chinatown, even though the neighborhood isn't the bustling center of Chinese culture it once was. The gate was built in the 1980s, has three levels, and is guarded by two lion statues.

★ Pittock Mansion

Although accessed by driving through a residential neighborhood of perfectly normal-sized houses, the **Pittock Mansion** (3229 NW Pittock Dr., 503/823-3623, www.pittockmansion.org, 10am-5pm daily July-Sept., 10am-4pm daily Feb.-June and Sept.-Jan., $10 adults, $9 seniors, $7 children 6-18, children under 6 free) lives up to its name with twenty-something rooms and a view to die for. Located on a hill inside a 46-acre park, the house was the brainchild of businessman and newspaper owner Henry Pittock, who got modern comforts like intercoms and a central vacuum system when the house was completed in 1914. Henry and his wife only got to live in the estate for a few years, and by the 1950s the family had to put it on the market; the city purchased the house and turned it into a landmark. The three-story staircase at the center is the house's most arresting feature—oh, to take a ride on those gleaming wooden bannisters—but it's hardly the only spectacle. Henry's shower is a wonder of hydraulics, with multiple sprays located at various heights (why don't we have a "liver spray" these days?) and a toe tester to gauge the temperature.

Besides the gift shop located in the former garage, the Pittock grounds include several benches and a green lawn

from top to bottom: inside the Portland Art Museum; the International Rose Test Garden; Pittock Mansion.

overlooking downtown Portland. Walks around the castle are free and worth the trek even when the house itself is closed.

Washington Park

Washington Park (head of SW Park Pl., http://washingtonparkpdx.org, 5am-10pm daily) makes up for its small size with tons of activities and attractions. It contains the International Rose Test Garden and Japanese Garden, Vietnam Veterans' and Holocaust memorials, and the **Hoyt Arboretum** (4000 SW Fairview Blvd., 503/865-8733, www.hoytarboretum.org, visitors center 9am-4pm Mon.-Fri., 11am-3pm Sat.-Sun., grounds 5am-9:30pm daily, free), a tree sanctuary and outdoor laboratory that offers 90-minute guided tours ($3) through the collections.

The **Children's Park,** located near the International Rose Test Garden, is a maze of brightly colored play sculptures. The **Washington Park and Zoo Railway** (10:30am-4pm daily, train $4, carousel $3) dates back to the 1950s when it was paid for using the proceeds of a children's book and by children selling "shares." The park begins in the **Oregon Zoo** (4001 SW Canyon Rd., 503/226-1561, www.oregonzoo.org, 9am-6pm daily June-Aug., 9am-4pm daily Sept.-Dec. and Mar.-May, 10am-4pm daily Jan.-Feb., $11.50 adults and children over 12, $10 seniors, $8.50 children 3-11, children under 3 free), Portland's first zoo, which started when a pharmacist bought two pet bears in the 1880s. Today it houses elephants, penguins, polar bears, and orangutans.

The **Portland Children's Museum** (4015 SW Canyon Rd., 503/223-6500, www.portlandcm.org, 9am-5pm daily, $10.75 adults and children, $9.75 seniors, children under 1 free) is full of hands-on exhibits for tots, like a Building Bridgetown area with tools and a clay studio for art projects. Because it's Portland, one area is for ecofriendly art projects and a tree house. The pet hospital exhibit has fake pets, but the water wheels run on real water. The museum is best for small tikes;

Oregon Museum of Science and Industry

once they're tall enough to see over the Zany Maze, it's less exciting. There are visiting exhibits as well, and a café with sandwiches, make-your-own salads, and a kids' menu with peanut butter-and-jelly sandwiches and macaroni.

When it's too wet outside to enjoy Washington Park's trees and gardens, the **World Forestry Center Discovery Museum** (4033 SW Canyon Rd., 503/228-1367, www.worldforestry.org, 10am-5pm daily Memorial Day-Labor Day, 10am-5pm Thurs.-Mon. Labor Day-Memorial Day, $7 adults, $6 seniors, $5 children 3-18, children under 3 free) is one way to experience the outdoors while inside. The museum, built in 1971, has exhibits on local and worldwide forests. A canopy lift ride ($4) offers a mini chairlift to show off what lives above the forest floor, and simulators show off what smoke jumping and timber harvesting are like. There's also a 1909 locomotive that was used to move timber hauls around the Pacific Northwest, and a petrified stump from a giant sequoia tree that's 5 million years old and weighs 10,000 pounds.

★ International Rose Test Garden

Although its name has a whiff of science, the **International Rose Test Garden** (850 SW Rose Garden Way, 503/227 7033, www.rosegardenstore.org, 7:30am-9pm daily, free) is a lush bacchanalia of roses, a hillside of thorns and blooms that's every bit as romantic as a rose garden should be. The Shakespeare Garden includes varieties mentioned in his works, as well as strains named for Shakespearean characters, and a giant grassy amphitheater hosts music concerts and plays. But the garden's name means something else— the 7,000 roses in 500 different varieties represent "the best and newest roses," many of which will bloom in early summer, just in time for the city's Rose Festival.

Portland Japanese Garden

The 5.5-acre **Portland Japanese Garden** (611 SW Kingston Ave., 503/223 1321, www.japanesegarden.com, noon-7pm Mon., 10am-7pm Tues.-Sun. spring-summer; noon-4pm Mon., 10am-4pm Tues.-Sun. fall-winter; $14.95 adults, $12.95 seniors, $11.95 students, $10.45 children 6-17, children under 6 free) shows off five styles of Japanese gardens, including the Flat Garden, with a raised porch for viewing, and the Sand and Stone Garden, made from a type of raked sand often found in Zen monasteries. Reach the garden from the parking lot in two ways: Ride a free shuttle up a short road (daily in summer, weekends the rest of the year), or climb a short trail through a Japanese gate before making a few switchbacks on the way to the entrance.

Southeast

★ Oregon Museum of Science and Industry

Its proper name is the **Oregon Museum of Science and Industry** (1945 SE Water Ave., 503/797-4000, www.omsi.edu, 9:30am-5:30pm daily, $14 adults, $10.75

Eastside Portland

0
0 500 yds
0 500 m

Ross Island

Willamette River

ROSS ISLAND BRIDGE

Springwater Corridor

MARQUAM BRIDGE

SW FRONT AVE

MORRISON BRIDGE

HAWTHORNE BRIDGE

BURNSIDE BRIDGE

Esplanade

BIKING

5

5

SE MARTIN LUTHER KING JR. BLVD

SE GRAND

OREGON MUSEUM OF SCIENCE AND INDUSTRY

McLOUGHLIN BLVD

SE MILWAUKIE AVE

ALADDIN THEATER ★

To Sellwood

To Crystal Springs Rhododendron Garden and Reed College

SE 8TH AVE

SE 17TH AVE

SE 21ST AVE

SE 28TH AVE

SE 33RD AVE

SE 39TH AVE

SE 42ND AVE

SE 52ND AVE

SE FOSTER RD

© AVALON TRAVEL

SE DIVISION

SE ELLIOT AVE

SE LADD AVE

SE 20TH AVE

SE 24TH AVE

SE 26TH AVE

SE POWELL BLVD

GLADSTONE ST

SOUTHEAST

Creston Park

CLINTON ST

SE HARRISON ST

SE MADISON ST

SE HAWTHORNE BLVD

SE YAMHILL

SE SALMON ST

SE MORRISON ST

SE STARK ST

SE ANKENY ST

E BURNSIDE ST

SE 11TH

SE 12TH

SE 20TH AVE

SE 22ND AVE

NE 12TH AVE

NE 20TH AVE

NE 28TH AVE

NE GLISAN ST

SE 30TH AVE

SE 35TH AVE

SE 35TH PL

LINCOLN ST

BELMONT ST

SE 43RD AVE

SE 49TH AVE

SE 50TH AVE

Laurelhurst Park

HISTORIC DISTRICT

OLYMPIA PROVISIONS

HAIR OF THE DOG BREWING

DOUG FIR/ JUPITER HOTEL

STREET CAR

GRAND CENTRAL BOWL

LE PIGEON

LUCKY LABRADOR BREWING CO

LARDO

CASTAGNA

NUESTRA COCINA

BAR AVIGNON

HOPWORKS URBAN BREWERY

HAWTHORNE PORTLAND HOSTEL

BLOCK + TACKLE/ ROE

POK POK

LAURETTA JEAN'S

ROMAN CANDLE BAKING COMPANY

BLUEBIRD GUESTHOUSE

WHISKEY SODA LOUNGE

AVA GENE'S

PHO VAN HAWTHORNE

THE WAFFLE WINDOW

3 DOORS DOWN

BRIDGEPORT ALE HOUSE

HAWTHORNE THEATER

BAGDAD THEATER/ BACK STAGE BAR

POR QUE NO?

WOODSMAN TAVERN

CLINTON STREET GUEST HOUSE

SCREEN DOOR

TUSK

NAVARRE

LAURELHURST MARKET

APIZZA SCHOLLS

HORSE BRASS PUB

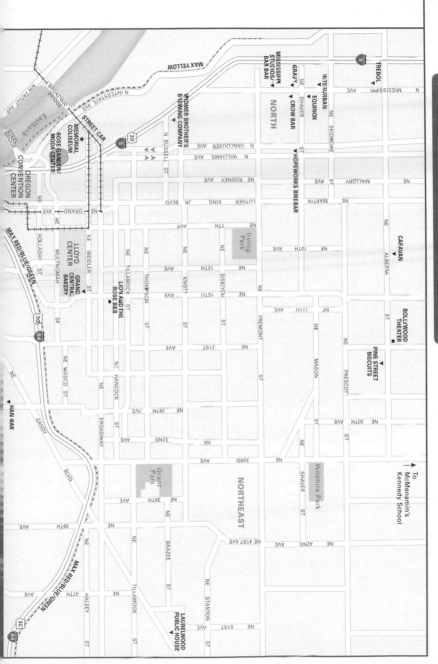

seniors, $9.75 children 3-13, children under 3 free, parking $5), but the active center just across the river from downtown is always called **OMSI**. With a mission to teach and inspire through science, OMSI is disguised as a giant playground, especially *Turbine Hall* with its industrial remnants, suspension bridge, ball room, robotic arm, and earthquake house. Large visiting exhibitions take up one wing of the museum, and a theater shows IMAX films. Just outside, the USS *Blueback,* a U.S. Navy submarine that appeared in *The Hunt for Red October,* is open for tours ($6.75).

Northeast/North
Rose Quarter
Unlike the rose garden in Washington Park, the **Rose Garden Arena** (1 N Center Court St., 503/235-8771, www.rosequarter.com) isn't pretty or delicate. Instead, it's a major arena that hosts the **Portland Trail Blazers** basketball team (www.nba.com/blazers) and the **Winterhawks** (www.winterhawks.com), a junior hockey team. It also serves as a performance space for some of the biggest arena music acts that travel to Portland. (As of 2013, the venue is technically called the Moda Center, though locals still call it the Rose Garden.)

Oregon Convention Center
The two glass spires of the **Oregon Convention Center** (777 NE Martin Luther King Jr. Blvd., 503/235-7575, www.oregoncc.org) almost look like they belong on a church, but the building is actually the largest convention center in the region. It holds travel, entertainment, and industry conventions throughout the year in a number of different spaces, including the Yard, Garden, and Patio Show in late winter and the Portland International Auto Show in February. The building also holds a number of art pieces, including one called *Ode to a Women's Restroom, Ode to a Men's Restroom* (guess where

you go to find that), a 40-foot dragon boat, and a giant Foucault pendulum.

Kennedy School
Ready to go back to school? Even if you're not staying the night, you can play for the day at the **Kennedy School** (5736 NE 33rd Ave., 503/249-7474, www.mcmenamins.com), a former elementary school transformed by the McMenamins into a hotel-playground to which even the locals flock. The hallways lead to a campus of fun spots, including an outdoor **soaking pool** (adults Mon.-Sun. 10am-8pm, minors 10am-6pm, $5)—bring your own towel—and the multistory **Boiler Room Bar** (Mon.-Thurs. 4pm-1am, Fri. 2pm-2:30am, Sat. noon-2:30am, Sun. noon-1am). Other smaller bars include the **Detention Bar** (Mon.-Thurs. 5pm-10pm, Fri. 5pm-midnight, Sat. 1pm-midnight, Sun. 1pm-10pm), which also sells cigars; **Honors Bar** (Mon.-Thurs. 5pm-10pm, Fri. 5pm-midnight, Sat. 1pm-midnight, Sun. 1pm-10pm), playing classical music; and the reggae-themed **Cypress Room** (Mon.-Thurs. 4pm-midnight, Fri. 3pm-1am, Sat. 1pm-1am, Sun. 1pm-midnight). **The Courtyard Restaurant** (7am-1am daily, $13-26) serves American fare, convenient if not particularly noteworthy—though it sometimes incorporates produce from the school's garden, and cinnamon rolls and breads are baked on the premises. Beers are from the Concordia Brewery in the building. Also on the property is a **movie theater** ($4 adults, $2 children 3-11, children under 3 free) in the school's old auditorium, where patrons sit on couches and lounge chairs and eat pub fare while drinking wine and beer. Kids are welcome at matinees.

Kennedy School is a bit farther from the core of the city, but worth the trip. From downtown, take I-5 North to exit 303, following Ainsworth Street to NE 33rd Street. Or hop on TriMet bus no. 17 heading toward Broadway.

The McMenamins and Portland History

When visiting Portland hotels, bars, and concert halls, one name keeps coming up: McMenamins. The company owns 30 pubs around the city, but it's not a chain, exactly. It all started with two brothers, Mike and Brian McMenamin, who had a passion for saving historical buildings and businesses. They opened their first pub in 1983, and they're now the fourth-largest producer of microbrews thanks to the 24 breweries they've purchased. They own hotels and restaurants throughout the Northwest, but most of their holdings are in Portland.

Not all McMenamins properties are historical, but many are. In Portland alone, they own **McMenamins Tavern & Pool** (1716 NW 23rd Ave., 503/227-0929, www.mcmenamins.com/tavern, 11am-11pm Mon.-Tues., 11am-midnight Wed.-Thurs., 11am-1am Fri.-Sat., noon-11pm Sun.), with two shuffleboard tables and a woodstove, and **Greater Trumps** (1520 SE 37th Ave., 503/235-4530, www.mcmenamins.com/greatertrumps, 3pm-midnight Mon.-Thurs., noon-1am Fri.-Sat., noon-midnight Sun.), a cigar bar next to its **Bagdad Theater** (page 262). The **Barley Mill Pub** (1629 SE Hawthorne Ave., 503/231-1492, www.mcmenamins.com/barleymill, 11am-midnight Mon.-Thurs., 11am-1am Fri.-Sat., noon-11pm Sun.), the brothers' first venture, is decorated in Grateful Dead paraphernalia and pinball machines.

Most hotels owned by the McMenamins are unusual in some way. The **Kennedy School** (page 286) used to be an elementary school and has blackboards in its guest rooms and a bar in the old boiler room. The **Crystal Hotel** (page 282) has a colorful past; the building was once a racketeering hub and, later, a gay bathhouse. Rooms are inspired by performances at the **Crystal Ballroom** (page 261), the live music venue across the street and also a McMenamins property. Don't miss the soaking pool in the hotel's basement, in a cozy bamboo-walled space. **Edgefield** (2126 SW Halsey St., Troutdale, 503/669-8610, www.mcmenamins.com/edgefield, $30 hostel, $50-115 shared bath, $155-175 private bath), located about 20 minutes east of downtown Portland, is a former farm that now has a hotel, hostel, garden, glassblowing studio, brewery, distillery, movie theater, golf course, music venue, and more. McMenamins properties are usually a mix of historical, artistic, and quixotic elements, and no two are exactly alike.

Sightseeing Tours

Navigating Portland isn't too challenging. The blocks are short, the sidewalks are wide, and there aren't any bad areas to accidentally wander into. But here are some alternatives to simply strolling the streets and blowing your cash on the excellent boutiques and restaurants (you can do that later).

Bus Tours

The bright pink Portland **Hop-On Hop-Off Trolley** (Pioneer Courthouse Square, SW Broadway and SW Yamhill St., 503/241-7373, www.graylineofportland.net, 9am-4pm daily July-Aug., 10am-4pm daily May-June and Sept.-Oct., $34 adults, $17 children 6-12, children under 6 free) is a good way to get around while sitting down. Open-air trolleys leave Pioneer Courthouse Square (the ticket booth is in the southwest corner, across from Nordstrom) on the hour, returning as late as 5:20pm. There are enclosed areas in which to ride, and in all parts of the trolley you can hear a narrated tour. Riders can leave at any of the 10 stops, which include the Oregon Zoo, OMSI, and Powell's.

For a slightly boozier ride around town, the **Brew Bus** (DoubleTree Hotel Lloyd Center, 1000 NE Multnomah Blvd., 503/647-0021, www.brewbus.com, 1:30pm Sat., $45) stops at breweries and brewpubs around town and includes up to two dozen beer samples.

Walking Tours

For a selection of outings in a variety of themes, look to **Portland Walking Tours** (503/774-4522, www.portlandwalking-tours.com, $23-59), which offers a basic Best of Portland route that hits up the most notable bridges, sculptures, and coffee shops, plus quirky only-in-Portland sights like skateboard lanes and a historical penny. The Underground Portland version looks at things both literally underground—the so-called Shanghai Tunnels in Portland's subterranean levels—and figuratively so, with sites related to the city's illicit past. The operators pride themselves on not trafficking in myths or legends, instead reporting real history and explaining away the untrue rumors that turned into urban legends. The Beyond Bizarre Ghost Tour was developed by a paranormal activity author and a clairvoyant, and participants are handed ghost detection equipment (an electromagnetic field meter, to be exact) and taught how to use it. There are no actors dressed in sheets jumping out from dark corners; however, there are ghost tales about dead prostitutes and haunted hotels, as well as discussion about ruling out hoaxes and hunting techniques. Tours start anywhere between 10am and 10pm and vary by day, lasting 45 minutes (for the Roses Gone Wild Tour) to 3 hours (for the Epicurean Excursion).

Forktown Food Tours (503/234-3663, www.forktown.com, $75-89) is a good way to get outside the downtown core. There is a Downtown and Pearl District version, which runs on Saturday afternoons and pops by seven dining spots. But the company also heads to the northwest area for an Alphabet District tour and across the river for the North Mississippi Avenue tour. With fewer than 15 people, groups pop into eateries or by food carts for complementary bites and drinks (wine and beer too). Tours last about three hours and can include up to 1.5 miles of walking, which isn't enough to work off what you'll eat. The company can accommodate most food restrictions with advance notice.

Entertainment and Events

Nightlife
★ Brewpubs and Taprooms

Portland won't drink just anything; one of its nicknames is Beervana for a reason. The city has an affinity for craft beer—generally beer made by smaller breweries—and more than 15 percent of the ale poured in the state was made in state. In fact, the state has the second most breweries per capita in the United States. Two of the oldest, Widmer Brothers Brewing and BridgePort Brewing, started in the 1980s, though Henry Weinhard began brewing here back in 1862. More hops, a major ingredient in beer, are grown in Washington and Oregon than anywhere else in the country, so that's one reason why home brewing and microbreweries are so popular here.

It's easy to create your own self-guided itinerary, but for tours check out **Brewvana** (pickups at DoubleTree Portland, 1000 NE Multnomah St., 503/729-6804, www.experience-brewvana.com, $65-79), which uses small buses equipped with mini fridges and beer murals to give brewery tours around the city.

Downtown

In a town of microbreweries, **Tugboat Brewing** (711 SW Ankeny St., 503/226-2508, www.d2m.com/tugwebsite, 5pm-10pm Mon., 4pm-midnight Tues.-Fri., 5pm-1am. Sat.) might be the smallest. It looks like just another divey bar, with nature documentaries playing on the only TV and bookshelves on the wall. Only beer and wine are served, but it offers a dozen pales, IPAs, porters, and stouts from around the region, not just its own beers. Food includes bar bites like nachos and pot stickers, but order only in a hunger emergency. The vibe is chill for a bar in the middle of downtown. Look for the Emmy Award on a shelf above the bar and ask the bartender to tell the story of how his father directed *Roots*.

At **Bailey's Taproom** (213 SW Broadway, 503/295-1004, www.baileystaproom.com, noon-midnight daily), the beers have a certain clean organization, with the tidy row of 24 taps and a giant TV of beer offerings with place of origin and alcohol content. Many are from Oregon and Washington, and almost a hundred more are available by the bottle. Old board games like hangman, Connect Four, and backgammon are available, but beer nerds will be busy enough tasting, judging, and tasting again. There's a good amount of seating under the exposed brick walls, but it gets loud in the evening.

Pearl District and Northwest

Perhaps Oregon's most well-known beer comes from **Deschutes Brewery** (210 NW 11th Ave., 503/296-4906, www.deschutesbrewery.com, 11am-11pm Sun.-Thurs., 11am-midnight Fri.-Sat.) in Bend, but it has a sizable brewpub in the Pearl District. The giant space has room to sell T-shirts and bike jerseys with the Black Butte Porter or Mirror Pond Pale Ale logos. The booths, tables, outdoor seating, and waiting areas can get packed. The 18 taps include variations on Deschutes classics and seasonal favorites. Northwesterners mark the change of season when the Deschutes Jubelale comes back every year. Food is hearty fare like a pretzel with porter-spiked mustard and flatbreads, but there's also an entire gluten-free menu.

The rotating taps at **BridgePort Brewpub** (1313 NW Marshall St., 503/241-3612, www.bridgeportbrew.com, 11:30am-11pm Tues.-Thurs.,

11:30am-midnight Fri.-Sat., 11:30am-10pm Sun.-Mon.) offer the brewery's own wares, like the triple-hopped Kingpin and a floral IPA. They really like hops in this joint: Hop Czar is a favorite, and seasonal beers often get hop heavy. The brewpub serves salads, pizzas, and hot, meaty entrées, and also displays local art on the walls.

Southeast

The British-style **Horse Brass Pub** (4534 SE Belmont St., 503/232-2202, www.horsebrass.com, 11:30am-2:30am daily) prides itself on its Imperial pints (that's 20 ounces) and English pub fare. It pours beers from around Portland and the world—with 59 taps, it's quite the spread—and also always has regular and cask-conditioned William Younger's Special Bitter from Rogue Ales, named for the pub owner's late brother. Food includes freshly made meat pies, Scotch eggs, and of course, fish-and-chips.

The tasting room at **Hair of the Dog Brewing** (61 SE Yamhill St., 503/232-6585, www.hairofthedog.com, 11:30am-10pm Fri.-Sat., 11:30am-8pm Sun.) is simple, with large wooden tables and a garage door that opens in good weather. The brewery specializes in bottle-conditioned beers that have a high alcohol content and can age like wine. There are also usually seven or eight beers on tap, plus a food menu that includes pan-roasted Brussels sprouts and Chuck Norris duck wings ("with a solid punch and a nice kick").

Sustainability is no joke at **Hopworks Urban Brewery** (2944 SE Powell Blvd., 503/232-4677, www.hopworksbeer.com, 11am-11pm Sun.-Thurs., 11am-midnight Fri.-Sat.). The beers are organic, and the brewery/brewpub composts and is completely powered by renewable energy sources. But for all the ecofriendliness, the beers pack a punch, particularly the popular IPA and Abominable Winter Ale (a.k.a. "The Beast").

With four locations around the city,

Lucky Labrador Brewing Company (915 SE Hawthorne Blvd., 503/236-3555, www.luckylab.com, 11am-midnight Mon.-Sat., noon-10pm Sun.) is a standby local beer pub for much of Portland. The Hawthorne location is where it all started in 1994, in an old warehouse space that now serves sandwiches and bento boxes, plus a house peanut curry. It has 12 taps of beer. With a name like Lucky Lab, it's no surprise the brewpub has a pet-friendly patio.

Northeast/North

Since Portland is a town that loves its two-wheeling, it's no wonder **Hopworks BikeBar** (3947 N Williams Ave., 503/287-6258, hopworksbeer.com/eat/bikebar, 11am-11pm Sun.-Thurs., 11am-midnight Fri.-Sat.), an outpost of Hopworks Urban Brewery, exists. The BikeBar serves creative beers, like one featuring oyster flavors, and is so family friendly it features a kids' menu and both an indoor play area and outdoor playground. Along with bike

directions on the website and plenty of bike parking, you'll find bike frames decorating the ceiling, bike tools, and bike takeout (specially packaged to be taken home by bicycle).

In a town of microbreweries, **Widmer Brothers Brewing Company** (929 N Russell St., 503/281-2437, www.widmer-brothers.com, 11am-10pm Sun.-Thurs., 11am-11pm Fri.-Sat.) is one of the best known and most successful—so much so that it's now part of the Craft Beer Alliance partially owned by Anheuser-Busch. Started in 1979 as soon as home brewing became legal in the state, Kurt and Rob Widmer managed to open a brewery only five years later. An experiment with leaving their Weizenbier unfiltered led to the first American-style *hefeweizen*. The brothers also claim to be the first American brewery to have a four-season beer list. They also launched the Oregon Brewer's Festival, making them something of godfathers among the Portland brewing scene. Free tours

Deschutes Brewery

are available of the brewery, but the pub has more than a dozen varieties on tap, including the brewery's first beer and, of course, their flagship *hefeweizen*.

Bars and Clubs
Downtown

The bar **Kask** (527 SW 12th Ave., 503/241-7163, www.grunerpdx.com/kask, 4pm-11pm daily) is adjacent to the alpine-themed Grüner restaurant (owned by a James Beard Award-winning chef), but has its own menu of cured meats and small plates. Despite the names and a small, well-curated beer and wine selection, the highlights aren't drinks that come in casks: The cocktail menu is extensive, divided by spirit, and experienced bartenders take their time with creations served on a bar made of a giant pile of rocks, next to walls lined with vintage chalkboards.

The **Multnomah Whiskey Library** (1124 SW Alder St., 503/954-1381, https://mwlpdx.com, 4pm-midnight

Mon.-Thurs., 4pm-1am Fri.-Sat.) might be the hardest library to access on the entire West Coast; members are the only ones who can make reservations, and the rest of us have to wait on a walk-up basis (which can mean very long waits on the ground floor under the main bar, in a separate bar called the Green Room). Oh, and there's a waitlist for memberships. But the special "hall pass" is a one-time reservation for $25, worth it if you have a single day and want to experience the 1,500-plus spirits and impeccable speakeasy decor. Bartenders can help select a whiskey you've never heard of that will become your new favorite.

Portland is known for its strip clubs (there's even one that serves vegan food), but none is more famous than **Mary's Club** (129 SW Broadway, 503/227-3023, www.marysclub.com, 11am-2:30am daily, $2 cover on weekends), where Courtney Love danced back in the 1980s. Mary's is more than 50 years old, claiming to be Portland's first topless joint. Its proprietor, who passed at the age of 90, is still memorialized on the readerboard out front. Look for its trademark retro neon-and-stars sign out front.

Although the pan-Asian cuisine at **Saucebox** (214 SW Broadway, 503/241-3393, www.saucebox.com, 4:30pm-midnight Tues.-Thurs., 4:30pm-2am Fri., 5pm-2am Sat.) is one of its calling cards, its cocktail program is the true highlight. It's so humble that one of its signature tipples is called "the best drink"—gin with mint and ginger brew. It infuses vodkas and gins in-house with Thai chili, watermelon, and kaffir lime, and bartenders will mix with any spirit from whiskey to sake. The ambience is calm and candlelit, but DJs spin in the space regularly.

Pearl District and Northwest

The **Teardrop Cocktail Lounge** (1015 NW Everett St., 503/445-8109, www.teardroplounge.com, 4pm-12:30am Sun.-Thurs., 4pm-2am Fri.-Sat.) doesn't skimp on naming drinks ($10-14). There's the

Misspent Youth with vodka and pear cider, or the Heartbreak Kid with herbaceous lemon vodka, black tea, and Lillet Blanc. They also borrow concoctions from bar books that date back to the 1860s. The round bar puts the bartenders on display as they carefully pound, chip, peel, crush, and pour while constructing the drinks. A brief menu of bites ($7-16) includes a pretzel baguette with bacon-mustard sauce and sweet-and-sour pork belly to pad your stomach, so the tipples don't make you tip over.

Southeast
Holocene (1001 SE Morrison St., 503/239-7639, www.holocene.org, hours vary) is located in an old warehouse space and is part music venue, part nightclub. Many nights have dance parties, others host music acts and multimedia art events. There's a regular '90s dance night that's been around for more than 10 years—so longer than the 1990s themselves—and led by a DJ with a PhD.

Northeast/North
Describing itself as a "new American saloon," **Interurban** (4057 N Mississippi Ave., 503/284-6669, www.interurbanpdx.com, 3pm-2:30am Mon.-Fri., 10am-2:30am Sat.-Sun.) combines cocktail culture with a relaxed neighborhood bar, more upscale than the owner's other joint in the neighborhood, the German **Prost!** (4237 N Mississippi Ave., 503/954-2674, http://prostportland.com, 11:30am-2:30am Mon.-Thurs., 11am-2:30am Fri.-Sun.). Tables are tiny, meant to fit drinks and only a few of the small bites from the menu, like bacon-wrapped shrimp cocktail and steak tartare. The back patio fills on sunny days, but the bar itself is the most social spot. Chat with the bartenders about the worldly beer and wine list, or consider a cocktail Jello shot, a strange combination of quality ingredients that is a college-party tradition. Children are allowed inside before 8pm.

The repetitively named **Bar Bar** (3939 N Mississippi Ave., 503/288-3895, www.mississippistudios.com, noon-2am daily) is part of Mississippi Studios, a live music venue, but still has a neighborhood bar aspect. Big windows open to the street, generally where a steady throng of concertgoers moves through. There are two outdoor patios, and a "secret garden" with a fire pit out back.

In a neighborhood that's becoming increasingly popular and polished, **Crow Bar** (3954 N Mississippi Ave., 503/280-7099, www.crowbarpdx.com, 3pm-2am daily) shows off some simple watering hole pleasures: pinball games, a jukebox, and specials for employees of other bars and restaurants. It even offers margaritas on tap. Works from local artists hang on the walls, elevating the bar well above a dive.

Gay and Lesbian
It's billed as the city's premier gay nightclub, but **C.C. Slaughters** (219 NW Davis St., 503/248-9135, www.ccslaughterspdx.com, 3pm-2am daily) in the Pearl District is the place for everyone to dance. It was originally a gay country-western bar and named for the first male born in the Republic of Texas (and a man rumored to be gay). Now it plays dance music and has Sunday-night drag shows. There's no regular cover, and a system allows dancers to text song requests directly to the DJ.

Scandals (1125 SW Stark St., 503/227-5887, www.scandalspdx.com, noon-2:30am daily) likes to call itself Portland's gay *Cheers* bar, and it has a history stretching back to 1979. It hosts karaoke nights, bands, and DJs and is generally known for its male crowd but is usually welcoming to women. Go for cheap drinks and the company, but not for the food. Sometimes there's dancing, but there's always pool to be played. Patio seating is available out front, and students get a food discount in the afternoons.

The **Embers Avenue** (110 NW Broadway, 503/222-3082, 11am-2am daily) is a show and dance club that often hosts drag shows and leather bingo. The hosts have monikers like Onalicious Mercury and Onyx Lynn. The bar has grubby corners, but service is generally good, and a fish tank (yes, full of fish) is under the bar. The back bar, the Avenue, opens at 9pm.

Live Music

The retro, mod **Doug Fir Lounge** (830 E Burnside St., 503/231-9663, www.dougfirlounge.com, 7am-2:30am daily) recalls Los Angeles or Palm Springs in the 1960s, but blended with a log cabin. The performance space holds only a few hundred people, so concerts stay intimate, and the bill usually features local singer-songwriters and indie bands. Though not in downtown, the attached Jupiter Hotel helps feed the busy restaurant, bar, and patio.

The **Mississippi Studios** (3939 N Mississippi Ave., 503/288-3895, www.mississippistudios.com, noon-2am daily) was, once upon a time, a Baptist church, but now it worships at the secular church of rock, pop, and indie hip-hop. The venue is small but flat, so the best viewpoints are up front or on a small balcony, which has a few chairs.

The long and storied history of the **Crystal Ballroom** (1332 W Burnside St., 503/225-0047, www.crystalballroompdx.com) includes a century of beat poets and police raids, Grateful Dead concerts, and Ike and Tina Turner shows. It has a unique "mechanical" dance floor and ornate curved windows, but you won't notice them or the chandeliers when the live music starts. Performing acts tend to be indie rock bands and singer-songwriters, but tribute shows to major bands and swing dances are also held in the space.

A number of bands have recorded live albums at **Roseland Theater** (8 NW 6th Ave., 971/230-0033, www.roselandpdx.com), which sits right between downtown and the Pearl District. Most concerts are standing room only, with limited seating on a balcony.

Graced with a giant vertical "Portland" marquee, the **Arlene Schnitzer Concert Hall** (1037 SW Broadway, 503/248-4335, www.portland5.com) sits in a 1928 building that once housed the Portland Public Theater, built in rococo revival style. Now the space hosts classical and jazz concerts, major lectures, visiting dance companies, the occasional ski flick, and big-name popular music acts. The Artbar & Bistro restaurant serves cocktails and a Northwest-inspired dinner menu before shows.

There's an intimate feel to the smallish **Hawthorne Theatre** (1507 SE 39th Ave., 503/233-7100, www.hawthornetheatre.com), but nothing delicate or precious. Smaller indie, punk, metal, and pop bands share nightly bills with DJs, and the space is just dark, hot, and sticky enough to earn a real rock 'n roll reputation.

The acts on stage at **Dante's** (350 W Burnside St., 503/345-7892, www.danteslive.com, 11am-2:30am daily) range from rock to cabaret and burlesque, making it one of the more eclectic live destinations in the city. Occasionally there's karaoke on stage with a band—called Karaoke from Hell—and it serves pizza by the slice.

When Portland's quintessential jazz club, Jimmy Mak's, closed in 2017 in the wake of the death of local legend Jimmy Makarounis, the city's music scene was in shock until the owners of Dante's opened a new venue called **Jack London Revue** (529 SW 4th Ave., 866/777-8932, http://jacklondonrevue.com). Located in the basement of the Rialto Poolroom Bar & Cafe, which boasts a poker lounge and an off-track gambling parlor, the Jack London Revue incorporates many of the musicians who were left without a stage when the old club closed. There are also new groups appearing regularly, not just jazz but indie rock and experimental and everything in between.

The Arts

The **Portland Center Stage** (Gerding Theater at the Armory, 128 NW 11th Ave., 503/445-3700, www.pcs.org) is a theater group that produces new and well-known plays and musicals and also hosts an annual playwriting festival. It performs in the Gerding Theater at the Armory, which gives public tours (503/445-3727) of the space that was built in 1891 and has served all number of functions since.

Unlike some of the city's older institutions, **Oregon Ballet Theatre** (Keller Auditorium, 222 SW Clay St., or Newmark Theatre, 1111 SW Broadway, 503/227-0977, www.obt.org) is fairly new, formed only in 1989. Still, the company has established itself in the city and performs classics like George Balanchine's *Nutcracker* along with premieres choreographed by the artist director. Dancers represent Portland's diversity, and the company performs at several spots around town, including the Tony Keller Auditorium and intimate Newmark Theatre.

The **Oregon Symphony** (Arlene Schnitzer Concert Hall, 1037 SW Broadway, 503/228-1353, www.orsymphony.org) was established more than 120 years ago—it's the oldest orchestra west of the Mississippi—and performs both classical symphony works and pops concerts, often performing with visiting pop singers. The symphony cares about reaching out—it offers $5 tickets to locals who receive state food assistance (as do other arts organizations in town). Students can get $10 tickets.

The **Portland Opera** (Keller Auditorium, 222 SW Clay St., 503/241-1802, www.portlandopera.org) starts its season with a Big Night concert, staging some of opera's biggest hits. The group tries to make its performances accessible,

hosting Q&A sessions with the general director after every performance and prepping audiences with pre-curtain talks an hour before the show. Subtitles— or rather supertitles, as they're properly called—are projected above the stage.

Cinema

The **Living Room Theaters** (341 SW 10th Ave., 971/222-2010, www.livingroomtheaters.com, $11 adults, $9 matinees, $8 students and seniors, $6 Mon.-Tues.) plays first-run movies, but tends toward the artsy and documentary type, not the blockbusters, though it's not unheard of for a comic book film to pay. The building has a sleek wooden style inside and out, with a bar serving a cheese plate and chicken skewers, plus drinks, which can be taken into the theaters. Seats have small tables and are large and comfortable, though screens are small, as befits an art house cinema. The café also has outdoor seating.

No, it's not a typo. **Bagdad Theater** (3702 SE Hawthorne Blvd., 503/236-9234, www.mcmenamins.com, $9.50 adults, $8 matinees, $6.50 children under 13) is spelled differently from the city in the Middle East. The theater was a former movie palace, built in 1927. (It once hosted the premiere of *One Flew Over the Cuckoo's Nest*.) Now renovated by the McMenamins group, the theater shows new-release movies amid its Arabian-style interior. The neon sign outside is one of the city's most striking marquees.

Unlike the theaters that have been used as such for decades, **Mission Theater** (1624 NW Glisan St., 503/223-4527, www.mcmenamins.com, $4 adults, $3 children, $2 matinees) was a former evangelical mission and a Longshoremen's union. The space now has a pulpit, screen, and balcony and hosts new movies as well as readings, lectures, a jazz series, and other performances. Sometimes the big screen shows live sporting events like *Monday Night Football* or Trailblazers basketball games. The attached pub serves

McMenamins beers, and children aren't permitted at movies that begin after 6pm.

Festivals and Events

Despite the name, the **Fertile Ground Festival** (www.fertilegroundpdx.org) in January isn't about farming, but art. The focus is on local artists and their latest creations, including new plays, films, and pieces of music. Recent years have seen more than 100 premieres across the city; passes good for all 11 days run about $50.

In the City of Roses, the **Portland Rose Festival** (503/227-2681, www.rosefestival.org, June) is a central event that's more than 100 years old. It takes place in early June, right about when the area's roses are in bloom (if the weather cooperates, that is). The Grand Floral Parade features marching bands, horseback riders, vintage cars, and dancers, plus floats made out of roses. It begins at Veterans Memorial Coliseum (300 N Winning Way), crosses the river at the Burnside Bridge, and zigzags around downtown before ending at Lincoln High School near SW Salmon Street and SW 14th Avenue. There's also dragon boat races, a Rose Festival Fleet Week featuring visiting naval and coast guard vessels, and a Starlight Parade the week before the Grand Floral Parade, plus an annual Spring Rose Show at the Lloyd Center Ice Rink (953 Lloyd Center, 503/777-4311, www.portlandrosesociety.org, $3).

The **World Naked Bike Ride** (South Park Blocks, SW Park Ave. from Salmon St. to Jackson St., www.pdxwnbr.org, June) takes place all around the world, but the Portland version is usually the biggest, with thousands of riders. Not everyone is fully nude, but some folks are. The theme is "bare as you dare," and cameras are banned at the start and end points. People ride to promote cycling, protest the country's dependence on oil, celebrate the nude lifestyle, and just for silly fun. It takes place at night, and a body-painting area usually operates near the start. One year the Portland Art Museum even opened up for participants, charging them a dollar for every piece of clothing they wore. A marching band kicks off the ride, and after parties continue into the night at the end. The ride is the signature event of the month-long **Pedalpalooza** (www.shift2bikes.org/pedalpalooza) in June, a series of bike-related events that incorporate everything from political protest to drinks and food to costumes and kazoos.

The annual **Portland Pride** (Waterfront Park, Naito Pkwy. between SW Harrison St. and NW Glisan St., 503/296-9788, www.pridenw.org, June) weekend celebrates local LGBTQ culture with a parade and festival on the waterfront, featuring live music and comedy performances.

One of the biggest blues festival in the country, the **Waterfront Blues Festival** (Waterfront Park, Naito Pkwy. between SW Harrison St. and NW Glisan St., 503/275-9750, www.waterfrontbluesfest.com, July) began as a concert to support Portland's homeless. Most of the festival can be accessed with a cheap ticket and two cans of food. The Oregon Potters Association sells handmade bowls to symbolize hunger, raising more money for food banks. It always occurs around the Fourth of July and includes the biggest fireworks show in the state, held over the Willamette River.

The **Oregon Brewers Festival** (Naito Pkwy. between SW Harrison St. and NW Glisan St., www.oregonbrewfest.com, admission free, tasting $7 plus $1 tokens) in July is one of the largest outdoor festivals on the West Coast, bringing more than 80,000 to Tom McCall Waterfront Park in late July for five days of craft beer tastings.

The giant food fest **Bite of Oregon** (Waterfront Park, Naito Pkwy. between SW Harrison St. and NW Glisan St., 503/248-0600, www.biteoforegon.com, Aug.) raises money for Special Olympics Oregon by selling tastes of Oregon food and drink. Restaurants from around the state bring more than a hundred dishes, and dozens of Oregon wineries and breweries pour tasting sizes. There's an Iron Chef Oregon competition and two stages of entertainment. Just remember to bring cash. In September, **Feast Portland** (Pioneer Courthouse Square, SW Broadway and SW Morrison St, 503/897-7773, https://feastportland.com) gathers local chefs to show off their culinary prowess, featuring a night market, competitions, and brunch events.

Labor Day weekend's **Art in the Pearl** (NW 8th Ave. between W Burnside and NW Glisan, 503/722-9017, www.artinthepearl.com, Sept.) includes rows of booths in the middle of the North Park Blocks in the Pearl District, featuring the work from more than a hundred artists, plus a World Music Stage with performances and a kids' pavilion. There's a food row for snacks, and a demonstration where groups show off wood carving,

metalwork, digital painting, papermaking, and more.

MusicFest NW (www.musicfestnw.com, Aug. or Sept.) is like a Northwest version of Austin's South by Southwest, with shows around the city in a variety of venues. The fest scores big names in the rock and pop worlds, and recent years have seen the addition of outdoor concerts in downtown's Pioneer Courthouse Square. A technology version of the festival, **TechFestNW** (www.techfestnw.com), held in March, has speakers, competitions, and panels about start-ups, media, and online design.

The **Time-Based Art Festival** (503/242-1419, http://pica.org/programs/tba-festival, Sept.), also known as TBA, is run by the Portland Institute for Contemporary Art. The mid-September event includes visual art exhibits that run for weeks, but most of the festival revolves around contemporary performances and installations in theaters, galleries, and public

a float at the Portland Rose Festival's annual parade

spaces, plus lectures and workshops. It might include a cabaret singer with the Oregon Symphony one night and a laser multimedia show the next.

Shopping

"Independent" is the watchword of Portland shops, which also tend to sell local and sustainable items. Clothing styles tend to have a vintage touch, while housewares are quirky and artsy. The lack of sales tax in Oregon makes it a shopping mecca. Look for Washington residents who've come down for a trip just to peruse the town's many fabulous boutiques.

Downtown
Clothing and Shoes

Steven Alan (1029 SW Stark St., 971/277-9585, www.stevenalan.com, 11am-7pm Mon. Sat., 11am-6pm Sun.) isn't

headquartered in Portland but has prime placement across from the Ace Hotel, in a pedestrian alleyway mall of stores known as the Union Way. The exposed roof trusses and skylights are a good match for Steven Alan's clean lines for men and expensive leather accessories. Head to the back for a wall of shirts whose patterns just bridge the line between hipster chic and practical style.

Also in the Union Way mall is **Will Leather Goods** (1022 W Burnside St., Unit N, 971/279-4698, www.willleathergoods.com, 11am-7pm daily), where the wares are new but the store is made from old mid-20th-century gym bleachers from a Portland-area college, an old Smokey the Bear sign, and an artfully rusty vintage cash register (a sign reminds shoppers that everything inside is indeed for sale; inquire about prices for the decor). There are belts and leather portfolios, as well as thick aprons appropriate for the avid chef or hardy backyard griller.

Animal Traffic (429 SW 10th Ave., 503/241-5427, www.animaltrafficpdx.com, 11am-6pm daily) first opened in the Mississippi district, selling outdoorsy sweaters and thick Western shirts, particularly brands like Pendleton and Minnetonka. Eventually it opened this downtown outpost, decorated with barn doors and wood beams from farm buildings. Besides the canvas knapsacks, men's coats, and women's vintage-style dresses, there's a spot to get measured for made-to-order White's Boots (a century-old company based in Spokane that once made rugged footwear for Northwest loggers).

With its headquarters just one town away in Beaverton, the flagship store for **Nike** (638 SW 5th Ave., 503/221-6453, www.nike.com, 10am-8pm Mon.-Sat., 11am-6pm Sun.) has to be impressive—appropriately, a gray statue of Michael Jordan making a dunk hangs from the ceiling. Walls of multicolored Nike sneakers surround racks of workout wear, and fancy display boxes explain the various technological wonders of particular lines of shoes in the three-store space.

In a town known for its vintage shopping, **Fat Fancy** (1013 SW Morrison St., 503/445-4353, www.fatfancyfashions. com, 11am-6pm Mon.-Fri., 11am-7pm Sat., noon-6pm Sun.) has a special niche: plus-size women. The proprietor was so passionate about the shop that she first started it in her studio apartment, inviting friends and acquaintances to shop next to her bed and other furniture, before moving to a basement space. Beth Ditto, fashion icon and singer in the Olympia band The Gossip, became a loyal customer, eventually making the real storefront possible. The new and vintage clothing represents a wide range of sizes and styles, from rockabilly chic to office wear; they've begun carrying plus-size men's clothing as well, along with shoes and accessories.

Radish Underground (414 SW 10th Ave., 503/928-6435, www.radishunderground.com, 11am-7pm Mon.-Sat., noon-6pm Sun.) is quintessential Portland shopping, combining a whimsical name with women's clothing from independent designers, many of them local, in a space decorated with a distressed floor and artful light fixtures. Styles are mostly clean and modern, and a handful of pieces—socks, T-shirts, some etched wooden cuff links—appeal to men as well.

Gift and Home

In a town full of tony home stores, **Canoe** (1136 SW Alder, 503/889-8545, www.canoeonline.net, 10am-6pm Tues.-Sat., 11am-5pm Sun.) is one of the best. The airy white store is flooded with daylight, and even the wood floor is pale and spotless. Most pieces could be either artworks or useful items. It's no wonder the store often pops up in national design and travel magazines. Locally made articles are highlighted, like the Eena canvas bags from Beckel Canvas that the store sells exclusively; they're trimmed with leather

and visible stitching. Linen tea towels with special wood-grain designs are almost too pretty to use on kitchen spills.

Tender Loving Empire (412 SW 10th Ave., 503/243-5859, www.tenderlovingempire.com, 11am-7pm daily) is more than a shop—it's a record label and screen-printing studio, and owners started it hoping to preserve a sense of community in Portland's bustling downtown. Murals by local artists are all over the store walls, and art pieces in the gallery are sold on consignment. Also find a selection of gifts like engraved spoons, scarves knitted to look like a fox, and screen-printed Onesies.

You could think of **Crafty Wonderland** (808 SW 10th Ave., 503/224-9097, www. craftywonderland.com, 10am-6pm Mon.-Sat., 11am-6pm Sun.) as a gift store, but one with a decidedly Portland bent. Find drinking glasses printed with mustaches and prints of the Oregon state shape. The greeting card selection is good but pricey, and a different local is highlighted in the "Artist of the Month" corner.

It might cost a lot to ship something home from **The Joinery** (922 SW Yamhill St, 800/259-6762, thejoinery.com, 10am-6pm Mon.-Sat., 11am-5pm Sun.), but the handcrafted furniture is the kind of piece that you'll hand down to your grandchildren one day. The wood pieces evoke the Pacific Northwest without feeling like Paul Bunyon's dorm furnishings.

Outdoor Gear

The two-story climbing rock at the Portland **REI** (1405 NW Johnson St., 503/221-1938, www.rei.com, 10am-9pm Mon.- Sat., 10am-7pm Sun.) is visible from the street and from both floors of retail space. The building boasts an eco-friendly design that made it one of the first retail spaces in the country to get a LEED Gold award. The store carries all the jackets, sleeping bags, hiking boots, and kayaks one would ever need on an outdoor excursion, and regular classes show off how to use the equipment. The store has a famously generous return policy, accepting any unsatisfactory gear for return or exchange within a year of purchase.

Though not a chain like REI, **U.S. Outdoor Store** (219 SW Broadway, 503/223-5937, www.usoutdoor.com, 9am-8pm Mon.-Fri., 10am-6pm Sat., 11am-5pm Sun.) carries nearly as many kinds of outdoor gear. A signpost on the ground level directs shoppers up or down to find snowboards, climbing gear, and rainproof everything.

Portland Outdoor Store (304 SW 3rd Ave., 503/222-1051, 9:30am-5:30pm Mon.-Sat.) bursts with personality, including a giant neon sign with a bucking cowboy on it. "Outdoor" has a different definition here—a western supply store with boots and saddles, plus Filson bags and Western shirts for anyone without a horse. The shop includes used gear, and clerks are chatty.

Pearl District and Northwest
Clothing and Shoes

The **Keen Garage** (505 NW 13th Ave., 971/200-4040, www.keenfootwear.com, 10am-7pm Mon.-Sat., 11am-5pm Sun.) is the flagship store for a local brand that makes hardy, weather-ready shoes and hiking boots. The warehouse space has polished wood floors, hanging blackboards, and display racks that move on pulleys and wheels. Best of all is the metal chute that emerges from the upstairs storage space, so boxes fly through the store on their way down to the cash register.

Sloan (738 NW 23rd Ave., 503/222-6666, www.sloanpdx.com, 11am-7pm Mon.-Fri., 10am-7pm Sat., 11am-6pm Sun.) is a boutique with women's clothing especially popular with the younger set. The shoe store next store is an extension of Sloan and offers contemporary styles.

Gift and Home

There's a little bit of everything in the giant former tire factory that is now

Cargo (380 NW 13th, 503/209-8349, www.cargoimportspdx.com, 11am-6pm daily). It has wooden furniture, paper lanterns, jewelry, fans, Chinese socks, wooden hand models, play masks, wind-up toys of a duck riding a tricycle—and so much more. The importer prides itself on bringing the entire globe to Portland, and one can spend hours in the crowded aisles, always finding a new basket of treasure.

Gourmet Goodies

The European-style **City Market Northwest** (735 NW 21st Ave., 503/221-3007, 9:30am-7pm daily) sells produce, wines, fresh pastas, and gourmet foodstuffs, all in a bright, cheery market. The people working the meat and cheese counters know what they're talking about.

Southeast
Clothing and Shoes

The jewel box of **Xtabay** (2515 SE Clinton St., 503/230-2899, www.xtabayvintage.blogspot.com, 11am-6pm daily) is a lovely salon of vintage women's wear, sorted by color and carefully tagged. Formal dresses are protected by plastic covers, and a separate bridal shop sells vintage wedding gowns. Hats and shoes from a dressier era line both sides of the small store. It's where to go for a *Mad Men* style fix, or just to remember how flattering the various styles of the past could be.

From the suit jackets to the snazzy shoes, **Wildfang** (1230 SE Grand Ave., 503/208-3631, www.wildfang.com, noon-6pm daily) is all about the tomboy look, dressing Portland's women in traditional male styles but with fun touches like Beyoncé prints and bright patterns. An exposed-wood space serves as a stage for hoodies, graphic T-shirts, and a very feminist jacket that announces "slay the patriarchy."

Gourmet Goodies

Even though the **Woodsman Tavern Market** (4529 SE Division St.,

Portlandia Keeps Portland Weird

Portland has been known for many things—bridges, roses, lumber—but since 2011 it has been known by a new nickname: Portlandia. The comedy TV show *Portlandia* riffs on the city's indie and alternative scene, ecofriendliness, and bike culture, calling it "the city where young people go to retire."

The show is a modest hit, but it's referenced often. The boutique **Land Gallery** (3925 N Mississippi Ave., 503/451-0689, www.landpdx.com, 10am-7pm daily) became famous as the site of the show's "Put a Bird on It" sketch, and the "Women & Women First" feminist bookstore is actually **In Other Words** (14 NE Killingsworth St., 503/232-6003, www. inotherwords.org, noon-7pm Tues.-Sat., 1pm-7pm Sun.).

The **Secrets of Portlandia Walking Tour** (SW 6th Ave. between SW Morrison St. and SW Yamhill St., 503/703-4282, www.secretsofportlandia.com, 11am daily May-Oct., free) is a free daily excursion that runs spring-fall, covering quirky attractions representative of Portland—like food cart pods, the Weather Machine (a public art piece that tells the weather), Mill Ends Park (the world's smallest park), and more. It passes the *"Keep Portland Weird"* sign that's painted on a building at 3158 East Burnside Street (the phrase is also on a lot of T-shirts and bumper stickers). The tours, done by Portland locals only for tips, are not directly affiliated with the show, but claim to reveal "Portland's obsession with beer, bikes, and beards."

Though recently popularized, the moniker "Portlandia" comes from a 1985 sculpture of a woman holding a trident, crouching down, and reaching out. It's located on the **Portland Building** designed by Michael Graves (SW 5th Ave. between SW Madison and SW Main St.) and is the second-largest copper statue of its kind in the United States—right behind the Statue of Liberty. Look up a few stories to see her. And when touring the city, any time you see a tattooed cyclist, an organic garden on a roof, or a random street performance by steampunk clowns, don't be surprised if someone says, "That's so *Portlandia*."

971/373-8267, www.woodsmantavern. com, 9am-7pm daily) is right next to the polished eatery with which it shares ownership, it's a much more casual shop, selling vinegars, oils, pastas, and jarred pickles, plus literary food journals. The space is small and lined with white tile, but it fits a butcher's counter, with cheeses and many meats smoked or cured locally, and a rotating selection of fish, sausage, and burgers. Sandwiches, salads, and soups are available to go.

Northeast/North
Books

In Other Words (14 NE Killingsworth St., 503/232-6003, www.inotherwords.org, noon-7pm Tues.-Sat., 1pm-7pm Sun.) is more than just a sketch on *Portlandia*. It's a feminist community center and bookstore, hosting events like reading groups that focus on feminist and queer science fiction, craft nights, yoga, dream discussion nights, and open mic nights. The lending library gathers radical books and feminist zines, and the store sells books on feminist issues as well as health, religion, gardening, and craft titles.

The small, independent **Broadway Books** (1714 NE Broadway, 503/284-1726, www.broadwaybooks.net, 10am-7pm Mon.-Sat., noon-5pm Sun.) has survived for more than 20 years, selling new and used books along with gifts, games, and journals. Compared to the cavernous Powell's, this shop is personal, cheerful, and happy to gift wrap for free. Staff recommendations are carefully selected, and locals enjoy a frequent buyer card that earns them a free book for every 12 they buy. Readings are held regularly.

Clothing and Shoes

The boutique **Flutter** (3948 N Mississippi Ave., 503/288-1649, www.flutterclutter. com, 11am-6pm Sun.-Wed, 11am-7pm Thurs.-Sat.) gets its name from "found objects and clutter," which it displays in a space with bright turquoise walls and chandeliers. There are vintage dresses and lots of jewelry, old mannequins artfully arranged, plus paper goods and pillows. It's all a little crammed together, as the name suggests. That sound in the back? Finches—yes, live birds—tweeting the day away in a big French birdcage.

Gift and Home

Land Gallery (3925 N Mississippi Ave., 503/451-0689, www.landpdx.com, 10am-7pm daily) will go down in history as the shop from the *Portlandia* sketch "Put a Bird on It," where the TV show's stars parodied the hipster practice of decorating housewares, tote bags, and clothing. And yes, the store does carry cute paper goods, socks, and T-shirts (most without birds on them), but it also has a gallery space that displays the works of independent Northwest artists.

Gourmet Goodies

Even though the neighborhood has good bars and breweries, **Bridgetown Beerhouse** (915 N Shaver St., 503/477-8763, noon-10pm Mon.-Thurs., noon-11pm Fri.-Sat., noon-8pm Sun.) simply offers bottled and canned beer, plus five taps for filling growlers. The craft beers they carry are carefully selected (but they admit to having cheap Pabst Blue Ribbon, too), and they care for the ales by filtering the UV light in the space, rotating the beers in the front of the case, and keeping them all at 38°F. It's also a pub with a simple wooden counter and a few wooden tables, so you can drink on-site.

Sports and Recreation

Parks
★ Forest Park

There's no singular entrance to **Forest Park** (NW 29th Ave. and Upshur St. to Newberry Rd., 503/223-5449, www.forestparkconservancy.org, 5am-10pm daily), and no one way to enjoy what is one of the largest city forests in the country. The 5,100 acres make up a chunk of wildness 30 miles long, one end only a few miles from downtown. Trails wind through the space partly designed by the famous Olmstead Brothers, land that was once surveyed by the Lewis and Clark expedition back in 1806. Dozens of mammals and birds live among the Douglas fir and maples trees, including deer, bobcats, woodpeckers, and coyotes, even migratory elk—and bear scat has even been sighted.

Despite plenty of space for stationary meditation in the thick forest, the trails are the rock stars of Forest Park. More than 80 miles, including old roads and fire lanes, are open to runners and hikers, with many accessible to bikers and equestrians. Dogs must be leashed. The **Wildwood Trail** alone is 30 miles long and passes the Stone House, a Works Progress Administration cabin from the 1930s, now gutted and used solely for scenic purposes. For a quick visit to the park, try the trail leaving from the **Audubon Society of Portland's Bird Sanctuary** (5151 NW Cornell Rd., 503/292-6855, www.audubonportland.org, 9am-5pm Mon.-Sat., 10am-5pm Sun.); the Pittock Mansion is a short hike downhill on the Wildwood Trail.

Director Park

In a city with nature-focused parks in the trees and on the river, **Director Park** (815 SW Park Ave., 503/823-8087, www.portlandoregon.gov, 5am-midnight daily) is a decidedly city spot, located right in the middle of downtown and featuring a large plaza with benches, as well as tables outside the **Elephants in the Park Café** (877 SW Taylor St., 503/937-1073, www. elephantsdeli.com, 11am-8pm daily, $7-13). A giant chess game has movable pawns and rooks the size of preschoolers. The terrace is covered by a tall glass roof, and the flat Teacher's Fountain area has arching jets popular with kids.

Tom McCall Waterfront Park

Located right on the Willamette River, the 30-acre **Tom McCall Waterfront Park** (Naito Pkwy. between SW Harrison St. and NW Glisan St., www.portlandoregon.gov, 5am-midnight daily) has views of the bridges that give Portland one of its nicknames. The site used to be Harbor Drive until former governor Tom McCall led a charge to remove the road and add a park in the 1970s. It has an esplanade walkway and a large lawn, which fills with spectators during the annual dragon boat races. Ornamental cherry trees, known for their annual burst into pink bloom, grow next to a sculpture that commemorates Portland's sister city in Japan.

Park highlights include the **Salmon Street Springs** water fountain, which shoots almost 5,000 gallons of water per minute (the springs' water patterns are controlled by computer), and the **Japanese American Historical Plaza.** The plaza is dedicated to the people who were put in internment camps during World War II, when the U.S. government decreed that everyone of Japanese descent, including American citizens, could be forced from their homes and into prison-like camps for security reasons (the government issued apologies and compensation in 1988). The plaza includes a sculpture called *Songs of Innocence, Songs of Experience* and a memorial garden.

Across the Willamette River from Tom McCall Waterfront Park, the east side of Portland gets a riverfront public space of its own in the **Eastbank Esplanade** (www. portlandoregon.gov). The path starts at the Steel Bridge, near where NE Oregon Street meets NE Lloyd Boulevard, and goes south past the Burnside Bridge, the Morrison Bridge, and the Hawthorne Bridge, ending south of OMSI where SE Caruthers Street meets SE Water Avenue. Along the 1.5-mile pedestrian and bike path are 22 interpretive panels and several pieces of public art, including one meant to represent the Shanghai tunnels that were once used to kidnap sailors and deliver them to waiting ships. Part is a floating walkway, the longest of its kind, with a public dock.

Mount Tabor Park

There's a volcanic cinder cone in the city of Portland at the east side's **Mount Tabor Park** (SE 60th Ave. and Salmon St., 503/823-2525, www.portlandoregon.gov, 5am-midnight daily), named for a mountain in Israel. This isn't to say that it looks like a volcano. The hill is now home to water reservoirs and a park with sparkling views. The nearly 200 acres contain playgrounds, a horseshoe pit, a stage, and tennis courts. The large statue is of Harvey W. Scott, an editor of *The Oregonian* in the 19th century, and made by the same man who carved Mount Rushmore. As for the volcanic cone underground, Mount Tabor is two million years old and hasn't erupted for at least 300,000 years—and isn't expected to do so again soon.

★ Biking

When someone lists the best U.S. cities for biking—*Bicycling* magazine, for instance—Portland always comes up at the very top of the list. By their count, in 2012 Portland had more cyclists per capita than anywhere else in America, and the city has dedicated bike lanes, bike parking everywhere from coffee shops to the airport, and its annual Naked Bike Ride is usually the best attended nude pedal in the world.

For easy cruises from downtown, depart from **Tom McCall Waterfront Park**

Day Trip to Mount Hood

The state's highest mountain is also a volcano that erupted in the mid-19th century. The pointy peak east of Portland is the city's own private mountain. It's not quite as big as Seattle's Mount Rainier but is closer to the city, a mere 60 miles or so. Head east from downtown Portland on I-84 to the town of Troutdale, exiting on NE 238th Drive, then turning left on NE Burnside Road and continuing on U.S. 26, following it east for about 40 miles. In the small settlement of Government Camp, a left turn leads to the 6-mile road leading to the prettiest spot at Mount Hood—besides the peak itself, of course—**Timberline Lodge** (27500 E Timberline Rd., Timberline Lodge, 503/272-3311, www.timberlinelodge. com, $160-290). Constructed by the Works Progress Administration in the 1930s from local trees and stones, the stately building was featured in the movie *The Shining*. It has 70 guest rooms, and the lobby has a three-story chimney with six fireplaces.

Skiing on Mount Hood is busiest on the southeast corner at **Mt. Hood Meadows** (14040 Hwy. 35, Mt. Hood, 503/337-2222, www.skihood.com, $89 adults, $54 seniors, $44 children 7-14, $10

children under 7). The resort has 11 chairlifts, including one that travels halfway up the mountain, night skiing, and a Nordic center. The skiing at **Timberline Lodge** ($68 adults, $56 youth 15-17, $42 seniors and children 7-14) often goes year-round, or at least once every month of the year. **Mt. Hood Skibowl** (87000 E Hwy. 26, Government Camp, 503/272-3206, www. skibowl.com, $54 adults, $35 seniors and children 7-12, children under 7 free) is smaller, with four chairlifts, but a slightly shorter drive. It also has night skiing and a **Winter Adventure Park** (Fri.-Sat., $79) with snow tubing, a zip line, and kiddie snowmobiles. Operating days and hours vary by season (generally open daily in ski season; weekends or Fri.-Sun. during shoulder seasons). Dates vary by year depending on when it snows.

Once the snows melt, the Mount Hood area becomes a hiker's and biker's destination, with 1,000 miles of trail in the **Mt. Hood National Forest,** plus campgrounds and fishing spots. Rangers at the **Zigzag Ranger District** (70220 E Hwy. 26, Zigzag, www.fs.usda.gov/mthood, 7:45am-4:30pm daily) can narrow down options and make recommendations based on seasonal availability.

(also the location of a number of bike rental spots). Head north along the water, under the Morrison and Burnside Bridges, then cross the Steel Bridge to reach the **Eastbank Esplanade** heading south. Cross the river again at Hawthorne Bridge for a 3-mile total loop.

For a longer ride, before crossing the Hawthorne Bridge continue south to pass OMSI, ending up at the Ross Island Bridge, the start of the **Springwater Corridor** (www.portlandoregon.gov), a former rail line. It's now a bike trail that goes all the way to the town of Boring, though a short section is on streets around Umatilla Boulevard. The first major stop on the route is **Oaks Bottom Wildlife Refuge** (SE 7th Ave. and

Sellwood Blvd., www.portlandoregon. gov), a meadows and wetlands park on the river. Ride all the way to **Powell Butte State Park** (16160 SE Powell Blvd., www. portlandoregon.gov), an extinct cinder cone volcano with hiking trails, picnic areas, and restrooms. It's about 13 miles east of downtown via U.S. 26.

Really want to escape the cars? Within Forest Park, you're protected from everything gas-powered. **Leif Erikson Drive** (Thurman park entrance: NW Thurman St. and NW Aspen Ave.) is an 11-mile dirt trail with forest views and just a taste of mountain biking's hard work—some rocks, some climbs.

The city is bike friendly, but cars can still present danger, and light rail trains and streetcars can catch pedalers unaware. Riding on sidewalks isn't allowed in downtown Portland, and bikes must yield to pedestrians on walkways like the Eastbank Esplanade. Helmets are required for riders under 16 but are recommended for everyone. Bikes can go on buses or MAX trains, but never leave one unattended without locking it up first. Bike maps are available on the city's website (www.portlandoregon.gov).

Bike Rentals

To rent a bicycle in Tom McCall Waterfront Park, look next to the Salmon Street Springs fountain for **Kerr Bikes** (1020 SW Naito Pkwy., 503/808-9955, www.albertinakerr.org, 11am-5pm daily Mar., 11am-5pm Mon.-Fri. and 11am-7pm Sat.-Sun. Apr., 9am-7pm Mon.-Fri. and 8am-7pm Sat.-Sun. May-June, 8am-8pm Mon.-Fri. and 8am-9pm Sat.-Sun. Jul.-Aug., 9am-7pm daily Sept., 11am-5pm Sat.-Sun. Oct., 9am-5pm Wed.-Sun. Nov.-Feb., bikes $10-16 per hour, surreys $25-35 per hour). It has regular, tandem, and kids' bikes, plus car-like four-seater surreys, trailers, and scooters. The "U-Fix-It" station has tools, lifts, and pumps for repairs to any cycle. All proceeds from the rentals support the Albertina Kerr group, a local nonprofit that benefits people with mental development disabilities, and folks from the foundation often work the bike rental kiosk. It's a good starting place for a gentle pedal around the waterfront, so ask about maps to gentle routes that stick to bike paths.

The city's biggest bike rental shop is **Waterfront Bicycles** (10 SW Ash St., 503/227-1719, www.waterfrontbikes. com, 10am-6pm Mon.-Fri., 9am-6pm Sat.-Sun., rentals $9-15 per hour, $30-100 per day), located just across from Tom McCall Waterfront Park. It has more than 100 cycles in its rental fleet, including three-speed cruisers with wicker baskets and ultralight road bikes (men's and women's models). It also offers a number of children's accessories like trailers, bike extensions, and child seats. Reserve online more than two days before rental or call within 48 hours.

At **Everybody's Bike Rentals & Tours** (305 NE Wygant St., 503/358-0152, www. pdxbikerentals.com, 10am-5pm daily May-Oct.), the bikes ($8-15 per hour) are notably light and easy to move up curbs or into one of the city's many bike parking spots. There are even vintage road bikes and fixies available so you don't stick out in the cool bike crowds of Portland. Tours ($39-59) come with a free 24-hour rental, making them an ideal starting point for wannabe city cyclists.

Bike Tours

You can tour the city with **Cycle Portland Bike Tours** (117 NW 2nd Ave., 503/902-5035, www.portlandbicycletours. com, $39-49 including bike rental). An Essential Portland Tour hits up the Park Blocks, the Pearl District, and Waterfront Park in an easy two-hour pedal, so you needn't be a seasoned road warrior, just comfortable cruising slowly near cars. The Bike-O-Rama! takes a more creative look at the city, focusing on bike culture itself. The bike-enthusiast guides show off the varieties of bike lanes and greenways and then discuss the various non-car transportation options in the city. And, of course, there's a brewery tour by bike.

Pedal Bike Tours (133 SW 2nd Ave., 503/243-2453, www.pedalbiketours.com, $59-99) does offer downtown and brewery tours, but its more exciting options include a Lava Tour to Mount Tabor, an extinct volcano that's actually within the city limits. The 20-plus-mile route and hills require you to be at least an intermediate cyclist.

Spectator Sports
Basketball

When Seattle lost its NBA franchise in 2008, the Portland **Trail Blazers** (Moda Center, 1 N Center Court St., 503/797-9619, www.nba.com/blazers, $11-220) became the only professional basketball team in the Northwest. They play in the building once known as the Rose Garden—now the Moda Center—and games often sell out. Although the team hasn't appeared in the NBA finals in decades, it has a fervent following.

Hockey

It has no NHL team, but the city is home to the Portland **Winterhawks** (503/236-4295, www.winterhawks.com, $15-55), a junior league team in the Western Hockey League that plays teams from Seattle, Spokane, Victoria, and elsewhere in games that go August-May. They split their home games between the **Moda Center** (1 N Center Court St.) and **Veterans Memorial Coliseum** (www.rosequarter.com) directly next door.

Roller Derby

The **Rose City Rollers** (www.rosecityrollers.com, $16-22) is a female flat-track roller derby league in Portland, made up of skaters known by nicknames like Nacho Lucky Day and Scald Eagle. Teams compete with each other or visiting roller derby teams at bouts year-round held at **Memorial Stadium** (300 N. Winning Way) and The Hanger at **Oaks Amusement Park** (7805 SE Oaks Park Way).

Soccer

Although the Portland **Timbers** (Jeld-Wen Field, 1844 SW Morrison St., 503/553-5400, www.portlandtimbers.com) have only been a Major League Soccer team since 2011, the team is part of a soccer renaissance in the Pacific Northwest. There's a healthy rivalry with the Seattle Sounders FC and Vancouver Whitecaps FC (and if you ask a rabid fan, particularly with the former). The organized Timber Army cheering section, filled with fans in green-and-white scarves, is raucous. The season begins in March and ends in October, but pre-season matches can start in January.

Food

What is the quintessential Portland meal? It's not of a particular cuisine, but it's probably locally and sustainably sourced, and it might even be served from the side of a food truck or from a counter. One of the most popular joints in town is a Thai restaurant that re-creates the street food of Bangkok, while the longest lines are at Salt & Straw ice cream on a hot summer day. (Seriously, you'll wait forever.) Great food isn't necessarily expensive in Portland, even though pricey tasting menus and fine French fare do exist here.

Downtown
Seafood

It's not a typo—**Jake's Famous Crawfish** (401 SW 12th Ave., 503/226-1419, www.mccormickandschmicks.com, 11:30am-11pm Mon.-Thurs., 11:30am-midnight Fri.-Sat., 3pm-10pm Sun., $20-47) has been around "since 1892" serving cedar plank salmon and steaks. The fish on the menu hails from Alaska, Hawaii, Washington, and of course, British Columbia, though the lobster tails do come all the way from Maine. Not a lot of crawfish on the menu, but you'll find them in the étouffée. The desserts—cobblers, truffle cake, and the decadent "chocolate bag" full of mousse—are just as rich. The sign outside is old-fashioned neon, and inside is a classic dining room with wood accents and stained glass.

American

In a city devoted to quirk and vintage style, **Higgins Restaurant** (1239 SW Broadway, 503/222-9070, www.higginsportland.com, 11:30am-midnight Mon.-Fri., 4pm-midnight Sat.-Sun., $25-40) is a refreshingly straightforward restaurant painted in soothing neutral tones—no antlers on the wall, no taxidermy by the door. The country-style menu is farm fare gone high end: a summer vegetable sandwich with sheep's milk feta, or risotto with chanterelles and squash, or a "whole pig plate" that includes sausage, roast loin, belly, and ribs. It's a grown-up's dinner out.

The building that holds **Raven & Rose** (1331 SW Broadway, 503/222-7673, www.ravenandrosepdx.com, 11:30am-2pm and 5pm-10pm Mon.-Fri., 10am-2pm and 5pm-10pm Sat., 10am-2pm and 4pm-9pm Sun., $12-36) used to be the carriage house for the Ladd Estate that stood in the middle of today's downtown Portland, but at three stories and with ornate exterior decorations in the English Stick style, it hardly looks like the garage. The 1st floor's main restaurant has regular seating, a stately bar, and four seats right at the kitchen where you can see chefs prepare the flatbread, meatballs, and mussels in the wood oven. Meals are simple but rich: buttermilk-fried rabbit, salmon with succotash, and beef short ribs with mashed potatoes and Yorkshire pudding. Try the Caesar salad, served with pieces of rabbit. Upstairs in the Rookery is another bar in a giant loft with exposed wooden beams, leather seating, and a pool table, which serves small bites from the kitchen.

Lines form to fill the metal chairs and reclaimed wood benches at ★ **Tasty N Alder** (580 SW 12th Ave., 503/621-9251, www.tastynalder.com, 9am-10pm Sun.-Thurs., 9am-11pm Fri.-Sat., $14-35) before it even opens for brunch (which it serves daily). Entrées include Korean fried chicken with house kimchi and Indonesian short rib, drawing from exotic influences but giving them a decidedly Portland, homegrown spin. Fries are fried in *washimi wagyu* beef tallow, and the burger comes with a hazelnut *romesco*. Decorations, besides the rustic light fixtures, are few, but the service is prompt.

Clyde Common (1014 SW Stark St., 503/228-3333, www.clydecommon. com, 3pm-12:45am daily, $14-29) is located right next to the lobby of the Ace Hotel, and it shares some of that joint's indie, hip feel. Decorated in rough-hewn wood and canvas, it nevertheless has an upscale, not outdoorsy feel. The liquor menu is mostly whiskeys and bourbon—what more do you need?—plus a little absinthe. Try snacks like truffle popcorn or roasted beets, or attack a full meal of ravioli or steak. But do speak up, as the din inside the busy joint fills with Ace guests, locals, and other very loud, very chatty young folks.

The green-sounding **Urban Farmer** (525 SW Morrison St., 8th Floor, 503/222-4900, www.urbanfarmerportland.com, 6:30am-3pm and 5pm-10pm Sun.-Thurs., 6:30am-3pm and 5pm-11pm Fri.-Sat., $29-80) is actually an "urban steakhouse" specializing in farmhouse fare like brioche French toast and duck breast. And then, of course, there's the steak, broken down by cut and origin, and each selection notes how the cows were fed: on Oregon grass for the 14-ounce rib eye, or on corn in California for the 14-ounce New York. The creamy spinach gratin makes the best pair for steak. The wine list has 350 bottles (many of them local), beers come from within Portland, and cocktails are made from Oregon spirits, plus the weekend brunch has a Bloody Mary bar. It's located in the Nines Hotel, on the 8th floor of a downtown building, in what feels like an outdoor patio that's actually surrounded by floors of hotel room windows.

If you miss mom's cooking while on the road, **Mother's Bistro** (212 SW Stark St., 503/464-1122, www.mothersbistro. com, 7am-9pm Tues.-Thurs., 7am-10pm Fri., 8am-10pm Sat., 8am-2:30pm Sun., $11-20) just makes sense—it serves traditional dishes you'd find at home, provided your home supper consisted of pork loin medallions with beer and caramelized onions or steak *frites*. Every month the restaurant features a different mother and her favorite dishes, done in her style. The Mother of the Month menus are often seasonal and hail from around the globe, and diners nominate favorite

Food Cart Revolution

some of Portland's many food carts

Almost every city has some kind of street food—hot dog stands, halal carts, ice cream trucks. But Portland takes it to another level, with more than 500 food carts around the city. Many are grouped in pods, which can have anywhere from three to dozens of different options. How do you know what's good? You wander, you look—and you just try something, since most food options are under $7.

The biggest food cart pod is the block between **SW 9th and SW 10th Avenues, and SW Alder and SW Washington Streets.** More than 60 food purveyors park here, making it the biggest single concentration of street food vendors in the country. Office workers fill the square at lunchtime, and while some carts open on weekends, not all will. If you don't want to eat while walk-

ing, head across the street to **O'Bryant Square** (SW Park Ave. and Washington St., www.portlandoregon.gov/parks). The brick half acre is not the lushest of city parks, but there are ledges to sit on while you wolf down a panini or bowl of pho. Another pod, at SW 3rd Avenue between SW Washington and Stark Streets, is close to Tom McCall Waterfront Park.

A **website** (www.foodcartsportland. com) lists the location of carts and pods, along with a link to a phone app that maps the locations. The host of the website leads 90-minute **tours** (www.foodcartsportland.com, tours@ foodcartsportland.com, $50, children under 12 free) Monday-Saturday around lunchtime, giving visitors a history of the food cart movement and tastes from a few carts.

moms on the restaurant's website. The space, too, is probably a little fancier than what you get at home—chandeliers hang over a bright, airy space on one side, and exposed brick walls face the bar on the Velvet Lounge side. There' a small play area for children—doesn't every home kitchen have one?

All the deli classics are at **Kenny and Zuke's Delicatessen** (1038 SW Stark St.,

503/222-3354, www.kennyandzukes.com, 7am-8pm Mon.-Thurs., 7am-9pm Fri., 8am-9pm Sat., 8am-8pm Sun., $11-18)— pastrami, chopped liver, cheese blintzes, and big Reuben sandwiches. The owner's pastrami, sold at a farmers market, was so popular he eventually opened a whole collection of Kenny and Zuke's spots around the city. Here all-day breakfast is served in the big corner space. Sit down to read the blackboards, or take an order at the counter to go, grabbing a bagel with a schmear for the road.

Coffee

Stumptown Coffee Roasters (128 SW 3rd Ave., 503/295-6144, www.stumptown-coffee.com, 6am-7pm Mon.-Fri., 7am-7pm Sat.-Sun.) used to be a small coffee roaster on Division Street when it opened in 1999, named for the logging industry. Founder Duane Sorenson delivered coffee to wholesale customers out of his own Ford Pinto. The company supported sustainable growth and trade practices—Sorenson became known for paying the highest per-pound price ever for beans in some Latin American countries. Eventually it became popular enough to open outposts around Portland, and then in cities like Seattle and New York, and in California. In 2015 the company was sold to the Peet's coffee chain, leading to some disappointment among those who liked the independent backstory. The 3rd Avenue space was the first Stumptown in the downtown area and epitomizes the chain's rustic aesthetic with exposed brick walls and wood counters, plus taps for their cold brew. Sit at the wall of magazines and stools where you can watch the baristas work.

Unlike the very hip Stumptown, **Case Study Coffee** (802 SW 10th Ave., 503/475-3979, www.casestudycoffee.com, 7am-6pm Mon.-Fri., 8am-6pm Sat.-Sun.) is more about the café vibe, with just two locations in the city and only this one in the downtown core. The wood coffee bar sits under a retro-futuristic light fixture, but everything else is sleek. It has all the chai lattes and cappuccinos and ice-brewed varieties we've come to expect from coffee shops, but a mug of house coffee starts at just $2.50. Food is just pastries, bagels, and granola.

The small **Courier Coffee Roasters** (923 SW Oak, 503/545-6444, www.couriercoffeeroasters.com, 7am-6pm Mon.-Fri., 9am-5pm Sat.-Sun.) is a small

shop that is everything Starbucks isn't—local, friendly, and unusual. Drinks are served in mason jars, and labels are hand stamped. You'll want to chat with the barista before you choose from the beans on hand. Coffee is made using reusable filters that are plated with 23-karat gold. Pastries and homemade granola bars are all made from locally sourced ingredients.

Dessert

It's a good thing ★ **Voodoo Doughnut** (22 SW 3rd Ave., 503/241-4704, www.voodoodoughnut.com, 24 hours daily, $1-4) never closes, because people are always looking for its signature weird doughnuts—maple bars with a strip of bacon on top, or treats topped with breakfast cereal or M&Ms. If you're looking for more than a sugar rush, order a wedding—they start at $35 for a nonlegal vow renewal ceremony (with no free treats) and go up to $325 for a legal ceremony and doughnuts for six people. Look for a brick building and a line outside. Cash only.

French

As the little sister restaurant to the fancier Le Pigeon, **Little Bird** (219 SW 6th Ave., 503/688-5952, www.littlebirdbistro.com, 11:30am-midnight Mon.-Fri., 5pm-midnight Sat.-Sun., $13-45) is allowed to be a little looser, so antlers hang on the walls across from deep red banquettes. Lunch includes casual French munchies like an oyster po'boy and *moules-frites,* and drinks come in half sizes—can you stop at just a half martini? Dinner features cassoulet of duck leg, pork belly, and sausage, and a chicken-fried trout, plus the burger off the Le Pigeon menu.

Pearl District and Northwest
Pacific Northwest

Paley's Place (1204 NW 21st Ave., 503/243-2403, www.paleysplace.net, 5:30pm-10pm Mon.-Thurs., 5pm-11pm Fri.-Sat., 5pm-10pm Sun., $15-30) doesn't look much like a restaurant at first glance, hidden behind trees in a Victorian building with a long porch. The chef has garnered attention from everyone from the James Beard Foundation to *Bon Appétit*, but the restaurant is still a sedate 50-seater that focuses on Pacific Northwest ingredients like wild salmon, potatoes, halibut, and mushrooms. The restaurant will serve half portions of main entrées so that tables can enjoy a greater selection of the menu.

American

Ready to experience the entire menu at **Little Big Burger** (122 NW 10th Ave., 503/274-9008, www.littlebigburger.com, 11am-10pm daily, $4.75)? It's cheeseburgers, hamburgers, veggie burgers, fries, sodas, and floats. That's it—so let's hope you were craving something on a bun. The burgers are a quarter pound and served on a brioche bun, a tiny, vertical mound that looks something like an overgrown slider (but not quite a grown-up burger). Fries are served with white truffle oil, a flavor some people love but others could do without, so make sure you know your position before you indulge. Fry sauce and ketchup are homemade, and floats are a combination of Tillamook ice cream and root beer.

Aslan

Though the spot was once an upscale Vietnamese restaurant named Silk, it was rebranded and reopened as **Pho Van Fresh** (1012 NW Glisan St., 503/248-2172, www. phovanfresh.com, 11am-10pm Mon.-Sat., $6-13); there are still a few old Silk favorites like the hoisin ribs on the menu. Like its predecessor, the new fast-casual eatery aims for authenticity, but leans heavily toward crowd favorites like fried Brussels sprouts and pork belly steamed buns—the banh mi are also popular. Pho, a Vietnamese rice noodle soup with vegetables, beef, or chicken, is the centerpiece, and the bar serves cocktails inspired by Asian flavors. Pho Van's original location is in southeast Portland, but this more central outpost pairs more easily with a day of downtown exploration.

Dessert

The ice cream empire of **Salt & Straw** (838 NW 23rd Ave., 971/271-8168, www. saltandstraw.com, 11am-11pm daily, $3.75-6.50) started as an ice cream pushcart, but since the owner had begun her career working at Fortune 500 businesses, it was no surprise that it quickly grew to a string of stores in Portland, San Francisco, and Seattle. Flavors combine the savory and sweet—the strawberry has balsamic vinegar in it, and the coffee flavor comes with bourbon. Try the pear with blue cheese or the sea salt ice cream with caramel ribbon for the classic flavor profile, or try a special flavor, developed with seasonal ingredients, sometimes by local chefs. There are sundaes and floats, but the scoops themselves are plenty complex; even if you're just getting chocolate, you can top your cone with finishing salt for an extra $0.50.

European

Olympia Provisions (1632 NW Thurman St., 503/894-8136, www.olympiaprovisions.com, 11am-10pm Mon.-Fri., 9am-10pm Sat.-Sun., $22-34) started as a meat maker, curing salami and winning awards for its European-style chorizo, *soppressata,* and other varieties. Now it has two restaurants whose menus go far beyond meat, with roasted veggies, crispy salmon, and gnocchi (don't worry—plenty of meat comes with the plate of bratwurst, kielbasa, and ham, and there's an entire charcuterie menu). The smaller, original location sits across the river, but this sunny space has more seating and lots of light, and the chef did a stint at Bouchon with Thomas Keller.

Peruvian

The multilevel **Andina** (1314 NW Glisan St., 503/228-9535, www.andinarestaurant.com, 11:30am-2:30pm and 4pm-9:30pm Sun.-Fri., 11:30am-2:30pm and

5pm-10:30pm. Sat., $21-40) feels smaller than it is once you sit down, more like a neighborhood tapas bar than the bustling warehouse restaurant it is. The Peruvian fare includes tapas and "novo-Andean" main courses like diver scallops, a quinoa dish that resembles risotto, slow-cooked lamb shank, and pork loin. Vegetarian, vegan, and gluten-free menus are also served. The bar has Latin-inspired live music performances, including a jazz trio, gypsy swing, and guitar-playing singer-songwriters.

Southeast
Pacific Northwest

The very modern, upscale ★ **Castagna** (1752 SE Hawthorne Blvd., 503/231-7373, www.castagnarestaurant.com, 5:30pm-10pm Wed.-Sat., $100-165) makes Pacific Northwest food artful and exciting. Menus are prix fixe, either a standard dinner of appetizer, salad, entrée, and dessert, or a chef's tasting menu of nine small courses—plan on several hours, as many as four, for that option. Wine pairings are extra. The chef, Justin Woodward, won the Rising Star Chef prize from the James Beard Foundation and is known for presenting his food with artistic and elaborate care. It is as fine a dining experience as you can find in town. Reservations are recommended, though the related ★ **Café Castagna** (503/231-9959, 5pm-10pm Tues.-Thurs., 5pm-11pm Fri.-Sat., 5pm-9:30pm Sun., $12-30) next door is more likely to handle walk-ins, and is overseen by the same star chef.

American

Stumptown founder Duane Sorenson turned to food and hard drink for **The Woodsman Tavern** (4537 SE Division St., 971/373-8264, www.woodsmantavern. com, 5pm-10pm Mon.-Fri., 9am-10pm Sat.-Sun, $16-60), a restaurant-bar on a quiet stretch of Division. Although meant to pay tribute to the logging industry, the space is more defined by its oysters on ice

and retro light fixtures than the woodsy landscape paintings crowding the walls. Main courses are heavy on the meat—pork shoulder, meatloaf sandwich—though starters are smaller and lighter. Fried chicken comes in a bucket with honey, and a special Oyster Hour is 5pm-6pm. The bar has 14 beers on taps and cocktails that seem high end, even when they're not—like the $7 Pickleback (Irish whiskey with a dram of pickle juice).

The **Roman Candle Baking Company** (3377 SE Division St., 971/302-6605, www.romancandlebaking.com, 7am-4pm daily) bakery smells faintly of flour, thanks to the pastries and breads ($4-9) cooked here. The space used to be a coffee processing site for Stumptown Coffee and has white tile walls and exposed wood beams. For a full meal turn to the pizza Bianca ($4-6 per slice, $28-44 per slab), a flatbread pizza made in a wood-fired oven and topped with locally sourced veggies and meats. Drinks include Italian sodas, wines, and coffee made in an elaborate espresso machine made of glass and copper tubes.

The small **Lauretta Jean's** (3402 SE Division St., 503/235-3119, www.laurettajean.com, 8am-10pm Sun.-Thurs., 8am-11pm Fri.-Sat., $7-11) serves pies and parfaits, plus craft cocktails in a sweet shop with pastel walls and small tables. Pies are shown off at the big glass case under the counter, but the menu has egg scrambles, biscuit sandwiches, and quiches in the morning and sandwiches and salads for lunch and dinner.

The treats at **The Waffle Window** (3610 SE Hawthorne Blvd., 971/255-0501, www. wafflewindow.com, 8am-6pm Sun.-Thurs., 8am-9pm Fri.-Sat., $3-8) aren't exactly breakfast or lunch on their own, which may only prompt you to rejoin the line after eating so that you can order again. It is indeed a window, located on the side of the Bread and Ink Café (with indoor seating there), and a covered outdoor seating area is right around the corner. The Liege sugar waffles are covered in sugar, dipped in dark chocolate, or topped with savory combos like mushroom and spinach or bacon and brie. For the spicy fans, the spicy bacon cheddar jalapeño waffle, topped with avocado-tomatillo salsa, is heavenly.

Asian

The chef behind Thai outpost ★ **Pok Pok** (3226 SE Division St., 503/232-1387, www.pokpokpdx.com, 11:30am-10pm daily, $11-19) is so well regarded, he won a James Beard award and opened three related branches in Portland and three in New York City. The original location has covered outdoor seating with colored lights, plus an upstairs dining room. The Southeast Asian food is meant to reflect the street and home cooking of Thailand, and many dishes are meant to be shared. It's not the pad Thai you may be used to; instead you'll find marinated baby back ribs, Chiang Mai sausage, and wild-caught prawns cooked with pork belly. Besides an extensive whiskey list and cocktail menu (including a Korean yuzu-honey hot toddy), there are non-alcoholic drinking vinegars, which are seasonal flavors mixed with soda water. Even the table water has flavor, that of the pandanus leaf. Reservations are only taken for groups larger than five, but if the wait is long, you can sneak in a drink at the related **Whiskey Soda Lounge** (3131 SE Division St., 503/232-0102, www.whiskeysodalounge.com, 4pm-midnight Sun.-Thurs., 4pm-1am Fri.-Sat.) across the street.

French

The French **Le Pigeon** (738 E Burnside St., 503/546-8796, www.lepigeon.com, 5pm-10pm daily, $24-35) has a short but impeccable menu, served as a five-course chef's tasting menu for $85. Starters include the likes of foie gras, glazed eel, and clam flatbread, with entrées of beef cheek bourguignon and rabbit blanquette. The unassuming small restaurant has bright white curtains and exposed brick walls

for an intimate farmhouse feel, and some tables are communal.

Italian

Although **Apizza Scholls** (4741 SE Hawthorne Blvd., 503/233-1286, www.apizzascholls.com, 5pm-9:30pm Mon.-Fri., 11:30am-2:30pm and 5pm-9:30pm Sat.-Sun., $19-26) serves pizza, don't think of it as a greasy pizza joint. Pies are made from dough that's handmade each day, which keeps the small restaurant from opening for lunch—when they run out of dough, they're done for the day. There's often a line, and servers ask how many pizzas you'll order when they add your name to the waiting list, but drinks, salads, and seating are available to patrons waiting for a table. The pizzas themselves have a ciabatta-like crust, so delicate the kitchen limits toppings to three per pie, and no more than two meats. House combinations include a margherita with anchovies or cured pork shoulder, cheese with truffle oil and sea salt, and a cheesy, sauceless concoction with house-cured bacon.

The charming ★ **Ava Gene's** (3377 SE Division St, 971/229-0571, avagenes.com, 5pm-10pm Mon-Thurs., 5pm-11pm Fri., 4:30pm-11pm Sat., 4:30pm-10pm Sun., $19-36) quickly gained a reputation as one of Portland's best restaurants. Its produce-minded Roman menu is served in a rather casual setting, and handmade pastas and mouthwatering vegetable dishes are the highlight. One of the restaurant's local purveyors is usually highlighted on each day's menu. Family-style dining is available if the whole table buys in ($75 pp). Pay attention to what the waitstaff highlights as the day's specials, since the seasonal nature of the menu means there are always surprises.

Mexican

Taco joint ★ **Por Que No?** (4635 SE Hawthorne Blvd., 503/954-3138, www.porquenotacos.com, 11am-10pm Mon.-Sat., 11am-9:30pm Sun., $5-13) is a prime example of the kind of eatery taking Portland by storm—you order at the counter, pay for your food and drinks, then find a table and wait for your food. But the Mexican restaurant is not merely fast-casual; the red-walled space is crammed with old paintings and funky decor, and meals are served with real silverware and in solid bowls and baskets. The tacos are made with house-made corn tortillas, and it's hard to pick one variety, or even three, but the *al pastor,* carnitas, and *pollo asada* are among the best. That and the line-caught cod *pescado* tacos are, or maybe the calamari ones. Bigger plates have tamales and salads, and you can start with flautas or fresh guacamole and house-made chips. Margaritas come in classic and pomegranate flavors.

Middle Eastern

The inside of beloved ★ **Tusk** (2448 E Burnside St., 503/894-8082, tuskpdx.com, 5pm-10pm Mon.-Wed., 5pm-midnight Thurs.-Fri., 10am-2pm and 5pm-midnight Sat., 10am-2pm and 5pm-10pm Sun., $15-40) is bright white, though the dishes themselves are filled with the colors of Middle Eastern cuisine and local produce. A new favorite regularly hailed as the best dinner in Portland, it's run by the same team behind Ava Gene's, and the two restaurants share an "aggressively seasonal" philosophy. Get several meat skewers or a big pork chop with veggies on the side, or simply sign up for the $50-per-plate chef's menu, called a "magic carpet ride."

Northeast/North
American

Almost all the produce served at **Navarre** (10 NE 28th Ave., 503/232-3555, http://navarreportland.blogspot.com, 4:30pm-10:30pm Mon.-Thurs., 4:30pm-11:30pm Fri., 9:30am-11:30pm Sat., 9:30am-10:30pm Sun., $23-35) is local—and when they say local, they mean fruits and vegetables grown within Portland's

Por Que No?

city limits. The wine list is crammed with Oregon vintages. For all the local sourcing, however, the menu has European inspirations, and they serve an excellent breakfast in the narrow space.

The **Laurelhurst Market** (3155 E Burnside St., 503/206-3097, www.laurelhurstmarket.com, 10am-10pm daily, $14-39) is a neighborhood brasserie, crowded with tables and serving a huge variety of steaks, salads, and sides. But it's also a butcher shop that sells hormone- and antibiotic-free meats and house-made sausages. Even if you're not looking to get your ham hocks to go, it's nice to know that your restaurant's kitchen has the very best cuts. The large modern space is a destination for meat eaters—salads and sides are on the menu, but nearly everything green is cooked with or topped with bacon.

At **Pine State Biscuits** (2204 NE Alberta St., 503/477-6605, www.pinestatebiscuits.com, 7am-3pm daily, $4-8), what started as a modest farmers market stand is now a sizable counter-service restaurant devoted to the biscuit. The buttermilk concoctions are served with sausage or mushroom gravy, and as any kind of sandwich you could want—fried chicken, steak club, pulled pork, or with egg. A few other Southern touches, like blueberry cornmeal pancakes and grits, round out the menu. Iron stools line a counter next to the open kitchen, and lights above look like mason jars, completing the homey look.

★ **Gravy** (3957 N Mississippi Ave., 503/287-8800, www.gravyrestaurant.com, 7:30am-3pm daily, $8-13) is so popular the lines get intense. Portions are massive, with hash made from corned beef, roast beef, and smoked salmon, and a Monte Cristo sandwich made on French toast. The hash browns are cooked into thick, crispy disks. Good luck finding the biscuit itself in the sea of sausage gravy. Grab coffee while you wait and expect to leave with a to-go box.

Asian

Getting into the delicious **Han Oak** (511 NE 24th Ave., http://hanoakpdx.com, 5:30pm-9pm Fri.-Sat., 5pm-10pm Sun.-Mon., $10-19) is a trial, but the lucky few can score reservations to the Friday and Saturday night prix fixe ($45), which is the primary way of dining here, full of whipped tofu, noodles, and pork belly—or maybe fried chicken or barbecue—from the Korean jewel. Leave time to find it; it's tucked into a courtyard like a secret hideaway. On Sundays and Mondays it serves dumplings a la carte, but the weekend dinners often change at the whim of the chef and owner.

Indian

The counter-service, bustling **Bollywood Theater** (2039 NE Alberta St., 971/200-4711, www.bollywoodtheaterpdx.com, 11am-10pm daily, $5-19) is Indian food inspired by Bombay street stands, right down to the steel cups and steel plates. It's so popular the line is usually out the

door (though it moves quickly, as do most of the hip new restaurants of this type in Portland). The menu has samosas and curry *thali* meals similar to what you'd find in other Indian takeout joints, while the Goan-style shrimp has curry leaves and chiles, and the *kati* rolls are like Indian burritos, with chicken, cheese, or beef wrapped in Indian flatbread with green chutney. Drinks include local beers, Indian beer on tap, and a Pimm's Cup cocktail.

Southern

Screen Door (2337 E Burnside St., 503/542-0880, www.screendoorrestaurant.com, 8am-2pm and 5:30pm-10pm Mon.-Fri., 9am-2:30pm and 5:30pm-10pm Sat., 9am-2:30pm and 5:30pm-9pm Sun., $12-18) serves cuisine inspired by the South, specifically the soul food traditions of the South Carolina Lowcountry, along with the Creole cuisine of New Orleans. Hushpuppies come with a pepper jelly dipping sauce, and fried okra plus mouthwatering buttermilk-fried chicken are also on the menu. The vegetarian sides include grits and sweet potato fries, but the collard greens? They're definitely not vegetarian—they're cooked with bacon and ham hocks. The restaurant is as casual as you'd expect from a place that serves pulled pork sandwiches, with boards on the walls and bright blue booths.

Accommodations

Most hotels in Portland try to show off some kind of character—a rock-and-roll aesthetic, or a fine-arts look complete with artwork in every room. Some cheaper hotels offer shared-bath accommodations, but they're not dingy rooming houses with crowded locker rooms—most patrons barely notice that their single-occupant bathroom is across the hall instead of across the room. Because parking is limited in the downtown core, most hotels charge steep prices for valet parking.

Downtown
Under $150

In case you forget what **Ace Hotel** (1022 SW Stark St., 503/228-2277, www.ace-hotel.com/portland, $125-195 shared bath, $175-345 private bath) is, giant distressed metal letters spell out HOTEL in the wood-paneled lobby. There's a cooler-than-thou vibe to the place, with record players in each room and handmade bikes available to rent. Low beds in white-walled rooms are covered with special wool Pendleton blankets that you'll be tempted to steal (but don't, they're for sale online). Some rooms share single hallway baths, while others have their own shower or claw-foot tub; all have TVs.

$150-250

The somewhat trippy ★ **Crystal Hotel** (303 SW 12th Ave., 503/972-2670, www.mcmenamins.com/crystalhotel, $155 shared bath, $215-235 private bath), part of the McMenamins empire, has mural-painted headboards on each bed, walls in dark colors, and thick black curtains—and each room is named for a band or performance from the live music venue Crystal Ballroom across the street, like songs by James Brown and the Flaming Lips. The 1911 building was once called the Majestic Hotel, which housed a rowdy gambling and drinking establishment, then a nightclub. Hall bathrooms are plentiful, so the European-style shared-bath rooms are a good bargain. There are reserved tickets for whatever's playing at the Crystal Ballroom; call ahead to score some for the night of your stay. Downstairs in a low-ceilinged room with bamboo walls is a soaking pool shaped like a big amoeba.

The artsy ★ **Hotel Lucia** (400 SW Broadway, 503/225-1717, www.hotellucia.com, $199-369) has a long, modern lobby with sculptures and framed photography on the walls; the hotel owns the world's largest collection of works by Pulitzer Prize-winning photographer David Hume Kennerly (he's also a Portland local). Rooms are generally modest but decorated in somber dark mahogany and black oak, and beds have pillow-top mattresses and come with a pillow menu. The location on Broadway is central but still fairly quiet. Attached to the hotel are two food spots: The upscale **Imperial** (410 SW Broadway, 503/228-7222, www.imperialpdx.com, 6:30am-2pm Mon.-Wed., 6:30am-2pm and 5pm-10pm Thurs., 6:30am-2pm and 5pm-11pm Fri., 8am-2pm and 5pm-11pm Sat., 8am-2pm and 5pm-10pm Sun.) has a large wood-fired grill and serves rib eyes, pork chops, and chanterelles cooked with bone marrow.

Over $250
Enter **The Benson** (309 SW Broadway, 503/228-2000, www.coasthotels.com, $198-450), and you'll be greeted by tall wooden pillars and a classic, marble-floored hotel lobby, so it's easy to see the century-old roots in the hotel. Rooms feature deluxe striped curtains and plush linens and bathrobes, and it's not unusual to see personal touches from the staff, like towels folded into the shapes of animals. The **Palm Court** (6:30am-close daily) in the lobby has live jazz music for much of the week and serves breakfast, lunch, and dinner and hosts two daily happy hours. Next door, **El Gaucho** (319 Broadway, 503/227-8794, 4:30pm-1am Mon.-Sat., 4pm-11pm Sun.) is an old-world steakhouse with a cigar room.

Hotel Rose (50 SW Morrison St., 866/866-7977, www.hotelroseportland.com, $179-389) has a mid-20th-century feel in the lobby, but purely modern rooms with large showers and memory-foam mattresses. Free bicycle rentals and gold umbrellas are also available. Its location on the east side of downtown, near the river, yields waterfront and cityscape views. The eatery downstairs, **Bottle + Kitchen** (503/484-1415, www.bottlekitchen.com, 6:30am-midnight Sun.-Thurs., 7am-noon Fri.-Sat.), features a New Zealand chef cooking globally inspired food with a local ethos.

The charming **Mark Spencer** (409 SW 11th Ave., 503/224-3293, www.markspencer.com, $289-329) is just a block away from the hipper Ace but has a more traditional vibe. The stately old building has rooms with exposed brick walls, and larger suites have fully equipped kitchens for longer stays. The overall vibe is not one of extravagance, but rooms are simple and comfortable. Swing by the lobby for free afternoon tea and cookies, then evening wine and cheese. Hybrid cars can park for half price. You can even bid for a room at a lower price online; enter your credit card information and propose a rate for a room, then wait for a response. If it's accepted, the card will be charged and the reservation is nonrefundable. Bid too low or for a booked night and you'll receive alternate suggestions.

The **Hotel Modera** (515 SW Clay St., 503/484-1084, www.hotelmodera.com, $279-319) claims to have more than 500 pieces of local art on its walls, and that's not counting the hotel itself, with its white mod lobby chairs and open fireplaces in the Nel Centro restaurant. Although billed as a boutique hotel, it has almost 175 rooms, all with Italian marble in the bathrooms and bath products made from Italian olive oils. Like most city hotels it doesn't have a swimming pool, but guests get free passes to the gym a block away. The **Nel Centro** (1408 SW 6th Ave., 503/484-1099, www.nelcentro.com, 6:30am-10:30am, 11:30am-2pm, and 5pm-9pm Mon.-Thurs., 6:30am-10:30am, 11:30am-2pm, and 5pm-10pm Fri., 7:30am-11:30am and 5pm-10pm Sat., 8am-2pm and 5pm-9pm Sun.) restaurant serves a menu inspired by the French and Italian Riviera, and has a large outdoor patio.

Walk into the **Sentinel Hotel** (614 SW 11th Ave., 503/224-3400, www.sentinelhotel.com, $209-429) and then look up—the hotel was built in 1909, and the intricate designs and glasswork on the ceiling are beautiful. Outside, art deco ornamentations adorn the building's exterior (though some think they look like robots). Rooms are done in calming neutrals with a few classic touches, like fireplaces and wood wardrobes, but mostly have modern amenities. Off the lobby, **Jake's Grill** (611 SW 10th Ave., 503/220-1850, www.mccormickandschmicks.com, 7am-11pm Mon.-Thurs., 7am-midnight Fri., 7:30am-midnight Sat., 7:30am-11pm Sun.) has basic grill fare and a bar, plus a giant mural that traces the history of the Lewis and Clark expedition. Lobby bar **Jackknife** (3pm-2am daily) serves champagne with a straw and a small menu of salads and sandwiches.

The name of the **Hotel deLuxe** (729 SW 15th Ave., 503/219-2094, www.hoteldeluxeportland.com, $189-359) isn't just about the fine amenities—though rooms are very nice—but rather the Hollywood color lab Deluxe, which is why the rooms and hallways feature black-and-white classic movie images. In the room are a number of menus—a pillow menu, a spiritual book menu, an iPod menu (borrow one with music from a particular genre), and even a pet spiritual menu, full of books on pet massage and psychology. The Pop-Up Cinema series screens classic films in a private screening room with historical touches and only 36 seats. Restaurants include the sedate **Gracie's** (503/222-2171, 6:30am-2pm and 5pm-9pm Mon.-Thurs., 6:30am-2pm and 5pm-10pm Fri., 8am-2pm and 5pm-10pm Sat., 8am-2pm and 5pm-9pm Sun.) and the hip **Driftwood Room** (503/820-2076, 2pm-11:30pm Sun.-Thurs., 2pm-12:30am Fri., noon-12:30am Sat.), which recalls a cocktail bar in the 1950s. For all the black-and-white glamour, rooms are bright and modern.

The stately **Hotel Vintage Plaza** (422 SW Broadway, 503/228-1212, www.vintageplaza.com, $166-401) is a solid combination of boutique property and chain hotel. Rooms are decorated in upscale linens and furniture with plush animal-print robes, but there's a personal touch with yoga mats in the rooms and daily wine hours in the lobby. Parking is $37 for valet service, but hybrid cars get 50 percent off. The Italian **Pazzo Ristorante** (627 SW Washington, 503/228-1515, www.pazzo.com, 7am-10:30am, 11:30am-2:30pm, and 5pm-9:30pm Mon.-Thurs., 7am-10:30am, 11:30am-2:30pm, and 5pm-10pm Fri., 8am-2pm and 5pm-10pm Sat., 8am-2pm and 5pm-9pm Sun.) is attached to the hotel.

Outside the ★ **Heathman Hotel** (1001 SW Broadway, 503/241-4100, http://portland.heathmanhotel.com, $170-408), the bellhop can't be missed—he is dressed in an elaborate orange getup that wouldn't look out of place on a Vatican guard. The boutique hotel is resolutely memorable, including a lending library with a catalog and more than 2,000 books, some first editions. Beds feature tentacle headboards that look either like the rising sun or a giant octopus, depending on your point of view, and you can select a bed type: featherbed, pillow top, or Tempur-Pedic. Signature suites are decorated in arts, literature, or symphony motifs, and a portion of the hotel's revenue goes to support a Portland arts organization.

The chic **Hotel Monaco** (506 SW Washington St., 503/222-0001, www.monaco-portland.com, $151-405) is almost aggressively hip—the walls are everything from dark red to wallpapered in whimsical bird patterns, and you can get a pet goldfish to stay in your room while you're there. (You even get to name him or her.) There are free loaner bicycles and a wine and microbrew hour every day at 5pm with free drinks. Most rooms have city views, and the hotel location is convenient for downtown dining and shopping. The in-house restaurant, the **Red Star Tavern** (503 SW Alder St., 503/222-0005, 6:30am-11am, 11:30am-2pm, and 5pm-10pm Mon.-Fri., 8am-2pm and 5pm-10pm Sat., 8am-2pm and 5pm-9pm

Sun.) serves casual American cuisine and has a long whiskey and bourbon list.

Nearly every room at the **RiverPlace Hotel** (1510 SW Harbor Way, 503/228-3233, www.riverplacehotel.com, $175-421) has a spectacular city, waterfront, or park view. Rooms are on the luxury end, with soft beds and softer bathrobes; even the smallest single rooms are sizable. Free bicycles are available in the lobby, and yoga mats are included in every room. Valet tickets include a free drink at the downstairs **Three Degrees Waterfront Bar and Grill** (503/295-6166, www.three-degreesportland.com, 7am-10:30am, 11:30am-2pm, and 5pm-9pm Mon.-Fri., 8am-2pm and 5pm-9pm Sat.-Sun.).

The rooms at **The Nines** (525 SW Morrison St., 877/229-9995, www.thenines.com, $373-411) start on, yes, the 9th floor of a downtown building that was once the headquarters of department store Meier & Frank. Striking art pieces mark the way from the elevator to the front desk. Rooms are decked with velvet couches, marble vanities, and rainforest showers—but they don't come cheap. The cozy library features billiards and a giant antler chandelier. Dining options include **Urban Farmer** (503/222-4900, www.urbanfarmerportland.com, 6:30am-3pm and 5pm-10pm Sun.-Thurs., 6:30am-3pm and 5pm-11pm Fri.-Sat.), a high-end steakhouse, while **Departure**'s (503/802-5370, http://departureportland.com, 4pm-midnight Sun.-Thurs., 4pm-1am Fri.-Sat.) Asian fusion menu and extensive sake offerings are served on two outdoor decks.

Pearl District and Northwest
Under $150

The **Northwest Portland Hostel** (425 NW 18th Ave., 503/241-2783, www.nwportlandhostel.com, $25-39 dorms, $69-88 private rooms without bathrooms) is actually four buildings with traditional hostel rooms and guesthouse rooms that more closely resemble a bed-and-breakfast. The Victorian main building is listed on the National Register of Historic Places and has both types of rooms, and smaller houses next door have more guesthouse rooms. The property boasts no curfew, free Wi-Fi, bike rentals, and an outdoor garden with a grill for guest use. The residential block is only a few blocks from the Pearl District, and the shopping and dining streets of Nob Hill are in the other direction.

Over $250

The **Inn at Northrup Station** (2025 NW Northrup St., 503/224-0543, www.northrupstation.com, $309-339) looks more like a condo development than a hotel from the outside with its balconies and palm-tree landscaping. The colors inside are brighter than a Miami dance party, with walls painted yellow and bedspreads a bright orange. An outdoor patio has the same tangerine and lime colors represented in the patio furniture. All rooms are suites with kitchens and dishwashers, some with ranges and full-size fridges. The sofas fold out to beds, adding more room in the sizable suites. The area is somewhat residential but close to a streetcar line and within walking distance of Northwest District restaurants and the Pearl District.

Southeast
Under $150

The **Hawthorne Portland Hostel** (3031 SE Hawthorne Blvd., 503/236-3380, www.portlandhostel.org, $28-37 dorms, $66-74 private rooms) has a calmer vibe than downtown hostels and is located in a 1909 house with a funky gazebo out front. There's a full kitchen, a few private rooms, and several dorm rooms. Meals on Sundays are potlucks for guests, and the hostel organizes pub crawls, travel talks, and garden work parties. Bikes are available to rent, and cyclists who ride their bikes into town get a $5 discount every night.

The charming **Bluebird Guesthouse** (3517 SE Division St., 503/238-4333,

Day Trip to Multnomah Falls

Though the entire Pacific Northwest is draped in waterfalls—thanks, rain!—Multnomah Falls, part of the Columbia River Gorge National Scenic Area, boasting a picturesque pillar of water and easy accessibility from Portland, is the area's most popular. The triple-decker falls, the longest of which is more than 500 feet, offers a prime photo op. Also here is the **Multnomah Falls Lodge** (53000 Historic Columbia River Hwy., 503/695-2376, www.multnomahfallslodge.com), a 1925 building that holds a restaurant and small **Forest Service visitors center** (9am-5pm daily).

To get to Multnomah Falls from downtown Portland, head east on I-84 and take the left-hand exit 31. When traffic doesn't clog the interstate, it takes about 45 minutes. If you have some time to spare, get off the interstate to take the leafy, moody scenic route to Multnomah

on the **Historic Columbia River Highway** (Route 30), which boasts numerous viewpoints and other waterfall options.

Note the parking lot at Multnomah Falls can be difficult to navigate, since drivers are coming from both directions and the falls are such an attraction. If you'd like to avoid it, an express shuttle called the **Columbia Gorge Express** (columbiagorgeexpress.com, $5 round-trip) offers round-trip service 10 times a day Friday-Sunday in the summer from **Gateway Transit Center** (9900 NE Multnomah Ave.).

The Eagle Creek Fire burned thousands of acres of the Columbia River Gorge National Scenic Area in 2017, but firefighting efforts saved Multnomah Falls. Evidence of the fires is visible in the forest that lines the Columbia River, and recovery is ongoing.

www.bluebirdguesthouse.com, $95-115 shared bath, $135-192 private bath) is the anti-hotel, with just seven rooms located in a 1910 house built in the Arts and Crafts style, complete with a porch out front. It offers free Wi-Fi and computer use, free parking, laundry, and a full kitchen available for guests. Social rooms are all painted a different bright, cheery color, and the guest rooms are named for authors like Gabriel García Márquez and Sherman Alexie. Some rooms have clawfoot tubs, and all feature antique furniture. Not all have private baths though, and basement rooms are located on a different floor from the shared baths.

$150-250

The motel bones underneath the heavily renovated ★ **Jupiter Hotel** (800 E Burnside St., 503/230-9200, www.jupiterhotel.com, $169-209) are visible, but they're overlaid with heavy layers of party chic. Room doors are blackboards that can be decorated (or used as message

boards for the cleaning crew). Ask for the "chill" side if you want quiet because the two floors of rooms on the "bar patio" side get more noise from the attached Doug Fir Lounge. Rooms come with low-to-the-ground beds and wall murals—and complementary condoms instead of pillow chocolates. Located a block from famed **Le Pigeon** (738 E Burnside St., 503/546-8796, http://lepigeon.com, 5pm-10pm daily) restaurant and next door to a busy live music venue, the area is nevertheless much quieter than the middle of downtown. Reaching other parts of the city likely requires a car, but the hotel has bikes and two ZipCars on-site for rent.

Northeast/North
$150-250

★ **Kennedy School** (5736 NE 33rd Ave., 503/249-3983, www.mcmenamins.com/kennedyschool, $155-225), run by the fun-loving McMenamins company, is housed in an actual elementary school built in 1915 that closed in 1997.

Classrooms were split in two to create 57 guest rooms, and some rooms have chalkboards still inside, which are low to the ground, of course, to accommodate elementary-aged students. Others have author themes, like the Ramona room and Sometimes a Great Notion room in tribute to local writers Beverly Cleary and Ken Kesey. Although the neighborhood around the school is pretty residential, there's plenty to do on campus. The building contains multiple bars; a restaurant serving breakfast, lunch, and dinner; an outdoor soaking pool (free for overnight guests); and a movie theater that plays second-run films, with old couches, cushy armchairs, and tables—the theater bar serves liquor and pub food.

Caravan-The Tiny House Hotel (5009 NE 11th Ave., 503/288-5225, www.tinyhousehotel.com, $165) is less a hotel than a tiny, impermanent commune, made up of small dwellings on wheels that range 100-200 square feet in size. Each has a bathroom with a shower and kitchenette, and all come with loft beds (some have a second sleeping surface below). The hotel is located in a small circle in a quiet area near Alberta Avenue, located behind a gate and wire fence; it used to be a parking lot for repossessed cars. Adirondack chairs are set up in the middle around a fire pit. The owners call the lot a kind of "urban campground" and hope to show off to visitors that caravan living in such small places is possible.

Lion and the Rose Victorian Bed & Breakfast (1810 NE 15th Ave., 800/955-1647, www.lionrose.com, $125-210 shared bath, $140-250 private bath) is located inside a 1906 Queen Anne mansion topped with a turret and decorated with intricate columns. Inside it's no less detailed, with parlors that live up to the name—think furniture you can't put your feet on. Breakfast is complementary, and free parking is generally easy to find in this residential neighborhood. Rooms have four-poster beds or decorative headboards, and most have floral wallpaper and antique furnishings. Some rooms have Jacuzzi tubs, and all have cable TV and wireless Internet access.

Information and Services

Visitor Information

Located in the middle of Pioneer Courthouse Square, **Travel Portland Visitor Information Center** (701 SW 6th Ave., 877/678-5263, www.travelportland. com, 8:30am-5:30pm Mon.-Fri., 10am-4pm Sat., 10am-2pm Sun. summer only) has maps and brochures, along with a window that vends tickets for the bus, MAX light rail, and streetcar.

Media and Communications

The city's daily newspaper is *The Oregonian* (www.oregonlive.com), one of the 25 biggest papers in the country. It has won five Pulitzer Prizes and is generally recognized as the area's newspaper of record, sold in newsstands and in newspaper boxes. However, those looking for information on a night out are better off scouring the streets for a box offering the free *Willamette Week* (www.wweek. com), an indie weekly that has covered local news and politics since 1974, but also has a hefty section on arts and music, including listings for the week's shows. Its website is also useful for planning a night out. The main newspaper's rival, *The Portland Mercury* (www.portland-mercury.com), has similar coverage and is a sister paper to Seattle's *The Stranger.* For a periodical with more feature stories and lengthier (though fewer) reviews, find *Portland Monthly* (www.portland-monthlymag.com), a magazine, at newsstands and bookstores. The magazine's website also has collections of best-of lists and event picks.

Services

The lobby of the **Portland Post Office** (715 NW Hoyt St., 503/294-2399, www. usps.com) in the Pearl District is open 24 hours, but they sell stamps only 8am-6:30pm Monday-Friday and 8:30am-5pm Saturday.

As one of several urgent care centers in the city, **ZoomCare** (900 SW 5th Ave., 503/608-3082, www.zoomcare.com, 8am-6pm Mon.-Fri.) has outposts throughout the city, including downtown; other locations are open on weekends. You can book a same-day appointment, get lab tests or a prescription, and even receive stitches and simple burn care. You pay a flat rate whether you bill to insurance or not (around $100 per visit). To treat more urgent and serious ailments, an emergency room is at **Providence Portland Medical Center** (4805 NE Glisan St., 503/215-1111, www.providence.org), but it's a few miles from downtown, so call 911 in an emergency rather than try to navigate the bus system.

Getting Around

Car

Car rentals are available from major vendors (Enterprise, Hertz, Avis, and more) at the Portland International Airport, but two options allow for short-term car rentals. **Car2Go** (1100 NW Glisan, 877/488-4224, www.car2go.com/en/portland, 9:30am-5:30pm Mon.-Fri., 10am-3pm Sat.) has tiny two-person Smart cars parked all around the city. Register at the Pearl District office or online in advance. You'll then receive a card that unlocks any vacant car2go and get billed by the minute (just $0.38 if below 150 miles in a single rental period) until you leave it anywhere within the zones. **Parking** is free in legal street spots. Find the empty cars via the company's app or website. It's an easy way to do a one-way trip, but the cars don't hold much luggage when a passenger sits in the front seat.

the Portland Streetcar

Taxi

With lots of one-way streets, streetcars, and pedestrian crossings, hiring a taxi doesn't guarantee a quick trip through downtown. However, when stranded in one of the westside parks, or eager to get to an eastside restaurant, they're much faster than the bus. Don't wait to flag one down on the street; call **Broadway Cab** (503/333-3333, www.broadwaycab. com), which also can be hailed online via its app, or by text at 571/309-5276. Or try **Radio Cab** (503/227-1212, www.radio-cab.net), which also has text (777222) and app options on its website.

Public Transit

The **TriMet** (503/238-7433, www.trimet. org) handles the bus, light rail, and commuter rail in Portland, and provides information on the Portland Streetcar (operated separately). Tickets ($2.50 adults, $1.25 seniors, $1.25 children 7-15, children under 7 free) are good for two hours of travel and work on any combination of vehicles. For anything over a single return trip, a one-day pass ($5 adults, $2.50 seniors, $2.50 children 7-15, children under 7 free) is worthwhile. Visitors with longer stays can invest in a seven-day pass ($26 adults, $7 seniors, $8 children 7-15, children under 7 free). Buses have the most reach, while the MAX (a light rail system that stands for Metropolitan Area Express) has four lines that go to the airport, the nearby towns of Beaverton, Hillsboro, and Gresham, and the Expo Center. All lines go through the Rose Quarter and Pioneer Square, and trains generally come about every 15 minutes, though they're less frequent at night.

The **Portland Streetcar** is more useful for travel in the city core. The North/South line goes from the waterfront through the city center and the Pearl District to the Northwest District. The Central Loop line heads from the city center across the river to the Convention Center and OMSI.

Although Portland is a fairly flat city, it has one way to travel by air—the **Portland Aerial Tram** (3303 SW Bond Ave., 503/865-8726, www.gobytram. com, 5:30am-9:30pm Mon.-Fri., 9am-5pm Sat., 1pm-5pm Sun. summer only, $4.70 adults round-trip, children under 7 free), which leaves every six minutes. However, its path isn't one usually frequented by tourists, from the waterfront south of downtown to the Oregon Health and Science University area. On a rainy day, however, it can be worth a ride for a dry look at the city.

Mount Rainier

Massive Mount Rainier is on Washington's license plates, on its state quarter, and in all of its prettiest pictures. But "The Mountain" is more than the state's mascot or backdrop.

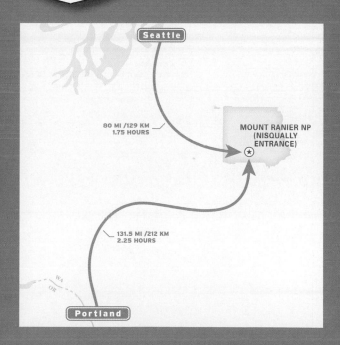

Seattle

80 MI /129 KM
1.75 HOURS

MOUNT RANIER NP
(NISQUALLY
ENTRANCE)

131.5 MI /212 KM
2.25 HOURS

WA
OR

Portland

Mount Rainier and Vicinity

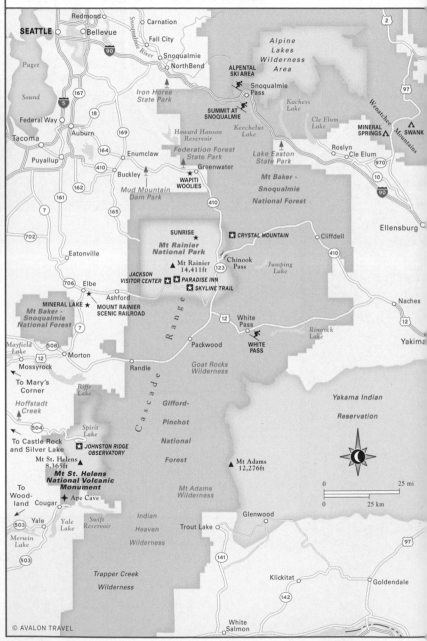

© AVALON TRAVEL

Highlights

★ **Jackson Visitor Center:** There's a reason this part of Mount Rainier National Park is called Paradise—come for the mountain views, but stay for natural history exhibits, hiking trails, and wildflower meadows that look like heaven (page 301).

★ **Paradise Inn:** The massive fireplaces and log ceiling in this historical hotel are worth a look even if you're not staying overnight (page 302).

★ **Skyline Trail:** This route along the flank of Mount Rainier offers up-close views of the state's massive peak, plus a sweat-inducing climb through meadows and volcanic rock (page 302).

★ **Crystal Mountain:** Ride in style to a killer viewpoint that just happens to have a gourmet restaurant (page 307).

★ **Johnston Ridge Observatory:** From this spot overlooking the crater of Mount St. Helens, it's possible to imagine the catastrophic 1980 eruption that changed this wilderness forever (page 319).

Mount Rainier is an active volcano beloved by outdoor enthusiasts, naturalists, and sightseers.

This behemoth has more glaciers than any other spot in the contiguous United States; mountain climbers claim that it has everything Mount Everest does, save the altitude. The peak is about 75 miles from Seattle so it can be visited as a day trip, but the problem is that on a pretty day it's hard to tear yourself away from the subalpine meadows and colossal glaciers. Stop by a visitors center for a quick view, but try to schedule an hour for a flat nature walk, an afternoon for a gondola ride or hike, or even a night to camp under the canopy of old-growth forest.

Mount Rainier is protected in a national park, and the forests that surround it are a patchwork of national forest, designated wilderness, logging land, and private holdings. The small towns support small fishing and recreation communities, but dining options—not to mention gas stations—are limited, though there are a number of fine, if rustic, hotels and cabins.

Getting to Mount Rainier

Driving from Seattle
80 miles, 1.75 hours

The **Nisqually Entrance** of Mount Rainier National Park is closest to the most popular activities. From Seattle, drive south on I-5 for 10 miles, and then turn east to follow I-405 north for 2 miles. Take exit 2 for Highway 167 South and continue driving south for about 20 miles. Near Puyallup, Highway 167 merges with Highway 512 for about 3 miles. Where Highway 512 continues west, take the Highway 161 exit south

toward Eatonville. Highway 161 ends at Eatonville in 23 miles. Turn left onto Center Street; after 0.5 mile, Center Street becomes the Alder Cutoff Road. Follow Alder Cutoff Road for 6.5 miles and then take a left onto Highway 7 (the National Park Highway). Highway 7 eventually becomes Highway 706, and after about 13 miles, you will arrive at the Nisqually Entrance.

85 miles, 2 hours

The **White River Entrance** is open seasonally (July-Sept.) and provides access to the Sunrise area of the park. From Seattle, drive south on I-5 for 10 miles, and then turn east to follow I-405 north for 2 miles. Take exit 2 for Highway 167 South. Drive south for a little less than 20 miles and take the exit for Highway 410 East. Follow Highway 410 east for 50 miles, through the town of Enumclaw and the small community of Greenwater, to the national park entrance.

Highway 410 south from the park entrance is only open from **May-November.** When this section of road is open, continue 5 miles and turn right to reach the White River Entrance and pay the fee to Sunrise. When that section of road is closed, you can drive through the national park without a fee, exiting on Highway 123 near Packwood.

Driving from Portland
131.5 miles, 2.25 hours

To reach the **Nisqually Entrance,** take I-5 north from Portland and drive 74 miles to exit 68 and U.S. 12. Follow U.S. 12 east for 31 miles to Morton, and then turn north onto Highway 7. Follow Highway 7 north for about 16 miles to where the road dead-ends in Elbe. Turn right (east) onto Highway 706 (the National Park Highway) and drive east almost 8 miles to the Nisqually Entrance.

155 miles, 2.5 hours

The **Ohanapecosh Entrance** is located in the southeast corner of the park on

Highway 123 (open seasonally May-Nov.). From Portland, take I-5 north and drive 74 miles to exit 68 and U.S. 12. Follow U.S. 12 east for 75 miles, passing through the town of Packwood. At the junction with Highway 123, turn left and follow Highway 123 north for 3.5 miles to the park entrance.

Mount Rainier National Park

Although the mountain has been an icon for centuries, it didn't become a national park until 1899. Naturalist John Muir visited the area and sang its praises, wowed by the wildflower meadows that surround it like a floral skirt. Today hundreds of climbers pay homage to the park's first champion at a camp halfway up the mountain named **Camp Muir.**

Visiting the Park

Mount Rainier National Park (360/569-2211, www.nps.gov/mora, $25 entrance fee per vehicle) consists of five main regions: Longmire, Paradise, Ohanapecosh, Sunrise, and the remote Carbon and Mowich area. Even though the park is open year-round, **summer** is by far its most popular season. Snowdrifts can linger in Paradise well into the summer, and the Sunrise visitors center doesn't generally open until July. August weekends are the most crowded in the national park, when wildflowers are at their peak and sunny days are more common.

Snowflakes begin falling in **September** or **October** and lead to serious accumulation—for many years the mountain held a world record for the most snowfall in a year, a record only broken by nearby Mount Baker. As thick snow blankets the park in **winter,** the narrow (but plowed) roads make for slow going and cars need chains, though the only attractions open are the Jackson Visitor Center (on weekends) and the National Park Inn.

Entrances

The park has two major entrances. The southwest Nisqually Entrance goes to the largest visitor destination at Paradise but first passes through the Longmire encampment. The northeast White River/Sunrise entrance (May-Nov.) leads to the visitors center at Sunrise. Entrance stations charge $25 per vehicle ($10 for walk-ins), which is good for up to seven days. Seniors age 62 and over can score a lifetime pass for $80, or an annual pass for $20.

The **Nisqually Entrance** is located in the southwest section of the park on Highway 706 approximately 6 miles from Ashford. The road from the entrance to Longmire stays open year-round (weather permitting) and provides the only winter access to the park. November 1-May 1 a gate closes the road from Longmire to Paradise (nightly at 5pm Mon.-Fri. and 7pm Sat.-Sun.) and may stay closed longer if snow builds up. All cars, including those with four-wheel drive, are required to carry chains November-May.

Sunrise and **White River** form the northeast entrance to the park. This entrance is accessed via Highway 410, 13.5 miles south of Greenwater. The road into the park is only open May-November; through access from Ohanapecosh and Longmire is available seasonally. The road from the White River Entrance station to Sunrise is open early July-October (weather permitting) and closes nightly from its junction with the White River Campground (open seasonally), reopening in the morning.

Other park entrances include the **Ohanapecosh Entrance,** the southeast entrance to the park. Packwood, 11 miles southwest, is the nearest gateway. Highway 123 from U.S. 12 is open May-November; this entrance is inaccessible the rest of the year.

Carbon River is the northwest entrance to the park; vehicles are not permitted past the entrance station. The Mowich Lake hike-in campground lies south of

One Day in Mount Rainier

A visit to Mount Rainier National Park is best enjoyed in summer, when the park roads are open and free of snow. Start by enjoying the drive to the Nisqually Entrance and grabbing breakfast at the café at **Whittaker's Motel and Historic Bunkhouse** (page 310). Once inside the park, drive the 6.5 miles to Longmire slowly, both to appreciate the thick forest and to take care on the road's tight turns. In Longmire, pop into the **Longmire Museum** (page 297) to learn about the family that once settled here, or walk the short **Trail of the Shadows** (page 297) through the meadows. Back on the road, drive 11 miles to Paradise as Mount Rainier looms larger. Grab lunch at the deli inside the **Jackson Visitor Center** (page 301), and then hit the trail to climb the **Skyline Trail** (page 302) to Panorama Point. The uphill hike is exhausting, but it's the best way to wander the Paradise meadows and Rainier's rocky flank.

Back at Paradise, check in to the **Paradise Inn** (page 302) and enjoy dinner in the lofty dining room. Curl up with a book in front of one of the lobby's giant wood-burning fireplaces before hitting the hay.

If You Have Time

After breakfast, take **Paradise Valley Road** (page 301) to Stevens Canyon Road and turn left. Drive 19 miles to Highway 123, stopping along the way for a picture at Reflection Lakes, just 3 miles after the turn. At the junction with Highway 123, turn left and continue 11 miles as the road becomes Highway 410, and in 3.5 miles turn left onto Sunrise Park Road and drive 15.5 miles to **Sunrise** (page 305). A burger from the snack stand is best enjoyed outside before hitting the 2-mile **Silver Forest Trail** (page 305) to the Emmons Glacier Overlook or a more ambitious hike on the **Burroughs Mountain Trail** (page 305) among the marmots.

Return to Highway 410 via Sunrise Park Road and turn left to exit the park in 4.5 miles. Turn right onto Crystal Mountain Boulevard and drive 8 miles to the ski resort of **Crystal Mountain** (page 307). Grab dinner at the **Snorting Elk Cellar** (page 308) or, if it's open, the **Summit House** (page 308) on top of the gondola.

To return to Seattle, drive the 8 miles back to Highway 410 and turn right. Follow Highway 410 north for 32.5 miles to Enumclaw, then continue west on Highway 410 for another 15 miles. At Sumner, take Highway 167 north for just under 20 miles to I-405. Follow I-405 south for 2 miles, and then take I-5 north for 10 miles to Seattle.

the Carbon River entrance, at the end of an unpaved road (mid-July to mid-Oct.) that may be difficult for some cars to navigate. A machine near the park entrance collects the entry fee.

Visitors Centers

Henry M. Jackson Memorial Visitor Center (360/569-6571, 10am-7pm daily June-Sept., 10am-4:30pm Sat.-Sun. Oct.-May) is located in Paradise and is the largest of the visitors centers in the area. It's always crowded on sunny summer days.

Other area visitors centers also have maps and rangers available to answer questions, as well as educational placards about wildlife. The **Longmire Information Center** (360/569-6575, 9am-5pm daily June-Sept., 9am-4:30pm daily Oct.-May) is located in the Longmire Museum and offers general visitor information. In the summer the **Longmire Wilderness Information Center** (360/569-6650, 7:30am-5pm daily mid-May-mid-Oct.) can also help with general visitor questions as well as provides further support on wilderness permit and backcountry questions. **Ohanapecosh Visitor Center** (360/569-6581, 9am-5pm daily June-Sept.) is in the southeast corner of the park on Highway 123. **Sunrise Visitor**

Center (360/663-2425, 10am-6pm daily July-Sept.) is in Sunrise. **Carbon River Ranger Station** (360/829-9639, 7:30am-5pm daily May-Sept., hours vary Oct.-Dec.) is in the Carbon and Mowich area.

Longmire

Enter the park on Highway 706. From there the road winds through forest and next to the Nisqually River, gaining elevation until it gets to the small gathering of buildings called **Longmire** (6.5 miles from Nisqually Entrance on Longmire-Paradise Rd.). James Longmire settled the area in 1883 and found a mineral springs nearby. Now it's one of the biggest recreation centers in the park. It holds the National Park Inn, a small general store full of gifts and snacks, a museum, a wilderness center, and historical displays in an old gas station. Most buildings are in the rustic national park style, made from large rocks and dark wood timbers.

Longmire Museum

Located in one of the historical stone and wood buildings that comprise Longmire, the **Longmire Museum** (360/569-6575, www.nps.gov/mora, 9am-4:30pm daily June-Sept.) is home to exhibits and photographs that trace the history of the area, including the Longmire family and their use of the area as a resort. Books and maps are available; when the museum is closed, some exhibits move to the Wilderness Information Center next door.

Hiking

A couple of short walks just off the road are options in the area. Six miles past Longmire, a one-way road provides a short detour to the **Ricksecker Point** parking area. Here you can take in views of the Tatoosh Range and the Paradise River before rejoining the road to Paradise. Located about 7.5 miles up the road from Longmire (and about 1 mile before Paradise), the 176-foot **Narada Falls** is an easy stroll just a couple of thousand feet from the road. Walk across the sturdy bridge and get a little damp from the spray. Picnic tables and restrooms are also available.

Trail of the Shadows

Distance: 0.7 mile round-trip
Duration: 30 minutes
Elevation gain: none
Effort: easy
Trailhead: across the street from the National Park Inn in Longmire

The Trail of the Shadows skirts one of the Longmire family's old cabins—it's actually a replica—and the mineral springs. Bear right after 0.5 mile. The first springs is ringed in rocks, and the second has a rusty color thanks to iron in the water. Look for placards explaining some of the natural history of the area. Complete the loop by taking a right at the last junction.

Rampart Ridge Trail

Distance: 4.5 miles round-trip
Duration: 2-3 hours
Elevation gain: 1,300 feet
Effort: moderate
Trailhead: across the street from the National Park Inn in Longmire

Start on the Trail of the Shadows, moving clockwise, but head left when you reach the intersection after 0.5 mile; it's marked with a small wooden sign. You'll head uphill through thick forest, hiking up switchbacks on a well-maintained dirt trail. Eventually the trail flattens out and heads north. Stop for a long snack or lunch break when Mount Rainier rises above you like a sentinel, its glaciers in full view. Continue on the loop until it bends down to Longmire again. Intersections are well signed.

Twin Firs Trail

Distance: 0.5 mile round-trip
Duration: 20 minutes
Elevation gain: 50 feet
Effort: easy
Trailhead: two miles west of Longmire, on the north side of the road

Mount Rainier National Park

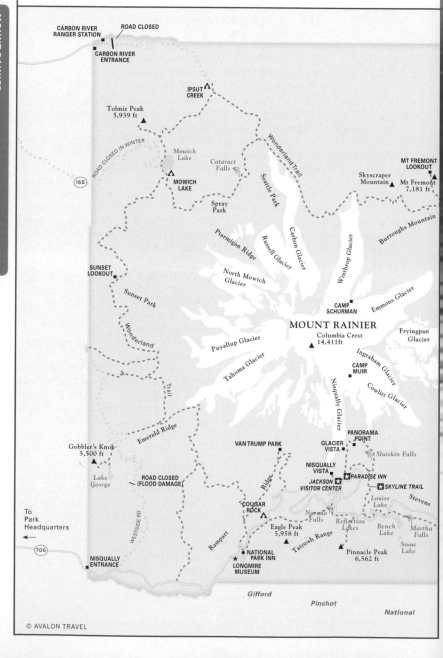

CARBON RIVER
RANGER STATION

ROAD CLOSED

CARBON RIVER
ENTRANCE

IPSUT
CREEK

Tolmie Peak
5,939 ft

ROAD CLOSED IN WINTER

*Mowich
Lake*

Cataract
Falls

Wonderland Trail

MT FREMONT
LOOKOUT

165

MOWICH
LAKE

Spray
Park

Seattle Park

Skyscraper
Mountain

Mt Fremont
7,181 ft

Ptarmigan Ridge

Russell Glacier

Carbon Glacier

Winthrop Glacier

Burroughs Mountain

SUNSET
LOOKOUT

Sunset Park

North Mowich
Glacier

CAMP
SCHURMAN

Emmons Glacier

Wonderland

Puyallup Glacier

MOUNT RAINIER
Columbia Crest
14,411ft

Fryingpan
Glacier

Tahoma Glacier

CAMP
MUIR

Ingraham Glacier

Trail

Cowlitz Glacier

Nisqually Glacier

Emerald Ridge

Gobbler's Knob
5,500 ft

VAN TRUMP PARK

GLACIER
VISTA

PANORAMA
POINT

Sluiskin Falls

*Lake
George*

ROAD CLOSED
(FLOOD DAMAGE)

Ridge

NISQUALLY
VISTA

JACKSON
VISITOR CENTER

PARADISE INN

SKYLINE TRAIL

*Louise
Lake*

To
Park
Headquarters

COUGAR
ROCK

Narada
Falls

Reflection
Lakes

Bench
Lake

Stevens

*Martha
Falls*

706

WESTSIDE RD

Rampart

Eagle Peak
5,958 ft

Tatoosh Range

Pinnacle Peak
6,562 ft

*Snow
Lake*

NISQUALLY
ENTRANCE

NATIONAL
PARK INN

LONGMIRE
MUSEUM

Gifford

Pinchot

National

© AVALON TRAVEL

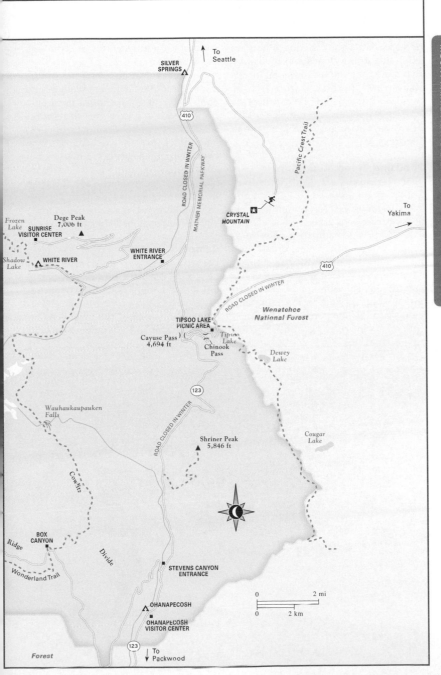

To Seattle

SILVER
SPRINGS

410

MATHER MEMORIAL PARKWAY

ROAD CLOSED IN WINTER

Pacific Crest Trail

CRYSTAL
MOUNTAIN

To
Yakima

Frozen
Lake

Dege Peak
7,006 ft

SUNRISE
VISITOR CENTER

Shadow
Lake

WHITE RIVER

WHITE RIVER
ENTRANCE

410

ROAD CLOSED IN WINTER

Wenatchee
National Forest

TIPSOO LAKE
PICNIC AREA

Cayuse Pass
4,694 ft

Tipsoo
Lake

Chinook
Pass

Dewey
Lake

123

Wauhaukaupauken
Falls

Shriner Peak
5,846 ft

Cougar
Lake

ROAD CLOSED IN WINTER

Cowlitz

BOX
CANYON

Ridge

Wonderland Trail

Divide

STEVENS CANYON
ENTRANCE

OHANAPECOSH

OHANAPECOSH
VISITOR CENTER

123

To
Packwood

Forest

0   2 mi

0   2 km

This loop travels through old-growth timber, including the namesake twin Douglas fir trees and cedar trees. Some of the greenery is giant, while others are small due to the floods and mudslides that can scour the meadows regularly. Kautz Creek burbles nearby, and the meadows burst with trillium when the snow melts. It's an easy ramble for kids or anyone who forgot to wear more than flip-flops.

Food and Accommodations

The **National Park Inn** (Paradise-Longmire Rd., 6 miles from Nisqually Entrance, 360/569-2275, www.mtrainier-guestservices.com, $126-177 shared bath, $177-263 private bath, open daily year-round) in Longmire is less grand than its Paradise cousin, but it has a cozier charm—plus it's open year-round. It has only 25 rooms in a building constructed in 1910 and has both a stone fireplace indoors and a long porch outside, lined with chairs for relaxing with ice cream or a hot chocolate (or beer). Rooms are simple, small, and not particularly modern, but rooms with a shared bath come with robes and slippers for trips through the hallway.

The casual **National Park Inn Dining Room** (7am-11am, 11:30am-4:30pm, and 5pm-7pm Sun.-Thurs., open until 8pm Fri.-Sat. year-round) serves straightforward hearty meals for lunch ($12-16) and dinner ($19-34) like pot roast, beef chili, and grilled cheese sandwiches, but the sweets—including blackberry cobbler and hot chocolate—are the best. Breakfasts ($9-14) include pancakes, biscuits and gravy, and eggs Benedict made with grilled portobello mushrooms.

Camping

Located just a couple miles past Longmire, **Cougar Rock Campground** (2 miles past Longmire on the Longmire-Paradise Rd., www.recreation.gov, May-Sept., $20) is one of the most popular places to camp in the state because of its

a climber at Mount Rainier near Paradise

proximity to Paradise. The 173 sites have access to flush toilets and an RV dump station, and five group sites ($60) can hold up to 40 people and five cars. There are no hookups, and RVs with generators must observe quiet hours. Across the road, a trail leads down to the Nisqually River, and a bridge crosses it to lead to a trail to Carter Falls. Ranger programs, sharing historical and natural information about the area, are held at a central amphitheater. Reservations are required in the busy summer months.

Information and Services

Longmire Information Center (360/569-6575, www.nps.gov/mora, 9am-5pm daily June-Sept., 9am-4:30pm daily Oct.-May), in the Longmire Museum, is the main visitor information center in the Longmire area.

In summer, the **Longmire Wilderness Information Center** (360/569-6650, www.nps.gov/mora, 7:30am-5pm daily mid-May-mid-Oct.) can answer a lot of the same questions as the Longmire Information Center, but it can also provide more technical information pertaining to wilderness permits and backcountry questions.

Paradise

From Longmire, **Paradise Road** continues to climb and crosses the Nisqually River; pull over at the **Christine Falls** parking lot to see a dramatic two-tiered waterfall and charming stone bridge. After 11 miles, the road approaches the tree line and you'll see lush subalpine meadows—this is Paradise, home to a hotel, visitors center, and climbing center.

During the approach from Longmire, keep to the left and follow signs for access to Paradise (the road runs both directions until Paradise). After passing the parking lots, the road becomes **Paradise Valley Road** and continues one-way in a scenic five minute loop. It runs under Mazama Ridge before meeting up again with the main Paradise-Longmire Road and Stevens Canyon Road, which continues east into the park.

Continue driving past Paradise and stop at **Inspiration Point.** The pull-out and viewpoint is located on Stevens Canyon Road (just past where it meets the Paradise-Longmire Road and Paradise Valley Road outlet). The views here stretch up Paradise Valley and across the Tatoosh Range. Continue along Stevens Canyon Road to Reflection Lakes, 3 miles from Paradise. These subalpine lakes are accessible from the roadside and are famous sites for photographers to capture Mount Rainier reflected in the icy-cold water.

★ Jackson Visitor Center

At the center of Paradise is the steep peaked roof of the **Henry M. Jackson Memorial Visitor Center** (Paradise Rd. E, 360/569-6571, www.nps.gov/mora, 10am-7pm daily June-Sept., 10am-4:30pm Sat.-Sun. Oct.-May), shaped so it doesn't hold the snow during the winter and an ideal refuge when the weather turns cold or

windy. It has a theater showing a short history film and displays about the area's natural history, plus a café and gift shop. Look for a relief map of the entire park, where you can see how the folds of smaller mountains surround Mount Rainier; the route mountaineers take to the top; and how little Tahoma, a side peak, manages to be dwarfed by its big sister even though it's one of the tallest points in the state. Note in the historical displays how the Paradise area has changed over the years; the meadows weren't always pristine, so it's important to observe posted signs when you wander outside. Even if you don't plan to hike, the visitors center—and, mostly, the view outside it—is worth a visit: Mount Rainier seems to rise right from the Paradise parking lot

★ Paradise Inn

Regardless of whether you're staying the night, the lobby of the **Paradise Inn** (98368 Paradise-Longmire Rd., 360/569-2275, www.mtrainierguestservices.com, May-Sept.) is a must-see. The long room, anchored by massive stone fireplaces at each end, is marked by regular exposed log beams. It's decorated with a 14-foot grandfather clock, built by the same German carpenter, and a piano, played by President Harry Truman during a visit. Couches and long wooden tables dot the lobby, often filled with as many recovering hikers and climbers—planning their next trek, or recounting their last one—as hotel guests, and you can enjoy drinks and food from the nearby snack bar. When the air turns chilly—that is, on all but the sunniest of summer days—the crackling fireplaces offer a chance to warm wind-scoured hands.

Hiking
Alta Vista Trail
Distance: 1.75 miles round-trip
Duration: 1.25 hours
Elevation gain: 600 feet
Effort: easy
Trailhead: lower or upper parking lot

Paradise's real treasures are outside. The short Alta Vista Trail that begins near the parking lot (look for trails branching uphill next to the Henry M. Jackson Memorial Visitor Center) is mostly paved to help preserve the fragile landscape of subalpine meadows, which burst in summer with purple lupine and orange-red Indian paintbrush. Follow the small signs as the trail heads subtly up toward Rainier, and don't step off the path. The Alta Vista Trail ends at a scenic overlook, after which you can turn around and return the way you came, but you can also add to the journey by taking the tiny spur paths that follow the meadows over small knolls and give slightly different views of Rainier's flanks. The trails here are a tangle of routes, so it's easy—and advisable—to wander on your return, provided the weather is clear enough to make your way back to the Paradise center by sight. Although Alta Vista might be a starting point, the pleasure of these paths is largely in the opportunities they offer for interesting meandering.

★ Skyline Trail
Distance: 4-5.5 miles round-trip
Duration: 2.5-4 hours
Elevation gain: 1,700 feet
Effort: strenuous
Trailhead: north side of the upper parking lot

Skyline is a comprehensive trail that includes the best meadows of Paradise, but climbs high enough for wider views of the entire park, plus closer looks at the vast snowfields and cracked glaciers on Rainier. The whole loop is well signed and has some of the best views of Mount Rainier and the jagged Tatoosh Range to the south. It starts at the same trailhead as Alta Vista, but most of the paved paths that lead uphill from the Paradise parking lot eventually funnel into Skyline; follow the small signs that sit at most trail intersections. The trail gradually inches higher along the flanks of the mountain, then gets steeper while the trees get less common, and finally tops out at Panorama Point (look for a bathroom that's been built into the rock here). It then heads east before swinging back to Paradise. Summit-bound climbers may pass by with large packs and ice axes. Be sure not to feed any wildlife, including chipmunks and the furry marmots that sun themselves on the large boulders of the mountainside. The entire 5.5-mile loop returns to Paradise via Sluiskin Falls, but there's a cutoff just past Panorama Point that will shorten the loop length to just 4 miles total (though you won't knock off any elevation gain). The cutoff and main route join again at roaring Myrtle Falls just above Paradise Inn.

Pinnacle Peak

Distance: 3 miles round-trip
Duration: 3 hours
Elevation gain: 1,150 feet
Effort: strenuous
Trailhead: across the road from Reflection Lakes
Directions: Take the Paradise-Longmire Road or the Paradise Valley Road to Stevens Canyon Road for three miles.

Escape some of the crowds by heading up a trail that gains some elevation, moving south of the road into the Tatoosh Range. It ends at the rocky Pinnacle Saddle and offers a spectacular view of Mount Rainier; climbing any farther requires scrambling experience and is not advised.

Bench and Snow Lakes

Distance: 2.5 miles round-trip
Duration: 2 hours
Elevation gain: 700 feet
Effort: moderate
Trailhead: 1.5 miles east of Paradise down Stevens Canyon Road

This is one of the most beautiful of the park's easier trails. You'll sometimes traverse wooden boardwalks over wet grass, as well as walk through wildflower meadows and eventually gain some elevation and skirt Bench Lake. Keep going until the trail ends at Snow Lake, fed by Unicorn Creek, about 1.25

miles from the trailhead, where there's a small backpacking campground. The trail is snow-covered at the start of summer and muddy until midsummer. The area is also popular with black bears—stay mindful and don't try to feed them.

Food and Accommodations

The stately old **Paradise Inn** (98368 Paradise-Longmire Rd., 360/569-2275, www.mtrainierguestservices.com, May-Sept., $119-155 shared bath) is one of the country's most distinguished national park lodges, built in 1916 and decorated with rustic woodwork by a German carpenter who wanted to evoke alpine styles. Many of the cedar logs were from a grove nearby that had been decimated in a fire. The original space had only a few dozen rooms, which today have shared hall bathrooms and cozy shapes under the steep roof. An annex built in 1920 added four floors of rooms, all of which have private bathrooms, though these are undergoing renovations through 2018; the main lodge rooms with shared bath will still be available during this time.

The attached **Paradise Inn Dining Room** (7am-9:30am, noon-2pm, and 5:30pm-8pm daily May-Sept., $17-35) is impressive in its elegant, rustic style. While it serves a wide array of seafood, small plates, steak, and a bourbon-buffalo meatloaf, the decor is more impressive than the flavors.

The **Paradise Camp Deli** (10am-6:45pm daily June-Sept., 11am-4pm Sat.-Sun. Oct.-May), in the Jackson Visitor Center, is a fast service restaurant serving salads, pizzas, and soft drinks. Enjoy soft-serve ice cream or coffee outside, or eat inside when the weather's bad.

Information and Services

The **Paradise Climbing Information Center** (360/569-6641, 7am-4pm daily May-Sept.), located in the historical Guide House, provides climbing permits for those attempting to summit Mount Rainier as well as backcountry hiking and camping permits. For information on day hiking or less advanced outdoor activities, visit the Jackson Visitor Center.

Ohanapecosh

The southeastern corner of the park is known as Ohanapecosh, named for a settlement of the Upper Cowlitz tribe. Ohanapecosh is located at an elevation of 2,000 feet, much lower than other areas in the park, and the old-growth forest here is likely to be free of rain when Paradise or Longmire are wet and soggy. The **Ohanapecosh Visitor Center** (360/569-6581, www.nps.gov/mora, 9am-5pm daily June-Sept.) provides services to the area. The Ohanapecosh Campground (the park's largest) operates May-October and provides picnic tables and bathrooms for visitors.

Ohanapecosh is located about 11.5 miles north of Packwood on U.S. 12 and is most accessible from Portland and points south. May-November, Ohanapecosh is accessible via a 19-mile drive from Paradise or a gorgeous 14-mile drive south of the White River Entrance. The park roads from Paradise and White River are closed in winter.

Hiking
Grove of the Patriarchs
Distance: 1.3 miles round-trip
Duration: 1 hour
Elevation gain: 100 feet
Effort: easy
Trailhead: 0.25 mile past the Stevens Canyon Entrance on Stevens Canyon Road

Sometimes you don't want a visitors center, or even an overwhelming view of the mountain—or maybe it's too cloudy to see the mountain anyway. In that case, the Grove of the Patriarchs Trail is an excellent way to get a taste of the wilderness in a short, flat, and very easy hike through old-growth forest. Signs point out cedar, western hemlock, and Douglas fir trees. Cross a suspension footbridge (*one at a time,* the sign warns) to gaze

up at 300-foot-tall trees more than 1,000 years old—which means that they sprouted in the time of Saint Francis of Assisi and Genghis Khan.

Silver Falls Loop
Distance: 3.8 miles round-trip
Duration: 2 hours
Elevation gain: 300 feet
Effort: easy
Trailhead: just north of the Stevens Canyon Entrance on Stevens Canyon Road, across from the Grove of the Patriarchs trailhead

This trail leads to a waterfall on the Ohanapecosh River that flows with glacial water; the name is a Native American one, from the groups who lived here long before the national park was formed. Start by moving south through the trees, reaching the falls in 0.5 mile. Anglers sometimes frequent the river, and woodpeckers are numerous in the area. Continue on the route south to Ohanapecosh Campground where, in the 1920s, a resort stood. None of those buildings remain, but the hot springs (not big enough for soaking) that first drew tourists here can still be seen along the Hot Springs Nature Trail, an easy 0.3-mile spur marked with interpretive signs that begins behind the old visitors center building at the campground and rejoins the Silver Falls Loop as it moves north.

Camping
Ohanapecosh Campground (Stevens Canyon Rd. near the intersection of Hwy. 123, www.recreation.gov, May-Oct., $20) is the largest of the park's campgrounds, with 188 sites, including two group spots ($60) and 10 walk-in campsites. The campground is set at 1,914 feet, a lower elevation than Cougar Rock or White River, and is more sheltered by trees. Amenities include water, flush toilets, and a dump station. There are no hookups, and RVs must observe quiet hours. Reservations are required in the busy summer months.

Sunrise

The park's Sunrise area got its name the obvious way—by offering a spectacular view of the mountain when the sun first emerges from the east. Located on the northeast side of the park and situated at the high elevation of 6,400 feet, Sunrise is covered in snow most of the year. This region is less developed than the west side of the mountain, with only a small visitors center, a nearby campground, picnic facilities, and limited food options. Sunrise Road stretches from the White River Entrance station to the Sunrise Visitor Center, and the road is usually open by mid-July and closes by October. Overnight visitors may camp at White River Campground, but are not permitted at Sunrise. The road between the visitors center and the campground closes nightly.

Sunrise is accessible via Highway 410. The region is about 50 miles (1.5 hours) south of the town of Enumclaw and is a two-hour drive from Paradise when the park road is open.

Sunrise Visitor Center

The **Sunrise Visitor Center** (Sunrise Rd., 360/663-2425, www.nps.gov/mora, 10am-6pm daily July-Sept.), on the northeast corner of the park, is even higher than Paradise, with views of the Emmons Glacier side of the peak, the White River Valley below, and Mount Baker and Glacier Peak up north. It's particularly spectacular at—what else—sunrise, especially from the **Sunrise Point** overlook on the road that approaches the wood-sided visitors center. Inside are more exhibits about the mountain and its history, and rangers lead programs and hikes. Services are less extensive than at Paradise, with only a snack bar and small bookstore.

Sights

As Highway 410 enters the national park, it becomes Mather Memorial Parkway. In 8 more miles, Mather Memorial Parkway

meets Highway 123 at Cayuse Pass (elevation 4,694 feet). Head east to continue along Mather Memorial Parkway for 3 miles to **Tipsoo Lake.** The lake is surrounded by glorious mountain meadows, and picnic tables offer a spot to sit and soak in the views.

Hiking

Hikes around Sunrise lead through the Yakima Park meadows and rocky expanses inhabited by mountain marmots and fuzzy white mountain goats.

Silver Forest Trail

Distance: 2 miles round-trip
Duration: 1 hour
Elevation gain: 150 feet
Effort: easy
Trailhead: south end of the Sunrise parking lot

At the Emmons Vista Overlook near the visitors center, look on the south side of the parking lot for the trailhead to the Silver Forest Trail, which offers great views with little elevation gain. In late summer, the meadows explode with wildflowers, including purple lupine and Indian paintbrush.

Burroughs Mountain Trail

Distance: 6 miles round-trip
Duration: 3 hours
Elevation gain: 1,200 feet
Effort: strenuous
Trailhead: south end of the Sunrise parking lot

From the same trailhead as the Silver Forest Trail, head west through meadows toward Frozen Lake, then turn at a large, well-signed intersection for the Burroughs Mountain Trail. With massive Rainier still looming in front, the rocky Burroughs mountains present a challenge of their own, mostly exposed to the hot sun as you climb their flanks. Reach the top of First Burroughs about three-quarters of a mile past Frozen Lake, then the even higher Second Burroughs a little more than a half mile past that. Turn here and return the way you came for the 6-mile hike, though the trail itself continues on for 2.2 miles (and loses a lot of elevation) to Glacier Basin Camp. Keep your eyes and ears peeled for the marmots that live in the area, who whistle to each other as they hide in the nooks between big boulders.

Sourdough Ridge

Distance: 3 miles round-trip
Duration: 1.5 hour
Elevation gain: 500 feet
Effort: moderate
Trailhead: north side of the Sunrise parking lot

Take a quick loop up a ridge above Sunrise with views of the mountains north of Rainier, such as Glacier Peak and Mount Baker. The trail splits less than a quarter mile from the trailhead and you can go in either direction. Explore the ridge, which offers opportunities to spot marmots, elk, mountain goats, and more.

Glacier Basin

Distance: 6.5 miles round-trip
Duration: 3 hours
Elevation gain: 1,700 feet
Effort: strenuous
Trailhead: White River Campground, in Loop D

The first part of this route is on an old mining road, but the wide, easy ramble quickly narrows to a conventional trail. The forest is home to a number of bears (give them space if you spot one), and at about 3 miles in, hikers can spot the rusty remnants of an old mine. Head just past the backcountry campsites to take in Glacier Basin, and see if you can spot climbers heading up the Interglacier at the end of the valley—they're likely heading to Camp Schurman, one of the two most popular base camps for Rainier summiters (the other is Camp Muir above Paradise).

Naches Peak Loop

Distance: 3.4 miles round-trip
Duration: 2.5 hours
Elevation gain: 600 feet
Effort: moderate
Trailhead: three miles south of the White River Entrance Station
Directions: Follow Highway 410 east for Tipsoo Lake and a parking lot.

Though only partially in the national park, this loop boasts big open alpine meadows, mountain views, and fewer hikers than routes out of Sunrise or Paradise. Don't expect to have the trail entirely to yourself, though, especially during wildflower season in late summer. You can hike in either direction, but a clockwise route provides the best vistas.

Food

The **Sunrise Day Lodge** (www.mtrainierguestservices.com, 10am-7pm daily June-Sept.) includes a small snack bar that serves grilled burgers and hot dogs, sandwiches, and soft-serve ice cream. Although there's space to eat inside, the view from the picnic tables outside overlooks the subalpine meadows that skirt Mount Rainier. An attached gift shop sells books and small souvenirs. The snack bar provides the only food service in the area and can open as late as July in especially snowy years.

Camping

The 112-site **White River Campground** (360/569-2211, www.nps.gov/mora, June-Sept., $20) lies 3 miles from Sunrise at 4,400 feet, a higher elevation than the other two major campgrounds in the park. A few of the 112 sites have prime locations next to the White River. Look for a historical patrol cabin located between two of the campsite loops to hear about the area's history at ranger programs by a campfire circle. Amenities include water and flush toilets, but no RV dump station (though RVs are allowed). Reservations are not accepted, so this is one of the few places you can still score a drive-up spot.

Though located outside the national park, the **Silver Springs Campground** (Highway 410, www.recreation.gov, May-Sept., $20-32) is just a mile west of the White River Entrance—useful when the White River Campground sites are all full. The forest here is full of old-growth cedar and western hemlock, and a small river flows through the 55 sites. Amenities include water, flush and vault toilets, and picnic tables; no electrical hookups are available.

Information and Services

The **White River Wilderness Information Center** (White River Entrance Station, 360/569-6670, 7:30am-5pm May-Oct.) can provide permit information for backcountry hikers and campers on the mountain's north side. Climbers attempting to summit Mount Rainier from the north side must register here.

The **Silver Creek Visitor Information Center** (69211 Hwy. 410 E, 360/663-2284, www.fs.usda.gov) is a classic log-cabin structure located about 1.5 miles north of the national park boundary. It's operated seasonally by the Snoqualmie Ranger District, with national forest rangers who can offer advice on recreation and informational materials.

Carbon and Mowich

The northwest corner of the park is the least accessible area of Mount Rainier National Park—except for the miles and miles of wilderness, of course. Highway 165 leaves Highway 410 west of Enumclaw in the town of Buckley and winds its way through rural landscape for 10.5 miles before Carbon River Road even begins. Then it's another 5.5 miles to the park entrance and the end of the road. The **Carbon River Ranger Station** (360/829-9639, www.nps.gov/mora, 7:30am-5pm daily May-Sept., hours vary Oct.-Dec.) operates seasonally.

The road from the entrance station into the park washed out in a flood, so visitors must park and hike or bike 4 miles to the picnic area on the Carbon River. It's another mile to **Ipsut Creek Campground** (backcountry permits required).

Mowich Lake Campground (first-come, first-served, mid-July to mid-Oct., free) is located on the park's deepest lake, accessed by staying on Highway 165 for an additional 17 miles after the Carbon River Road cutoff. The road is open in summer only, and many sections are unpaved or difficult for small vehicles. The campground has 10 primitive, tent-only sites; there is no water, and campfires are prohibited.

★ Crystal Mountain

Sprawling **Crystal Mountain Resort** (33914 Crystal Mountain Blvd., 360/663-2265, www.crystalmountainresort.com, $74 adults, $50 seniors and children 11-17, children under 11 free, $8 for gondola) is the biggest ski resort in the state and has Washington's only gondola. It has bunny hills, new chairlifts, and backcountry skiing. The jib park is for trick skiers and snowboarders and has a giant airbag for aerial tricks ($5-25)—though anyone attempting to flip onto the cushion has to sign a waiver and wear a helmet. Rent ski equipment at the base ($45 adults, $35 children), or visit a dedicated boot shop for fittings and adjustment.

Non-skiers can do more than just sip hot chocolate at the base lodge: **Snowshoe tours** ($65) include equipment rental and a cheese fondue dinner, plus a guide for the trek along a ridge near the summit. Scenic rides on the **Mount Rainier Gondola** (10am-5pm Sun.-Fri., 10am-7pm Sat., closed fall and spring, $23 adults, $18 seniors, $12 children 4-12, children under 3 free) allow anyone to see the top, with a climb of 2,500 feet in less than 10 minutes in an enclosed car—but be warned that in winter the wind up top can be unforgiving.

Even though Crystal Mountain Resort is best known as a ski destination, the gondola runs during summer to carry hikers and sightseers up the hill. Guided hikes (11am and 1 pm Fri.-Sun. summer, weather permitting) with a U.S. Forest Service ranger are free with a gondola ticket, as are wildflower hikes with naturalists; head to the top of the gondola and look for a meetup sign. A disc golf course is free, at least if you're willing to hike uphill to hit all 27 baskets (otherwise buy a gondola ticket and work your way down). The **Mountain Shop,** at the base, rents lawn games like bocce and croquet, and a taco truck is parked outside on weekends. Find maps of hikes at the Mountain Shop as well; unsurprisingly, they're all downhill from the top of the lifts.

If you're not looking to walk yourself, **Chinook Pass Outfitters** (800/726-3631, www.crystalmountainoutfitters.com, 8am-6pm daily in season, $35-180) leads horseback riding trips from parking lot C. Overnight and fishing trips are also available.

Food

The Austrian theme of the Alpine Inn at Crystal Mountain extends to the in-house restaurant, the **Snorting Elk Cellar** (33818 Crystal Mountain Blvd., 888/754-6400, www.crystalhotels.com, 11am-10pm daily summer; 11am-10pm Sun.-Thurs, 11am-midnight Fri.-Sat. winter, $11-30). Low arched ceilings cover a fireplace and walls painted in floral designs that wouldn't be out of place at any Oktoberfest. Seattle brewery Elysian creates the bar's namesake beer, but there are plenty of other taps for après-ski or après-hike visits. The menu leans toward hearty fare like stone-fired pizzas and thick sandwiches. The hot-drinks menu includes a hot toddy, hot buttered rum, hot spiced wine, and a drink called the Face Plant—imagine a rummy hot chocolate with peppermint schnapps and whipped cream.

You can't get much higher than the **Summit House** (33914 Crystal Mountain Blvd., 360/663-3085, www.crystalmountainresort.com, 10:30am-4:30pm Sun.-Fri. and 10:30am-6:30pm Sat. summer, 10:30am-2:45pm daily weather permitting winter, $18-32) and still get waiter service—from 6,872 feet at the top

of Crystal Mountain, Summit House claims to be Washington's highest restaurant (and no one's arguing). Located at the top of the Mount Rainier Gondola, it's a meal that requires serious planning. Skiers swarm the area during winter months, and the wind is significant. Even in summer, clouds can obscure the spectacular Mount Rainier view, and sunset dinners mean a flashlight-led walk back to the gondola. Still, the wood-trimmed dining room with stone fireplace and antler chandeliers is worth the trip, and the menu includes gourmet fondue, fish specials, and filet mignon. Reservations and a gondola ticket are required. Hours can vary from year to year, so it's a good idea to check the Crystal Mountain website for the most up-to-date hours.

Accommodations

Of the three hotels at the base of the Crystal Mountain ski area, **Alpine Inn** (33818 Crystal Mountain Blvd., 360/663-2262, www.crystalhotels.com, $145-290) has the most charm. The exterior is all Bavarian, complete with bright green shutters and a large porch, and the hotel itself is located across the creek from the parking lot. Inside, a small fireplace anchors the lobby, and the hallways are lined with vintage black-and-white photos of skiers with wooden equipment and jaunty old ski outfits. Rooms are small but come in combinations with a sleeper sofa or bunk beds to accommodate families. Most don't have a TV or phone—the mountain is your entertainment.

The simpler **Village Inn** (33818 Crystal Mountain Blvd., 360/663-2262, www.crystalhotels.com, $205-240), just across the parking lot, has rooms only with a queen bed or two twins. Headboards are made of thick wooden logs, and rooms have balconies facing the ski mountain. Rooms come with refrigerators and, unlike the Alpine Inn across the way, a TV. But like the Alpine Inn, it's a short walk to the Mount Rainier Gondola.

The **Alta Crystal Resort** (68317 Hwy. 410, 360/663-2500, www.altacrystalresort.com, $299-350) isn't at Crystal at all, but rather down the road a few miles. It's a small complex of suites, some two stories with two bedrooms. All have wood-burning fireplaces and either a kitchenette or full kitchen, and rooms aren't cramped. A large honeymoon cabin is on a creek and located away from the rest of the buildings. Steam rises from the hot tub and heated pool (set to 90 degrees F. in the winter), and a recreation lodge holds board games and a foosball table. Unlike some cabins in the area, the hotel has indoor distractions like wireless Internet and cable television, plus movie rentals and meals to cook in the room, but also holds campfires, s'more making, and other evening activities during weekends, holidays, and summer months.

Gateways

Ashford

Don't be fooled by its tiny size, or even the fact that there's no "town" of Ashford at all, just a loose string of business and houses stretched over a few miles of highway. It's the last chance for food and hotels outside Mount Rainier National Park's southwest **Nisqually Entrance,** and the entire area has art, culinary, and outdoor surprises.

Ashford sits in the Nisqually River Valley, anchored by the river that begins on a glacier on Mount Rainier and travels to Puget Sound near Olympia. It's home to two of the three companies that offer guided climbs of Mount Rainier, and it's not unusual to see crowds of mountaineers loading into vans for the drive up to Paradise.

Ex Nihilo

The **Recycled Spirits of Iron** (Hwy. 706, 4 miles west of Ashford, www.danielklennert.com, hours vary, free) is a singular attraction, one that represents the artistic output of sculptor Dan Klennert. Klennert calls his home collection Ex Nihilo, or "something out of nothing." His works appear throughout the state, but Klennert's home is his greatest accomplishment—the junk he collects in scrap yards and industrial sites has become a lawn of strange animals and dancing figures: a giant seahorse created out of horseshoes and deer and dinosaurs made from salvaged metal and wood. He'll use an animal skull in one sculpture, then take his blowtorch to a rusty old sprocket for another. Entrance to see the approximately 50 sculptures is free, though donation boxes are posted (separate ones for Democrats and Republicans). Opening hours are irregular, mostly when Klennert is around to open the front gates.

Entertainment and Events

The **Rainier Mountain Festival** (30027 Hwy. 706 E, Ashford, 800/238-5756) takes place at "Rainier Base Camp" at Whittaker's Bunkhouse over a weekend in the middle of September, combining a trail run with films, music performances, food, and a gear sale as the guide outfit unloads the stuff it rented to clients all summer. Famous alpine climbers, including the Whittaker brothers, sign books and take photos. You don't have to be a climber to enjoy the festival, but kids can get the mountain bug by ascending the rock wall for free.

It's not all climbing ropes and ice axes in Ashford. The early winter **Mount Rainier Fall Wine Festival** (Mt. Rainier Lions Grand Tasting Hall, 27726 Hwy. 706 E, Ashford, 877/617-9951, www.road-to-paradise.com, Nov. or Dec., $25) celebrates the finer side of mountain life, highlighting Washington wines and microbrews. Entrance to the indoor event comes with a wine glass and tickets for 10 tastes. Children are welcome (to attend, not to drink), and rooms booked in the area during the festival weekend come with one free entry.

Shopping

If you forgot anything important for a hiking trip, like sunglasses or a headlamp, **Whittaker Mountaineering** (30027 Hwy. 706 E, Ashford, 800/238-5756, 7am-8pm Wed.-Mon., 7am-6pm Tues. summer, 9am-5pm daily winter) rents and sells trail gear. But don't be scared off by all the hardcore climbers about the place—they can give advice on taking a small stroll in the Rainier area.

The little red **Painter Art Beads** (30517 Hwy. 706 E, Ashford, 360/569-2644, www.painterartbeads.com) is open irregular hours but has a quirky combination of wares: lots of beads, some crystals, original art by proprietor Joan Painter, and some jewelry—plus a beaded tapestry and the cast of a Bigfoot footprint.

The building that houses **Ashford Creek Pottery** (30510 Hwy. 706 E, Ashford, 360/569-1000, www.ashfordcreekpottery.com, 10am-6pm daily summer, 10am-6pm Sat.-Sun. winter) was once a snowplow shed, but it now holds the works of local potters and painters. One, Dee Molenaar, is a local legend, having penned a well-read history of Rainier and worked as a local guide; his paintings and maps grace many National Park Service brochures and signs. Also find books about the region (sometimes signed when the authors are local), a book room with author portraits, and stained-glass artwork.

Food

The menu at **Copper Creek Restaurant** (35707 Hwy. 706, Ashford, 360/569-2799, www.coppercreekinn.com, 8am-9pm Mon.-Thurs., 7am-9pm Sat.-Sun. summer; 11am-7pm Mon.-Fri., 8am-8pm Sat., 8am-7pm Sun. spring and fall; 11am-7pm Mon. and Thurs.-Fri., 8am-8pm Sat., 8am-7pm Sun. winter, $12-28) has two parts—the part that's blackberry pie, and the part that isn't. The fare is varied, with veggie burgers, biscuits, and gravy to feed hungry hikers, and lemon chicken. The bright red spot, complete with white shutters, first began as a gas station in the 1920s and has been a restaurant since the 1940s, but now its blackberry pies take top billing. They sit on cooling racks near the counter, demanding to be served a la mode. Sure, there are plenty of sweet options, including cinnamon rolls and blackberry butter for the rolls, and the gift shop is full of blackberry syrup and local gifts. But leaving without a slice of pie just seems wrong.

Is it odd to find a Nepali restaurant like **Wildberry** (37718 Hwy. 706, Ashford, 360/569-2277, www.rainierwildberry.com, 11am-8pm daily, $11-30) in the middle of rural Washington State? Not if you consider that Mount Rainier is a training ground for climbers heading to Mount Everest, K2, and other famous climbs in Nepal—and Everest climbing sherpas are known to serve as Rainier mountaineering guides. The fare resembles Indian food in its curries, but with slightly different spices: Sherpa Stew is a thick, meaty concoction with dumplings, and Sherpa Tea is flavored with cardamom and cinnamon. The owners had a restaurant near Mount Everest Base Camp, and they enjoy putting yak on the menu next to American options like burgers and fish. But it's the *thali*-style meals—served on a tray with veggies, rice, a naan-like bread, soup, and other dishes—that warm the belly on a windy Rainier day.

At the Whittaker Motel and Historic Bunkhouse, the **Rainier BaseCamp Grill** (30205 Hwy. 706, Ashford, 360/569-2439, www.whittakersbunkhouse.com, 11am-8pm daily summer only, $7-21) has hardier fare like burgers, pizzas, and beers.

Accommodations

The **Whittaker's Motel and Historic Bunkhouse** (30205 Hwy. 706, Ashford, 360/569-2439, www.whittakersbunkhouse.com, $35 dorms, $90-145 private rooms) is the closest thing to a center of town in Ashford. The complex is made up of several buildings next to "Rainier Base

Camp," home base for the climbing guide company Rainier Mountaineering, Inc., started by Lou Whittaker in 1969. He and his wife bought a 1908 bunkhouse used by loggers and millworkers in National, a town three miles away, and moved it to its current location. The bunkhouse beds are popular with Rainier climbers preparing for their ascent and have no bedding, but the other rooms have private baths and normal hotel amenities. The hot tub can help relax post-hike muscles, and the **Whittaker Café** (6:45am-8pm daily summer, 8am-6pm Fri.-Sun. winter) sells coffee and snacks. The national park is just up the road, and several hidden gems are around the property. A tall sculpture, much like a totem pole, towers over the bunkhouse in front, and from a trail behind the parking lot, visitors can reach a tranquil reflecting pool and a memorial to fallen mountain guides made from old ice axes. Follow a trail up the hill about a half mile. It leads to a bench—actually a salvaged ski-mountain chair—overlooking the valley.

The rooms at **Copper Creek Inn** (35707 Hwy. 706 E, Ashford, 360/569-2799, www.coppercreekinn.com, $89-295) have even more to offer than proximity to their restaurant's specialty blackberry pie. One cabin behind the diner is directly on Copper Creek, with two acres of land and no other buildings within sight. Several other cabins have private hot tubs, and some are big enough to sleep 12; other tiny cabins sleep 3 but have detached bathrooms. An art studio cabin even comes with an easel and art supplies, as it was once the studio of a local artist. The cabins are best for couples looking for privacy since there's little to tie the separate buildings together. Suites in the restaurant building itself feel more like a hotel.

When hobbits vacation, they probably go to a place like **Wellspring** (54922 Kernahan Rd. E, Ashford, 360/569-2514, www.wellspringspa.com, $95-195), a collection of cabins in the woods. The

dwellings have feather beds and fireplaces, some with lofts and hammocks, and either a full kitchen or kitchenette. It gets even more creative: The Trail's End tent is next to a nature trail (but has a woodstove inside—this isn't roughing it), and the Timbuktu hut is decorated in an African safari theme. The Treehouse is what it sounds like, located 15 feet above the ground and containing a queen bed. Below it is a little patio and private bathroom, but for all its charm, only adults are allowed up.

Wellspring also includes a spa, two outdoor hot tubs, and a sauna (and one guest room that gets exclusive access to a hot tub after dark). A gazebo and wood-fired grill is available for guests hoping to cook dinner outside. A small info board next to the garden out front includes instructions for checking in—and finding the staff around the spacious grounds.

Camping

Campers with reservations make a beeline into the national park for sites at one of its three car campgrounds, but outside the boundaries, other options may be less crowded. The **Big Creek Campground** (Skate Creek Rd., 5 miles south of Hwy. 706, 541/338-7869, www.reserveamerica. com, May-Sept., $18-30) takes reservations and has three pull-through sites for RVs under 22 feet. Located in the Gifford Pinchot National Forest, the campground has thick trees, and some sites abut the burbling Big Creek. Look for the start of the Osbourne Mountain Trail, a route that heads steeply uphill for views of Mount Rainier and the Nisqually Valley.

Getting There

Ashford is 80 miles south of Seattle. From Seattle, take I-5 south for 10 miles and exit onto I-405 North. Once on I-405, take exit 2 onto Highway 167 South. Drive south for a little more than 20 miles, and then take Highway 512 west for 3 miles. Take the Highway 161 exit toward Eatonville; you'll reach that small town in about 23 miles. From Eatonville, turn left onto Center Street, which becomes Alder Cutoff Road. Follow Alder Cutoff Road for 6.5 miles to its junction with Highway 7. Turn left onto Highway 7, which becomes the National Park Highway. In 4.5 miles is the small settlement of Elbe; stay east onto Highway 706 and continue 8 more miles to Ashford.

Elbe

Just a few miles up the road, west of Ashford and the park's **Nisqually Entrance,** is the tiny town of Elbe, good for a coffee stop, train ride, or one of the **last gas stations** before the park.

Mineral Lake Resort

Nearby Mineral Lake is billed as the "Home of the 10-pound trout" and hosts a popular fishing derby every April. The **Mineral Lake Resort** (148 Mineral Hill Rd., Mineral, 360/492-5367, www.minerallakeresort.com) offers boat rentals ($20-120) and dock fishing, including pole or crayfish pot rental ($5). A bait and tackle shop on the resort's dock also sells snacks and ice. The lake is well stocked with rainbow and steelhead trout, among others, and crayfish are plentiful when the weather is warm. The resort has cabins ($88-108) that come without amenities like bedding or Wi-Fi.

Mount Rainier Scenic Railroad

Mount Rainier Scenic Railroad (54124 Mountain Hwy. E, Elbe, www.mrsr.com, 888/783-2611, $41-54 adults, $21-34 children 4-12, children under 4 free) is a bit of a misnomer. The rails don't get much closer to the peak itself than the actual depot in Elbe. But the "scenic" part of the moniker is no lie. The route to Mineral has views of Rainier, or the closer forested hills when the clouds get in the way. The trip is along a section once used by the Chicago, Milwaukee, St. Paul & Pacific Railroad, and is about 40 minutes each way. You're pulled along by vintage steam locomotives and sit on wood benches in open-air cars when the weather allows. (But this is Washington, after all, so there is an enclosed coach car for the inevitable days of drizzle.) There are also regular themed rides, including a Christmas trip and Civil War history trip. Bring a picnic for the break between the ride to Mineral and back, or indulge your inner rail buff at the train and logging museum, where admission is included for the price of the ticket. It includes an engine you can climb inside and a look at the locomotive restoration being done by the volunteers who largely operate the railway, plus dioramas and tools.

Accommodations

The Ritz it's not. The rooms of the **Hobo Inn** (54106 Hwy. 7, Elbe, 360/569-2500, www.rrdiner.com, $115) are actually individual train cabooses, parked next to the Mount Rainier Scenic Railroad in the whistle-stop town of Elbe. The whimsical little hotel has loads of vintage charm, and you can climb up to look out the cupola lookouts on top of some of the cabooses. But despite some funky touches, inside the rooms can be musty and they have small bathrooms. Breakfast is included—in the dining car, obviously. Skip the dinner here and try something up the road in Ashford.

The **Mineral Lake Lodge** (195 Mineral Hill Rd., Mineral, 360/492-5253, http://minerallakelodge.com, $119-145 shared bath, $157 private bath, no children under 12) is off the beaten path, a three-story hotel built by a Scandinavian out of cedar in 1906. It has served as both sanitarium and gambling hall (and maybe even brothel) in the years when logging, mines, and lumber mills supported the area. Rooms are bed-and-breakfast style, with quilts on the beds and bric-a-brac on the walls. Half have their own bathrooms, and half share the hall bathrooms. Mount Rainier is visible across the lake from the hotel's wraparound porch or fire pit, and a cedar sauna sits out back. The private waterfront and dock are for the hotel, though boat rentals are just down the shore at the public beach. Just across the street is the smallest post office in the continental United States, or what used to be. The wooden structure was built in the 19th century and is little bigger than an outhouse; attached to the now-empty building is a white sign nearly half its size, describing the post office's history.

Eatonville
Alder Lake Park

Between Eatonville and Elbe, **Alder Lake Park** (50324 School Rd., Eatonville, 360/569-2778, www.mytpu.org, parking $5 summer) offers water recreation like fishing and boating, plus picnic areas and camping on the seven-mile-long Alder Lake. The giant concrete Alder Dam forms the reservoir, and at 330 feet high, the dam was one of the tallest in the world when it was constructed in 1945. Its turbine generators create electricity for Tacoma Power. Drive to the end of the road inside the main entrance for a view of the dam. Before that you'll pass almost 50 picnic sites, a playground, a day-use shower house, and a swimming beach (but remember that these waters come from a glacier and certainly are not warm). Boat launches are at this main area and at the Rocky Point Campground, accessed four miles east on Highway 7. The park includes a day-use area at the summer-only Sunny Beach Point, about half a mile south on the highway, with a swimming beach, picnic tables, and grills. The park boasts four **campgrounds** (888/226-7688, $23-33) with a total of 173 sites.

Alder Lake is stocked with kokanee, a kind of sockeye salmon, but also has varieties of crappie, bass, and catfish. Of course, the glacial silt in the lake can complicate things, so plan lures accordingly. Find bait at **Elbe Mall and Sporting Goods** (54011 Hwy. 7 E, Elbe, 360/569-2772, 5am-8pm daily).

Northwest Trek Wildlife Park

Plenty of wild animals roam the Rainier area, but nowhere are they more concentrated than at **Northwest Trek Wildlife Park** (11610 Trek Dr. E, Eatonville, 360/832-6117, www.nwtrek.org, 9:30am-4pm Mon.-Fri., 9:30am-5pm Sat.-Sun. mid-Mar. to June and Sept.-Oct., 9:30am-3pm Fri.-Sun. Nov.-Mar., $22.25 adults, $20.25 seniors, $14.25 children 5-12, $10.25 children 3-4, children under 3 free). The county-run property is dedicated to wildlife conservation through education and, in certain cases, raising animals for release into the wild. Trams drive through a free-range area of almost 500 acres, where bison, mountain goats, elk, and other animals wander freely. The 50-minute ride includes a tour guide, and it's rather like a safari, Washington-style.

Other enclosures dedicated to bears, bobcats, and wolves are viewed from a footpath. Naturalists bring animals out onto three stages for short educational sessions, and a family discovery center provides sheltered exhibits and activities. An old trapper cabin teaches kids about all aspects of wildlife research with computer models and binoculars. A zip line and high-ropes course is strung above the park but requires a reservation and special ticket ($21-70).

Pioneer Farm Museum

The **Pioneer Farm Museum** (7716 Ohop Valley Rd. E, Eatonville, 360/832-6300, www.pioneerfarmmuseum.org, 11:15am-4pm daily mid-June to early Sept., 11:15am-4pm Sat.-Sun. Mar. to mid-June and late Sept.-Nov., $11 adults, $10 seniors and children) promises a "hands-on homestead" that teaches kids about 19th-century settlers' life in the Ohop Valley and the Coast Salish culture that was already well established in the area. Experience the outdoor space through a 90-minute farm tour, and try your hand at working in a blacksmith shop or barn. The 90-minute Ohop Indian Village tour has activities—like bow-and-arrow shooting, dressing up, and jewelry making—for every season of life among the Coast Salish people. The gift shop is in the original 1887 log cabin homestead, but no food is for sale.

Greenwater and Enumclaw

It's a stretch to call Greenwater a town, with only a handful of buildings visible from the road, plus many more houses and cabins hidden from sight. But it's the only real stop on Highway 140 between the town of Enumclaw and the **White River/Sunrise Entrance** on the northeast side of Mount Rainier National Park. Mountain stops along the way include Crystal Mountain Resort, just outside the park, and Sunrise Visitor Center in the national park proper. Despite its name, Greenwater sits on the White River, which braids through gravel and rock with milky, glacial water. What's green is the forest, which slowly changes from regularly logged parcels to dappled, preserved acres as you approach the national park.

To rent equipment before you hit Crystal Mountain, try **Greenwater Skis** (58703 Hwy. 410 E, Greenwater, 360/663-2235, www.greenwaterskis.com, 8:30am-5pm Mon.-Thurs., 8am-6pm Fri., 7am-6pm Sat.-Sun., $35-50).

Federation Forest State Park

The 619 acres of the **Federation Forest State Park** (Hwy. 410 near milepost 41, 360/902-8844, www.parks.wa.gov, 8am-dusk daily summer, closed winter) are some of the best places to see classic old-growth Washington forest, thick with Douglas firs, western hemlock, and western red cedar. The park was protected with help from the General Federation of Women's Clubs in the mid-1940s. Nature trails leave from the interpretive center, and a picnic area sits next to the White River. On the Hobbit Trail or Naches Trail, find the **Hobbit House,** remnants of a tiny children's village, complete with a small mailbox and little fences. (It's not easy to find, located on a poorly maintained trail, so keep your eyes peeled.) The park is located on Highway 410, about 16 miles east of Enumclaw.

Suntop Lookout

The **Suntop Lookout** (Mount Baker-Snoqualmie National Forest, Forest Road 7315, near milepost 49 on Highway 410, parking $5) is no easy viewpoint—it's a 10-mile drive up to a point more than 5,000 feet in elevation, just 10 miles from Mount Rainier. The structure was built in the early 1930s and has a picnic area adjacent to it. On a clear day, you can see the Olympic Mountains and Mount Baker near the Canadian border. Just don't look down because the drop off one side is about 3,000 feet. Suntop is one of the few fire lookouts that can be reached by car, but only in the summer—once the road closes in winter, you'll need snowshoes or cross-country skis.

Mountain Biking

The rough terrain around Mount Rainier provides plenty of challenge to any level of biker. Rent wheels at **Enumclaw Ski and Mountain Sports** (240 Roosevelt Ave. E, Enumclaw, 360/825-6910, http://skiandbicycle.com, 10am-6pm Mon.-Fri., 9am-4pm Sat., 10am-3pm Sun. summer, 7:30am-6pm Mon.-Fri., 7am-6pm Sat.-Sun. winter, $35-55 per day). Then head to **Mud Mountain Dam Park** (Mud Mountain Rd., www.nws.usace.army.mil, 9am-4pm Mon.-Fri.), a recreational area with a rim trail popular with experienced bikers. Bikes can roll down the ski trails on Crystal Mountain during the summer but aren't allowed on the gondola, so bikers must earn the downhill trip with a serious pedal up.

Wapiti Woolies

Just try walking out of **Wapiti Woolies** (58414 Hwy. 410, Greenwater, 360/663-2268, www.wapitiwoolies.com, 9am-6pm Mon.-Fri., 8am-7pm Sat.-Sun.) without a hat. The store used to make its own custom hats and still carries some headwear under its own name, but now it carries racks of hats from many brands, many in the ear-flap style reminiscent of Scandinavia. Look for pictures on the wall of mountain climbers and professional skiers who have worn Wapiti creations on ascents in the Himalayas or Alaska. The store also carries other outdoor wear, including sweaters, and has a café in back serving coffee and ice cream.

Getting There
Enumclaw lies 40 miles southeast of Seattle. From Seattle, take I-5 South for 10 miles to I-405 North and continue 2 miles. Exit onto Highway 167 South and continue south for a little less than 20 miles. Take the Highway 410 East exit, and stay on Highway 410 for 15 miles to reach Enumclaw. Greenwater is 21 miles farther south on Highway 410.

From Sunrise, Greenwater is about 13 miles north of the national park exit, and Enumclaw lies another 21 miles farther north. From Sunrise, follow Highway 410 West out of the park; the road from Sunrise to the park boundary is only open May-November. Highway 410 from the park boundary north is open year-round and is usually in good condition, since skiers make their way to nearby Crystal Mountain even during the biggest snows.

Packwood
There's absolutely nothing fancy about Packwood, but it serves as an entry point to all kinds of recreation—skiing, hunting, fishing, and hiking—at the southeast **Ohanapecosh Entrance** to the park. The town was named for William Packwood, one of the first Caucasian people in the area, who came with James Longmire to trace a wagon road across the Cascade Mountains. The area is known for its communities of elk, which graze around town. A large flea market takes place every Labor Day all around town.

White Pass Country Museum
The **White Pass Country Museum** (12990 Hwy. 12, 360/494-4422, Packwood, www.whitepasscountrymuseum.org, noon-5pm Thurs.-Sat. summer, noon-4pm Sat. winter, $2 adults, $1 children) has small-town charm but is little more than a repository for a handful of local artifacts. But the story pole outside is a lovely artwork made by a local chainsaw artist, topped with a snow goose to represent a local Native American elder who lived to be 115 years old. Look for a bearded man, meant to be the town's namesake.

White Pass Ski Area
Originally a small family mountain, the **White Pass Ski Area** (48935 Hwy. 12, Naches, 509/672-3100, www.skiwhitepass.com, $63 adults, $43 children 7-15, $5 children under 7 and seniors over 73) was expanded in late 2010, making it one of the state's bigger ski destinations. The resort has a terrain park, night skiing, and ski rentals ($32 adults, $22 seniors and children). Directly across the highway is a network of 11 miles of groomed Nordic trails ($15), departing on the side of Leech Lake (prettier than it sounds). Rent skis or snowshoes ($14-19 adults, $14 seniors and children), take a lesson ($45 including rental), and get trail information at the yurt near the parking lot.

Morton Logging Jubilee
The early August **Morton Logging Jubilee** (451 Knittles Way, Morton, 360/523-4049, www.loggersjubilee.com) is billed as "The Granddaddy of All Logging Shows." It began in the 1930s, celebrating the area's biggest industry. It kicks off with the coronation of the Queen and then has a 10K run, bed races, a grand parade, and a street dance. The festival includes lawnmower races through a track lined with hay bales, a tradition that's decades old—the event actually includes time trials, and according to the official rules, "brakes are legal,

but not mandatory." And, of course, there is the logging show, with speed climbing, tree topping, logrolling, axe throwing, and more.

Food

In the small town of Packwood, **Blue Spruce Saloon** (13019 Hwy. 12, Packwood, 360/494-5605, 11am-midnight Mon.-Thurs., 6am-2am Fri.-Sat., 6am-midnight Sun., $9-12) is the destination for anyone in desperate need of straightforward burgers, beer, or both. The jukebox plays classics, the liquor pours are generous, and the special sauce on the burgers elevates the grub just above normal dive-bar status (but don't try the Bigfoot one-pound burger unless you're really, really hungry). The joint serves breakfast on weekend mornings, but for the best ambience, try to hit it on a karaoke night.

The pies are straightforward at **Cruiser's Pizza** (13028 Hwy. 12, Packwood, 360/494-5400, www.eatcruiserspizza.com, 9am-9pm Mon.-Fri., 8am-10pm Sat., 8am-9pm Sun., $10-26)—though the cashews on the Packwood Special is a bit unusual, and the restaurant itself is pretty bare, with counter service and arcade games. The rest of the menu includes everything from a fishwich to gizzards, but stick with a burger or pizza.

A good coffee joint like **Mountain Goat Coffee Company** (105 E Main St., Packwood, 360/494-5600, 7am-5pm daily, $1-4) is essential in any mountain town, but this hometown joint also delivers creative savory scones and fresh muffins baked on-site, and sells local crafts that hang on the walls. A long wooden bench sits outside, near where a farm stand sets up in the warm months.

Accommodations

Built in 1912, the **Hotel Packwood** (104 Main St., Packwood, 360/494-5431, www.packwoodwa.com, $29-49 shared bath, $49 private bath) has all the trappings of a vintage property—wraparound veranda, wood siding, and mostly shared bathrooms. Rooms are very sparse, but the iron beds add a tiny touch of charm, and elk are known to wander through the parking lot.

The **Cowlitz River Lodge** (13069 Hwy. 12, Packwood, 360/494-4444, www.escapetothemountains.com, $90-130) excels in straightforward motel style: basic rooms and adequate service. A fireplace in the lobby spruces up the place, and the location is just removed enough from the road that you don't quite feel like you're sleeping on the highway. The hotel has wireless Internet and laundry facilities.

With pillars made from river rock out front, the **Crest Trail Lodge** (12729 Hwy. 12, Packwood, 800-477-5339, http://whitepasstravel.com/cresttrail, $129-139) is a cheery addition to the small town of Packwood. Free breakfast includes waffles, biscuits and gravy, and other hot offerings, and complimentary nightcaps are poured in the evening.

Camping

Although the name of the **1896 Homestead** (U.S. 12 and Huntington Rd., 360/496-8283, www.packwoodonline.com, $15) sounds pastoral, it's a sparse parking spot for RVs, but elk sometimes wander the area. Flea markets crowd the site on Memorial Day and Labor Day weekends. Some parking spots are directly next to the (very tiny) Packwood Airport.

La Wis Wis Campground (U.S. 12, 5 miles east of Packwood and right before the national park entrance, 541/338-7869, www.reserveamerica.com, May-Sept., $20-38) has a whopping 122 sites, including a few walk-in tent sites away from the fray. The narrow parking spots and lack of hookups discourage most RV drivers, so the campground is largely tent campers. The most popular sites are those directly on the Ohanapecosh River. Reservations can be made online.

Getting There

Packwood lies almost 12 miles south of the Ohanapecosh Entrance on U.S. 12. To reach the entrance, take U.S. 12 north for 7.5 miles and turn left onto Highway 123 (road closed Nov.-May). Follow Highway 123 north for 3.5 miles to the turnoff for Ohanapecosh Campground.

To reach Packwood from Portland (70 miles) or Seattle (97 miles), take I-5 to exit 68 and follow U.S. 12 east for 64.5 miles to Packwood.

Mount St. Helens

Mount Rainier is no simple lump of rock. It's an active volcano, one of the largest in the country. What does that mean? Just ask any local about May 18, 1980, when nearby Mount St. Helens erupted—and consider that Mount Rainier could do the same.

Mount St. Helens is located 35 miles south of Mount Rainier and is a somewhat smaller 8,365 feet to Rainier's 14,410 feet. In March 1980, steam and ash started spitting out the peak of St. Helens, and a bulge—signifying an upcoming eruption—formed on the side. On May 18 the hot magma erupted out of the mountain, along with hot gas and rock. Trees for 6 miles were flattened like dominos, and an ash cloud traveled 15 miles up. Ash fell like snow all over the state (and as far east as the Great Plains), and lahars—volcanic mudslides—rushed down river valleys. The resulting landscape looked something like the surface of the moon, and St. Helens went from a pointy peak to a wide, flat crater.

Although 57 people were killed by the eruption, the most famous casualty was Harry Truman (no relation to the 33rd U.S. president). Truman was a cantankerous 83-year-old who refused to leave his lodge (or his 16 cats) at Spirit Lake, near the base of the volcano. He gave a number of interviews in the months before the eruption as experts begged him to leave,

but his responses were mostly too laden with profanity to print or air.

Today Mount St. Helens is a **National Volcanic Monument** (www.fs.usda.gov/mountsthelens) administered by the forest service. There's no fee to access the area.

West Side

Highway 504 (Spirit Lake Highway) runs more than 50 miles from I-5 to the base of Mount St. Helens near Spirit Lake, and is the most popular route into the monument. The road was reconstructed after the eruption, and moved farther off the valley floor in order to avoid destruction in case of a future event. The route from I-5 runs mostly through the rural countryside and over bridges that cross the Toutle River. Approximately 25 miles from I-5, the volcano appears. Notice how smaller trees and a land shaped by mudflows show evidence of the 1980 blast zone.

In 20 miles, the road passes Coldwater Lake and begins to climb amid the rocky hillsides. It ends more than 4,200 feet above sea level at Johnston Ridge. From this viewpoint, you can see not just the outer profile of the mountain, but the crater that formed in the middle, 5 miles away.

In winter, Highway 504 closes after Coldwater Lake, near milepost 45.

Visitors Centers

A visit to Mount St. Helens National Volcanic Monument today shows just how much the landscape has recovered in the last few decades and how the land also still holds scars. The **Weyerhaeuser Forest Learning Center** (Milepost 33, Hwy. 504, www.weyerhaeuser.com, 10am-4pm Fri.-Wed. May-Sept., free) was opened by the Weyerhaeuser logging company to highlight the company's replanting efforts, and is a good spot for viewing elk. With the closing of a county-owned visitors center in 2017, the best stop is the state-run **Mount St. Helens Visitor Center** (3029 Spirit Lake Hwy., Castle Rock, 360/274-0962, http://parks.state.wa.us/245/Mount-St-Helens,

Mount St. Helens National Volcanic Monument

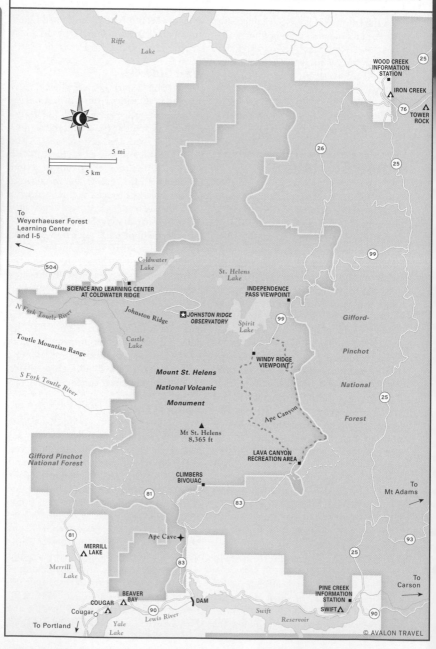

Riffe Lake

WOOD CREEK INFORMATION STATION 25

IRON CREEK

76 TOWER ROCK

26

25

0   5 mi
0   5 km

99

To Weyerhaeuser Forest Learning Center and I-5

Coldwater Lake

504

SCIENCE AND LEARNING CENTER AT COLDWATER RIDGE

St. Helens Lake

INDEPENDENCE PASS VIEWPOINT

JOHNSTON RIDGE OBSERVATORY

Johnston Ridge

N Fork Toutle River

Spirit Lake

99

Gifford-

WINDY RIDGE VIEWPOINT

Castle Lake

Toutle Mountian Range

Pinchot

S Fork Toutle River

Mount St. Helens National Volcanic Monument

Ape Canyon

National

25

Forest

Mt St. Helens 8,365 ft

LAVA CANYON RECREATION AREA

Gifford Pinchot National Forest

CLIMBERS BIVOUAC

To Mt Adams

81

83

Ape Cave

93

81

MERRILL LAKE

25

To Carson

Merrill Lake

83

BEAVER BAY

COUGAR

DAM

Cougar

90

PINE CREEK INFORMATION STATION

Lewis River

Swift Reservoir

SWIFT

90

To Portland

Yale Lake

© AVALON TRAVEL

9am-4pm daily Mar. 1-May 15 and Sept. 16-Oct. 31, 9am-5pm daily May 16-Sept. 15, 9am-4pm Thurs.-Mon. Nov. 1-Feb. 28, $5 adults, $2.50 children 7-17, children under 7 free) in Silver Lake, which has a seismograph and step-in model of the volcano.

Coldwater Lake

Anglers and kayakers dot the surface of Coldwater Lake (Hwy. 504, 45 miles east of I-5). The lake was created when the eruption reshaped the Washington topography. To understand the process that created the lake, walk along the **Birth of a Lake Interpretive Trail,** a brief 0.5 mile with illustrated signs.

Access to the trails, picnic area, and lake is $8 per person per day. Fishing for rainbow trout is restricted to anglers with single barbless hooks and in boats without gasoline motors, and limited to only one fish more than 16 inches long. A state license is required.

Mount St. Helens Science and Learning Center

The **Mount St. Helens Science and Learning Center** (19000 Spirit Lake Hwy., 360/274-2114, www.mshslc.org, 10am-6pm Sat.-Sun. mid-May to Nov., 10am-4pm Sat.-Sun. winter, weather permitting) at Coldwater is mostly used for education programs and private events, but there is an information desk in the building and picnic areas outside. The center is located at milepost 43 on Highway 504. Snowfall may close the road, but Highway 504 is usually open as far as Coldwater Lake.

★ Johnston Ridge Observatory

At the very end of Spirit Lake Highway is the site where USGS volcanologist David Johnston was camping when Mount St. Helens blew its top. The **Johnston Ridge Observatory** (24000 Spirit Lake Hwy., 360/274-2140, www.fs.usda.gov, 10am-6pm daily mid-May to Oct., $8 adults, children under 15 free) has videos about

the eruption and a giant viewing deck where you can see the lava dome and crater (pay your entrance fee before you start snapping photos). A light-up model of the mountain shows where and how the lava flowed, and some displays focus on the serious and catastrophic loss of life in the area. Outside, an amphitheater with fantastic views holds summer music concerts.

Hiking
Hummocks Trail
Distance: 2.4 miles round-trip
Duration: 1.5 hours
Elevation gain: 100 feet
Effort: easy
Trailhead: 2.2 miles past the Mount St. Helens Science and Learning Center

Named for the steep hills and mounds formed by the debris as it moved through the valley after the eruption, the Hummocks Trail is a popular loop route for kids who need a break on the long drive to the mountain. There are interpretive signs along the first 0.25 mile, and then the trail winds through ponds and wetlands—and the hummocks. Look for elk and birds on the trail.

Eruption Trail
Distance: 0.5 mile round-trip
Duration: 0.5 hour
Elevation gain: 25 feet
Effort: easy
Trailhead: main parking lot at Johnston Ridge Observatory

This paved trail from the end-of-the-road visitors center shows off not only the lava dome and crater, but the plain of pumice (or volcanic rock) that formed from the eruption, as well as the landslides. Look for informational placards and a memorial to those who died in the blast, as well as wildflowers in the dry, ashy dirt.

Getting There

Access to the west side of Mount St. Helens is from I-5, 57 miles north of Portland and 116 miles south of Seattle.

From I-5, take exit 49 to the town of Castle Rock, and then follow Highway 504 east for approximately 50 miles to the Johnson Ridge Observatory.

To reach the Johnston Ridge Observatory area on the west side of Mount St. Helens from Mount Rainier, exit the national park through the Nisqually Entrance and follow Highway 706 for 10 miles to the town of Elbe. Turn left onto Highway 7 and follow it south for 17 miles to U.S. 12, then drive 31 miles west to I-5 South. Stay on the interstate for only one exit, exiting 5 miles south at Highway 505. Follow Highway 505 and signs for 16 miles to Highway 504, then turn left and take winding Highway 504 for 37 miles to the Johnston Ridge Observatory. The drive takes about three hours without traffic.

South Side

Highway 503 offers access to recreational activities on the south side of Mount St. Helens. The town of **Cougar,** about 30 miles east of I-5 on Highway 503, serves as a base for trips to Lava Canyon and the Ape Caves, plus has permits and access for climbers attempting to summit Mount St. Helens.

Visitors Centers

The **Pine Creek Information Station** (15311 Forest Rd. 90, Cougar, 9am-6pm daily May-Sept.) is a summer-only stop located about 18 miles east of Cougar. Volunteers offer maps and guidance for visiting the south side of Mount St. Helens, and picnic areas and restrooms are available (only open seasonally), as well as a spot to buy bottled water. Some trails in the area require recreation passes, which can be obtained here as well.

Ape Cave

The **Ape Cave Lava Tube** (Forest Rd. 8303, www.fs.usda.gov/mountsthelens, 10am-5pm daily June-Sept., $5 parking, $5 lantern rental) is the third-longest lava

Mount St. Helens National Volcanic Monument

tube in North America. A trip here offers evidence that lava has been carving up this landscape for almost 2,000 years.

Inside the cave, unaccompanied visitors usually walk the muddy floor of the **Lower Cave Trail** (1.6 miles round-trip). The more difficult **Upper Ape Cave Trail** (3 miles round-trip) includes an eight-foot lava fall and a "skylight" hole that opens to the surface.

A light source is required for trips into the cave, so visitors should bring one flashlight per person (rangers suggest two) or rent a lantern during summer. It gets cold underground, so wear layers and sturdy shoes. To prevent the spread of white-nose syndrome (a bat disease), rangers are on hand to encourage visitors to decontaminate their shoes and clothing.

To reach Ape Cave from Cougar, follow Forest Road 90 east for 3 miles. Turn left onto Forest Road 83 and continue approximately 1.5 miles to Forest Road 8303. Turn left and drive 1 mile to the Ape Cave entrance. In winter, cars must park at the Trail of Two Forests trailhead and hike 1 mile to the cave.

Lava Canyon

Lava Canyon operates as a trailhead and interpretive site, with a viewpoint that overlooks Mount St. Helens, a canyon, and a waterfall. From the viewing platform, look for the layers of lava from an ancient eruption. It's a steep walk back up the paved trail to the parking lot.

To reach Lava Canyon from Cougar, follow Forest Road 90 east for 3 miles. Turn left onto Forest Road 83 and continue for 15 miles. The last 15 minutes of this drive can take the better part of an hour because of the small wilderness roads. A recreation pass is required to park here.

Hiking

Trail of Two Forests

Distance: 0.25 mile round-trip

Duration: 20 minutes

Elevation gain: none

Effort: easy

Trailhead: one mile before Ape Cave, right at the intersection of Forest Roads 83 and 8303

While visiting the Ape Cave Lava Tube, add a boardwalk stroll along the Trail of Two Forests. The short trail shows off the old-growth Douglas fir forest as well as the recovering forest that grew after the 1980 eruption. The parking lot is open year-round and serves as the trailhead to the Ape Cave in the winter. A parking fee or recreation pass is required.

June Lake

Distance: 2.8 miles round-trip

Duration: 2 hours

Elevation gain: 450 feet

Effort: moderate

Trailhead: Forest Road 83, about 10 miles from its junction with Forest Road 90

There's little elevation gain to June Lake, but it passes through forests and lava flows. A 70-foot waterfall tumbles into the lake at about 1.3 miles into the hike.

Unlike many stops in the area, access here does not require a parking pass.

Climbing

How do you summit a mountain that no longer has a summit? Thousands of people do it every year at Mount St. Helens, ascending to the crater rim at 8,365 feet. The climb itself is nontechnical, but it's a strenuous trip that can take anywhere from 7-12 hours. In winter, the snow cornices around the crater are very dangerous, and anyone in the area should be prepared for ash fall.

Permits ($22 Apr.-Oct., free Nov.-Mar.) are required for every climb above 4,800 feet and can be purchased online from the **Mount St. Helens Institute** (http://mshinstitute.org), which also offers guided climbs ($225-300). For climbing April-October, permits must be secured in advance; permits typically go on sale in February and sell out. If you're lucky enough to score one, you can pick up your permit at **Lone Fir Resort** (16806 Lewis River Rd., Cougar, 360/238-5210, www.lonefirresort.com). In winter, self-registration is required.

Those attempting a climb in the summer start their trek at the **Climbers Bivouac Trailhead.** To reach the trailhead from I-5, take Highway 503/Lewis River Road east for 31 miles, then turn onto Forest Road 90 and continue 3.5 miles. Turn left onto Forest Road 83 and drive 3 miles, turning left onto Forest Road 81. Continue 1.7 miles, then turn onto the gravel Forest Road 830 and look for the trailhead sign 2.5 miles farther. Note that some roads close in winter.

Camping

There is no camping within the Mount St. Helens National Volcanic Monument, which encompasses the mountain, Spirit Lake, and much of the surrounding area to the north, including Coldwater Lake. Most area camping is found outside the monument borders on the South Side. Privately managed **Cougar Park**

Mount St. Helens crater from the rim

& Campground (reservations accepted at 360/238-5251, www.pacificorp.com, Memorial Day-Labor Day, $21) has 45 sites for tents or RVs and one group site, as well as showers, a boat ramp, and a swimming area in the Yale Reservoir. **Beaver Bay Camp** (503/813-6666, www. pacificorp.com, late Apr.-Sept., $21) has 63 tent sites and one group site, as well as a swimming area and showers. All sites are first-come, first-served. Both camps are located on Highway 503/Lewis River Road about 34 miles east of I-5, just past the town of Cougar. Alcohol is not permitted at either location.

    Merrill Lake Campground (www.dnr. wa.gov, spring-fall) is located in the town of Ariel, north of Cougar. This walk-in campground has nine tent sites and a day-use area with a boat launch and picnic area. All sites are first-come, first-served, and there is no drinking water. From the town of Cougar, follow Forest Road 81 north for almost 6 miles to the Merrill Lake Campground. A state

recreation pass (866/320-9933, www. discoverpass.wa.gov, $10 one day, $30 annual) is required.

Getting There

Mount St. Helens and the town of Cougar, Washington, are approximately 50 miles northeast of Portland, Oregon. From Portland, take I-5 north for 29 miles to Woodland, Washington. Take exit 21 for Highway 503 (or Lewis River Road) and follow it as it heads east along the Lewis River, passing Lake Merwin and Yale Lake before reaching the small town of Cougar in 28 miles.

    To reach the south side of Mount St. Helens from Mount Rainier, exit the national park through the Nisqually Entrance and follow Highway 706 for 10 miles to the town of Elbe. Turn left onto Highway 7 and follow it south for 17 miles to U.S. 12, then drive 31 miles west to I-5 South. Stay on the interstate for 45 miles heading south to the town of Woodland, taking exit 22 for the Old Pacific Highway and driving west for 1 mile. Turn left on East Scott Avenue, and then immediately take a left on Lewis River Road, also known as Highway 503. Follow it for 27.5 miles to the town of Cougar. Without traffic, it takes about 2.5 hours to reach Cougar from the edge of Mount Rainier National Park.

    At one point, Highway 503 bends south, but signed traffic toward Mount St. Helens continues straight on Lewis River Road. Lewis River Road becomes Forest Road 90 just past Cougar; 3 miles farther, Forest Road 83 breaks left and heads north toward the mountain. Forest Road 90 is plowed and remains open well past the Forest Road 83 cutoff (to around Pine Creek Information Center) in winter, but big snows can affect access. Forest Road 83 is open to past Ape Cave year-round and provides access to sno-parks, but often closes before the June Lake trailhead.

Essentials

Getting There

Car

When driving around the Pacific Northwest, orient yourself using **I-5,** the major interstate highway that runs north to south, parallel (but far inland) from the Pacific coast. It's by far the quickest route from Portland to Seattle and Seattle to Vancouver, though it stops at the U.S.-Canada border. Running east to west across the United States is **I-90,** which crosses the country from Seattle all the way to Chicago and Boston. In Oregon, **I-84** travels northwest from Salt Lake City to Portland. In Canada, **Highway 1,** or the Trans-Canada Highway, runs east-west, making it less useful for a traveler adding Vancouver to a Washington and Oregon trip.

Interstate highways generally have speed limits of 60 or 70 miles per hour and are the fastest, but not the most scenic route—though mountain passes are beautiful no matter the size of the road. Interstates are also prone to traffic congestion near cities, especially in mornings and late afternoons when business commuters are on the roads.

Closer to the coast, **U.S. 101** curves around the top of the Olympic Peninsula and then continues south near the Pacific coast all the way to the Oregon-California border and beyond. In some places it's a scenic wonder on the very edge of the rocky cliffs; at other times, the road travels far inland to the rural Pacific Northwest. Much of that stretch is a single lane in each direction, which requires careful attention from drivers. Slow down around curves and keep an eye out for cyclists on the small shoulders.

Crossing the Border

There are two vehicle border crossings between the United States and Canada. The primary crossing is the **Peace Arch** (noncommercial vehicles, 24 hours daily), located at the end of I-5. Peace Arch is a state park on the U.S. side and a provincial park on the Canada side. The buildings are surrounded by manicured lawns, sculptures, and a giant white arch to mark the border.

A few miles away is the **Pacific Highway Crossing** (commercial vehicles, 24 hours daily), also known informally as Truck Customs. The terminus is located off I-5 at Exit 275, where U.S. Highway 543 meets Canadian Highway 15. This crossing is less scenic than the Peace Arch but is often faster. Reader boards on either side will note the wait times for each crossing.

Americans traveling into Canada need proof of citizenship, typically a passport. Likewise, a passport or equivalent documentation (such as military orders or a permanent resident card) is required to enter the United States. Canadians can reenter Canada with a birth certificate and photo identification, but a passport is recommended.

Border officials may ask for vehicle registration papers. For rental cars, the appropriate paperwork from the rental agency should suffice. Be sure to check with the rental company that international travel is approved for your vehicle. For U.S. rental cars brought into Canada, drivers may need a Canadian Non-Resident Insurance Card, issued by the rental company. For Canadians renting cars and crossing the border, there may be limits on how much time they can spend outside the country. Drivers are required to show proof of insurance in both countries. Frequent travelers can preregister with programs like NEXUS, SENTRI, or FAST (www.cbp.gov) for faster service.

Air
Seattle

There is no "Seattle Airport." When approaching the Emerald City, flights land at the **Sea-Tac International Airport** (SEA, 17801 International Blvd., 800/544-1965, www.portseattle.org/sea-tac), so named because it sits between the cities of Seattle and Tacoma. Although its name is half and half, it's undeniably the Seattle airport and lies about 15 miles south of the city.

The vast majority of visitors that fly to the Seattle area come to Sea-Tac. A few flights from Boeing Field (a mostly private airport near downtown) go to San Juan Island, Orcas Island, and Port Angeles on the Olympic Peninsula through **Kenmore Air** (866/435-9524, www.kenmoreair.com). Kenmore also runs floatplane trips that leave from Lake Union to Victoria, Port Angeles, and spots all around the San Juan Islands. In Everett, north of Seattle, commercial flights from **Paine Field** (3220 100th St. SW, www.painefield.com) are expected to begin in 2018 but will likely only include short commuter flights within the Northwest.

The **Bellingham International Airport** (BLI, 4255 Mitchell Way, www.portofbellingham.com) is just 20 miles south of the Canadian border and about 95 miles north of Seattle. It's generally thought of as a regional option for those living in the area and a low-cost option for travelers from Vancouver and Seattle who don't mind the extra drive.

Airport Transportation

To reach downtown Seattle from the airport via public transportation, take the **Central Link light rail** (888/889-6368, www.soundtransit.org). The train runs to Westlake Center in downtown Seattle with stops in neighborhoods like Columbia City, Rainier Beach, the International District, and the stadium area; it then continues on to Capitol Hill and the University of Washington. The trip from the airport to Westlake is about 40 minutes, and passengers can buy tickets ($3 each way for a full trip) at the station before boarding. (Don't try to board without a ticket because fare enforcement staff will regularly board the train to make sure everyone has a valid ticket.) Trains arrive every 7-15 minutes and operate 5am-1am Monday-Saturday and 6am-midnight Sunday. The station is located across from the main airport terminal; exit on the mezzanine level to the parking garage and follow signs for the Link Light Rail.

Taxis depart Sea-Tac airport on the third level of the parking garage; look for a row of yellow cabs. A dispatcher is usually managing the line. A set fare of $40 covers trips from the downtown Seattle district to the airport; the trip from the airport to downtown is not set, but will cost about the same. Ride sharing services like **Uber** (www.uber.com) and **Lyft** (www.lyft.com) will pick up from the airport in a designated area of the 3rd floor of the parking garage; look for signs. Cabs are subject to the same traffic considerations as private cars, and congestion on I-5 can be intense. Trips from the airport to downtown Seattle can take as little as 20 minutes or over an hour during rush hour.

Shuttle vans can also take travelers to downtown Seattle or throughout the city. **Shuttle Express** (425/981-7000, http://shuttleexpress.hudsonltd.net, $18) organizes trips to hotels or the convention center in downtown Seattle. Advance reservations are not required but are recommended, especially during peak travel times.

Car Rentals
The **car rental center** (3150 S. 160th St., www.portseattle.org/sea-tac) is separate from the main airport, accessible via regular shuttles that leave outside the baggage-claim area. The

energy-efficient facility holds 13 different car rental companies, and shuttles run 24 hours a day.

Vancouver
The large **Vancouver International Airport** (YVR, 3211 Grant McConachie Way, Richmond, 604/207-7077, www.yvr.ca) is located in the city of Richmond, just 11 kilometers southwest of Vancouver. As Canada's westernmost major airport, it provides service to Australia, New Zealand, Asia, and Europe, as well as much of North America.

If you're stuck at the airport or miss your flight, the **Fairmont Vancouver Airport** (3111 Grant McConachie Way, 604/207-5200, www.fairmont.com/vancouver-airport-richmond) is walkable from the terminal and has nearly 400 rooms with airport and runway views.

Airport Transportation
The **Canada Line** (604/953-3333, www.translink.bc.ca) is a rapid-transit rail system that takes travelers from the airport to downtown Vancouver in less than 30 minutes. Service runs 5am-1am daily, and adult tickets cost $4.10 (plus $5 for the Canada Line YVR AddFare).

Long-distance buses leave from the airport to Whistler, Victoria, and around Washington State. **Pacific Coach Lines** (800/661-1725, www.pacificcoach.com) provides service to Whistler and Victoria; tickets are available in the International terminal on Level 2. **QuickShuttle** (800/665-2122, www.quickcoach.com) connects to U.S. cities such as Bellingham and Seattle; reservations can be made online.

Taxis from the airport to downtown Vancouver cost about $35. A number of downtown Vancouver hotels also run courtesy shuttles.

Car Rentals
Most car rentals at the airport are located within the terminal on the ground floor. The drive to downtown Vancouver takes

about 20 minutes when there's no traffic, but longer during morning and evening rush hours.

Portland

Although Portland is the smallest of the Pacific Northwest's major cities, the **Portland International Airport** (PDX, 7000 NE Airport Way, 503/460-4234, www.pdx.com) remains a thriving airport, located 12 miles northeast of the city near the Columbia River. Flights depart for Asia, Europe, and U.S. destinations including Hawaii and Alaska. Nonstop service within Oregon is available to North Bend, Medford, Eugene, Klamath Falls, Redmond, and Pendleton.

Airport Transportation

The **TriMet/MAX Light Rail** (503/238-7433, www.trimet.org) Red Line trains reach downtown Portland from the airport in less than 40 minutes. Trains run 4:45am-11:45pm daily, and the adult fare costs $2.50. **White Van Shuttle** (503/774-9755, www.whitevanshuttle.com) provides daily shuttle service from the airport to locations within Portland. Reservations are required and can be made online; extra people are only $5 each.

Taxis are also available at the airport, and trips between the airport and downtown Portland run about $35. Many hotels offer courtesy shuttles downtown; for a list, visit www.portofportland.com.

Car Rentals

Car rental companies are located at the airport across from the baggage-claim area. More are located just off the airport grounds, accessible by pickup vans on the airport's lower roadway.

Train

Several major **Amtrak** (800/872-7245, www.amtrak.com) lines run through the Pacific Northwest. Most trains offer wireless Internet access and bistro cars that serve a limited menu and drinks.

- *Cascades:* Travels from Vancouver, BC, to Eugene in central Oregon with stops in Seattle and Portland. (Business Class seats on the *Cascades* trains offer more room.)

- *Coast Starlight:* Travels from Seattle to Portland continuing on to Los Angeles. For longer trips, sleeper cars offer "roomettes" with simple bunk beds and larger rooms with private bathrooms.

- *Empire Builder:* This east-west line connects both Portland and Seattle to Chicago and Milwaukee; it has sleeper accommodations, but no wireless Internet.

Bus

Greyhound (800/231-2222, www.greyhound.com) operates routes between Vancouver, Portland, and Seattle, as well as Olympic Peninsula destinations such as Port Angeles, Sequim, and Port Townsend, and Oregon Coast spots such as Cannon Beach, Florence, and Astoria. However, service outside of major cities may not be common, and public transportation within those regions is limited. Travelers without cars in those areas may find it difficult to reach sights and services.

Although owned by Greyhound, **Boltbus** (877/265-8287, www.boltbus.com) is more popular with younger travelers. Buses travel from central train stations in Vancouver, Seattle, and Portland, and continue down to major cities in California. Fares start low, as little as $1 for a trip, but those deals sell out quickly. Buses offer plug-ins and wireless Internet, as well as reserved seating.

Road Rules

Car and RV Rental

Seattle, Portland, and Vancouver airports have car rental counters from a variety of companies, including **Avis** (888/583-6369, www.avis.com), **Dollar** (800/800-5252, www.dollar.com), **Hertz** (800/654-3131, www.hertz.com), and **National** (www.nationalcar.com), with other companies represented in nearby off-airport locations. Cars can be booked online directly from the car rental company or through a reputable travel website such as **Expedia** (www.expedia.com) or **Kayak** (www.kayak.com). Prices can fluctuate wildly throughout the year, spiking during summer travel season, winter holidays, and large conventions, but generally a weekend car rental in Seattle runs about $25-40 per day, Vancouver $14-30 per day (in U.S. dollars), and Portland $17-40 per day.

While prices and requirements vary, you'll generally need a credit card and driver's license, and must be over the age of 25. The age requirement may be waived if you have plane tickets to and from the local airport. Drivers with licenses issued in a language other than English may be required to show an International Driver's License in addition to their own. If you plan to drop your rental car at a location other than where you picked it up, there may be additional fees involved, particularly if you cross the border into Canada, and requirements may differ for citizens of different countries.

The narrow, winding roads of the Pacific Northwest mountains and coastal areas may be difficult to navigate in a large RV, while the bigger cities have few campgrounds nearby with RV-ready services. Nevertheless, RVs can be a handy way to explore the far-flung regions of the Northwest. RV rentals may include mileage charges, required additional insurance, charges for generator use while the vehicle is off, and one-way fees. Operating a smaller RV may not be more difficult than operating a normal large SUV or truck, but larger recreational vehicles take some practice—and drivers need to remember that they won't fit in many drive-through windows, tunnels, and parking garages. Companies like **Cruise America** (www.cruiseamerica.com) do rentals in Seattle, Portland, and Vancouver; **Campervan North America** (www.campervannorthamerica.com) rents out of Seattle and **RV Northwest** (www.rvnorthwest.com) rents out of Portland. Few RV rental agencies are close to the airport, though many will provide airport pickups and drop-offs by request.

Driving Rules

Seat belts are required in Oregon, Washington, and British Columbia for every passenger in a car, with special **child seats** and booster seats required for children under the age of 8 or less than 40 pounds. Children must also ride in the backseat if less than 13 years of age in Washington. **Texting and cell phone use** is strongly prohibited in both states and British Columbia, and drivers can be cited even if fiddling with a phone for directions while behind the wheel.

In Washington and British Columbia, **tolls** are usually automatically billed rather than collected at a stationary toll booth—a camera takes a photo of your license plate, and you later receive a bill; if you're in a rental car, expect your rental company to bill you. Cash for tolls is generally only necessary on the toll bridges between Oregon and Washington, all located on the Columbia River far east of Portland. In Washington, some **HOV** (high-occupancy vehicle) lanes can be used by a single driver if a toll is paid, while British Columbia sometimes allow single drivers in electric-powered vehicles to travel HOV lanes.

Note that in Oregon, only gas station attendants are allowed to pump gas; there's **no self-service.**

In British Columbia, speeds are listed in **kilometers per hour** rather than miles per hour. A **flashing green light** signifies that the intersection may have a pedestrian crossing, and the driver must give the right-of-way before turning. International drivers can use their international license for only 90 days before they are required to get a Canadian one.

Although **cannabis** is now legal for recreational use in Washington and Oregon, driving under its influence is illegal, and crossing state lines with it is against federal law. It's also against the law to cross into Canada while in possession of the substance.

Motorcyclists are required to hold a special license and drive with a helmet, and may be subject to requirements on lights and sound levels. **Lane-splitting** is prohibited in Washington, Oregon, and British Columbia. Washington motorcyclists must have eye protection. Although **bicyclists** are subject to the same rules as car drivers, their much more vulnerable state means extra care needs to be taken in areas with bike traffic. Slow down when coming up behind a bicyclist and pass on the left only when oncoming traffic allows.

Road Conditions

Mountain roads are prone to seasonal closures, and it's illegal to forgo **snow chains** when requirements are posted. To prepare for a trip in the winter months, check the official departments of transportation websites: the **Washington State Department of Transportation** (www. wsdot.wa.gov), **Oregon Department of Transportation** (www.oregon.gov/ odot), and **British Columbia Ministry of Transportation** (www.drivebc.ca). Pass cameras, which show live feeds of snow and ice levels, backups, and accidents on Oregon roads are at **TripCheck** (www. tripcheck.com).

In Washington and Oregon, drivers can call 511 from a phone to get recordings of major **traffic information.** In British Columbia, the number is 800/550-4997. In the case of a **roadside emergency,** drivers should call 911 (in both the U.S. and Canada) to reach police and emergency services. For nonemergency cases, like a breakdown or flat

tire, Americans can prepay for services from **AAA** (800/222-4357, www.aaa.com); in Canada it's **CAA** (888/268-2222, www. caa.ca). Subscriptions are required.

Visas and Officialdom

Passports and Visas

When visiting the United States or Canada from another country, a valid passport is required. Depending upon your country of origin, a visa may also be required when visiting the United States. For a complete list of countries exempt from U.S. visa requirements, visit http:// travel.state.gov/visa.

Canadian citizens can visit the United States without a visa, but must show a passport or enhanced driver's license at the border. All car, train, and bus crossings may require questioning from border-control agents about the purpose of the visit, destination (including hotel address), and purchases made while in the country. To protect the agricultural industries of each country from the spread of pests and disease, the transportation of fresh fruit and plants may be prohibited. More information on crossing into the United States can be found at www. cbp.gov.

American citizens and permanent residents must show identification such as a passport or a U.S. Permanent Resident Card when crossing the border into Canada. A list of countries whose passport holders do not require a visa to visit Canada is available at www.cic.gc.ca/english/visit. There is a limit on the amount of alcohol and tobacco visitors can bring into each country.

Embassies

When traveling to the United States or Canada from another country, the embassy from your home country can help in the event of a lost passport or unexpected troubles. Embassies for many countries can be found in Vancouver,

Seattle, and Portland. To find an embassy within the United States, visit www.state.gov/s/cpr/rls. For an embassy in Canada, visit www.international.gc.ca.

Customs

When entering the United States or Canada by plane, you will have to fill out a customs form. Be sure to have handy the information on your destination—name, address, and phone number. There are limits on the gifts you can bring into the country as well as the amount of tobacco and alcohol you can bring.

If you take prescription medications, bring documentation for your medicines. Medicines that require the use of syringes should be packed in checked luggage along with proper documentation. Find exact regulations on customs and duties for the United States online at www.cbp.gov; for Canada, visit http://caen-keep-exploring.canada.travel/travel-info/customs-and-duty.

Travel Tips

Alcohol and Smoking

The **drinking age** in the United States is 21 years old, and most bars and restaurants will ask for identification for anyone who looks close to that age. Almost all grocery stores and liquor stores will require identification as well.

Bars in Seattle stay open until about 2am and often close earlier on weeknights. Laws regarding when alcohol can last be served are very strict, but some dance clubs will stay open later after their bars have stopped serving alcohol. In the rest of Washington, select bars may stay open late, but many close at midnight or 1am. Oregon has a similar pattern, with bars in Portland serving drinks until 2:30am, but establishments elsewhere close earlier. The drinking age in British Columbia—the province that holds Vancouver and Victoria—is 19 years old. Bars can serve alcohol until

3am, though many bars have earlier closing times.

Smoking in bars, restaurants, and indoor places is prohibited. Some towns and state parks prohibit smoking in outdoor public places, including many in the Seattle area. Cigarettes are not sold to anyone under the age of 18, and identification is required. Canada has many of the same restrictions for smoking as the United States; for example, it is illegal to smoke in Vancouver parks and beaches.

In 2012, possession of **marijuana** for recreational use became legal in Washington State, and Oregon followed suit in 2015. That doesn't mean it's a free-for-all, however. Adults age 21 or older can possess up to one ounce of marijuana, but cannot smoke in a public place. Stores selling marijuana are slowly becoming a reality as the state works out regulations and taxation. However, marijuana is still illegal on federal lands. Recreational use of cannabis is slated for legalization in British Columbia in 2018.

Traveling with Children

The Pacific Northwest is a wonderful destination for families because of its affordability, relaxed pace, and large number of activities for children. Most of the region's cities have parks, zoos, children's museums, and aquariums that cater especially to kids, as well as educational destinations such as Portland's OMSI and Seattle's Pacific Science Center. Look for family rates at museums and at gardens that require admission.

When traveling with children in the Pacific Northwest, be sure to make plans that include indoor stops. Kids can get stir-crazy in the event of a rainy day, which is common in the area. But there is also a prevalence of creative transportation options in the region: Rides on ferries, trams, and light-rail trains can be exciting for travelers of any age. Most hotels will happily accept children and can offer rooms away from noisy bars or events. Be sure to check before booking a bed-and-breakfast room, as some establishments may limit guests to adults only.

When visiting the beaches of Washington, Oregon, and British Columbia, take care with small children around the water. Pacific Ocean waves are very strong, and the cold water and undertow can be deadly for even experienced swimmers—most beaches in Washington and Oregon are for strolling, not swimming. Tides can come in quickly, stranding slow walkers or even erasing a beach. On shores with beautiful rocks to explore, the footholds around tidal pools are slippery. Avoid climbing rocks unless necessary, both to protect the wildlife and to avoid deadly injuries.

Senior Travelers

Many older travelers will find discounts at bars, restaurants, museums, and transportation options around the Pacific Northwest. Age requirements vary and go by different names: For instance, the MAX light rail in Portland calls riders over 65 "Honored Citizens," and they pay less than half a normal adult fare. At hotels, ask for senior rates when booking. American travelers can also get discounts with membership in the AARP.

Gay and Lesbian Travelers

The Pacific Northwest in both the United States and Canada is generally very friendly to gay and lesbian travelers. That warmth is sometimes less evident, but by no means absent, in smaller towns and more rural areas. The three large cities—Vancouver, Seattle, and Portland—hold annual pride parades.

Seattle hosts the **LGBT Visitors Center** (614 Broadway E, www.thegsba.org) at a small information stand inside a bank on Capitol Hill, which distributes maps of the area.

Gay marriage is legal in Canada and across the United States, but early adoption in Washington State brought an influx of LGBT destination weddings to the area. Check local city hall websites for more about the process of obtaining a wedding license.

Information and Services
Money

All businesses in Washington and Oregon accept the U.S. dollar ($), and most businesses, including taxi cabs, will accept major credit cards like Visa and MasterCard. Other cards, such as American Express and Discover, are often accepted as well. Currency exchange businesses are available in most airports, downtown areas of major cities, and in banks around the region. ATMs are prevalent.

The Canadian dollar (C$) is not interchangeable with the U.S. dollar; check currency exchange businesses or online for the current exchange rate. A limited number of businesses in downtown Vancouver and Victoria or near the U.S. border may accept U.S. currency, often returning change in Canadian money. However, it's best not to rely on that, and you may not get the best exchange rate. Note that banks may charge fees for using credit cards in countries other than where they were issued.

Travelers will be pleased to discover that the State of Oregon does not charge a general sales tax.

Maps and Tourist Information

When planning a trip to the Pacific Northwest, come prepared with a number of maps. City maps of Vancouver, Seattle, Victoria, and Portland are ideal for navigating the often-confusing waterfront cities. Routes to the Oregon Coast and Olympic Peninsula will require state maps of Washington and Oregon; the best versions are available at a book or travel store, or from **AAA** (www.aaa.com). What's more, the drive through Canada to Vancouver, while not difficult, can be stressful for drivers without a map to reassure them.

For travelers expecting to use GPS or

cell phone route-finding, note that the service may not be available in rural areas of the coast and Olympic Peninsula, or in Canada with some service plans. Many towns have visitors centers with some form of free map, but reliable highway maps are a must to pack for a road trip in the area.

Health and Safety

In both the United States and Canada, emergency services can be reached by dialing 911 from any phone. Although help is likely to be slower to arrive in rural areas, most of western Washington and Oregon, as well as southwestern British Columbia, is well saturated with hospitals and other emergency resources.

When hiking or doing outdoor activities, be sure to note the conditions before attempting an outing. Cell phone service may be spotty or nonexistent, so go in prepared to handle any conditions, and inform others of your plan before you depart. Stop by visitors centers or park offices to ask about regulations and advisories.

Resources

Washington
Experience WA
www.experiencewa.com
Experience WA has travel resources for the entire state, including statewide restaurant listings and access to the Washington State Visitors' Guide.

Mount Rainier National Park
www.nps.gov/mora
The official park website has up-to-date hours and conditions for the park, as well as permit and activity information. Check here for road conditions in winter.

Olympic National Park
www.nps.gov/olym
The national park website has maps, camping information, conditions, and

suggestions of how to approach the sprawling park.

Olympic Peninsula
www.olympicpeninsula.org
A travel website for the region has activity ideas and photo galleries.

Visit Rainier
www.visitrainier.com
A tourism website for the area has listings for businesses around Mount Rainier National Park, as well as campground listings, calendars, and outdoor activity ideas.

Visit Seattle
www.visitseattle.org
The official tourism site for the city has maps, listings, trip ideas, and ticket deals.

Washington Department of Transportation
www.wsdot.wa.gov
The official state website for transportation has road conditions, traffic updates and cameras, and planned closures, plus information on ferry times, waits, and fares.

Oregon
Travel Oregon
www.traveloregon.com
The state's official tourism website has photos, trip ideas, and listing information, but its beautiful design is best suited to inspiration during planning.

Travel Portland
www.travelportland.com
The city's official travel website has accommodation listings and itinerary ideas, plus promotions and access to the visitors' guide.

TripCheck
www.tripcheck.com
The traveler's wing of the Oregon Department of Transportation offers an easy-to-use map of traffic cameras and construction alerts.

Canada

Destination British Columbia
www.hellobc.com

The official website for the province has event calendars, itinerary ideas, and hotel listings.

Tourism Victoria
www.tourismvictoria.com

The city's official website shares museum listings and featured events.

Tourism Vancouver
www.tourismvancouver.com

The City of Vancouver's official travel website has listings and itineraries, plus descriptions of major neighborhoods and promotional deals.

INDEX

WXYZ

INDEX

LIST OF MAPS

PHOTO CREDITS

MOON NATIONAL PARKS

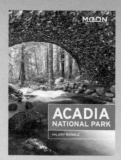

ACADIA
NATIONAL PARK
HILARY NANGLE

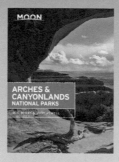

ARCHES &
CANYONLANDS
NATIONAL PARKS
W. C. McRAE & JUDY JEWELL

BANFF
NATIONAL PARK
ANDREW HEMPSTEAD

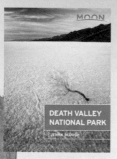

DEATH VALLEY
NATIONAL PARK
JENNA BLOUGH

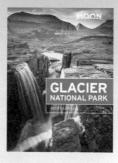

GLACIER
NATIONAL PARK
BECKY LOMAX

GRAND
CANYON
KATHLEEN BRYANT

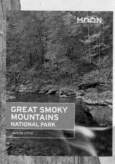

GREAT SMOKY
MOUNTAINS
NATIONAL PARK
JASON FRYE

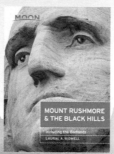

MOUNT RUSHMORE
& THE BLACK HILLS
including the Badlands
LAURAL A. BIDWELL

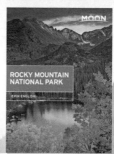

ROCKY MOUNTAIN
NATIONAL PARK
ERIN ENGLISH

In these books:

- Full coverage of gateway cities and towns
- Itineraries from one day to multiple weeks
- Advice on where to stay (or camp) in and around the parks

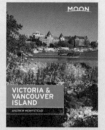

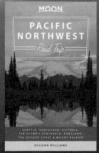